.

Altruistically Inclined?

Economics, Cognition, and Society

This series provides a forum for theoretical and empirical investigations of social phenomena. It promotes works that focus on the interactions among cognitive processes, individual behavior, and social outcomes. It is especially open to interdisciplinary books that are genuinely integrative.

Editor: Timur Kuran

Editorial Board: Tyler Cowen   Advisory Board: James M. Buchanan
                 Diego Gambetta   Albert O. Hirschman
                 Avner Greif   Thomas C. Schelling
                 Viktor Vanberg

Altruistically Inclined?

The Behavioral Sciences,
Evolutionary Theory, and the
Origins of Reciprocity

Alexander J. Field

Ann Arbor

THE UNIVERSITY OF MICHIGAN PRESS

Copyright © by the University of Michigan 2001
All rights reserved
Published in the United States of America by
The University of Michigan Press
Manufactured in the United States of America
⊗ Printed on acid-free paper

2004   2003   2002   2001   4   3   2   1

A CIP catalog record for this book is available from the British Library.

Library of Congress Cataloging-in-Publication Data

Field, Alexander J.
    Altruistically inclined? : the behavioral sciences, evolutionary
theory, and the origins of reciprocity / Alexander J. Field.
        p. cm. — (Economics, cognition, and society)
    Includes bibliographical references and index.
    ISBN 0-472-11224-4 (cloth : alk. paper)
    1. Altruism.   2. Genetic psychology.   3. Social groups.   I.
Title.   II. Series.
BF637.H4 F54 2001
155.7—dc21   2001002648

To my son, Jamie, for his love of history,
and my daughter, Emily, for her love of philosophy

Contents

Preface

Two strangers meet far from the reach of organized society. Each must decide quickly whether to attack, or await the action of the other. Together, they are better off choosing restraint and thus opening up possibilities for mutually beneficial intercourse. Desires for both self-protection and possible wealth enhancement, however, impel each of them toward an initial and immediate aggressive move.

The parable of the good Samaritan reminds us that failure to help can be hurtful. We can easily overlook the symmetrical point: since we are vulnerable to injury from all but the weakest, *failure to harm can be helpful.* In holding in check our ability to damage or destroy, we help our counterparty, both because she has avoided injury at our hands and because she now faces opportunities for gains at our expense that would otherwise have been unavailable. And in forgoing potential gains and exposing ourselves to otherwise avoidable risks, we have harmed ourselves. A surprising but inescapable conclusion: failure to harm can be *altruistic.*

Are we altruistically inclined? Are we, in spite of the counsel of prudence and the temptations of greed, often predisposed, in situations such as that described above, to give up the option of making a first aggressive move? If it is in our nature to be so inclined, how can this possibly be, given what we know of the operation of evolutionary forces?

Discussions of human altruism often have a nebulous and ill-defined quality to them. People commonly question what altruistic behavior is and whether it can truly be distinguished from what is selfish. But in a biological context, altruism has a very precise meaning: behavior by an individual organism that reduces its own reproductive fitness while improving the reproductive fitness of at least one other member of the same species (conspecific). Reproductive fitness affects the relative frequency with which an individual's genes appear in the next generation's gene pool.

Like Robert Frank's book *Passions within Reason* (1988), this book takes as a starting point the proposition that altruistic behavior is an important empirical category. Like Frank's work, this book explores evolutionary explanations of this phenomenon. But unlike Frank, this book considers the possibility that natural selection—the fundamental motor of evolutionary dynamics—has operated at the group as well as the individual level. Group selection occurs when selection differentially rewards members of a group as a consequence of the frequency of some trait within it, for example, when groups with higher frequencies of those altruistically predisposed grow more rapidly.

Group selection is not a new idea, but has only slowly been reemerging from an intellectual doghouse. The evolutionary models that most people carry around in their heads start with the premise that natural selection operates exclusively at the level of the individual organism. This poses a fundamental problem for the explanation of altruistic behavior, since by definition, altruism cannot be favored if selection operates only at the individual level.

Much of the history of the social and biological sciences since the 1960s has involved attempts to resolve this apparent contradiction. Considerable progress has been made in understanding altruistic behavior toward kin: for example, the sacrifices that parents make for their children. The theory of inclusive fitness, pioneered by the late William Hamilton, emphasizes that selection occurs ultimately at the level of the gene and, since parents share half their genes with each of their children, sacrifice for offspring may favor genes predisposing to such behavior, even if the sacrifice is not in the material interest of the parent.

The explanation of altruistic behavior toward non-kin is more difficult. The degree of genetic relatedness drops off quickly (second cousins share only 1/32 of their genes). Since altruistic behavior favors the fitness of other conspecific(s) at the expense of the actor, it is hard to see how predispositions to behave altruistically toward non-kin could spread or even survive. Were they to arise through mutation or genetic recombination, such tendencies would seem inevitably to decline in frequency and eventually disappear over time through the operation of natural selection.

If group selection processes are operative, however, it is possible, within a population periodically dividing into smaller groups, for behavioral predispositions to be shrinking in frequency within each individual group, while they are increasing in frequency within the global population. This possibility, admittedly counterintuitive, arises when there is a positive covariance between the frequency of altruists within a group and the rate at which it grows. Thus while altruistic behavior will engender reduced reproductive fitness for the organism exhibiting it within each group, genes predisposing to it can be increasing over time within the global population. The possibility enables us to understand how altruistic tendencies could be favored by evolutionary processes even when they are, by definition, disadvantaged within each individual group.

Most social scientists admit the relevance of altruism in considering relations among kin. But in relations among non-kin, interest seems to reign supreme, and suggestions that altruistic predispositions have a role to play are, if not rejected, then greeted with considerable skepticism. This presumption persists in the face of considerable evidence, experimental and observational, inconsistent with it. Part of the explanation for this is that we have tended to focus on what sustains or maintains ongoing interaction, as opposed to what allows it to originate.

Altruism may not be necessary to sustain relations of reciprocity. But altruism is necessary for them to originate. The description of a contingently cooperative strategy (Tit-for-Tat, for example) will be formally identical in an environment in which it or similar strategies prevail at low frequency and an environment in which it prevails at high frequency. But whether or not such a strategy is altruistic in an evolutionary sense depends on the frequency of such tendencies and others within the general population. In this respect, inclinations toward such strategies differ from the predispositions of parents to sacrifice for their children, which are altruistic irrespective of the prevalence of such tendencies among others.

My interest in what holds human groups together began with dissertation research more than a quarter of a century ago (Field 1974). That work gave little attention to the possible contribution of evolutionarily determined inclinations in allowing reciprocal, cooperative relations to develop. It seemed pretty obvious that natural selection, by favoring those who helped themselves, meant that Darwin was a problem to be overcome, not part of the solution.

The intervening years led to revisiting the question periodically, exploring and elaborating on the role of institutions and norms in influencing behavior (Field 1981, 1984, 1991). As was true for my dissertation, and in line with conventional social science thinking, none of these articles considers genetically or biologically mediated influences on our abilities to initiate and sustain social and, ultimately, economic intercourse.

A change in perspective was precipitated by a year-long sabbatical at the Social Science History Institute at Stanford University in 1997–98. The break afforded me an opportunity to read broadly and without distraction in a number of areas, some familiar and some entirely new. The process caused a number of inchoate ideas to develop and coalesce in directions not entirely anticipated.

I emerged with a reevaluation of how we can effectively tackle this problem, one whose logic and evidentiary foundation I think important for social and behavioral scientists to seriously consider. It is now far clearer than it was in the 1970s that the natural sciences do more than simply define a problem that the social sciences must resolve. A more nuanced Darwinian approach can enable us to organize and interpret the results of experimental and other research in ways that facilitate understanding of biological influences both on universal human behavioral propensities and on the structure of our cognitive faculties whereby we acquire knowledge about the world. These in turn can help us understand the emergence of normative structures without which the origins of reciprocity and complex social organization would be impossible.

Evolutionary, biological reasoning has been frequently misused in the past, sometimes in horrific ways, and many readers will approach it with reservation. It is important to enumerate several factors that argue in favor of our being more receptive to it. First, research and, especially, theorizing in this area are, in general, more nuanced and somewhat less prone to overreaching than was the case twenty-five years ago. In particular, there is now more emphasis on understanding genetic influences on human cognitive structure and behavior as reflecting adaptation to the relatively stable ancestral environment of hunter-gatherer existence (a period of at least two million years duration), as well as earlier, and less emphasis on attempts to interpret behavior subsequent to the Neolithic revolution (a period of ten or eleven thousand years at most) as necessarily reflecting adaptation to encountered environments. Second, the understanding of and scientific consensus about the levels at which natural selection can and does operate have been refined as the result of observational, experimental, and theoretical research, as have been assumptions about the interrelationships and balance between "innate" and learned cognitive and behavioral mechanisms. Third, the fruitfulness of inquiry into biological influences on human behavior and cognition has been steadily reinforced by an accretion of observational and experimental data and of new ways of interpreting such data.

Overall progress in these areas over a quarter century is striking in comparison with what one observes in the social and behavioral sciences, and suggests that research along these lines, and perhaps along these lines alone, offers the possibility of transcending the most significant and persisting fault line within them. That divide separates the sociological-anthropological tradition, with its emphasis on culture, norms, institutions, ideology, and emergent properties, from the economic approach, with its assumption of rational choice, and ambivalence toward or outright rejection of all of these concepts.

Research by heterodox scholars has tried to bridge this gap. But many *on both sides of it* remain skeptical that these efforts can lead to a scientifically progressive research agenda. This book is intended for those who, like me, have thought hard about these issues and have often been stymied. Many of us are committed in our work to approaches with explanatory deficiencies that at some level we acknowledge. The argument and analysis should be of interest to those identifying with either the rational choice or the sociological tradition. But it tries to move beyond the ultimately unproductive opposition of one to the other. Rethinking the implications of evolutionary theory and processes, and in particular relaxing the assumption that natural selection operates only at the level of the individual organism, leads to a rethinking of the strengths and limitations of each. In the context of serious consideration of experimental and observational evidence, it lays groundwork not only for some rapprochement within the social sciences but also, more generally, between the biological and behavioral sciences. This integration, however, entails a different set of implications than those traditionally drawn by advocates of such unification.

Some background in game theory is helpful in understanding the arguments developed here. This is not because game theory, any more than the rational choice approach of which it represents an extension, provides a universal key to understanding human behavior. But in recent years it has become almost impossible to discuss or engage developments in social science, and, increasingly, biological science, without employing its idiom. The main use of game theory in this book is as a means of organizing our thinking about what would be likely outcomes if interacting individuals were strictly self-interested and/or if natural selection operated only at the level of the individual organism.

Since the main focus is on areas where game theory doesn't predict well, it would not be fair to say that the emphasis here is principally on the application of game theory to the social or biological sciences. Those interested in work with more emphasis along these lines, which also treats the experimental literature, should consult Anivash Dixit and Susan Skeath's *Games of Strategy* (1999), Herbert Gintis's *Game Theory Evolving* (2000), or a number of other recent texts.

This book is more wide ranging in scope, more focused on the implications of evolutionary approaches, broadly conceived, for our understanding of essential human predispositions. In exploring the cognitive underpinnings of these tendencies, I also emphasize what has come to be called modularity. Modularity refers to cognitive adaptations, which employ different neurobiological machinery, use different reasoning algorithms, and may lead to different behavioral outcomes depending upon the domain encountered.

As a result of millions of years of selection, humans possess powerful reasoning modules that facilitate foraging and its modern equivalents. These include facility at Bayesian learning—necessary for forming "rational" expectations—as well as competence at, for example, maximizing goals such as caloric yield in allocating time among alternative activities.

The mathematics of constrained maximization, central to economic theory, provides a useful metaphor for modeling the operation of such modules. But in the realm of strategic interaction, as the experimental and observational evidence makes clear, humans possess other algorithms and action inclinations that are equally and in some cases more important in influencing behavior.

The idea of cognitive and behavioral modularity helps explicate a variety of otherwise anomalous observations. But, like group selection, it is not one that has been widely considered within the social sciences. As a consequence, either is likely to be embraced only after the most careful consideration. This book recognizes the appeal of the familiar, and that we may be drawn to certain explanatory frameworks because of their expressive qualities or their aesthetic appeal, rather than simply their explanatory or predictive power. But it is written under the assumption that evidence and argument ultimately matter, and that the vast majority of scholars in our disciplines are interested in these issues and committed to traditional scientific methods in addressing them.

The arguments here vary in complexity, but many are quite subtle. It is easy to be glib when discussing such matters as essential human predispositions, and when there has been a choice I have erred on the side of providing documentation and seeking clarity of exposition. This makes for a lengthier volume but one I hope will ultimately have more impact. The ideas, models, and analyses explored represent serious attempts at understanding fundamental social phenomena. To analyze them deeply, even if at times critically, is to acknowledge the serious efforts made by scholars to understand these problems.

In striking a balance between being too elliptical and making certain my meaning is understood, some redundancies have crept in. For those readers who get my drift immediately, some tolerance is sought for those less well versed in the technicalities. For those who do not, close reading will perhaps make an argument become clear in a way it had not been before.

Readers approaching this study with a jaundiced view of economics or rational choice theory may question much in the first part of the book as belaboring the obvious. In defense, I can only say that the appeal of the methods associated with this tradition remains very strong in modern behavioral and social science, and that those employing them have a justified sense that they explore the implications of some very powerful human predispositions. Only by carefully delineating the restricted applicability of the underlying models can one hope to make headway in articulating the case for alternative and complementary approaches.

Regardless of one's starting point, it is almost inevitable that some aspects of this book will challenge firmly held, perhaps unexamined, assumptions. It is helpful to keep in mind that what is obvious and easily accepted by one person may represent a challenge to a deeply entrenched presumption or point of view to another. One of the objectives of this work has been to soften some of the divergences in perspective that define disciplinary divides, and this can only be done by probing fundamentals. The research and writing of this book have been extraordinarily enriching for me and advanced my thinking significantly. I hope readers will share in and benefit from those experiences.

When contemplating a work attempting to cover a broad range of material, one often dips into sections where the knowledge base is strong. If details and analysis seem on target, we read further. The book aims to survive this test from a range of entry points. It covers multiple literatures, and considerable effort has been made to get the details right in each of them. For those whose ideas or arguments are inadvertently misinterpreted, my apologies in advance.

Following a prologue, the first chapter develops the main issues and evidence that occupy the study. Chapter 2 discusses the logic and mathematics of group selection models. Chapters 3 and 4 consider other explorations of altruistic behavior, including work by Robert Trivers, John Maynard-Smith, Robert Axelrod, and Robert Frank. Chapter 5 covers arguments and evidence underlying the concept of modularity. Chapter 6 addresses the heuristics and biases research program and its more limited relevance to the issues addressed here. Chapter 7 considers heterodox utility functions and differences between historical and social scientific explanations, and looks to a more integrated future.

My intent in these chapters is to probe, enlighten, and ultimately persuade. My hope is not that readers will, in light of what is written here, immediately abandon their current lines of inquiry, but rather that they will emerge with a better sense of where efforts fit within a larger scientific enterprise.

I owe debts of gratitude to a wide range of individuals who have read and commented on part or all of this work in manuscript. Particular thanks are due to Paul David; Mark Field; Deborah Garvey; Herbert Gintis; Avner Greif; John Heineke; Jack Hirshleifer; Larry Iannaccone; Terence Kealey; Robert Keohane; Michael Kevane; Daniel Klein; Timur Kuran; Deirdre McCloskey; Ross Miller; Douglass North; Robert Numan; Mel Reder; Tom Russell; Bill Sundstrom; Rick Szostak; Gavin Wright; and participants in seminars at Stanford University, Santa Clara University, the University of California at Berkeley, the University of California at Davis, and the August 2000 Knexus symposium at Stanford.

My wife, Valerie, approaching the work as an intelligent layperson, asked the toughest questions, insisting I define terms I took for common knowledge, or clarify exposition I thought was clear. If the book is more accessible to a wider audience, she deserves much of the credit. My greatest acknowledgment is to her and my children, for tolerating over an extended period what surely seemed to them abstruse preoccupations. I hope, in the end, they will understand what has concerned me.

Prologue: The World's First Prisoner's Dilemma Experiment

By the time Thomas Hobbes published *Leviathan* in 1651, his observation of the English Civil War had led him to develop an intuitive understanding of the Prisoner's Dilemma, and his analysis of and solution to it underlay what would become one of the most influential treatises in Western political theory. In a state of nature, he argued, individuals would find it mutually beneficial to agree to restrain their tendencies toward mutual harm and deception but, having entered into such agreements, would experience an overweening incentive to violate them, and would in fact do so. The agreements, in consequence, would not be worth the paper they were written on or the airtime consumed in their negotiation. The introduction of a coercive state with a monopoly on the use of force, to which individuals would voluntarily submit, was, in his view, the only satisfactory remedy.[1]

The clear identification of this most fundamental political and social question—how and why groupings of apparently egoistic individuals extending beyond kin avoid degenerating into a war of all against all—was a seventeenth century achievement. But the systematic investigation of what is to date the most widely studied strategic game does not begin until 1950. In that year the Prisoner's Dilemma (PD) was first formally described by Merrill Flood and Melvin Dresher, two researchers at the RAND Corporation in Santa Monica, California. Flood and Dresher described a game in which each of two players chooses between "cooperating" or "defecting," and in which the best outcome for the players considered as a pair is not the best for each considered individually.

At roughly the same time, John Nash, a brilliant mathematics graduate student at Princeton, defined a solution concept[2] for a broad class of

---

1. "Such gentler virtues as justice, equity, mercy, and in sum, *doing unto others as we would be done to,* without the terror to cause them to be observed, are contrary to our natural passions. . . . And covenants, without the sword, are but words and of no strength to secure a man at all" (Hobbes [1651] 1909, chap. 17).

2. A solution concept adduces a set of assumptions about human behavior and expectations formation, intended to be intuitively plausible, that restricts the outcome or set of outcomes players are likely to reach in situations of strategic interaction.

games of this type, one characterizing no regret noncooperative[3] equilibria that are today referred to by his name. A Nash equilibrium is a strategy profile such that each player's play is the best response to that of the other.

In this instance, a strategy profile is simply a pairwise listing of the plays of the counterparties. In two player single play Prisoner's Dilemma games, there are four possible profiles: cooperate-cooperate, cooperate-defect, defect-cooperate, and defect-defect. The first element of each pair indicates the play of the first player, the second that of the second player. The unique Nash equilibrium, as the examples that follow illustrate, is the *last* of these pairs, because for that profile, neither player has available a better response to the play of the other. When analysis indicates the existence of a unique equilibrium, theory has provided us with an unambiguous prediction of the outcome of an interaction, assuming the strategic options and payoffs have been appropriately characterized and the assumptions about how people will behave are realistic.

In the single play PD game, mutual defection leads to a Nash equilibrium. But the theoretical appeal of the strategy is even stronger, because for each player defection is also *strictly dominant*. This means that it results in a higher payoff irrespective of the choice of the counterparty. Whether one's counterparty makes the normatively "wrong" play of cooperate, or the "correct" play of defect, one's best choice ex post is to have defected.[4]

Following Flood and Dresher's initial description, the Princeton mathematician (and Nash's thesis supervisor) Albert Tucker popularized the PD in its canonical form, in the process giving it its distinctive name. Here is one version. Two prisoners have jointly committed a crime but

---

3. The equilibrium is sometimes referred to as "no regret" because since neither player has available a better response to the action of the other, there should be, for each individual, no ex post desire to have played differently. In their seminal work, von Neumann and Morgenstern (1944) thoroughly analyzed two player zero sum games, games in which what one wins the other loses. The Prisoner's Dilemma is not such a game: one of the outcomes (cooperate-cooperate) is Pareto superior to another (defect-defect), in the sense that both players are better off in the first as compared with the second. von Neumann and Morgenstern also suggested ways to analyze non–zero sum games, in which players were able (through some unexplained mechanism) to enter into enforceable agreements among each other (this came to be known as "cooperative" game theory). Nash took the analysis of non–zero sum games in a different direction, analyzing outcomes in which such agreements were not possible. The distinction between cooperative and noncooperative games originated in Nash's doctoral dissertation.

4. A Nash equilibrium need not necessarily involve a pair or set of strategies each of which is strictly dominant. Each strategy in the equilibrium might well be the best response to the other. But if one's counterparty had "foolishly" played differently, in some cases, such as in the two player fixed and known duration game, it could have paid to select a different strategy. In the two player single play PD game, these concerns need not occupy a player.

agreed beforehand that if caught neither will admit involvement. The district attorney tries to entice each of them with a deal: "If you confess [defect from your original agreement] and your partner does not, you'll go free but your partner gets five years. If you both confess it's three years in jail for each of you. If you both persist in denying involvement, I'll put you away for a year on a minor and unrelated offense." The prisoners are, in a sense, in the same situation as Hobbes's individuals prior to the formation of Leviathan, because although they may be dealing with a representative of a powerful state (the district attorney), in this instance the state is not interested in enforcing their agreement. Indeed, the reverse is true.

The dilemma, a function of the insidious incentives dangled, is that regardless of what the other chooses, each prisoner is, from a self-interest standpoint, better off confessing, yet if both refrain from so doing, each will get off with less jail time (one year each) than if both confess (three years each). Not confessing, however, exposes a player to the risk of the longest—five-year—prison term. Moreover, if a player believes his counterparty will not confess, he may be tempted by the desire to go free, and therefore defect at the counterparty's expense.

Three of the four strategy profiles are efficient in this sense: comparing the jail terms in any of these three with those associated with each of the alternatives, neither player can be made better off without making the other worse off. The Nash equilibrium is the only profile that does not have this quality. It is the only Pareto *inferior* outcome, because, in comparison to it, cooperate-cooperate yields less jail time for each. The cooperate-cooperate profile (the prisoners are cooperating with each other, not the authorities) is the best of the three efficient outcomes for the two players considered jointly, because it minimizes the total amount of jail time. But players are sorely tempted, and encouraged by prudence, to move in directions that will not result in this outcome.

The dilemma can be made more dramatic by raising the stakes. Imagine the players as revolutionaries and, as a means of concentrating our minds, replace the five-year sentence with death by firing squad.

TABLE 1. A Prisoner's Dilemma with High Stakes

	Sentence	
Strategy Profile	Vladimir	Joe
Vladimir remains silent; Joe remains silent	1 year	1 year
Vladimir remains silent; Joe confesses	firing squad	free!
Vladimir confesses; Joe remains silent	free!	firing squad
Vladimir confesses; Joe confesses**	3 years	3 years

Vladimir thinks that Joe will remain loyal and keep his mouth shut, and hates to betray him, but, as he has been known to say, in order to make a revolution one has to break a few eggs. Joe reasons identically, so they end up in jail for three years, rather than the one-year sentence each could have obtained had both remained silent. Or, fearing that Joe will betray him, Vladimir spills the beans out of simple prudential self-preservation, with Joe reasoning in the same fashion. In either event, the outcome (**) is the same: defect-defect is the unique Nash equilibrium because it is the only strategy profile for which each player's play is the best response to that of the other.

The fact that the rational pursuit of individual interest apparently drives players to the one Pareto inferior profile helps account for the enduring scholarly and popular interest in the game. The conclusion appears to violate widely held intuitions that interactions of egoistic agents lead to mutually beneficial outcomes, a central tenet of economic thinking. Obviously, the context of such interactions must matter. For many, the Prisoner's Dilemma resonates as a metaphor for real world dilemmas periodically confronted, and references to it can easily creep into day-to-day conversation, particularly among those with exposure to modern analytical social science.[5]

To Hobbes it was as clear as a geometric proof that the Prisoner's Dilemma could not be surmounted in the absence of an all-powerful ruler. Nevertheless, because humans often rebel at the conclusion that defection is the normatively "correct" play in these instances, the exploration of situations appropriately modeled as PDs poses problems for social scientists interested in predicting behavior. Flood and Dresher were concerned not just with the counsel of game theory. They also wanted to know how humans, sophisticated humans, would actually play the game. To this end, they recruited Armen Alchian, a member of the UCLA economics department, and John Williams, chair of RAND's math department and future author of *The Compleat Strategyst*.[6] In the first ever Prisoner's Dilemma experiment, Alchian and Williams played one hundred games, one after the other. The theoretical convention is then to understand the entire sequence as one game, with each of the pairs of plays defined as a stage. In

---

5. Flood and Dresher's experiment involved asymmetric returns to the two players and points, not jail terms, but the ranking of the payoffs associated with the different strategy profiles is identical. The game and the dilemma it captures have spawned an enormous theoretical and empirical literature (Roth 1995a; Poundstone 1992, 8; Nassar 1998, chap. 13).

6. In this, the most popular study the RAND Corporation has ever published, Williams avoids discussion of the Prisoner's Dilemma. He presumably wished to emphasize the explanatory successes of game theory and chose not to dwell on this instance where its predictions are poor and its counsel so problematic (Williams 1954).

a two player game of fixed and known duration, which this was, the unique Nash equilibrium is for each player to defect in each of its one hundred stages. Assuming Alchian and Williams believed each other to be rational, and were committed themselves to playing rationally, continuous defection was the only defensible strategy for either.

In this inaugural experiment, however, the two subjects behaved quite differently from what theory counseled. Contrary to the predictions suggested by Nash's analysis, and in spite of his initial defection, *Alchian cooperated sixty-eight times; Williams did so seventy-eight times.* The players achieved mutual cooperation (cooperate-cooperate), which is jointly better for the players than mutual defection, although defection is always individually superior, in sixty of the hundred stages (Flood 1958, 5–26; Poundstone 1992, 107–16).

Nash's subsequent life history has been almost cinematic in its pathos, a testimony to the complexities of a human psyche his work attempts to model in more unidimensional terms. In 1959 he succumbed to severe mental illness, resigned his tenured professorship at MIT, and for several decades haunted the halls of Princeton and the Institute for Advanced Study, a shadow of his former self. In the last decade, he has recovered, at least partially, and, in a poignant moment, shared the Nobel Prize in economics in 1994 with John Harsanyi and Reinhard Selten (Nassar 1998). In 1950, however, Nash was visiting RAND and at the top of his intellectual form. When he heard about Flood and Dresher's results, which deconfirmed his predictions, he wrote a note to the experimenters that was eventually included in their final technical report. The note included this remarkable and somewhat plaintive comment about the observed behavior of (the hardly naive) Alchian and Williams: "I would have thought them more rational" (Flood 1958, 16; Roth 1995a, 8–9).

Nash's comment raises profound issues about what it means for humans to be intelligent, smart, or rational. Since humans are generally viewed as more intelligent and smarter than other animals, it leads, in a related fashion, to questions about the evolutionary contribution of larger cranial capacity, generally viewed as facilitating rational choice, to the achievement of cooperative outcomes. Because the social sciences are today so heavily influenced by the rational choice tradition, it compels us to ask what factors or considerations might predispose people to play cooperate in such circumstances.

Defining Rationality

To be useful, the word *rational* must be defined with precision. I will formally understand an action to be rational if it satisfies two criteria, the first concerning how and on what basis beliefs are formed, the second how actions are chosen. A rational choice must be based first of all on beliefs about the state of the world that have been arrived at rationally. I am distinguishing here between beliefs as values or preferences and beliefs as factual or probabilistic propositions, meaning the latter. A rational actor should devote an "optimal" amount of resources and energy to acquiring or improving on the relevant information set, and then apply the best available cognitive algorithms, logical and/or statistical, in arriving at these beliefs about the actual or likely state of the world (on the practical implementation of this, see Gigerenzer and Todd 1999; on the concept of a rational expectation as one embodying all "available" information, see Muth 1961).

It would not, for example, be rational to conclude that today it will be sunny because so it was last Thursday, when one could easily open the shades and see the approach of storm clouds. In this instance, assuming there are real costs if it rains and one predicts sunny skies, insufficient resources have been devoted to acquiring information, and the expectation or forecasting algorithm employed is suboptimal: it would generally be better to forecast today's weather using yesterday's, or better yet, this morning's, rather than last Thursday's.

Second, conditional on beliefs arrived at rationally, a rational actor should choose so as optimally (with the greatest likelihood) to satisfy his or her desires or preferences. If one believes it will rain, and one wishes to stay dry, one should choose to take an umbrella. Assuming that we can usefully view most human behavior as purposive (there is an important argument—see Lane 1996—that some is simply expressive), and thus behavior reflects instrumental choice of means to achieve ends, what characterizes these ends? Most economic models assume that preferences are stable over time; invariant with respect to how formally identical choices are presented; transitive (if A is preferred to B and B to C, A must be preferred to C); that they cover all possible outcomes; and perhaps most generally, that they are egoistic: reflective of the desires of the individual.

The assumption of egoism is critical in rational choice models, and it is important to explore the implications of how it is understood. In order for a rational choice model to be refutable, it must do more than simply maintain that individuals act in satisfaction of their desires—clearly a tautology. Almost any behavior can, after the fact, be "explained" within the context of that definition. Precisely because the formulation is so flexible, it leads away from models capable of making out-of-sample predictions.[7]

---

7. The language is drawn from the statistical literature. The idea is that for a model to be tested scientifically, it must be confronted with data other than that used to generate it.

Consequently, a theory based on this broad understanding of rationality can't scientifically be tested. It becomes easy to provide rationales for behavior already observed, but difficult to specify circumstances under which a theory of rational choice can be rejected.

While the tautological definition can still claim to be based on egoistic preferences, it imposes few restrictions on what they are. As David Hume said, "'tis not contrary to reason to prefer the destruction of the world to the scratching of my finger" (quoted in Leslie 1996, 156). Nor, in principle, does it require that preferences be stable or transitive. If your preferences are different tomorrow than they were today, or five minutes ago, who is to say that your tastes are to be disputed? If you choose to act in ways that benefit others and harm yourself, who is to say that the behavior does not satisfy some deep seated psychological need and is thus actually egoistic? Thus, using the broader definition, one really has no choice but to conclude that the widow who throws herself on her husband's funeral pyre is being completely rational.

I don't attempt to engage the tautological version of the theory empirically, because it is not so engageable. Instead, I characterize the standard economic model as predicting, among actions that might be termed rational, those that efficiently advance the material welfare of the actor (see Kavka 1986, 35; Samuelson 1993, 143; Elster 1999b, 142–43; Frank 2000, xxiv). This narrowing of the definition enables us to posit behavior by an agent that would, based on external observation, be inconsistent with rational choice. We can identify as irrational the choice of death over life or, assuming zero disposal costs, less to more (Arrow 1951, 136). Such a modeling approach can claim scientific status because it generates predictions that might not be realized.[8]

There is an additional advantage for our purposes in adopting this stronger definition of rationality. Choosing life over death and more wealth over less will tend to increase an organism's reproductive fitness. Choosing this definition has the consequence of aligning rationality

---

8. There is an intermediate position, one that theorists such as Gary Becker would probably characterize themselves as holding, in which one allows greater variation in goals, but continues to insist that preferences be *stable, transitive,* and *invariant.* Such an approach can also be defended as scientific because it is possible to imagine or observe behavior of individuals at variance with these postulates. What I have termed "the standard model" embodies a stronger version of rationality, and there are several ways in which it can be tested: by searching for revealed intransitive preferences, for choices influenced by irrelevant considerations, or for choice of less over more. In focusing on decision making under uncertainty, the heuristics and biases literature has generally pursued the first two of these (see chap. 6). My focus will be on the third and on well-defined environments in which the behavior of counterparties remains the only real source of uncertainty. In some cases, such as the responder's choice in a sequential move ultimatum or dictator game, even that source of uncertainty is removed.

closely with the type of behavior likely to be favored by the individual level view of natural selection. Consequently, when we say that an action is rational, we will also be saying, in evolutionary terms, that predispositions toward it would have been favored by individual level selection. Conversely, when we say that an action is irrational because it is altruistic, we will be saying that predispositions toward it would have required selection above the individual level in order to become established in populations.[9]

Because rationality is so highly valued in Western culture, we often find ourselves pulled in the direction of embracing its broader, more encompassing definition, one less likely to be inconsistent with observation. This is a temptation that must be resisted if we wish to retain scientific aspirations. In many instances we may wish desperately to believe that altruistic behavior is rational in the stronger sense. But this cannot be so, because biologically altruistic behavior by definition damages the relative fitness of the actor, whereas rational behavior, as defined here, efficiently advances our material well-being. If behavior that benefits others turns out to benefit us as well, it is not altruistic but has, by definition, become mutualistic.

Were Alchian and Williams Rational?

There is every reason to conclude that the beliefs held by Alchian and Williams about the game they were playing were rational. As far as we can tell they fully understood its rules and the payoffs to the different strategy profiles, and understood that the other understood this: the beliefs each held were common knowledge. The assumption of rationality as defined earlier implies that, if the payoffs had been accurately characterized, each player should have defected at the outset and continued along the same path. This they did not do.

What did Flood and Dresher's two subjects think as they played this game? We have good evidence on this. Besides recording the sequence of plays in the game, the experimenters asked their subjects to keep a written log of their thoughts prior to each move. On the first play, Alchian defected, reasoning that Williams surely would as well, and therefore if he (Alchian) cooperated, it would mean a certain win for his counterparty. As Williams made his initial, and to Alchian confounding, cooperative move, he wrote down, regarding Alchian, "I hope he's bright," observing, as he (Williams) tried cooperation again a second time, "He isn't, but maybe he'll wise up."

---

9. It is not accidental that the individual level view of evolution is often advanced as explanation for why the strong version of rationality should be accepted.

Eventually, to a remarkable degree, Alchian did "wise up," to the evident satisfaction of Williams but not Nash. Nash was unhappy both with Alchian's and Williams's choices in the experiment and with Flood and Dresher's design, protesting that it permitted too much interaction among the players, and that one would see behavior closer to that predicted by his (Nash's) analysis if players were rotated through a number of simultaneously operating games and thereby deprived of knowledge of previous play against a particular opponent. That objection, of course, is obviously irrelevant in a single play PD game and, as subsequent analysis showed, irrelevant for a repeated game of fixed and known duration, as was the Flood and Dresher design, so long as one assumed all counterparties were rational. Why? Mutual defection should clearly take place in the very last stage because at that point each player faces the equivalent of a single game, for which defect is a strictly dominant strategy. Having apparently resolved uncertainty about the outcome of the final stage, players should conclude that it would be rational to defect on the penultimate play, and, continuing to reason by backward induction, eventually conclude that it would be rational to defect on the very first play and all that follow (Luce and Raiffa 1957, 94–102; Kreps et al. 1982, 246).

This argument may strike readers less familiar with the game theory literature as somehow wrong, because most people are unprepared to reason more than two or three steps by backward induction (Camerer 1997). But its logic is unimpeachable. Estimates or forecasts of counterparty play derived from preplay conversation or observation of past behavior are simply not relevant from the standpoint of canonical game theory in choosing one's best strategy in this game, if one assumes one's counterparty is also rational.

There is considerable evidence, however, that such considerations do influence how humans actually behave in these kinds of interactions. Many readers, indeed, placed in a controlled environment and asked to play one-shot or fixed and known duration PDs, would, like the two subjects discussed earlier, probably not act in the way counseled by theory. The use of game theory in this instance is to specify very precisely what rational self-interested players should do. It is to force the issue of what the underlying cognitive and behavioral assumptions really imply in these situations. The predictions made by theory unavoidably call attention to the implications of the evidence that many subjects, as did Alchian and Williams, systematically ignore the counsel of theory, and in so doing avoid Pareto inferior outcomes. But, as Nash observed and complained, in so doing they are not choosing according to the precepts of rational choice theory.

Since that first experiment, the propensity among high proportions of subjects to play cooperate, even in single play PD games, has been confirmed experimentally hundreds of times (for a summary, see Roth 1995a, 27). The willingness to do so, because it offers the counterparty an otherwise unavailable opportunity to benefit, and exposes the player to an otherwise avoidable risk of loss, is a form of individual sacrifice that will unequivocally benefit the counterparty. By playing cooperate, one grants to a counterparty an option to obtain the highest possible payoff in the game (in the examples, freedom), at the cost of imposing on oneself the lowest possible payoff (in the first example, five years jail time, in the second, death). Such behavior, because it creates beneficial opportunities for an unrelated conspecific and imposes avoidable risks on the actor, is altruistic from a biological standpoint, unambiguously so in a one-shot game. And, when the choice of cooperate is made in a controlled experimental environment in which there can be no expectation that the game will be indefinitely repeated, the play simply cannot satisfy the criteria of economic rationality as defined earlier.[10]

Why, in this very first PD experiment, did the two subjects each choose voluntarily, more than two-thirds of the time, to play in a way that cannot be defended as rational according to standard economic criteria? This question is particularly striking given Alchian's and Williams's familiarity with logic, mathematics, and economic theory. Subsequent studies have deepened our understanding of its dimensions, but the nature of this behavioral predisposition—a puzzling anomaly from the standpoint of the standard economic model—has been evident from the very start of experimental research on human strategic interaction, if it was not so before. Is it possible that there is something common in our constitutive features that facilitates solution of these dilemmas? If so, how could it possibly have arisen?

Toward an Improved Behavioral Science

This book is concerned with fundamental aspects of human nature, and with the attempts by economists and other social scientists to identify its essential features and explore its implications. At a practical level it asks how we can proceed in developing a behavioral science with improved predictive capabilities. In particular, what should be our practice when the predictions of a theory are repeatedly deconfirmed—as they are here—by experimental and observational evidence? The answer will appear to many to be obvious—*modify the theory or model such that its predictions bear a closer correspondence to observable data*—and one can appeal to Milton

---

10. In the fixed and known duration game, this conclusion depends on the assumption that counterparties are rational. In the one-shot game, the conclusion that defect is the only rational play is independent of how the counterparty chooses. See chapter 1.

Friedman and many others in support of this course of action. Friedman claims that the gold standard for evaluating a model or hypothesis is *prediction:* out-of-sample prediction, no doubt, with success defined according to the purposes for which the model was intended, but prediction nonetheless (1953, 40).

Within the field of philosophy of science, however, matters are rarely so simple or straightforward. To illustrate this, consider the views of Ronald Coase, another University of Chicago Nobelist. Coase argues that we should and do prefer models that accurately capture features of (give insight into) how a process works, *even if they don't predict well.*[11]

Both Friedman and Coase advance defensible positions, and if one proceeds carefully it is possible to reconcile them so that they are not necessarily in conflict.[12] Nevertheless, this reconciliation is a delicate business, and the attempt eclectically and unreflexively to hold both positions can easily degenerate into jeopardizing any claim that what we are doing is science. In particular, the habit of moving almost at will between them, embracing prediction until it fails and then championing the Coase view, particularly where intuition is the standard for judging the degree of "insight" provided, reflects a methodological opportunism that can easily render the practice of behavioral science impervious to the appearance of deconfirming evidence. In the limit, it creates a practice that simply cannot justify the designator *science,* regardless of what definition we may choose. It leads to disciplines that are inward looking, often contemptuous of work in other areas, yet ultimately insecure in their status as sciences. This diagnosis can most easily be made with respect to economics (Reder 1999) but can be applied as well to other social sciences, whether or not they fully embrace the rational choice paradigm (on anthropology, see Sperber 1996, 16; on political science, see Green and Shapiro 1994, x–xi, and Lane 1996, 123–26; on sociology, see Rule 1997).

Friedman's views are often adduced to counter suggestions that we should revise or reject an economic model because its assumptions are unrealistic. But when models *consistently predict poorly* it is both appropriate and necessary for us to scrutinize the behavioral assumptions that underlie them. Friedman's dictum that we abstain from considering such

---

11. "Faced with a choice between a theory which predicts well but gives us little insight into how the system works and one which gives us this insight and predicts badly, I would choose the latter, and I am inclined to think that most economists would do the same" (Coase 1982, 6).

12. The domain over which the prediction criterion is evaluated is critical. If the domain is narrow, a model may pass the Friedman test—perhaps not surprising, if it has been constructed in part based on data from that domain—but we might still credit the Coasian view on the grounds that it will lay the groundwork for the construction of a model that in the longer run will perform better by Friedman's criterion over a broader purview.

issues can be applicable only as long as the model delivers the predictive goods.[13] It is one thing, as a scientist, to back away from Karl Popper's view that a single deconfirming experiment or piece of evidence can or should be grounds for jettisoning a model (Lakatos 1970). It is another to be unable or unwilling to specify any conceivable empirical observation or series of observations that would lead to the modification of one's theory. Yet in a number of areas of social science we have come close to this.

A casual attitude toward evidence in justifying model assumptions, sometimes observed among rational choice or microeconomic theorists, is reflected in the influential writings of Lionel Robbins.

> The propositions of economic theory, like all scientific theory, are obviously deductions from a set of postulates. And the chief of these postulates are all assumptions involving in some way simple and indisputable facts of experience. . . . These are not postulates the existence of whose counterpart in reality admits of extensive dispute once their nature is fully realized. *We do not need controlled experiments to establish their validity:* they are so much stuff of our everyday experience that they have only to be recognized as obvious. (my italics) (Robbins [1932] 1984, 78–79)[14]

Robbins was referring to such indisputable "facts" as the existence of scarcity, but his reasoning has often been applied by rational choice theorists to the basic assumptions we make about human behavior.

Scientific advance often involves probing beneath the surface of what appears obvious. The striking results of the very first Prisoner's Dilemma experiment are the tip of a much larger iceberg. They are complemented by a growing body of experimental evidence, as well as a wide range of field observation. These data confirm repeatedly that the standard economic model predicts poorly in a range of domains, particularly those involving strategic interaction. Under these circumstances we are naturally and

---

13. See Friedman 1996 for arguments in favor of and (mostly) against the position advanced here. This edited book, in conjunction with Green and Shapiro 1994, to which it is a response, provides a sophisticated and methodologically informed discussion of the contributions of rational choice models within political science. My views on philosophy of science closely mirror those expressed in Green and Shapiro 1996 (255–61).

14. See also Koopmans 1957 (131). Koopmans advocated separating theory entirely from observation "for the protection of both" (cited in McCloskey 2000, 217). Both Robbins and Koopmans are discussed in Hildenbrand 1999 (39); both have for decades been standard methodological references for graduate students in economics. Popper's emphasis on the requirement that scientific propositions generate refutable hypotheses was forcefully introduced to an economics audience by Hutchinson (1938). Most economists accept the position in principle but are often less consistent in adhering to it in practice. See also Lewin 1994.

justifiably drawn to examining the model's underpinnings. So long as our vehicle gets us where we want to go, we can perhaps eschew interest in how it operates. But when that condition no longer holds, we need, as it were, to look under the hood.

The underpinnings of the standard economic model, including the common assumption of psychological egoism, comprise an implicit theory of human nature. Following Gregory Kavka (1986, 29–31), I view such a theory as a description of a set of cognitive and behavioral predispositions possessed by all or nearly all human beings, tendencies alterable through changes in the natural or social environment only with great difficulty. Given that the standard model performs poorly in certain domains, we may legitimately inquire whether its cognitive and behavioral assumptions—its implicit theory of human nature—are adequate enough, complete enough, or realistic enough for the task at hand.

The Coase position does, after all, and in contrast to Friedman, evidence an interest in how the engine operates. But if we are to select emendations or alterations to the assumptions reflected in the standard economic model, the criteria for so doing should be more systematic than intuition, ultimately no more an adequate guide in developing alternatives than a justification for sticking with a poorly performing model. Persisting in regarding the mechanism(s) producing behavior as a black box, and continuing to rely only on our intuition, we are likely to end up with emended models that provide ex post rationales for anomalous observations but lack out-of-sample predictive power because they have not adequately captured relevant cognitive or behavioral mechanisms.

In many cases we can do better predictively than has the standard model by considering what the black box was designed for, how natural selection achieved this, and the relevance both of experimental data focused on its mechanisms and what scientists who have opened it up can tell us about its workings. This position meets resistance from those who, like Robbins, do not wish to be bothered with experimental results, evolutionary theory and history, or research in such areas as neuroanatomy and neuroscience. But this stance returns us to the untenable position of being unwilling to modify a model that suffers repeated predictive failure because its postulates are assumed to be axiomatic.

A close and dear relative of mine once maintained with great conviction that the accelerator of an automobile was connected directly to its speedometer. This model had intuitive appeal, and so long as one did not focus on the consequences of revving the engine in neutral, or coasting down a hill with the engine off, it predicted reasonably well. As one might imagine, however, performing either of these actions produced anomalous observations.

Persistent failures of prediction compel those scientifically inclined to explore, consider, or develop alternate models. But can intuition alone be relied upon to provide the appropriate emendations? Is it not a better strategy to dirty one's hands by getting under the hood? In the case of the automobile speedometer, this involved thinking about what the speedometer was designed for, perhaps even tracing the cable emanating from it to its origin.

The principle illustrated is general. Developing alternatives in the behavioral sciences, or justifying staying with an existing approach, needs to be done in other than a casual fashion if we are to move forward in developing disciplines with improved predictive power. All relevant evidence should be brought to bear. A dismissive attitude toward the value of empirical data in general and controlled experiments in particular in evaluating the validity of cognitive or behavioral assumptions handicaps this effort.

In progressive sciences, the identification of predictive weaknesses or anomalies within existing theoretical approaches has historically proved an effective way station in developing alternative or revised frameworks generally viewed as superior. A growing body of research on human subjects, both experimental and observational, now makes it possible more specifically and less tentatively to identify domains wherein the standard economic model performs poorly, and to calibrate these regularities to give us some idea of what kinds of deviations we are likely to see, and under what conditions we are likely to see them. Observing, identifying, and categorizing these anomalies, and clarifying their scope through further observation and experimentation—methods common to the sciences—are processes that can help organize and discipline our consideration of alternative sets of behavioral or cognitive assumptions (for similar argument, see Ostrom 1998; van Damme 1999, 187; or Schelling 1960, 162–63).

The methodology advocated is modern—not postmodern, except to the degree that these philosophical currents incorporate a necessary pragmatism. Francis Bacon protested against scholastics, who continued to deduce "new scientific conclusions from premises insufficiently founded, as all the premises of the natural sciences must be, on the evidence of the senses" (Gross 1990, 88). He proposed an empiricism based on the experimental method: a "double scale or ladder, ascendant and descendent; ascending from experiments to the inventions of causes, and descending from causes to the invention of new experiments" (Bacon 1973, 90–91). Science is, to be sure, conducted by humans with all their frailties, and we should not fetishize its procedures. Its modes of reasoning rely heavily on induction, which, since David Hume, we have known has no firm philosophical foundation. As Bertrand Russell put it, "Domestic animals expect food when they see the person who usually feeds them. We know that all these rather crude expectations of uniformity are liable to be misleading. The man who has fed the chicken every day throughout his life at last wrings its neck instead" (1974, 21).

Yet in recognizing the foibles of scientists and the weaknesses of scientific methods, there is no need to celebrate these weaknesses. From a pragmatic standpoint, scientific methodologies have been extraordinarily productive of real advances in knowledge in biology, chemistry, physics, geology, and many other natural sciences. To claim otherwise calls into question much of the epistemological foundation of the modern world. Since humans are part of the natural world, there is no reason in principle why the understanding of our behavior should not be amenable to similar methods. Our behavior is not inherently less tractable. In many instances, it is easier to predict using simple statistical algorithms, at least in the aggregate, than are some other natural phenomena such as the weather.

The alternative of allowing the social sciences to continue down insular roads in the direction of a new scholasticism is not to be preferred. Advances in the behavioral sciences are likely to arrive, and indeed are arriving, from the systematic organization and production of evidence, both experimental and observational, in continual dialogue with speculations about causes, not disciplines devoted to the deduction of new "scientific" conclusions from premises insufficiently founded. *If the social sciences are to be truly social, they must remain in close dialogue with empirical evidence.* And if they are to be scientific, the evidence must be treated in a systematic way.

These approaches offer the promise of producing behavioral models with superior predictive power. But ultimately we would like to do more. We would like to understand why: to understand mechanism and, in the final analysis, origin. Why does the standard model perform relatively well in some domains and poorly in others? I believe the perspectives of evolutionary history and theory can be of great assistance here, by helping us understand what our essential cognitive and behavioral predispositions were designed for, and how that design took place.

Scope, Objectives, and Audience

The principles advocated here and the research program to which they give rise conflict with established ways of doing business within the social sciences. Nevertheless, the ingredients for such a program are emerging in a range of different intellectual locales, with relevant advances occurring in areas both within and outside of the social sciences. Many of these, and the opportunities afforded by them, have been recognized only slowly, particularly across disciplinary boundaries, and especially where traditions of insularity are strong.

It is now possible for us to reference a range of literatures beyond the purview of traditional social science in evaluating and selecting a set of cognitive and behavioral assumptions for models of human behavior that are likely in the longer run to perform better according to the Friedman criterion. These include, in addition to the experimental work, a number of areas in the natural sciences that have witnessed important, in some cases very rapid recent progress, including molecular biology, in particular that underlying genetics; neurobiology and neuroanatomy; evolutionary theory and history; and ethology. By exploring these literatures in a focused, analytically rigorous, and empirically disciplined fashion, I hope, within the behavioral sciences, to bring to bear in an intelligent fashion the results of recent research in the natural, particularly biological, sciences, but also, perhaps even more important, to encourage a greater unity of purpose among the social sciences.

Many parts of this story can be found elsewhere, and the extensive bibliography provides an entry to these bodies of work. A distinguishing feature of this exploration, however, is the joint consideration of two controversial and related ideas: the operation of multilevel (including group) selection within early human evolutionary processes, and the likelihood of modularity: domain specific adaptations in our cognitive mechanisms and behavioral predispositions. Both of these ideas reflect traffic up and down Bacon's twin ladders, as we attempt to understand what underlies the results of the world's first PD experiment and those that followed.

These ideas are developed in the light of the growing body of experimental research involving human subjects, one carried forward by behavioral scientists trained in a variety of disciplinary traditions, including economics, psychology, sociology, and political science. And they are considered within the context of two well-established traditions within the social sciences: the sociological/anthropological and the economic or rational choice. These traditions are similar in sometimes surprising ways.[15] But in other important respects they differ, and indeed, those trained within one have frequently been at loggerheads with adherents of the other. Whereas it is possible to cite instances of apostates now embracing a framework formerly anathema, it is unclear what the overall net migration has been.

In any event, charting such flows misses the point, because this book

---

15. There are analogues, for example, between structural-functional explanation in sociology and anthropology and economists' explanation of institutional selection with reference to efficiency properties.

does not argue that either of these traditions offers the one true and correct foundation for social science, or that progress is to be measured by tabulating intellectual demography. I do claim that in the final analysis the approach we adopt should be determined by evidence and logic, that the divide between these two traditions is both symptomatic of and contributor to the insularities of the social sciences, and that it needs to be bridged.

The construction of that bridge requires alterations in foundational assumptions in both camps. The task is complicated because those operating within the sociological/anthropological tradition have been deeply suspicious of any discussion of biological influences on cognition or behavior, seeing it as a threat to the autonomy of central theoretical concepts such as culture or social structure. Rational choice theorists' understanding of the import of evolutionary theory for their work, on the other hand, has been typically limited by adherence to what one might call pop Darwinism, which at the outset conceives of natural selection as operating exclusively at the level of the individual organism. Pop Darwinism has provided a background reinforcer for the belief that the behavioral postulates of the standard economic model are axiomatic.

Bridging these traditions requires a catholic approach, but one that retains willingness to recognize deficiencies on *either* side of the divide: the side one builds from and the side one builds to. Previous attempts have foundered, I believe, on an inability to develop and maintain a consistent critical perspective. With this challenge of intellectual civil engineering in mind, literatures from political science, psychology, sociology, anthropology, history, law, and philosophy are addressed, although the point of departure and principal point of reference is economics, the most self-consciously "Darwinian" of the social sciences. Although some basic familiarity with the empirical and theoretical literature in game theory is a helpful starting point, the book is written with the intent that it might be read with interest and profit by scholars and students in any of these disciplines, as well as by educated lay readers with exposure to contemporary currents in modern behavioral science.

Having stated some of the book's aspirations, it is important as well to stress its limitations. It may be helpful, for example, to make clear at the outset that this is not principally a work in moral philosophy or ethics— concerned with whether we should cooperate or reciprocate, for example. It is about what we as humans actually do, and about essential predispositions that enabled human or hominid ancestors to live successfully in groups extending beyond immediate kin.[16] Second, its main interest is in

---

16. Hominids include *Homo sapiens,* his immediate predecessors, such as *Homo erectus,* and other extinct species, such as *Homo neanderthalensis.* Hominoids include all these plus apes, anthropoids all hominoids plus monkeys, and primates all anthropoids plus prosimilans.

universal features of human societies, not primarily in cultural variation and its consequences.

The Case for Human Universals

Human groups have differed greatly in their toleration or encouragement of cannibalism, slavery, human sacrifice, interminable feuding, head-hunting, female genital mutilation, violent and painful male initiation rights, and ceremonial rape, to name just a few of the culturally variable practices Robert Edgerton documents in his book *Sick Societies* (1992). Edgerton reminds us, in sometimes excruciatingly painful detail, that the consequences of such variation can be significant and, within broad limits, that cultural practices may be maladaptive as well as adaptive or neutral for a group considered as a whole.

More generally, societies have differed greatly in their political cultures; in their treatment of women, children, and the aged; in their stratification; and in their tolerance of inequality of all sorts. Timur Kuran (1995) has developed models that help us understand why that variation, and the course of development of a particular society's political culture, such as that in Eastern Europe or the shah's Iran, is so difficult to predict. It is precisely the inability to make such predictions that he advances as confirmation of the validity of his analysis.[17] Consistent with these conclusions, I argue that such variation can, after the fact, only be explained historically, a point returned to in chapter 7. No general theory of the determinants of cultural or political variation is here proposed.

Rather, it is the origin of cultural universals, in particular the degree to which they have in part a biological foundation, that I explore. The idea that there are such universals conflicts with deeply held views, particularly in sociology and anthropology. The principle of relativism, indeed, has been so firmly embraced in anthropology that many define the field as the study of culture rather than the study of humans (see Brown 1991).

In the last half century, a variety of research and evidence has made more legitimate the consideration of human universals. Noam Chomsky's work on universal grammar (1957), discussed in chapter 5, has been influential, as has been Paul Ekman and Wallace V. Friesen's on human facial expressions (1975). Ekman and Friesen showed members of preliterate New Guinean tribes photographs of Americans who were angry,

---

17. His analysis does, however, contain refutable hypotheses. For example, he predicts that sudden unexpected regime changes are more likely to occur in repressive regimes that do not allow the results of polling data to be made public.

happy, or afraid, and asked them to select one that matched a story such as "she is about to fight." Even though subjects had no prior experience with U.S. culture, they were able to match photo with affect with little difficulty, providing compelling evidence that a subset of facial expressions comprises a universal human language.

On a more informal level one might mention as well the remarkable documentary *First Contact,* which appeared in 1983. The film is based on footage taken by three Australian gold prospectors who in 1930 unexpectedly encountered over a million highland New Guinean tribespeople who had had no prior contact with the outside world. The gestures and facial expressions of these individuals, their ability quickly to establish a rough understanding with the intruders, and their success in coming to terms with westerners and Western civilization, as evident in interviews a half century later, is highly suggestive of a core universality in human cognitive and behavioral mechanisms.

Ekman and Friesen's work suggests that a subset of our facial expressions is ultimately governed by biological machinery built according to a common set of genetic instructions, Chomsky's that we are biologically prepared to learn language according to a set of deep structural rules. It appears as well that the taxonomies we use for animals and plants have a hardwired component. Scott Atran's cross-cultural evidence suggests that all human are born with a set of categories for classifying living things that corresponds very closely to outlines of the Linnaean system. In contrast, uniformities in "folk biologies" have no counterpart in taxonomies of inanimate objects, many of which have been part of the human environment only in recent centuries or millennia (Atran 1990, 1998). His argument is that evolutionary advantage accrued to organisms born with preformatted categories for recurring features of the natural world. For items of more recent provenance, we lack this head start, and must expend energy devising and transmitting filing systems, which are consequently more culturally variable.

In another classic study, Brent Berlin and Paul Kay showed that the demarcations of colors in different societies do not reflect arbitrary divisions of a continuously variable visible spectrum. Although cultures use different sets of words to characterize colors, the colors to which these words correspond are not randomly distributed. Rather, they cluster around red, blue, green, and yellow. Subjects from a culture that lacks color words learn such words better if they correspond to these colors. These focal points have a neurobiological substrate in the sensitivities in the retina's color cones and the lateral geniculate body of the thalamus, where nerve cells carrying information between the eye and the visual cortex are divided into four types, apparently corresponding to the four principal colors humans discriminate (Berlin and Kay 1969; Lumsden and Wilson 1983, 65–67).

A second type of study has critically revisited seminal contributions in the cultural relativism canon. Here one can cite Derek Freeman's (1983) deconstruction of Margaret Mead's study of adolescence in Samoa, as well as Ekkehart Malotki's demolition of the Whorf-Sapir hypothesis insofar as it applies to the Hopi conception of time, published in the same year. The Whorf-Sapir hypothesis argued, basically, that variation in language structures or determines variation in consciousness. Contrary to their claims, however, it turns out that the Hopi conception of time is not very different from yours or mine, and the Hopi language is not lacking in words to describe it (Malotki 1983).

These and other works, in conjunction with evidence available in the Human Relations Area Files (HRAF),[18] provide grounds for questioning the fundamental principle of relativism, that culture is an emergent property, distinct from the humans whose behavior it organizes, and consequently cannot be explained with reference to characteristics of individuals. If this principle is accepted, evolutionary processes as Darwin understood them cannot influence culture, since biological attributes apply only to individuals. If we begin with the principle of relativism as foundational for the study of society and culture, we will be predisposed against acknowledging common features (universals) in human societies, since such commonalities must then be attributed to a statistically unlikely set of coincidences.

Nevertheless, the evidence for some universals, both cognitive and behavioral, is substantial and growing. This book does not consider or attempt a comprehensive catalog (for efforts in this direction, see Edgerton 1992, 65–67). Rather, the focus is on an important few necessary to allow complex social organization to originate. Underlying *any* organized social interaction beyond the level of immediate kin rests a set of predispositions that enables solution of the problem Hobbes identified. Experimental evidence will be used to document them systematically. The argument is strengthened, however, when we can go beyond simple enumeration and show not only how these predispositions came to be but

---

18. These files, the collection and writing of which began at Yale University in the 1930s, were originally intended to document cross-cultural variability. But they have also provided a database whereby hypotheses regarding universals may be systematically considered. An organization dedicated to making these materials available for scholarly research was established at Yale in 1949. Further information may be obtained at <www.yale.edu/hraf>.

also the workings of the black box(es) that produce them. Here is where analyses of group selection and cognitive modularity, respectively, enter.

Altruism as Failure to Harm

The proximate concerns of this book are to explain selection for and persistence of altruistic behavior toward non-kin, to understand the cognitive adaptations that enable it, and to consider how such predispositions should be incorporated in behavioral models. The ultimate concern is the origin of complex social organization, understood to mean networks of social and economic relations extending beyond those involving immediate kin.[19] The two are linked because the development of these relations requires and presupposes a complex of behavioral predispositions, the primus inter pares of which, because it is the sine qua non, is a propensity to play cooperate in single play PDs. This predisposition means most fundamentally the practice of forgoing the option of first strike when encountering an unrelated individual.

In a one-shot PD game, a predisposition to play cooperate is unambiguously altruistic. Once one moves to the fixed and known duration game, the altruistic character of cooperative or contingently cooperative strategies becomes dependent on the frequency of individuals practicing similar strategies within the population from which one's counterparty is drawn. We are accustomed to thinking of the biologically altruistic character of a strategy as dependent only on the description of the strategy itself. This is typically the case for altruism toward kin, such as the sacrifices a parent makes for his or her children. But it is not true for predispositions that foster the development of relations of reciprocity among non-kin.

The distinction is critical in understanding why continuing interactions that are *empirically* of mutual benefit may nevertheless originate as the result of biologically altruistic behavior. Thus, it may empirically be beneficial to play a contingently cooperative strategy in a fixed and known duration PD, as turned out to be the case for Alchian and Williams. But such strategies benefit those who follow them only when others play them

19. My use of the term "complex" is different from that of authors who contrast organization of more "advanced" societies with the simpler forms characterizing hunter-gatherer groups (Diamond 1997). The distinction I make is between the simpler social organization that characterizes the family, whether involving two parents or simply mother-offspring groupings, and more "complex" groups of non-kin. The survival of mammalian species requires parental interaction at the time of conception and for varying periods of parenting. Many mammalian species, however, unlike humans, lead otherwise solitary lives. Mammals aside, parental care among animals is unusual, observed elsewhere only among birds and some reptiles, such as crocodiles.

as well. Such strategies are unlikely to be favored by individual level selection when they prevail at low frequencies. Consequently, at low frequencies they are likely to be biologically altruistic.

Similarly, although the play of cooperate in a one-shot game is unambiguously altruistic, it will not be as detrimental to the actor as theory suggests if others play similarly. The high frequencies of strategies in a population that end up rewarding contingently cooperative play in the fixed and known duration game, or make cooperate not as detrimental as theory suggests it will be in the one-shot game, cannot simply be taken as givens. We need to understand the evolutionary mechanisms that have allowed altruistic predispositions to become established in populations, enabling the development of ongoing social interaction that may then no longer require them for maintenance. What altruism initiates, interest can help sustain.

Still, history affords numerous instances of betrayal and treachery and of individuals or group leaders who have with premeditation launched unprovoked attacks on others. Similarly, some humans *will* play defect in one-shot Prisoner's Dilemmas, even in the context of preplay communication. In light of the litany of cruel practices enumerated in *Sick Societies,* one might ask how we can even consider the possibility that altruistic predispositions underlie complex social organization. The answer is in part that the alternative—ruling such predispositions out of bounds on a priori grounds—is indefensible given the experimental evidence. Some subjects, *but often only a minority,* will play defect in a one-shot PD, far from the 100 percent predicted by theory. Hewing closely to the Nash model leaves unexplained a wide body of experimental and observational data. Moreover, it leaves a gaping hole in our explanations of how organized society beyond kin, whatever the form it has eventually taken, arose.

This work features a broader understanding of altruistic predispositions than is common in the literature. The canonical instance of altruism toward non-kin is taken to be failure to harm, rather than the affirmative acts of assistance with which the concept is typically identified. Failure to harm, where one has powerful capabilities to do so, can be as beneficial to another organism as active assistance.[20] Readers whose intuition tells them their altruistic behavior is limited to kin have, perhaps without reflection, limited attention to affirmative assistance, rightly perceived as a

---

20. Some of those concerned by the relatively weak inclination to render affirmative assistance to non-kin have advocated laws mandating aid if it can be provided at minimal cost by the assister. In doing so they have emphasized that failure to help can be hurtful. What this analysis overlooks is that failure to harm can be helpful. For a review of research on the inclination to render affirmative assistance to non-kin, and the conditions likely to induce it, see Hunt 1990.

weaker predisposition. That is one reason we spend so much time commenting on, praising, being surprised at, and, in many instances, reciprocating unexpected acts of kindness or assistance. They are remarked upon precisely because they are remarkable—above and beyond what is normally expected.

On the other hand, most of the time humans do not walk down the street or along a back country trail and return amazed, exclaiming that no one tried to rob or murder them. We are not in general grateful for altruism of the failure to harm type, *because we generally expect it.* An exception is when credible threats to harm are made and then not carried out—as in hostage situations, in which captives end up bonding with their captors in a seemingly irrational fashion (de Waal 1989, 237).

If we think deeply about the categorical imperative, it becomes clear that what we expect of non-kin is disproportionately weighted toward the former. When we encounter strangers our greatest expectation of others is that they not harm us (and our duty to them is perceived as symmetric). This is not a trivial matter, as anyone who has experienced a situation in which social organization has disintegrated can attest. We are generally surprised, shocked, angered, terrified if this is not the case. We are pleasantly surprised if affirmative assistance is offered and typically only mildly disappointed if it is not, because we do not as a matter of course expect strangers to render affirmative assistance, particularly where we are obviously capable of taking care of ourselves, nor are humans as inclined to proffer such aid in symmetrical situations.

Some of this, of course, is culturally variable, and the degree to which people live in fear of unprovoked attack has varied considerably among societies and over time. As I will discuss subsequently, there is a dark side to humans' ability to form reciprocal bonds among non-kin. Nevertheless, the imbalance in the strength of these two variants of altruistic inclination is defensible as a general proposition and mirrors the asymmetry between the ease with which humans can take another's life and the difficulty of actually saving one by doing other than refraining from taking it.

If one doubts this, perform the following thought experiment. Imagine yourself for an interval of time placed among a random sample of 100 human adults with whom you have had no previous interchange and with whom you expect none in the future. Ask yourself what fraction, a, of these individuals you expect to launch unprovoked attacks on you, and what fraction, b, would render affirmative assistance should you suddenly be obviously in need. I submit that although these estimates will vary among respondents based on personal history and other considerations, for each individual a will invariably exceed b, and that in relations among non-kin an individual's welfare depends as much, and arguably more so, on *a* than it does on *b*. Most ethical and many legal systems emphasize that we have a stronger duty to avoid harming others than we do to provide them affirmative assistance, here articulating and reinforcing what I see as essential predispositions.[21]

The imagined situation of two unrelated individuals encountering each other, each potentially dangerous to the other, is, as Hobbes understood, a classic Prisoner's Dilemma. Without providing a satisfactory explanation of how that dilemma is resolved, one cannot begin to address the development of the range of reciprocal behaviors that results eventually in complex social organization, whose altruistic origin is largely disguised by the benefits individuals typically receive from living cooperatively within larger groups.

Altruism is defined in evolutionary terms as behavior that reduces the fitness of the actor and increases that of another organism. Failure to strike first—giving up the first move in a game that may or may not be one shot—qualifies as such behavior, because the organism loses the advantage that accrues to the offense and, by so doing, renders itself more vulnerable to an attack from its counterparty. Such behavior satisfies the formal definition of altruism as much as does an affirmative act of assistance involving such risk and represents, I argue, its more empirically important form.

No satisfactory explanation within economics or political science has emerged for why rational players should cooperate in a single play or fixed and known duration Prisoner's Dilemma game, assuming both players wish efficiently to maximize their material welfare. Similarly, in evolutionary theory, no one has provided, within an exclusively individual level selection framework, a satisfactory explanation for how a predisposition to refrain from first strike in such situations could have survived the forces that would operate against it upon its emergence at low frequencies in a population. Upon first emergence, indefinitely repeated interaction could not be assumed or expected, and the payoff to the cooperator in a defect-cooperate profile might be death. In spite of this, the predisposition is real, there is a substantial body of observational and experimental evidence for it in human populations, and its persistence and survival can be accounted for by admitting selection at levels above the individual.

Although sympathetic to the position that most adaptations are pop-

---

21. I am attempting here to characterize the relative strength of essential predispositions, reflected to a large degree in common normative structures. As Lorenz notes, the most important imperatives of Mosaic (and all other) law are in fact prohibitions, not commandments (1966, 110). I do not mean to suggest that the strength of their manifestation cannot be altered by training and socialization. Religions will often try to encourage more affirmative assistance, at least to coreligionists, and military training may be necessary to overcome aversion to initiating locally unprovoked attacks.

ulation or species typical, I do not claim that the genotypic determinants of this predisposition have necessarily evolved to the point of fixation: polymorphism[22] is possible and deviant tendencies may persist at low and stable levels. Moreover, in any individual the predispositions identified must, almost certainly, be evoked by environmental cues and can be extinguished or attenuated in their absence or in the presence of different ones. Differences in culture, particularly the political culture of a group or region, can and will have important influences on how these tendencies are manifested (Bar-Tal and Leiser 1981).[23] More generally, their expression will be affected by one's personal history as an infant, child, adolescent, and adult (Lewis, Amini, and Lannon 2000). But these environmental influences flesh out a structure whose scaffolding, like that of the human body, is constructed according to a genetic blueprint, one with variation but remarkable commonality across the human species.

To the degree that we may view some of these predispositions as morally praiseworthy, it is hard to improve on Aristotle in specifying the respective roles of nature and nurture in determining them: "The virtues are neither innate nor contrary to nature. They come to us because we are fitted by nature to receive them; but we perfect them by training or habit" (Aristotle 1963, 303, cited in Binmore 1994, 26). The difficult evolutionary issue, however, not of concern to Aristotle, is how we became "fitted by nature" to receive them.

Summary Plan

Two big ideas, that of modularity in cognition and that of multiple levels of selection in evolution, are central to this book, as is a novel and broader conception of altruism emphasizing failure to harm as its canonical form. The idea of modularity in cognition refers to the conception, championed by structural linguists and evolutionary psychologists, that the mind is not a single, general-purpose computer but a network of systems, some

---

22. Fixation refers to achievement of 100 percent frequency for an allele or a group of alleles that begins in a population at a lesser frequency (Cavalli-Sforza, Menozzi, and Piazza 1994, 6). The consequence of fixation is that the design feature encoded by the allele(s) is now species typical. The basic layout of the human eye or stomach is species typical; eye color, on the other hand, exhibits multiple forms (polymorphism). D. S. Wilson (1994) criticizes Cosmides and Tooby for pushing too hard on the prevalence of species typical design—emphasizing that polymorphism can and does survive in the presence of frequency dependent selection (see chap. 2).

23. As both Aristotle and Hobbes observed, our ability to consider and choose different forms of political structure, a function of our reason and speech, critically distinguishes our social existence from that of the social insects (ants, bees, and termites) (Wrong 1994, 2). Edgerton (1992, 2) provides vivid reminders of the consequences of some of those differences.

domain general and others functionally specialized to particular domains.[24] Just as our body contains specialized internal organs, so too does our brain. The effect of the operation of these mental organs can be observed experimentally and in field data, and increasingly the locus of different subsystems can be mapped through techniques of neurobiology and clinical and experimental neuroanatomy (see chap. 5).

The other big idea (see chap. 2) is that natural selection can sometimes operate at levels above that of the individual organism—and that such a mechanism has permitted the evolution in humans of behavioral and associated cognitive modules critical for the development of complex social organization. These include predispositions to play cooperate when in one-shot PDs and, when repeated interactions have been established, to punish violators of social rules or norms even when so doing cannot be rationalized ex ante as in the interest of the organism.

A concern with these issues, and a need for models in the behavioral sciences with better predictive and explanatory power, is motivated by consideration of a broad range of experimental evidence from Prisoner's Dilemma, public goods, ultimatum, and dictator experiments, and field data ranging from voter participation rates in national elections to the control of international conflict. These issues are discussed within the context of two important and often conflicting traditions in social science: the sociological/anthropological and the economic. Chapter 1 details this evidence and expands on the issues involved in its explanation.

Chapter 2 discusses the logic, mathematics, evidential foundation, and intellectual background of evolutionary models embodying multilevel selection and their role in understanding human altruism. Chapters 3 and 4 address alternate explanations for the emergence of complex social organization. Chapter 3 considers Robert Trivers's model of reciprocal altruism, the concept of social norms, and research in evolutionary game theory, particularly that of John Maynard-Smith and Robert Axelrod. Chapter 4 deconstructs Robert Frank's 1988 book *Passions within Reason,* illustrating the problems that result when attempting to explain altruistic behavior within an economic/evolutionary framework limiting selection to the individual level.

Chapter 5 covers research in a diverse range of fields, including paleontology, molecular biology, ethology (in particular the study of close animal relations), infant cognition, language acquisition and structure, neurobiology, and neuroanatomy. Collectively, these studies underlie the case for modularity in the cognitive and behavioral mechanisms that organize

---

24. For example, people may reason about and react differently to a formally identical logical problem when it concerns social relations than when it does not (see chaps. 5 and 6).

our social relations. The chapter proposes a different solution to the problem Konrad Lorenz posed in *On Aggression* (1966), one that emphasizes the existence in humans of hardwired restraints on intraspecific violence.[25] The final section of the chapter provides a detailed discussion of experimental work by Leda Cosmides and John Tooby on "cheater detection" modules, the cognitive underpinnings of a behavioral predisposition to punish violators of social norms, a key pillar, along with a willingness to give up the option of first strike, of Tit-for-Tat.

Chapter 6 addresses the second major interdisciplinary conversation engaged in by economists over the last quarter century: that with the heuristics and biases research program pioneered by the psychologists Daniel Kahneman and the late Amos Tversky and introduced to economists through the work of Richard Thaler and others. Their work has encouraged social scientists to be more receptive to the results of experimental research and introduced the concept of framing to our vocabulary. In so doing it has opened our minds to the possibility that modularity is an important phenomenon. For example, we may think and behave differently depending on whether or not a situation is framed as one involving strategic interaction. But its lack of an explicitly evolutionary perspective and its focus on decision theory and in particular judgment under uncertainty, irrelevant for the PD and a number of other games of strategic interaction, limit its ability to resolve the issues addressed here. Within the domains it does address, moreover, the program is currently suffering from an explosion of heuristics—behavioral rules of thumb—a development that has tended to reduce the predictive value of any one of them considered individually. The chapter illustrates this through a discussion of the application of behavioral economics[26] in finance, one of the hottest current areas of research within this program.

The concluding section, chapter 7, considers the place of economics/rational choice models within an empirically based and evolutionarily informed behavioral science and how its self-conception and practice might differ were the two big ideas adduced in this introduction fully accepted. In so doing, it returns to the question of how we should distinguish between historical and social scientific explanation.

---

25. The original title of this manuscript was "On Altruism," which I thought a clever and subtle allusion to Lorenz's work, which everyone read when I was in college. It was such a subtle reference, however, that most readers missed it, although fully recognizing it once it was pointed out. Another rejected candidate was "Altruism as Failure to Harm."

26. "Behavioral economics" should not be confused with behaviorist psychology. Behavioral economics emphasizes the study of what individuals actually do, as opposed to what economic theory predicts they will do or counsels they should do. Behavioral economists have no inherent aversion to the concept of modularity, which implies domain specific mental organs. Such a concept, however, is anathema for behaviorist psychologists.

CHAPTER 1

Evidence and Logic

This chapter develops broad contours of the book's argument, adduces additional experimental and observational evidence, and establishes foundations for the more detailed treatments of chapters 2 through 6. It extends the prologue's discussion of the limits of rational choice theory as well as the sociological/anthropological approach in understanding the empirical evidence, themes developed in detail in chapters 3 and 4. It addresses the relevance to these questions of the heuristics and biases research program, the subject of chapter 6. And it contextualizes the key elements of the alternate route proposed to the solution of the Hobbesian problem, the concepts of multilevel selection and modularity, the subjects of chapters 2 and 5. The emphasis is on the relationship of these concepts to, respectively, traditional evolutionary biology and behaviorist psychology.

On the empirical side, the chapter summarizes experimental results beyond those involving PD games, including those concerned with the voluntary provision of public goods, ultimatum, centipede, and dictator games. It probes the claim that failure to harm is the canonical form of human altruism, and thus that the phenomenon is more widespread than commonly appreciated, through the historical consideration of what appears to be the strongest countercase: war and genocide, in particular the war of extermination against the Jews conducted by the Third Reich. It discusses the interactions of nation-states, which operate in the absence of the coercive ruler Hobbes identified as necessary to solve the PD. Finally, in addressing why democracies do not fight each other, the chapter reaffirms that variations in political culture will influence the expression of essential predispositions. Born though we are with similar biological scaffolding, our continuing efforts to fashion, refashion, maintain, and change political structures have real consequences.

The Limits of Game Theory

As the prologue suggested, game theory, the branch of microeconomic theory addressing strategic interaction, faces severe difficulties in accounting for observed behavior in Prisoner's Dilemmas. In the single play game

29

the unique Nash equilibrium is for each player to defect, but many players do otherwise. When games are repeated a fixed and known number of times, defecting at every stage remains the unique Nash equilibrium, although the strategy is no longer strictly dominant. If there is some probability one's counterparty might not be entirely rational, or might tremble a bit, it could pay (be rational) to employ other strategies (Kreps et al. 1982).

This conclusion does not, however, follow if both players are assumed rational. Nevertheless, many sophisticated subjects cooperate throughout much of a finitely repeated game, the Alchian-Williams pairing a case in point. Models of single play and of finitely repeated PD games engaged in by rational players therefore imply unique equilibria and lead to clean, unambiguous predictions of behavior, predictions consistently at variance with the experimental evidence.

More complex models do raise the possibility of explaining the persistence of cooperative outcomes within a rational choice framework. When PD games are repeated indefinitely, there may exist Nash equilibria involving some degree of cooperation, provided players do not discount future payoffs too much (Fudenberg and Maskin 1986; Fudenberg and Tirole 1991, chap. 5). The discount rate matters because the higher it is, the less important are later stages of the game, and the closer the interaction comes to being equivalent to a single play game. If we accept these assumptions, it is possible to "rationalize" how cooperative outcomes are *sustained* as an outcome of egoistic choice. Unfortunately, these models feature multiple equilibria, and not all of them involve cooperation. If we are interested in prediction, what grounds do we have for knowing which one will obtain? In what sense has theory predicted or explained a particular outcome?

These conclusions, widely understood, help account for the strong predilection of game theorists (e.g., Binmore 1994, 1998a) to begin by assuming an environment of indefinitely repeated interaction. If one is interested in squaring theory with data, having a model that at least allows for the possibility of cooperation as an outcome is surely preferable to one that precludes it.

One must keep in mind, however, that what is being accounted for is the maintenance of an equilibrium, not its origin. Moreover, the applicability of the underlying assumption to real world situations is often questionable. A marriage may be modeled as involving indefinitely repeated interaction, but since in principle either party may end it, each has the option, at his or her own initiative, of converting the interaction into one of fixed and known duration. Moreover, the marriage may well have begun with an interaction that, ex ante, looked to both parties as if it would be one time (one night?). How did the time horizon get extended? The same considerations apply with greater and lesser force to many other continuing relationships that began with meetings that could well have ended as one-time encounters only. One-shot dilemmas existed in the past and continue to confront us today. We need to understand why they did not and do not defeat us more often.[1]

To summarize: (1) If we are rational and egoistic, we can only choose defect in single play PD games, regardless of what we believe will be the play of our counterparty. The strict dominance of the strategy of defection means that even if we think our counterparty will irrationally choose cooperate, as a rational agent, we should play defect. Our ability to forecast counterparty play is irrelevant—worthless—because that estimate cannot affect our choice. (2) In repeated games of fixed and known duration, rational agents can, assuming their counterparty is also rational, only choose continuous defect: a strategy that requires defecting at each stage of the game. Continuous defect by both parties forms the unique Nash equilibrium profile, although if we thought our counterparty might be irrational, it could make sense to play a different strategy. (3) *If* the duration of interaction is indefinite, it becomes possible for mutual cooperation to be sustained as a Nash equilibrium, although so can mutual defection and many other profiles. (4) The predictive or explanatory utility of the conclusion of this last point, by no means clear cut, must be further qualified because the assumption of indefinitely repeated interaction—an environment in which neither party can control the timing of an unknown endpoint—can be at best approximately true when characterizing any real social interaction.

The longer and more indefinite the horizon of interaction, the more possibilities open up that rational egoistic behavior can sustain cooperative equilibria. But which is cause and which effect? Do indefinite horizons of interaction explain cooperative outcomes, or does (and did) our ability to reach cooperative solutions in single play games help explain their extension into extra innings?

---

1. Bendor and Swistak (1997, 294) express a commonly held view when they observe that one period games with a single stage "are games of little substantive importance." I disagree. It is true that in day-to-day life with my family or at work, I engage in interactions that have long and indefinite time horizons. But every time I venture on the freeway, walk down the main street of a new city, get onto a crowded subway car, or hike down a sparsely traveled backcountry trail, I engage in encounters that are, in all likelihood, one shot. The "social structure" that makes the assumption of indefinitely repeated interaction realistic is one we are continually creating and re-creating. It is not some reified force that exists separately from the humans whose behavior and preferences generate and sustain it, although it may be perceived as such, a perception that is strengthened when multiple parties are involved. See also Barry and Hardin 1982 (385).

Even were the assumption of indefinite interaction more widely applicable, we would want to understand how environments in which it could reasonably be assumed developed in the first place. A central and unresolved problem in strategic analysis, therefore, the one that Hobbes identified, is explaining how rational individuals transition from single play environments to those where repetition may more reasonably be anticipated. A central challenge in evolutionary analysis is accounting for the increase from low to high frequencies in cooperative predispositions within populations in which humans interact.

In addressing how these transitions came about, and come about, we will need to consider, in a manner inconsistent with the standard economic approach, whether humans possess essential tendencies that might contravene the counsel of logic and mathematics, predisposing them, in one-shot interactions, to play cooperate, a strictly dominated strategy. If we have these tendencies, we need to understand how we acquired them. The suggested solution to the problem of transition lies outside of the realm of strategic analysis as commonly understood. It lies rather in the realm of evolutionary theory, albeit a more nuanced version of it than that with which most people are familiar.

Hobbes's enduring contribution was in posing the problem; his resolution of it, however, for reasons to be discussed, is inadequate. So too is that of other social contract theorists, including John Locke and Jean-Jacques Rousseau. Locke's solution emphasizes mutuality of interest, which anticipates the arguments of economists and game theorists but confuses an account of how cooperation may be sustained with an explanation of how it originated. The same can be said for Rousseau's analysis, which stresses consensus on norms, anticipating key sociological arguments (Wrong 1994, 9). Where do norms come from if we begin with single play interaction? The problem of the origin of complex social organization is recapitulated every time individuals face the challenge of building an ongoing personal relationship. Norms specific to a relationship develop and are reinforced and sustained by continued interaction. They cannot explain the ability of a pair of individuals to move from one-time to ongoing intercourse because they arise as the consequence of that outcome. The same will be true of norms organizing multiparty interaction.

Experimental Methods

Experimental methods are particularly useful for exploring these issues because they allow the study of behavior in single play situations, where considerations of reputation and the anticipation of repetition may be controlled for. The resulting body of research in this area is now so large, generally so carefully conducted, and so consistent in many of its findings that it commands our attention, even if we are initially inclined to be skeptical of what it can tell us. A leitmotiv in what follows is the contrast between the predictions (and counsel) of canonical game theory as applied to such games, and what the evidence reveals.

Economists have tended to adopt a rather unvariegated view of human nature, sometimes questioning whether it is even meaningful to talk about altruistic or nonrational behavioral tendencies among humans, particularly where such behavior involves non-kin. When pressed, the underlying assumptions about rationality and egoism often turn out to involve a tautology: the presumption that individuals act in satisfaction of their own desires. If narrower and potentially refutable definitions are adopted, leading to the presumption that people act efficiently to advance their material interests, then Prisoner's Dilemma experiments form part of a body of experimental results that leads us to reject this view as universally applicable across all domains.

They point in a different direction, in particular toward the conclusion that predispositions to engage in other-regarding behavior toward non-kin form part of a range of essential human characteristics.[2] These inclinations can be difficult to identify through field observation alone. Ambiguity arises because where group beneficial behavior is mutualistic, it is consistent with egoistic as well as altruistic inclinations.[3] What field observation may sometimes only hint at, however, experimental methods can pinpoint. Under controlled conditions altruistic and nonrational predispositions are isolable and identifiable and represent, I will argue, part of the legacy of the evolutionary trajectory that produced the human genotype.

The evidence suggests, for example, that as the result of a long history of natural selection, we are born, hardwired, with the fundamentals of a PD solution module, a module with both cognitive and behavioral dimensions. It follows that there is an essential biological component to what is universal about human societies, although our reason and speech have

2. Use of the Aristotelian term here is designed to differentiate the approach from behaviorist views common in the social sciences, which imply that almost all action can be explained with reference to circumstance and past learning, rather than inherent inclinations. The proposed methodology for identifying these traits is empiricist. I make no claim that nonrational predispositions are necessarily morally praiseworthy, although they often are.

3. Both Locke and Adam Smith in the *Wealth of Nations* ([1776] 1937) can be read as articulating mutualistic accounts of how cooperation is sustained. Mutualistic behavior benefits others as well as the actor. It is in the interest of the actor and in the interest of the group of which the actor is part. Altruistic behavior imposes a fitness cost on the actor but benefits at least one other conspecific. The term *mutualism* is most commonly applied to interactions between species but can also be used to apply to behavior among conspecifics.

given us the ability, within that framework, to develop different political cultures. An understanding of the solution of the basic problem of order, however, precedes exploration of the consequences of such differences. How natural selection could have allowed a PD solution and related modules to survive is a principal concern of chapter 2.

Beyond the Prisoner's Dilemma: Public Goods, Ultimatum, and Dictator Games

Predispositions that cannot be squared with criteria of rational action manifest themselves in a broad range of contexts beyond those Flood and Dresher examined. Studies of the voluntary provision of public goods, to take a related example, show an irreducible propensity among some subjects voluntarily to provide such goods, in spite of Nash equilibrium analysis, which counsels and predicts universal free riding (Ledyard 1995).

Such experiments typically involve a group of subjects, say, seven, each of whom is given a sum of money, say, $10, and told they can either keep it or (secretly) deposit it in a group account whose total will be, say, doubled and then equally divided among the group. The best of the Pareto efficient solutions for the individuals considered as a group is for everyone to put the entire sum in the collective account, enabling each in this instance to double his or her endowment. But the unique Nash equilibrium solution is for each to put nothing in the account, in which case everyone ends up with his or her original $10. Each individual following the egoistic Nash-prescribed strategy hopes he or she will be the only one failing to contribute and will thus be able to free ride on the voluntary contributions of others. Contributing to the common pool is a risky strategy since, in the worst case, if one is the only contributor, one will end up with substantially less than if one had retained the entire initial endowment. Such voluntary contributions can legitimately be characterized as altruistic, because they result in a benefit to others and, whatever the contribution profile of the other players, an individual would, ex post, have done better by contributing nothing. In these experiments, an outcome involving any positive amount of voluntary contribution cannot be a Nash equilibrium.

Nevertheless, some subjects persist in rejecting the prescriptive counsel of game theory, even when it is clear they fully understand it. Although contribution rates can be manipulated experimentally by, for example, altering the magnitude of temptations for defection, *such rates cannot be driven to zero.* Moreover, such rates can be increased by providing opportunities for preplay communication even though, in the absence of enforceable agreements, such opportunities should, according to theory, have no effect on the outcome. Remarkably, contribution rates sometimes rise, rather than fall, as group sizes are increased or, in learning experiments, as the number of iterations is increased (Hoffman, McCabe, and Smith 1998, 340; Ostrom 1998). In a variety of political and economic arenas, such as managing common resources or dealing with shirking where groups are jointly responsible for work output, this research has important implications. Free riding, though a very real phenomenon, is not as inexorably insurmountable as rational choice theory suggests it will be.

Consider a variant of the design with somewhat more restrictive strategy options. Robyn Dawes has conducted experiments in which groups of individuals (e.g., seven) were given choices of keeping $6 or having $12 distributed in equal shares to the other six players ($2 to each). The strictly dominant strategy for each player is to retain the $6, but if all distribute to each other, each ends up with $12. Dawes found in his experiments a hard core of 25 to 50 percent of subjects who would altruistically distribute even under the most unfavorable circumstances; that rate went up dramatically if relevant communication was permitted, even where choice was anonymous and subjects could be more or less guaranteed they would never see each other again (Dawes 1988, 197).[4]

Behavior in these experiments, just like that in the PDs discussed in the prologue, is not rationalizable from the standpoint of normative game theory. It is the watermark left on our phenotypes by evolutionary pressures that selected for cooperation toward non-kin, through mechanisms, including group level selection, described in chapter 2.

Some field observation is unambiguous in its consistency with these conclusions. A large literature in political science, for example, is devoted to the explication and prediction of voting behavior based on the assumption that citizens are rational. Its soft underbelly is the phenomenon of voting itself.[5] Voting takes time and energy. The likelihood that one vote will influence a national election outcome is very small, unless one happens perhaps to be a Supreme Court Justice. Yet in spite of what is apparently an unfavorable benefit-cost ratio, tens of millions of people vote in national elections. Participation rates in the United States have fallen from a peak of 80 percent of eligible voters at the end of the nineteenth century. But rates today continue in the range of 50 percent, in spite of a substan-

---

4. The effect of preplay communication existed only when players communicated about the choice and believed the results of cooperation would go to the group of which they were part. However, if groups were initially told the group would share the benefits of cooperation, but were subsequently told the benefits would go to strangers, some carryover of cooperation above the 25–50 percent baseline could still be observed.

5. The political scientist Morris Fiorina calls this "the paradox that ate rational choice theory" (Fiorina 1990). Joking about the paradox doesn't eliminate it!

tial expansion of the electorate, which now includes women, an increased share of African Americans, and eighteen to twenty-one year olds. Facilitated in part by the Nineteenth, Twenty-fourth, and Twenty-sixth Amendments to the U.S. Constitution, voting in national elections as a proportion of the total population has actually risen during the twentieth century from under 20 percent to its current rate of around 40 percent.[6] In the 1992 U.S. presidential election, the number of those voting exceeded 101 million. At this writing, returns are not final for the 2000 election, but it appears as if participation will have exceeded 104 million.

If one views broad based participation in democratic decision making as providing a benefit shared by many in society, then we have a clear illustration here of the paradox of the voluntary provision of public goods. Political scientists in the rational choice tradition have performed triple somersaults trying to account for these data, without much success (see Green and Shapiro 1994, chap. 4). Ordinary citizens in Western democracies, along with media commentators, are also deeply involved in this effort, as we sometimes try to provide an instrumental interpretation of or rationale for behavior that can ultimately only be viewed as expressive. Witness for example serious discussions of whether or not one should "throw one's vote away" on a third party candidate. If one accepts that there is an infinitesimal probability of one's vote affecting the outcome of a national election, it is difficult to see how this discussion can be taken seriously, if it is intended literally.

My intent here is to point out (a) that people do vote and (b) that we often "rationalize" behavior by persuading ourselves that this is an activity that can be analyzed as if it were pursued on instrumental grounds. The tendency to engage in such self-deception is a special occupational hazard for those operating within a rational choice tradition. I use the term *hazard* advisedly, however, because the predisposition may serve socially useful purposes, as in the case of voting but also, for example, in nuclear strategy. It is common to worry that a counterparty might "irrationally" launch a first strike. Given our belief in the normative and predictive value of the rationality assumption, it is simply too frightening to confront head-on the conclusion that if we and our counterparty are rational, first strike might be the only theoretically defensible option for either of us. The logic of this possibility is discussed in greater detail in chapter 4.

---

6. In 1900, the top three presidential candidates received approximately 13.8 million votes; U.S. population was about 75 million. In 1992, the top three candidates received over 101 million votes; U.S. population was about 250 million. Data are from *Historical Statistics of the United States* and *Statistical Abstract of the United States* (1999). In the last three decades, participation among the *voting age* population has fluctuated around the 50 percent level (*Statistical Abstract* 1999, 280; table 8.1).

Willingness to Punish

The evidence from single play PD experiments, both two player and those involving the multiplayer provision of public goods, confirms a widespread human tendency to play cooperate, even in the absence of any anticipation of repetition. This does not mean that people who choose to do so are indifferent to what their counterparties play. In two stage experiments involving public goods, if, after the first stage, subjects are given an opportunity to punish defectors, at some cost to themselves, they will do so. This is true even when group composition changes every round, so that such behavior cannot be motivated by the hope that one will benefit from the greater cooperation in future plays of those punished (Ostrom, Walker, and Gardner 1992; Fehr and Gächter 2000).

Fehr and Gächter's work is particularly striking in demonstrating that humans are predisposed to punish rule violators for reasons that can have nothing to do with a desire to establish a "reputation" for toughness or vindictiveness. The unique Nash equilibrium in the games they study should be one involving no punishment, since the costs are borne by the punishers and the possible benefits (of altered behavior on the part of the punishees) are received mostly or entirely by others.

A willingness to punish defectors, or those perceived as such, even when such behavior cannot serve the interest of the punisher, is also evident in asymmetric bargaining, or ultimatum games. In ultimatum games, discussed in more detail in chapter 4, a proposer is given a sum of money, say $10, and told she may propose a division of this amount between herself and another subject. The catch is that if the other subject rejects the proposed division, neither receives anything. If $0.01 is the minimum denomination, the unique subgame perfect Nash equilibrium is for the proposer to suggest $0.01 for the other subject and $9.99 for herself.[7] But proposals for anything less than about $3 for the other subject are routinely rejected. These are typically single play games, so the rejecter cannot be "efficiently advancing his or her material welfare" by apparently preferring nothing to something.

---

7. Any proposed division can be the consequence of a pair of strategies that satisfies the Nash equilibrium criterion. If the responder's preannounced strategy is to reject all offers below $3, then an offer of $3 completes a Nash equilibrium profile (each is the optimal reply to the other). But this equilibrium is not "subgame perfect," because the threat of rejecting a lower offer is not credible *if* one believes counterparty behavior to be rational, an assumption generally viewed as inconsistent with preferring nothing to something. Subgame perfect equilibrium, an equilibrium "refinement" due to Reinhard Selten (1965), requires that the outcome in each of a series of stages in a sequential game be itself a Nash equilibrium. It thus precludes strategies that, in initial stages, involve threats of behavior in subsequent stages that, if carried out, would be irrational.

These experiments have been run in a number of countries around the world, including some in the third world, such as Indonesia, where the dollar stakes, although small, represent a more sizable fraction (as much as three months worth) of annual income (Cameron 1999; Camerer 2002). The results in other countries are similar, although some cultural differences have been identified. Israelis, for example, play somewhat closer to the Nash/Selten prediction (Roth et al. 1991), although the probability that an offer is refused differs little cross-culturally.

Another sequential move game with startling experimental outcomes is centipede, so called because of the appearance of the diagram of possible plays in it. The experimenter puts, say, a dollar on the table. Player A can either take it or leave it. If she takes it, the game is over. If money is left on the table, a dollar is added. Player B can then either take the $2, in which case the game is over, or leave it, in which case the experimenter adds another dollar. Both players know in advance that when a limit, say, $10, is reached, no more will be added. Since A expects that player B will take the $10 should they get to the final stage, it is clear, reasoning by backward induction, that the only rational decision for A is to take the dollar at the outset. Every time a player leaves money on the table, she is behaving altruistically, because the action gives the counterparty an otherwise unavailable option to obtain a higher payoff, at the risk for the actor of ending up with nothing. The only way leaving money on the table can be rational is if one assumes one's counterparty is not. Experimental evidence overwhelmingly contradicts the prediction that play will never move beyond the first stage.

The results of dictator games provide perhaps the starkest confirmation of altruistic and irrational behavior among humans. In dictator games, subjects are provided with a sum of money and asked to divide it with a counterparty, often with the opportunity to remain completely anonymous (Eckel and Grossman 1996). In contrast to an ultimatum game, in which a counterparty's refusal to accept an offered division means that neither party gets anything, in a dictator game the offerer keeps his or her share regardless of whether or not the counterparty accepts the proposed division. Although some subjects will keep all of the money, not all will. Indeed, in recent experiments *only 20 percent* of subjects kept all the money: a more frequent outcome was to split it down the middle, with the remaining offers distributed roughly evenly between 50 and 0 percent (Forsythe et al. 1994). Again, these rates can be manipulated through different experimental treatments, but they cannot be driven to zero. Such behavior can easily be made consistent with tautological egoism, the presumption that people act in satisfaction of their own desires, by altering in an appropriate but ex post fashion the arguments of the utility function each is presumed to maximize (see Fehr and Schmidt 1999).[8] But it cannot be viewed as consistent with the hypothesis that people act so as efficiently to advance their material self-interest.

These baseline levels of cooperation in PD games, voluntary contribution and defector punishment in public goods experiments, rejection of positive offers in ultimatum and dictator games, and play beyond the first stage in centipede games are all anomalies vis-à-vis the behavior an analysis of Nash equilibria predicts. In each of these experimental domains, research provides repeated laboratory confirmation of what is intuitively clear to most humans. Our behavioral decision processes cannot be governed entirely by those presumed in the standard economic/rational choice model or canonical game theory. Other predispositions are operative, including some warranting the descriptor *altruistic,* and although some of these are more likely to be displayed toward family members, their expression is not restricted to kin. The empirically observed disjunctures between behavior and theoretical prediction are real. And they are important, I argue, because the human propensities that underlie them form the foundation upon which has been built social organization beyond groups of immediate kin.[9]

In many situations for which the Prisoner's Dilemma is a useful metaphor, the payoff realized by a cooperator in the face of a counterparty's defection can involve death, a point Hobbes understood well. Restraint on defection—altruistic because of the avoidable risks it imposes on the cooperator and the opportunities for gain presented to the counter-

---

8. It is unlikely that a concern with fairness is all that is involved in the results of ultimatum games experiments (see chap. 4). Falk, Fehr, and Fischbacher (1999) have already questioned the adequacy of the Fehr and Schmidt model (1999): other, less praiseworthy other-regarding motives, such as envy, are almost certainly implicated.

9. For a contrary view, see Ken Binmore. He and others believe that the behavior observed in one-shot experimental games "survives because it is needed to sustain equilibria in *repeated* games. . . . Nor should we be surprised if the physiological and psychological mechanisms that have evolved to sustain equilibria in repeated games should somehow be triggered inappropriately in one-shot situations" (1994, 183). In other words, people bring to these games rules of thumb derived from their day-to-day experience and need practice in order to learn how to play them correctly. Theorists who follow this route argue that the experimental stakes are too small (but see Cameron 1995) or emphasize that repetition produces movement toward the Nash predictions. But any positive deviation remains a violation of the normative predictions, and in experimental research involving strategic interaction/bargaining, such deviations remain substantial, even where subjects are experienced. Binmore's statement that "In the long run, behavior tends to converge on whatever the equilibrium of the game under study happens to be" (1994, 185–86) seems to be based as much on faith as it is on evidence, at least in strategic interaction/bargaining games. The frequency of cooperation in the Alchian-Williams pairing *increased* as the subjects "learned how to play" (see subsequent discussion), and they were scarcely naive when they started. Presumably Binmore shares Nash's reaction to their behavior.

party—is therefore essential in enabling the transition from environments of single play interaction to ones where repetition may be anticipated. It is among an important range of predispositions that *enables* complex social interaction. Some of the central questions posed in this book are how, from an evolutionary standpoint, we came as a species to possess them, what is their specific character, and what cognitive and neurobiological mechanisms underlie them.

The Sociological Tradition and the Role of History

Some of the limitations of game theory and the rational choice approach in understanding these results have now been laid out. What of the sociological/anthropological tradition? This alternative tradition and its associated concepts (norms, culture, social structure), although helpful descriptively, offers only limited assistance from an explanatory perspective. Understanding these limits opens the way for consideration of evolutionary/biological influences on predispositions reflected in cultural universals.

Like sociologists and anthropologists, economic historians and students of comparative systems, because of the nature of their subject matter, consider the consequences of variation in institutions, culture, and norms in ways that economists conducting analysis within structures assumed stable can often sidestep. A recurring question has been whether such concepts can explain what rational choice theory apparently does not. A critical issue in addressing such variation is whether or not it is necessarily efficient or adaptive. If so, institutions and norms are ultimately inconsequential, because they are derivative and reflective of more fundamental determinants.

Economists, sociologists, anthropologists, and sociobiologists have, within disciplines, not spoken with unanimity on this issue. The structural-functional approach in sociology/anthropology, early work in the new institutional economics, and sociobiological analyses in the 1970s all tended to start with the presumption that norms or institutions were efficient or adaptive. In the last two decades, however, there has been movement among scholars in each of these disciplines away from that position.

The answer one gives to this question has important implications. If norms and institutions are reflective of currently available resources and technologies, then knowledge of past states of the system cannot add value in explaining them. If they are not necessarily so reflective, then historical analysis, historical explanation, and historical data all become relevant. Once one admits a role for historical influence, the possibility of maladaptation, within limits, arises.

Since the evolutionary process that gave rise to the hardwired predispositions underlying universals is ultimately historical, the issue is not whether or not we need historical explanation, but rather the time frame over which it is to be invoked. The historical explanation of human universals takes place in a distant evolutionary past. The role of historical considerations in accounting for political and institutional variation is charted over a much more recent time frame, in units of years or decades rather than hundreds of thousands or millions of years. In trying to predict human behavior, it is important to distinguish between the explanatory role of essential human predispositions, unchanged for at least thirty thousand years, and the influence of cultural variability on their expression.

The determinants and consequences of behavior not strictly self-interested were central concerns in my dissertation research. My thesis investigated the economic returns realized from socializing schoolchildren in nineteenth century Massachusetts as well as helping them learn reasoning skills and master particular domains of knowledge in public (common) schools.[10] It was difficult to understand the common school revival dating from the late 1830s using a standard human capital model. In such a model, increased derived demand for cognitive skills raises the private return to schooling, leading, in a democracy, to political pressure for tax-subsidized primary education. The problem with this story was that the necessary trends in the demand for skills simply are not evident until perhaps the end of the nineteenth century.

In contrast, the documentary record suggested that, in the context of universal male suffrage, elite perceptions of external benefits associated with school provision (greater willingness among schooled children to be punctual, respond positively to authority figures outside of the family, and respect others' property and persons) were critical in terms of political motivation, regardless of what may have been the long term, perhaps unintended, economic consequences of compulsory, tax-supported education. The thesis emphasized the economic benefits from effective socialization but eschewed a simple rational choice model of its provision. As is common in the area of economic history, the scholarship reflected an attempt to bring to bear concepts and tools from a variety of the social sciences on a historical problem. These themes continue to be developed and explored in broader comparative contexts by other scholars (Lindert 1999; Engerman, Mariscal, and Sokoloff 1999).

The analysis of the role of schools as agents of socialization is, of course, not at issue in this book. What is of concern is the larger question

---

10. Field 1974, 1976a, 1976b, 1979b, 1980. See also Field 1978 on labor market context and 1979c for extension of the model to British data.

of the mechanisms responsible for the control among humans of intra-specific harm, and the extent to which this restraint is influenced by hard-wired (biological) predispositions, the result of evolutionary processes. A satisfactory explanation of how that control is achieved is necessary for a coherent account of the origin of complex social organization.

Sociologists and anthropologists have emphasized culture, norms, and institutions in accounting for that restraint, but have generally eschewed an interest in their microfoundations and in particular the possibility that biological processes might have an influence on them. The appeal of these concepts is their apparent ability to address phenomena for which microeconomic theory, premised on strictly self-interested agents, often seems inadequate. Receptivity to elements of the sociological/anthropological tradition among specialists in economic history, economic development, comparative systems, and other subdisciplines, along with the appeal of rational choice approaches among growing contingents within sociology, anthropology, and political science, is indicative of the fact that the influence of the two core social scientific traditions identified does not map precisely onto departmental or disciplinary affiliations.

A chapter of my thesis ("On the Explanation of Rules Using Rational Choice Models") focused specifically on the limitations of standard economic models in explaining the origin of social rules, and was eventually published as a separate article (1979a). These themes were extended in an *Explorations in Economic History* paper (Field 1981) critical of Douglass North and Robert Paul Thomas's attempt to provide in 158 pages a systematic account of institutional variation in Europe over an eight-hundred-year period based solely on variation in such "economic" variables as technologies and land-labor ratios (North and Thomas 1973). High land-labor ratios led to conditions of free labor (as North and Thomas pointed out for Europe) except where they did not (in the U.S. South or Eastern Europe), and, I argued, one needed to introduce variation in social norms or structure to close the model and account for such variation.[11] My 1984 *Economic Development and Cultural Change* paper more explicitly addressed the need for norms to close microeconomic models, with emphasis on game theoretical models and in particular the analysis of

---

11. Evsey Domar, for example, had used *high* land-labor ratios to account for coerced labor regimes (slavery) in the U.S. South as well as the recrudescence of feudalism in eastern Europe after the great plague (Domar 1970). North no longer assumes that institutions are necessarily efficient, opening the door to the possibility of maladaptation and its consequences (North 1990). In his more recent research he places much more emphasis on the role of ideology and beliefs in accounting for cultural variation, a position consistent, for example, with that taken by Kuran.

games of coordination (those that involve, e.g., the choice of which side of the road to drive on) as well as the more emotionally complex PD games.

This emphasis on norms counterpoised the traditions of classical sociology and anthropology to those of economics. The view of social structure as emergent and "superorganic" is evident in Durkheim's work and in anthropological writings such as those of A. L. Kroeber, and was forcefully articulated by Talcott Parsons in his earliest and most influential book, *The Structure of Social Action* (1937), a work that directly engages the development of economic theory. Parsons took Hobbes as his starting point but, in lieu of Hobbes's coercive state, adduced a shared and autonomous normative structure as the cement of society.

My appeal to social norms, in the tradition of these disciplines, did not offer a systematic explanation of their origin but instead insisted that we explicitly acknowledge the limits of our knowledge. This was far better, I thought, than offering incomplete models that claimed to do more. My 1991 article "Do Legal Systems Matter?" argued that although "functional" constraints imposed limits on the norms or institutions (structure) that could persist, within that range, idiosyncratic variation in legal rules or norms could have real and potentially significant economic effects, in ways extending beyond those involving transactions costs emphasized by Ronald Coase.[12]

That is, while technologies and resource endowments might restrict the range of institutional regimes in a particular region at a particular time to those with survival potential, they did not narrow it to one. Structural-functionalism was simply not powerful enough to explain the prevalence of a particular institutional regime from within that restricted set. A variety of case specific factors, in other words, historical explanation, would invariably also be necessary for such an account, and the work of anthropologists, sociologists, historians, and students of comparative political institutions was critical for that characterization. Finally, the historically specific selection from within the set mattered for economic performance, in ways that economic historians were well situated to analyze.[13]

This position is consistent with the more recent work of North (1990);

---

12. Coase (1960) argued that in the absence of transactions costs, the particular assignment of individual property rights would have no effect on the sectoral allocations of inputs or composition of output.

13. They mattered because institutions could not simply be viewed as epiphenomenal. Once institutional structures were "selected," they could persist for idiosyncratic and indeterminate periods of time, in spite of changes in underlying resources, available technologies, or demographic factors. Or they might change, sometimes suddenly, in the absence of alteration in such "underlying" factors. Thus, from both a cross-sectional and a time series perspective, institutions could differ while underlying conditions were similar and could be similar while underlying conditions differed. Appreciation of the consequences of institutional

with game theoretic work showing that inefficient conventions, once established, may persist (Sugden 1989); with Kuran's analysis (1995) of interactions of public and private opinion; and with a developing strain of thinking emphasizing path dependency that has been applied principally to arguments about technology (Arthur 1989; David 1985). The path dependency literature retains the assumption of rationality and does not explore the possible implications of cognitive modularity for decision making. Like the arguments of this book, however, it emphasizes the importance of distinguishing between the explanation of origin and the explanation of stability. Path dependency stresses the need to adduce historical accident in explaining retrospectively a particular trajectory. So does evolutionary analysis, but the relevant time frame for these "accidents" is much earlier insofar as it applies to universal norms.

Although any evolutionary account is by necessity historical, the role of evolutionary forces in changing our wiring has been inconsequential in the eleven thousand years since the beginnings of the Neolithic revolution. By that time we were, biologically, essentially what we are now,[14] and my concern is understanding how evolutionary legacies help account for a set of altruistic inclinations and a subset of norms, common to all human groups, that reflect them. I return in chapter 7 for a more extended discussion of the meaning of historical explanation.

In the meantime, my focus is on why the traditional use of the norms approach does not push the analysis far enough and why I now believe that the rejection of methodological individualism, with which this approach is typically associated, is unwarranted. For economists, "primitives" of theory have traditionally been recognized as tastes, technologies, and endowments. My work insisted, as did that of many others within and outside of economics, that one needed a fourth: rules, norms, or institutions. The unanswered, indeed, unasked, question, however, has been

---

variation has been reinforced by observation of the breakdown of the former Soviet Union and the strong recent interest in the role of institutional design in affecting economic performance in transition economies. In a similar vein, Laporta et al. (1998) consider the consequences of historical variation in legal systems (English, French, German, and Scandinavian) for financial structure and economic performance.

14. By this I mean that our biological potential is essentially unchanged. Experimental research has now shown that experience, and the learning that goes with it, physically changes brain tissue at the molecular level by enhancing linkages between concurrently firing neurons (Ahissar et al. 1992). This confirms the theory of how neural networks encode memory first proposed by Douglass Hebb in 1949. Because his experience has been different, the average adult human's brain today is physically different from that of Cro-Magnon man. But the differences are analogous to the molecular realignment that takes place when data are recorded on a hard disk. The basic specifications of the drive, to extend the analogy, are what they were before the Neolithic revolution.

whether it is possible to account more systematically for the origin of those norms or rules that appear more or less invariant: in the Aristotelian sense, *essentially* human. In particular, does one need a somewhat different approach for understanding norms that are essentially human and those, the subject of cultural anthropology or comparative political economy, that characterize what differs among societies?

Although the sociological/anthropological tradition has championed the relevance of norms, it has from its origins distinguished itself from the rational choice approach with the view that the whole is greater than the sum of the parts and cannot be understood with reference to them alone. Consequently, adherents have manifested great reluctance to explore any microlevel, and thus possibly biological or genetically influenced, underpinnings of cognition, culture, or social structure. In contrast, rational choice theory has enthusiastically endorsed methodological individualism, appealing to Darwin in support of it, but its resulting models of strategic interaction, as we have seen, exhibit great predictive inaccuracy. Something apparently is missing.

Evolutionary Theory and Levels of Selection

When, in the past, economists have been dissatisfied with the gap between observed human behavior and the predictions of normative models, they have typically turned in one of two directions: toward evolutionary models, or toward the heuristics and biases program in psychology pioneered by Daniel Kahneman and Amos Tversky. These conversations have not, however, resolved puzzles encountered when trying to fathom the logic of human behavior and social relations. Why do substantial numbers of experimental subjects play cooperate in fixed duration (in the limit *single play*) Prisoner's Dilemma games, even after, and indeed in some instances more frequently after, the payoffs have been carefully articulated (Rapaport and Chammah 1965, 53–54; Dawes 1988; Dawes and Thaler 1988)? Why did sophisticated students of game theory submit strategies like Tit-for-Tat[15] to the first Axelrod (1984) computer tournament, and why did such strategies do so well (see chap. 3)?

There are a couple of explanations for the failure to make more progress. First, the evolutionary models accessed have, in a sense, been artificially restricted to permit selection to occur only at the level of the individual organism. The evolutionary biologists' "consensus" position

---

15. Tit-for-Tat, which cooperates in the first stage and then matches a counterparty's play on subsequent moves, is normatively irrational in a two player PD game of fixed and known duration, assuming one believes one's counterparty to be rational.

that selection above the level of the individual organism was empirically unimportant had been translated, through the equivalent of a bad game of telephone, into the economists' understanding that it was impossible: simply inconsistent with the principles of natural selection. Thus these models lead over and over again into the same culs-de-sac encountered in exploring rational choice models where such choice is defined as that which efficiently advances the material welfare of the actor.

When one recognizes, in the context of multilevel models, that natural selection can sometimes favor behavioral predispositions not in the interest of the individual organism manifesting them, provided such predispositions give the gene(s) inducing them a fitness advantage, it becomes possible to tell a coherent story about the origin of restraints on defection and other behavioral tendencies essential to the emergence of complex social organization. Necessary conditions for this to happen, addressed in chapter 2, include populations that separate into groups (e.g., of thirty to one hundred individuals) for one or several generations, a positive covariance between group growth rates and the frequency of the altruistic trait(s) within each group, and a periodic dispersion back into a general population and re-formation into new groups through exogamy and/or group splintering and recombination. Under such conditions a group beneficial trait may, remarkably, be declining in frequency within every group but, over time, increase in global population frequency.[16]

Allowing for the possibility of multilevel or group selection is not equivalent to proving that such selection was operative in Pleistocene hominid populations or earlier, a task made difficult by the fragmentary nature of the archaeological and paleontological record. It is nonetheless critical that we adopt an explanatory framework, consistent with known evolutionary mechanisms, that permits an adequate account of human predispositions observable in modern experimental data.

Multilevel selection models provide a plausible explanation of the origin of key human behavioral propensities, an explanation that has proved maddeningly difficult within evolutionary frameworks allowing selection only at the level of the individual organism. Multilevel selection models make use of evolutionary mechanisms recognized by Darwin and indeed encouraged by him for the explanation of the behaviors at issue here. Finally, such mechanisms can be precisely described theoretically, and have been documented in a number of species both experimentally and observationally.

For reasons detailed in chapter 2, a strong consensus among biolo-

---

16. This is an instance of the Simpson paradox (Simpson 1951), explicated through the use of the Price equations discussed in chapter 2.

gists in the 1970s and 1980s attributed minimal empirical importance to group selection. That consensus has broken down in the past decade, and the treatment of the levels at which selection may occur is more catholic than it was even relatively recently (Wade 1978; Boyd and Richerson 1990; Wilson and Sober 1994; Sober and Wilson 1998). In particular, dismissal of the empirical likelihood of selection above the level of kin groups anywhere within the biological realm, now or in the past, common fifteen years ago, is less frequent and, where it appears, more restrained. Theoretical refinements, in particular contributions by George Price (1970, 1972), evidence from both experiments and field observation, and extended and often heated discourse have been responsible for this change.

Resistance to such models has been reinforced by belief that existing rational choice and/or individual level evolutionary explanations are adequate for the explanation of cooperative behavior. Chapters 3 and 4 dispute that view, emphasizing the need to distinguish carefully between accounts of the maintenance of "end state" equilibria and the explanation of the dynamic trajectories that led to them.

Recent game theoretic investigations of cooperation have tended to explore behavior within an environment in which indefinitely repeated interaction may be assumed. The corresponding assumption within evolutionary models has been of a very large population with pairs of individuals repeatedly selected at random to play the game (Sugden 1998, 86). One or the other of these assumptions defines the preferred work space for game theorists (see Binmore 1994, 1998a) and creates necessary but not sufficient conditions for cooperation to be sustained in an environment in which individuals can be assumed to be rational and/or in which selection operates only at the level of the individual organism. These conditions are only necessary because of the likelihood of multiple equilibria in such models.

If one believes that the appropriate metaphor for the "original state" is an environment in which interaction is characterized by one-shot PDs, then one must provide a coherent account of the transition from that state to an environment in which it becomes realistic to assume a pattern of indefinitely repeated interaction—or of a large population repeatedly interacting with each other. In order to address the issue of transition we must explain why an organism would play cooperate in a one-shot PD and/or why a predisposition to do so would not be extinguished by the operation of natural selection. The modeling of the original state as involving one-shot Prisoner's Dilemmas is particularly appropriate when dealing with predator species capable of visiting serious harm on each other, an issue addressed more extensively in discussion of Konrad Lorenz's views on the evolution of restraints on intraspecific harm (chap. 5). The assumption retains considerable and justifiable appeal in philosophy, political science, and economics (Kavka 1986), and well-established traditions in these fields take it for granted that the one-shot PD is the appropriate metaphor for the original state.

As has been noted, experimental evidence going back to Flood and Dresher shows a widespread willingness to play cooperate in single play or fixed and known duration PDs. Two common interpretations of this evidence have emerged, each of which in a different way seeks to preserve the assumption that humans are rational. One concludes that since it is obviously *not* rational to play cooperate in a one-shot PD game, and since we assume that humans are rational, we should be highly skeptical of experimental evidence suggesting the contrary and certainly not predict or make policy based on these data (Binmore 1994). The other approach reasons that since experimental evidence overwhelmingly shows that some individuals *will* play cooperate even in a one-shot PD, and since we assume that humans are rational, it must therefore be rational for them to do so (see, in general, Gauthier 1986; or for application to the phenomenon of voting, the large literature summarized in Green and Shapiro 1994, chap. 4).

But neither line of argument is satisfactory. The first approach dismisses a large and growing body of experimental and observational evidence. It is difficult to accept the idea that experimental "anomalies" simply reflect the importation of rules of thumb honed in environments of indefinitely repeated interaction (Binmore 1994).[17] Humans do play cooperate in single play PDs, even when they are scarcely naive, fully understand the game, and are guaranteed complete anonymity. Such a predisposition is, moreover, essential in any account of the transition from one-shot environments to those where repeated and indefinite interaction may reasonably be presumed.

The latter approach, on the other hand, concluding that it is somehow rational to play cooperate in a one-shot PD, has been effectively criticized by Binmore (1994, chap. 3), who argues persuasively that if the term *rational* is to retain meaning, it cannot describe the implementation of a strictly dominated strategy.[18]

---

17. The argument that experimental subjects have been "contaminated" through their prior social experiences cuts both ways. Suppose 65 percent of experimental subjects play cooperate in one-shot PDs with opportunity for preplay communication. Binmore's view is that this majority has not had time to adjust to the experimental environment. But what of the other 35 percent? Could one not equally well conclude that some of those playing defection are applying rules of thumb honed in the competitive marketplace (competition is not a tort; cooperation in restraint of trade is a felony)? Evidence that economics students play closer to Nash equilibrium predictions might support this view.

18. Contra Binmore, I interpret the deviations from Nash equilibrium play in one-shot PDs as reflecting an essential human behavioral predisposition. But like Binmore, I reject the suggestion of Gauthier and others that it is rational to play a strictly dominated strategy. I personally may be prepared to do so but will not defend the play as rational.

An advantage of moving to an evolutionary framework is that we can dispense with the question of whether or not a behavior is rational. All that now matters is whether it favors gene(s) predisposing to it. Adoption of an evolutionary approach does not, however, in and of itself resolve the conundrum. In particular, if at the outset the model precludes any role for group selection, it enables no more progress on the problem than do rational choice models. Many analyses such as that offered by Trivers (1971) claim to provide an account of transition within a framework admitting selection only at the individual level, but, as chapter 3 argues, all Trivers actually establishes is how an equilibrium involving reciprocity, once attained, can be sustained by individual level selection or, for that matter, rational choice.

If we define rationality narrowly and precisely, and we have accurately characterized the payoffs in a game, it cannot be rational in a one-shot PD game to play cooperate, a strictly dominated strategy. Similarly, if the payoffs to a single play PD game are viewed as affecting fitness, it cannot be possible for a predisposition to play cooperate to be favored at low frequencies in an evolutionary model of one-shot interaction (pairs of individuals chosen repeatedly at random to play such games) with selection limited to the level of the individual organism.

The Inverse Genetic Fallacy

The work of Robert Trivers (1971), Robert Axelrod (1984), and Robert Frank (1988) is representative of an existing and widely cited body of research originating within both the biological and the social sciences that claims or appears to prove otherwise, or, as Binmore puts it, to square the circle (1994, 173). All of these analyses appeal to evolutionary models that explicitly preclude selection above the level of the individual organism. Each claims to provide accounts of the origin of altruistic, cooperative, or other-regarding behavior among non-kin.

But the appearance is an illusion, because each of these efforts suffers in varying degrees from the inverse genetic fallacy.[19] Each confuses a demonstration that, within models assuming either individual level selection alone, or rational (egoistic) choice, mutualistic behaviors once established can persist with a demonstration that the origin of cooperative behavior in the context of one-shot encounters has been accounted for. In

---

19. The genetic fallacy is the attribution to a mature organism or phenomenon of a feature characteristic of its development. I characterize the inverse genetic fallacy as the reverse attribution: in this instance the inappropriate attribution of mechanisms that may be sustaining cooperation to the explanation of its origin. Both the original and its inverse are sometimes termed "the" genetic fallacy (Flew 1979, 130). I am indebted to Mel Reder for suggesting this formulation.

two player game theoretic models assuming rational choice, cooperative outcomes are made possible, although not guaranteed, by the assumption of indefinitely repeated interaction. In evolutionary game theory models, cooperative outcomes are made possible, although not guaranteed, by the assumption of a large population repeatedly interacting with each other. And getting to a point where it is reasonable to make either of these assumptions remains a central part of the explanatory challenge we face.

It is possible, of course, that economists, political scientists, philosophers, and biologists simply have not thought long enough or hard enough about the problem. Given the attention devoted to individual level selection/rational choice approaches, however, it is my conclusion, and Binmore's—this is an area of strong agreement—that the routes lead inevitably into the same cul-de-sac. If we restrict evolutionary models to those allowing selection only at the individual level, we cannot get beyond the dilemma of a one-shot PD. Binmore's solution, however, is simply to declare that this is not the right problem and move on. His position is that if we wish to account for the persistence of complex social organization, we must retain the behavioral assumption that individuals are narrowly egoistic and begin with the environmental assumption of indefinite interaction (Binmore 1998a, 10).

Binmore's ability to provide individual level/egoistic explanations of how cooperative outcomes can maintain themselves once established is, however, purchased at a considerable price. In particular, there is now no place for an account of the replicator dynamic that might convert an original state environment of one-shot PDs into an environment of indefinitely repeated interaction.[20] Why? Because the problem is assumed away at the outset. Binmore's approach, although forthright and intellectually coherent, can offer no help in addressing the problem of origin. We need to reflect on this as we evaluate future directions for research.

The experimental results summarized at the start of this chapter remind us that the predictions of Nash equilibrium analysis are contradicted even when one controls for reputational effects, by assuring anonymity, or the effects of repetition, when one studies single play games. Such factors are commonly adduced to explain human willingness to engage in apparently other-regarding behavior, but even after controlling for them, the behavior persists.

We are therefore offered a choice in dealing with the issue of transition: (1) continue to pour treasure and intellectual resources into what is a losing battle (account for cooperative play in one-shot PDs using individ-

20. The technical definition of the replicator dynamic is that a strategy's growth rate is a linear function of its payoff relative to the average payoff (Young 1998, 27; Taylor and Jonker 1978).

ual level/rational choice explanations), (2) abandon the problem (this is essentially Binmore's solution) because it cannot be resolved in a fashion one finds intellectually congenial, or (3) favor lines of inquiry that admit rather than try to explain away behavioral predispositions that could lead to the play of cooperate in a one-shot PD, and attempt to provide accounts of their origin consistent with known biological mechanisms.

What are some of the key predispositions that must be accounted for? The most central is a willingness to refrain from defection in PD games, a predisposition historically essential in the conversion of single play games, over time, into ones in which indefinite interaction may reasonably be presumed. As horizons of expected interaction increase, a predisposition to retaliate after what is perceived as a defection, even when such retaliation may be detrimental to the fitness of the individual organism, also becomes important. Finally, as interactions persist and become more multilateral, a willingness to retaliate against third parties, even when the agent retaliating is not the one against whom the original attack was directed, becomes relevant. In sum, we need *restraint* on primary (unprovoked) aggression and *predisposition toward* secondary (retaliatory) action. The first cannot satisfy any standard criterion of economic rationality, and the second cannot be rational from the standpoint of subgame perfection (see chap. 4).

Yet each of these predispositions has been well documented in experimental research, the first in the play of cooperate in one-shot PDs and the second, for example, in the rejection of positive offers in single play ultimatum games. With respect to retaliation against third parties, roughly three-quarters of experimental subjects in an ultimatum game will reject an opportunity to split $12 50/50 with someone who has previously made an offer they deem too low to a third party, preferring to split $10 50/50 with someone who has previously made what they view as an acceptable offer to a third party (Kahneman, Knetsch, and Thaler 1986; see also Boyd and Richerson 1992). Tit-for-Tat, a strategy with strong descriptive and some normative resonance in research on human behavior (see Axelrod 1984), combines two of these tendencies, requiring the practice of giving up the option of first strike, an ability to monitor defections, and a predisposition to punish them.[21]

In a context of one-shot games the behavioral predisposition (forgo-

---

21. In a two person game of indefinite length, cooperative behavior can be sustained as a rational choice equilibrium, but not one that is unique. If the predispositions underlying TFT are among those central to the transition from an environment of one-shot PDs to one in which indefinite interaction can be presumed, the hardwired legacies of that transition might be thought of as a "focal point," contributing to humans' ability to coordinate on this as opposed to other possible equilibria. Once we move to a multiplayer ecology, matters become even more complex. See Hirshleifer and Martinez-Coll 1988 and more recently Bendor and Swistak 1997 for explorations of what can and cannot be concluded under these conditions.

ing first strike) that lays the foundation for complex social organization cannot be rationalized as in the interest of the organism. In evolutionary terms, particularly if the payoff to the cooperator in a cooperate-defect profile is death, the persistence of genes favoring such behavior following their emergence at low frequencies cannot be accounted for on the basis of selection at the level of the individual organism. Cooperation in the one-shot game is unambiguously altruistic.

Assume that this inclination has allowed the development of repeat interaction among a group of cooperators. What of a propensity to retaliate against defecting invaders? Iteration allows a big increase in the complexities of the strategy space. But one can easily appreciate that at low frequencies, such a retaliatory inclination would be altruistic, benefiting other third parties at cost to oneself. Punishing defectors is costly, and it pays to free ride and let others play the sheriff. Upon first emergence, such an inclination would also not be favored by individual level selection.

Although these inclinations are critical for the origin and development of complex social organization, once that has been attained, they may seem transparently rational and self-serving as well as of benefit to others. But how can these inclinations be altruistic if they end up benefiting the actor who undertakes them? The answer is that they cannot. In an infinitely repeated game, a contingently cooperative strategy will be altruistic when practiced in an environment in which the frequency of cooperative strategies in the population from which one's counterparty is drawn is low. But it will cease to be so as the frequencies of such strategies rise.

If one walks into a room of players one believes with high probability to be full of Tit-for-Tat players, particularly if they will interpret an attack on one as an attack on all (this was the foundational language for the North Atlantic Treaty Organization), it certainly seems rational, even for a purely egoistic actor, to behave in a manner observationally indistinguishable from everyone else. The argument can be made more vivid by assuming everyone is packing heat and carrying gold. In such circumstances one will conclude that it is rational, contingent on beliefs about the strategies to be played by others, to behave in a manner that is apparently "moral" or other regarding, even if one is completely "amoral" and exclusively self-regarding (Andreoni and Miller 1993). The self-regarding invader will, to the extent that all other players are truly Tit-for-Tat, find herself favored, ex post, by such other-regarding behavior. And if there is any concern that the native population may punish those who do not punish, one will go along and join in punishing the behavior of any less astute invader.

From an evolutionary standpoint, this favoring of strategies widespread in a population is an instance of frequency dependent selection. Such selection can sustain an equilibrium characterized by behavior that would be altruistic were it practiced in an environment in which it obtained at lower frequency, even though all of the selection will be occurring at the level of the individual organism. At high frequency, behavior that would be altruistic at low frequency can become mutualistic, benefiting both the individual and others in the group.

Why is it then necessary to consider a role for group level selection, if the behaviors of interest, such as restraint on first strike, can be accounted for without appealing to it? An adequate account of such behavior requires that we explain not just persistence as the consequence of frequency dependent selection, but also origin (Dugatkin 1998, 41). How did such behavioral predispositions move from low to high frequency in a population? From an evolutionary standpoint, they will not be favored by individual level selection if they suddenly appear at low frequencies, in which case they will be unambiguously altruistic.

Yet the experimental data suggest very strongly that propensities enabling cooperation represent essential human characteristics operative even in one-shot interactions. Recall that many of the experiments control for the effects of iteration or concern with reputation that figure so prominently in explanations of how cooperative behavior is sustained by egoistic individuals and/or selection at the level of the individual organism alone. It is apparent from the experimental evidence that we have acquired predispositions (and we must have done so through evolutionary mechanisms) that in certain circumstances or domains short-circuit or contraindicate behavior that our rational faculties would counsel.

How else are we to interpret the persistent rejection of positive offers in ultimatum games? The willingness to leave money on the table in a centipede game? The behavior of over 101 million citizens who voted in the 1992 presidential election and over 104 million in the most recent contest? Finally, how else are we to interpret the behavior of Williams, and eventually Alchian, that so troubled Nash? It cannot be because they were naive or did not understand the structure of the game at the outset. Do we wish to argue that each thought the other irrational? An alternative hypothesis is that they were "oversocialized." Binmore suggests that subjects need time to break away from culturally reinforced habits of play in games of repeated interaction, time to "learn" how to play "correctly," that is, according to the Nash prediction.

Let us take Binmore's hypothesis seriously and examine more closely the data from the Alchian-Williams experiment. After all, if any subjects had the capacity to learn how to play "correctly," it should have been they. If we divide their hundred plays into groups of ten, here is the changing frequency of cooperate (the number of cooperative plays out of ten in each decile) for each of the two players.

TABLE 2.   Cooperative Play in the First Finite Duration PD Experiment

	1–10	11–20	21–30	31–40	41–50	51–60	61–70	71–80	81–90	91–100
Alchian	1	6	5	7	8	8	7	9	9	8
Williams	4	6	6	8	9	10	7	10	9	9

Source: Poundstone 1992, 108–17.

There is no evidence here that they moved systematically closer to the Nash prediction as the game proceeded. In fact, we observe the contrary.

Modularity in Cognition and Behavior

There are two distinct ways in which the action of an egoistic actor may fail to satisfy the criterion of rationality (see the prologue). It may fail because the action is conditioned on beliefs that have not been arrived at rationally, either because a "nonoptimal" amount of energy and resources has been devoted to acquiring and processing information relevant for forming them, or because they have not been reached using the best available logical and/or statistical algorithms. An action may also fail to satisfy the criterion because, conditional on some beliefs, it does not efficiently advance the material welfare of the individual. The first type of "failure" involves primarily cognition, the second, choice.

Failures of rationality of the first sort are the main focus of the heuristics and biases research program, addressed more systematically in chapter 6. The experimental behavior catalogued at the start of this chapter, however, represents failure of the second type. Why? Because there is little reason in any of these experiments to conclude that the beliefs possessed by subjects about the structure of the games were in any way irrational or even subject to any uncertainty. And we must use the term *"failure"* here advisedly. It has a pejorative connotation, and we may hesitate before concluding that it would be desirable if each and every one of these "failures" were eliminated.

Both laboratory evidence and field observation suggest that "failures" of both types are real and are sufficiently common that they may reflect human predispositions that can reasonably be termed essential. If that is so, the hypothesis that human cognition and behavior are influenced by a modular design of mental organs, with modules functionally specialized to particular domains, may help us understand why.[22] The

---

22. The concept of a mental organ is originally due to Chomsky. A domain is understood to mean a particular type of encountered environment.

proposition is not easily entertained, however, because it presents a challenge to our self-conception as possessors of an integrated learning and reasoning capability applicable across all encountered environments that in most cases does or should drive behavior.

Subject to the assumption of a limited number of innate drives (to eat, to drink, to procreate), behaviorist psychologists, and, implicitly, many social scientists, have tended to assume that human action is determined in the following manner. Within any specified category of behavior (operants), infants engage initially in an essentially random range of actions. Those that produce pleasure are reinforced, and thereby the behavior that led to them is conditioned. This is known in the psychology literature as the law of effect.

The passive stimulus-response connection central to behaviorism has been softened somewhat with an emphasis on a conscious hypothesis testing mechanism that intermediates between the two (e.g., Bower and Trabaso 1963). But the dominant perspective within academic psychology, at least for the last half century, has nevertheless conceived of the mind as a general purpose tabulator devoted, through such calculations, to efficiently advancing the material interest of its possessor. Our faculties for acquiring and processing information are assumed to be dedicated, almost exclusively, to computing correlations between actions and sensations, maintaining updated tables of conditional probabilities, and choosing actions based on those that best satisfy the organism's desires. The behaviorist model assumes that the function of the mind is to assist the organism in making choices that are rational, in the sense in which that term was defined in the prologue.

The model of learning based on classical and operant conditioning embodies the principle of equipotentiality, which assumes that learning mechanisms are similar irrespective of the character of the stimuli, the responses, or the reinforcers. It assumes we are not born with "preformatted" taxonomic or conceptual categories but are equally receptive to any range of sensory input. In conjunction with the assumption of a very limited number of innate drives, the model gives environmental influences enormous and almost exclusive power in influencing behavior. Ivan Pavlov, in his Nobel Prize–winning experiments with ringing bells and salivating dogs, showed that involuntary reflexes could be associated with new stimuli and thereafter be reliably produced by such stimuli. B. F. Skinner, behaviorism's most famous exponent, demonstrated repeatedly how voluntary responses could be associated with rewards and thereby increase in frequency. Their experimental results, and those of many others, reinforce a presumption that tabulated frequencies of conjoint (associated) occurrences and extrapolations to similar situations (reasoning by resemblance) govern human belief about how the world works and, by indicating the direction in which pleasure can be obtained, determine behavior. From the standpoint of behaviorism, the most important hard-wiring is a general ability to learn through the correlation of actions with reinforcing consequences.

The behaviorist tradition in U.S. psychology advanced by John Watson, the anthropological perspective associated with Franz Boas and Alfred Kroeber, and the development of European sociology reflected in the writings of Emile Durkheim are all closely associated with this view of cognition and the determination of human behavior. Without giving the matter a great deal of thought, most economists implicitly accept this view, which derives originally from the seventeenth and eighteenth century writings of Hobbes, John Locke, and David Hume and characterizes an undeniably important learning mechanism. What is increasingly at issue, however, are the claims that our knowledge base arises *exclusively* through this association of pleasant or unpleasant sensory experiences with behaviors and that consequently our mind at birth can usefully be pictured as a blank slate, a tabula rasa as Locke put it, on which experience writes.

A powerful set of experiments in the 1960s by John Garcia and his colleagues challenged the fundamental principle of equipotentiality. Garcia found that he could easily get rats to associate tastes with nausea induced by X rays and to associate lights or sound with electric shocks but that it was very difficult to get them to associate tastes with electric shocks or nausea with lights or sounds (Garcia and Koelling 1966). In other words, rats seem to be differentially prepared to make certain types of associations. Garcia's work struck at the heart of behaviorist psychology and received a very hostile initial reception.[23] But its implications have by now been more broadly accepted.

A closely related area of controversy concerns the extent to which innate drives, representing evolutionarily favored strategies that are wholly or partly unconditioned, influence behavior. The larger are the variety and power of innate drives, the more restricted is the scope for environmental influence on or modification of behavior.

Where have economists typically stood on these issues? With its common assumptions that tastes are stable, given, and not to be disputed, the field allows for a somewhat broader role for inborn drives than a Skinnerian might feel comfortable with. With very limited exceptions, behaviorists concern themselves only with behavior and its antecedent conditions

---

23. Garcia's original paper was turned down by top journals, and one reviewer dismissed the results of a subsequent paper as "no more likely than birdshit in a cuckoo clock" (Seligman and Hager 1972, 15).

(response and stimulus, respectively), eschewing discussion of consciousness, the actual process of cognition, or motives. In contrast, the standard economic model imposes fewer restrictions on variation in motives and encourages us to focus on how these motives, along with beliefs and how we acquire them, determine action.

On the other hand, the differences between the standard economic model and that common in behaviorist psychology can easily be overstated, since economists, unable to observe tastes directly, try to deduce them from behavior, using the principle of revealed preference. The economic assumption that individuals maximize utility subject to constraint in no way conflicts with the behaviorist model of operant conditioning, which specifies that individuals choose actions that produce pleasure and avoid those that do not. Nor is there conflict with the economist's instrumental interpretation of rationality as involving the effective choice of means to attain ends.

Finally, with respect to the assumed cognitive and learning mechanisms, there is little variance between the two approaches: the tabula rasa assumption is as consistent with the standard economic model as it is with traditions in U.S. psychology, sociology, and anthropology.[24] Indeed, in all of these disciplines there is little allowance, within dominant research paradigms, for the possibility that learning mechanisms might be specialized to particular domains, in other words, that equipotentiality might be violated. In all but economics the significance of innate behavioral predispositions is downplayed, with economists displaying somewhat more flexibility with regard to their role (beyond drinking, eating, and procreating) in influencing behavior.

The work of Leda Cosmides and John Tooby builds on the work of Garcia, Ekman, and Berlin and Kay in forcing one to question the adequacy of these views of cognition and the determination of behavior. It does so both through its attack on the Standard Social Science Model, shocking in its undifferentiated lumping together of economics with sociology and anthropology as target, and in the authors' experimental work, which shows evidence of a powerful "cheater detection module" in

---

24. The differences between the economist's perspective and that of a behaviorist can be illustrated as follows. An economist believes some people are born liking oranges, some liking apples. A behaviorist would grudgingly grant that people are born liking to eat but believes that it is possible, through appropriate reinforcement, to condition an infant to like apples or oranges at will. The economist and the behaviorist share a common view about how knowledge of oranges, apples, and where to find them is acquired and doubt that we are differentially prepared to learn about certain kinds of fruit. Perhaps this is so with respect to this domain. The question is whether the principle of equipotentiality can be maintained as a cognitive axiom.

humans, a module that at times improves performance on problems involving the propositional calculus, although in other contexts worsening it (Tooby and Cosmides 1992; Cosmides and Tooby 1992). Their research develops the implications for social science in general and economics in particular of extending the modularity central to the work of Noam Chomsky on language acquisition as well as the well-developed research program in visual perception to the area of social relations. Chapter 5 surveys evidence from a number of disciplines supporting this approach.

Modularity—the idea that cognitive processes or behavioral choice mechanisms may be functionally specialized to deal with particular domains of knowledge or types of situations—is relevant not only in thinking about the mechanisms whereby we acquire beliefs about the nature and structure of the world but also in understanding how apparently inconsistent behavioral predispositions may simultaneously characterize, and thereby appear to coexist within, the same individual. That possibility has bedeviled economists, who generally assume the self is unitary, with consistent preferences invariant to encountered environments (Kuran 1995, 43). If our cognition is modular, with mental organs specialized to particular domains and closely linked to particular behaviors, then it becomes plausible to hypothesize that we possess apparently inconsistent predispositions that pull in different directions, with the outcome probabilistically dependent on the type of situation (domain) encountered, in a manner that may or may not leave the actor with any sense of behaving inconsistently.

The issues here go beyond concerns about the number and/or power of innate drives. Some hardwiring for drives is accepted, grudgingly, even by strict behaviorists. A behaviorist psychologist or an economist may differ regarding their range but will generally agree on at least a basic subset. Moreover, he or she will assume that such goals are pursued with means that are rational. This implies that, where relevant, expectations are conditioned by past stimulus/response pairings and means (behaviors) are selected in pursuit of the satisfaction of these ends.

Restraint on first strike, cheater detection modules, or predispositions to follow through on retaliation threats even when such threats have failed to deter reflect hardwiring at a different level. These behaviors generally fail the criterion of rationality, and if they are essentially human, they involve hardwiring of instruments (means), not just ends. This poses a more serious challenge to modern social science than simply navigating among different views regarding the range and power of innate drives. It goes beyond demonstrations of violations of equipotentiality. And it addresses a different type of rationality failure from that which principally concerns researchers in the heuristics and biases program.

Behavioral economists, whose contributions challenge different aspects of the standard economic model, in particular transitivity and the invariance postulates, have at times seemed comfortable with what could be interpreted as a modular approach.[25] But what has increasingly been lacking in this work is a clearer specification of the relationship between encountered domains and the probabilities of different predispositions asserting themselves. Absent that, we run the risk of developing long menus of predispositions (heuristics and biases), some of which operate in opposing directions and one or more of which can, after the fact, be selected to "account" for almost any behavior or judgment. Unless these deficiencies can be overcome, these models will have only limited ability to predict human behavior, even in an aleatory manner (see chap. 6).[26]

The work done by Cosmides and Tooby is not subject to this criticism. On the basis of a series of carefully designed experiments, they make a compelling case that reasoning involving problems in propositional logic differs in systematic and predictable ways whenever the domain of social rules is encountered. While their research on cheater detection is first and foremost a study in cognition, the specialized cognitive processes it identifies are implicitly associated with behavioral predispositions to punish violators of social rules, propensities apparently hardwired and not necessarily in the organism's individual interest.[27] They stress the implications of their research for our understanding of the process of cognition and in particular for the support their work provides for a modular approach. My argument, however, places equal emphasis on the *behavior* with which this specialized module is associated (a propensity to seek out and punish violators of social rules) and the evolutionary explanation of its origin. The cheater detection module (a cognitive adaptation) exists in service of a cheater punishment module, an adaptation at the behavioral

---

25. See for example Thaler and Shefrin 1981, which posits, within a single individual, a rational "planner" coexisting with a more emotional "doer."

26. The distinction between aleatory and epistemic explanation is emphasized in Beach, Barnes, and Christensen-Zalanski 1986. Epistemic reasoning, which clinical psychologists generally employ, treats each individual as unique, not as a member of a larger class for which base rate data may be relevant in predicting behavior. Aleatory reasoning involves the attempt inductively (or, as in games of chance, analytically) to forecast events probabilistically. In general, social scientists aspire to aleatory but not epistemic predictions of human behavior.

27. Such behavior is not necessarily in the organism's individual interest because it would always "pay" to free ride: to let others use up valuable energy punishing transgressions of social rules (which might contribute to a more favorable reproductive environment for the collectivity). The issues involving the rationality of punishing defection differ in scale from those associated with the rationality of nuclear retaliation after a devastating first strike, but they involve the same basic concerns. These issues, which have been only partially explored by Cosmides and Tooby, are discussed in more detail in chapters 3 and 4.

level, for which substantial experimental evidence is available (see the earlier discussion of Kahneman, Knetsch, and Thaler 1986; Fehr and Gächter 2000).[28] Cosmides and Tooby argue that such predispositions would have been favored by natural selection, but they do not systematically explore the level at which selection favoring them would have had to have occurred.

To the extent that we treat social rules as public goods, a willingness voluntarily, and at some positive fitness or welfare cost, to punish violators can be seen as closely related to the irreducible willingness to make voluntary contributions to public goods discussed in the first section of this chapter. Just as the origin of that willingness is difficult to account for within individual selection models, so too is the propensity to seek out and punish "cheaters." We may react ambivalently to observing the collective punishment of violations of social norms, particularly when, because of differences in political culture, we are ambivalent about the norm itself. We are generally less ambivalent when witnessing the punishing of codifying norms that reinforce essentially universal human predispositions. Thus regardless of culture, few will experience ambivalence witnessing punishment of an unprovoked and premeditated murder, or a father's abuse of his daughter, although westerners may feel ambivalence at the punishment of a woman who appears without a veil in an Islamic country, and there may be widespread revulsion at actions designed to enforce a practice of female genital mutilation. But in each of these cases the predispositions underlying and enabling these behaviors are cut from the same cloth as those that generate, in more antiseptic experimental environments, a voluntary willingness to provide public goods.

A willingness to seek out and punish violators of social norms, although essential, is not, however, the most important foundation for complex social organization. A propensity to punish defections presumes there are established rules or norms from which one can defect. Without a history of repeated interaction, there can be no trust or norm to be violated, just as in an iterated PD game, retaliation has no meaning absent a prior record of cooperative outcomes. Accounting for a predisposition to play cooperate in one-shot PDs is therefore an explanatory challenge that must, logically, be given first priority.

I go beyond Cosmides and Tooby in arguing that a propensity to practice restraint on defection (the PD solution module) has as much evi-

---

28. The Cosmides and Tooby research program represents a shift from the earlier sociobiological emphasis on selection for behavior to an emphasis on cognitive adaptations, from Darwinian behaviorism to Darwinian psychology, as Sterelny and Griffiths put it (1999, 324–28). The two are, however, related, since cognitive adaptations clearly may have important influences on behavior.

dential foundation and evolutionary rationale as the predispositions associated with detecting and punishing cheaters that they have identified.[29] In both instances we have, apparently, specialized cognitive processes associated with behavioral propensities specialized to particular domains. In both instances we have behavioral evidence consistent with the operation of neurobiological subsystems persistently capable of overriding the counsel of our rational (self-serving) faculties. Both propensities are critical in understanding the origin of complex social organization (although forgoing first strike is logically prior), and both would have to have been favored by evolutionary forces above the level of the individual organism.

Although influenced by and sympathetic to the research of Cosmides and Tooby, my argument is not simply an extension of their framework. Whereas Cosmides and Tooby appear to view the problem of the origin of social organization as largely "solved" by the Trivers model of reciprocal altruism, augmented perhaps by their cheater detection module, I do not. This is because the Trivers model, which claims to operate only at the individual level of selection, does not adequately explain how a willingness to play cooperate in what might well be one-shot PDs could survive were it to appear initially at low frequencies where indefinitely repeated interaction cannot be assumed (see chap. 3). We need to extend the concept of modularity to encompass the cognitive underpinnings of a propensity to play cooperate in a one-shot PD and more explicitly consider the nature of evolutionary mechanisms that permitted such a module to survive and spread. In other words, we should entertain the likelihood of a PD solution module, along with a cheater detection/punishment module. According to this line of argument, then, Cosmides and Tooby have not pushed modularity far enough in developing a coherent account of the origin of complex social organization.

Modularity and the Kahneman and Tversky Program

It seems initially ironic that one of the key targets of Cosmides and Tooby was the Kahneman and Tversky program, which has attracted considerable attention among economists and is discussed in detail in chapter 6. When Leda Cosmides first explored the "elusive content effect" in experiments involving the Wason selection test, the principal existing explana-

---

29. The term *first mover altruism* is sometimes used to mean any cooperative move in a PD or PD-like game, whether or not the game is single play or repeated and whether or not moves are entered sequentially (as in the game of trust) or simultaneously. For that reason, I refer to it more generally as *first move(r) altruism*. A propensity to make such moves, and the cognitive and behavioral mechanisms responsible for them, is what I have in mind in referring to a PD solution module.

tions involved decision making based on the "availability" heuristic and the tendency to seek confirming, rather than deconfirming, evidence, both staples of Kahneman and Tversky reasoning.[30] The irony was that if anyone's research had raised doubts among economists with regard to the proposition that our brain operated like a smoothly functioning computer, it was that of Tversky and Kahneman (1974). Although they initially followed in the Herbert Simon tradition of emphasizing how these heuristics often worked tolerably well, the overwhelming preponderance of their research and that which it inspired has stressed the reverse: the existence of systematic biases and their consequences.[31] All the biases that their research program apparently documented made it look like our "wet computers" had some seriously frayed insulation inside.

Again, if we think of rational choice as involving both the formation of rational beliefs or expectations and the rational selection (choice) of actions conditional on those beliefs and the organism's desires, it is clear that the Kahneman and Tversky program is principally concerned with defects in the first stage (the title of their 1982 book, with Slovic, is *Judgment under Uncertainty*). To the degree that their work studies action, it is most relevant for decision theory (the study of games against nature).[32] The "defects" reflected in the experimental data summarized at the start of this chapter do not involve failures in the formation of rational beliefs. And they do not involve games against nature. Thus it may not be surprising if the work of Kahneman and Tversky ends up shedding relatively little light on why Alchian and Williams behaved the way they did.

At the same time, in many cases judgment (belief or expectation for-

---

30. The Wason selection task measures competency in solving problems of logical inference involving statements of the *if p then q* type (see chap. 5). The "elusive content effect" is a reference to the title of Cosmides's 1985 doctoral dissertation in psychology at Harvard. It refers to the fact that performance varies according to the differing content of logically equivalent problems. Within the Kahneman and Tversky framework, the "availability" heuristic explains exceptionally good performance as resulting from content with which subjects were familiar or that was similar to other problems with which they were familiar. Poor performance is attributed to a human tendency to search for evidence confirming, rather than deconfirming a conditional statement (rule) (Cosmides, 1985; Camerer 1995, 609).

31. "In general these heuristics are quite useful, but sometimes they lead to severe and systematic errors" (Tversky and Kahneman 1974, 1124). Compare with the more consistently negative emphasis on the role of biases in Dawes 1988 (7): "The basic point of this book is that we often think in automatic ways about choice situations, that these automatic thinking processes can be described by certain psychological rules ("heuristics"), and that they systematically lead us to make poorer choices than we would by thinking in a more controlled manner about our decisions."

32. In technical terms, a game against nature involves optimization against a fixed environment—not one that may be trying to figure out what you are going to do and altering its behavior in response to such calculations.

mation) and choice are intimately linked, and to the degree that the Kahneman and Tversky program has identified truly universal judgmental defects, or biases, we should pay close attention to them. Because of the multiplication of posited heuristics and biases, however, there are increasing grounds for concern about the extent to which the research program they have inspired has succeeded in this effort. A troubling general question, for example, is why evolution should have endowed us with such a poorly functioning set of belief or expectation formation algorithms, particularly for the important inductive task of statistical inference, a highly desirable capability in updating conditional probabilities in interactions with the nonhuman as well as human environment.

Binmore, in general, vigorously resists crediting experimental research with demonstrating systematic deviations in human capabilities and/or predispositions from those implied by the assumptions that individuals make rational choices. The one exception he is prepared to grant is, ironically, in this area. He sees the results of the Kahneman and Tversky program as showing "perhaps that real people have little natural capacity for statistics. . . . As a consequence, it is in this area that I believe modeling *homo sapiens* as *homo economicus* has least to recommend it" (Binmore 1994, 273–74). In the domain where Binmore is most receptive to crediting the experimental research, however, my argument, following Gigerenzer, Cosmides, and Tooby (see chap. 6), expresses doubt as to whether the deficiencies in our statistical capabilities are as significant as some experimenters have suggested they are.

The key difference between the Cosmides and Tooby approach to modularity and the Kahneman and Tversky research program has been the explicitly evolutionary perspective in the former, a perspective that emphasized asking first what the mind was "designed" for before postulating research hypotheses. It is also clear that this approach, whether serendipitously or not, has permitted these researchers to hit experimental pay dirt. That fact is one of the strongest pieces of evidence in support of their approach.

A new body of research is now emerging, questioning why evolution should have made us such poor intuitive statisticians, particularly in the light of research on animal foraging indicating that birds and bumblebees, among others, seem quite good at these tasks (Stephens and Krebs 1986, chap. 9).[33] The fact that the specialized neurobiology of animals is supe-

---

33. Human memory capacity, although remarkable, is exceeded along some dimensions by that possessed by animals. A humpback whale can sing a song thirty minutes long and then repeat it note for note without error. Honeybee workers, after only limited conditioning, will remember the locations of up to five beds of flowers and at precisely what time of day they will yield nectar. One species of sparrow can remember ten thousand hiding

rior to ours in certain dimensions does not automatically call into question the Kahneman and Tversky conclusions. Our senses of smell and hearing are, after all, markedly inferior to those of dogs and many other animals. Still, the findings provide pause, given the centrality of efficient foraging to the survival of our ancestors. As they evolved, hominids, along with many animals, faced issues of foraging for food as well as dealing with other organisms, problems that benefit from, as Stephen Pinker puts it, "complex algorithms for multivariate, nonstationary time series analysis (predicting when events will occur, based on their history of occurrences)" (1997, 182). From an evolutionary perspective, then, there is a presumption that humans should be relatively good at keeping track of histories of occurrences, updating them, and basing decisions on updated conditional probabilities. The ability to tabulate such frequencies and perform such calculations is central to the traditional behaviorist model of cognition that, although diminished in scope or compartmentalized by the emphasis on modularity, remains an essential human learning mechanism.

New experimental results suggest that some of the results within the Kahneman and Tversky program are the consequence of presenting problems in an information format the easy processing of which the brain has not been selected for. In many cases, the way problems have been posed to subjects within the heuristics and biases literature has been a bit like asking a hand calculator to process binary numbers, or insisting that children do long division with roman numerals. When problems are restated in formats that humans can more easily process (for reasons that are comprehensible from an evolutionary perspective) many of these biases go away. In particular, human subjects do much better processing data on frequencies than they do in reasoning about single event probabilities (Gigerenzer 1991; Gigerenzer and Hoffrage 1995; Cosmides and Tooby 1996).

Obviously, proficiency in maintaining and updating frequency tables was extraordinarily valuable in the search for food, that is, in interactions with the nonhuman environment. A key question is whether the tools that make us good decision theorists are also relevant for how we interact with other humans. Canonical game theory answers this question, in a number

---

places for its food caches. Beyond simple feats of memory, animal learning competencies can be quite remarkable. Birds navigate thousands of miles using celestial navigation. They have to *learn* the position of the North Star, because of the "wobbling" of the celestial poles, a twenty-seven-thousand-year cycle known as the precession of the equinoxes that takes place too quickly to permit evolutionary hardwiring. They do so by staring at the sky and noting the point around which all the stars appear to rotate. Learning the nearby constellations they are then able in subsequent periods to keep a steady bearing (Lumsden and Wilson 1983, 105; Pinker 1997, 181). At the same time, although animals are generally quite good at foraging, they appear to exhibit the same violations of expected utility theory as do humans (Camerer 1995, 641).

of instances, in the negative. In choosing how to play in a one-shot PD, it should not matter whether we are good at predicting whether our counterparty will cooperate, since defect is a strictly dominant strategy. In reality, good statistical intuition probably complements behavioral propensities toward cooperation in one-shot PDs in helping to account for the origin of complex social organization beyond the family unit, as well of course as being extremely useful in foraging.

While both Cosmides and Tooby and Kahneman and Tversky can be interpreted as consistent with a modular approach to cognition, the Cosmides and Tooby approach privileges modules that would have been reinforced by natural selection in the environment of evolutionary adaptiveness[34] and is skeptical of those for which there is no coherent evolutionary rationale. For the latter, the approach has mandated careful scrutiny of experimental design and further testing, again, with quite striking results. Thus while on the one hand pressing us to consider the importance of domain specific modules in human reasoning about social relations, their work and that of others also pushes us to accept, contrary to Kahneman and Tversky, that we are, after all, rather good intuitive statisticians (a domain general competency) provided inputs and outputs to Bayes' theorem are in frequency terms, rather than in terms of subjective probabilities of single events (see chap. 6).

Thus there appears to be a paradox. In order to construct a coherent theory of human behavior, in particular those aspects related to social relations, we may need on the one hand to adopt a view of cognition that extends the results from language acquisition and visual perception to other arenas, a view that sees the brain as an interconnected set of information appliances, exhibiting a modularized design, with many of the component neurobiological subsystems specialized to particular domains of cognition.[35] At the same time, the body of research that has perhaps done most to sensitize economists to the possibility of modularity, that there may be cognitive processes that systematically short-circuit "normal" human reasoning, such as Bayesian inference, may have to be questioned.[36]

---

34. This awkward phrase refers to the roughly two-million-year period of Pleistocene hunter-gatherer existence that presaged the Neolithic revolution.

35. This model necessarily represents a challenge to behaviorist models of cognition, and indeed, it was in opposition to Skinner's interpretation of the acquisition of language that Chomsky first developed his insights embodying concepts of modularity and specialized mental organs (Chomsky [1957] 1965, 1959).

36. This argument reflects one of several ways in which the heuristics and bias program and the research in behavioral economics to which it has given rise provide a challenge to the standard economic model that is only partially successful as foundation for a comprehensive empirically based behavioral science. See chapter 6.

The resolution to this apparent paradox is this. Domain specific reasoning or behavioral modules have been selected for because they represented an adaptation to environmental challenges that recurred over thousands of generations of Pleistocene existence or earlier. An example is aversion to sexual relations among children reared together. By hardwiring these modules into the human brain, evolution spares us the necessity of trying to learn these lessons again every generation. On the other hand, not all challenges to survival and procreation recur generation after generation in the same form. Natural selection has also endowed us with certain domain general learning technologies, including the ability to be good intuitive statisticians, provided the data are presented in formats we have been selected for to interpret well, because these skills are central to addressing the life cycle–specific challenges that confronted and confront individuals, challenges whose details varied from individual to individual and generation to generation (this position is at variance with that adopted by Binmore 1994, 152).

These domain general competencies lie at the heart of the traditional learning model reflected in behaviorism, one that has achieved many successes in accounting for both human and animal behavior. My intent, and I believe that of Cosmides and Tooby, is not to reject the relevance of this mechanism but rather to recognize that it is more limited in scope than its most ardent supporters have suggested. My argument goes beyond Cosmides and Tooby, however, in emphasizing behavioral as well as cognitive modules. Certain of these modules give rise to altruistic behavioral predispositions that, definitionally, could not have been favored by individual level selection upon initial appearance.

These two principles, involving first, more flexible thinking about the levels at which natural selection has influenced gene frequencies in human populations (an issue about which Cosmides and Tooby have conventional views) and second, rethinking the scope of domain general and domain specific cognitive competencies (where they do not), provide the basis for a coherent account of the origin of complex social organization and a sounder foundation on which to build a more progressive empirically grounded social and behavioral science.

Model-Behavior Interaction and the Making of Rational Judgments

Evidence that the models of human behavior we advance may, to a limited degree, affect behavior itself adds complexity to but does not render nugatory the task of developing and adopting accurate models, a point reinforced to me while drafting this book. At one point one of my children said, offhand, after reading a particularly depressing article in *Newsweek,* that "People will do anything for money." At one level, my daughter did not really mean this. But at another level, her view reflected a model of human behavior actively advanced in the media, the result of drawing out the implications of rational choice theory, narrowly defined, to its logical conclusion. It was Nash's model.

Since I had been pondering these issues, my response was more reflective than it otherwise might have been. "No," I said, "people will do many things for money, but it is not true that they will do anything for money." The standard economic model, as here characterized, assumes that people will act efficiently to advance their material interest. My statement reflected a view that this hypothesis was refutable, at least if it was viewed as universally applicable across all domains, and that there were some domains, particularly those involving strategic interaction, where it was often a very poor predictor. I considered and consider the statement to be based on a broad range of experimental and observational evidence and consistent with the logic of evolutionary theory, if one allows for selection above the level of the individual organism. It does not reflect wishful thinking that might somehow be self-validating, or a teleological view of human nature lacking scientific support, or simply an attempt to balance an inaccurate model with one known to be equally inaccurate.[37]

Our duty as behavioral scientists (and as parents) accurately to characterize the phenomena we examine or describe is complicated because the object of inquiry in this instance is the behavior of our own species. What if modeling behavior in certain ways changes it? Experimental evidence has shown that the study of economics (specifically, price theory) pushes subjects' behavior closer to the Nash equilibrium prediction in games of strategic interaction (Frank 2000, xxv). Cooperation rates in PD games and voluntary contribution rates among students who have studied economics are lower than among students who have not (but they are not zero) (Marwell and Ames 1981; Frank, Gilovich, and Regan 1993b, 1996). These results are not simply a matter of self-selection, since the differences with respect to the general student population are not observed in students who will but have not yet taken the economics course (Frank, Gilovich, and Regan 1993b, 170). There is also evidence that economists are less prone to make charitable contributions than are other social scientists. One interpretation is that economic students have an essentially cor-

---

37. By *teleological* I mean an argument from design: the claim that our eye is a marvel of engineering because it was *in fact* designed; humans have the behavioral tendencies they do because they were designed to have these tendencies. The power of evolutionary theory has been its provision of an alternate mechanism—natural selection—to explain the appearance of complex design.

rect view of the world but have discovered through course work the joys and wealth-enhancing benefits of free riding. A second view is that students taught the rational choice model have adopted a positive (and according to this book, false) view of the world consistent with the assumption that the average person follows its normative counsel. Defection, then, becomes justifiable as a matter of prudence, rather than just greed.

Either interpretation legitimately feeds concern that models cannot be formulated without altering the behavior they are intended to illuminate or explain—a potentially serious objection to the proposition that scientific methods should or can be applied to the study of human behavior. Indeed, utopians or reformers might seize on these results and argue that if this is the result of allowing students to study economics, there is full justification, as a counterweight, in disseminating a putatively positive view of human nature consistent with romantic idealism on the grounds that it too could be self-fulfilling. Neither the proposal nor the reasoning underlying it can be dismissed out of hand. But each has important defects.

First, the analysis incorrectly presumes that cooperative behavior is necessarily morally praiseworthy, whereas selfish behavior is not. In some instances we may applaud selfish behavior and censure that which is cooperative. Second, cooperative or contingently cooperative behavior is not necessarily altruistic: this may depend on frequencies of different strategies in the population. Favoring a model of human nature that maintains people are more or less altruistic than they are because of belief the model can and should be self-fulfilling reads too much into model-phenomenon interaction that, although perhaps real, is of limited empirical importance. In the final analysis, allowing what we think should be to influence statements of what is creates a volatile brew that not only threatens the rationale for our endeavors but may also explode in ways not anticipated. The best strategy from a scientific perspective is simply not to pull intellectual punches and to try to keep discussion of how people ought to behave or society ought to be structured on a different page.

The description of the human ethogram[38] suggested in this book reflects neither a tendency toward unconditional altruism of which utopians and romantics are often enamored nor the strict egoism underlying the hardheaded rational choice approach. Humans, in general, refrain from first strike, but they will also commonly retaliate if attacked and sometimes retaliate even if third parties are attacked.

Evidence in favor of model-behavior interaction can seem to threaten

---

38. *Ethogram* is a term used by students of animal species to signify a complete list and description of naturally occurring behaviors characteristic of a particular species, often illustrated pictorially.

to obliterate the traditional lines separating positive and normative social science (for recognition of this concern in political science, see Green and Shapiro 1996, 270). But to embrace uncritically this blurring of distinctions as a description of "how science really operates" opens the door to a descent into relativism and subjectivism from which scientific methods cannot emerge intact. It is true that the pursuit of an objective study of human behavior rests on some shaky philosophic foundations. But the alternative of abdicating that pursuit is worse.

If the phenomena of model-behavior interaction is real, we need to know how large an effect it creates and why. In answering that question, evidence still matters, and experimental and observational techniques used in the natural sciences are still relevant to the study of human behavior. It is not true that anything goes.[39] Our generalizations about and our predictions regarding human behavior should be *rational* in the sense in which we apply the term to human judgment: they should make use of all available information processed according to the best available logical and statistical algorithms. A rational prediction may be that less than 100 percent, perhaps substantially less than 100 percent, of experimental subjects will defect in one-shot PDs. In other words, a rational prediction may forecast behavior other than what rational choice theory, as understood by Nash, would predict.

In this context, rational forecasts are what we mean by truth, which is what we should seek to impart to our children. At the same time, we may attempt to instill in them certain types of nonconsequentialist ethical precepts.[40] My interest, both as a parent and as a behavioral scientist, is not in arguing that people are more altruistic than they are, in hopes of producing a self-fulfilling prophecy. At the same time, I have no hesitation in countering, with data, logic, and argument, inaccurate models that suggest we are less altruistic than we are (for a similar point of view, see Ostrom 1998, 7, 18). If we are to assume that there is an inherent altruistic compo-

---

39. If any of these statements is false, we should abandon at once any references to behavioral *science* or social *science* and refrain from submitting further applications to the National *Science* Foundation. Thus while sympathetic to Deirdre McCloskey's recent attempts to have economists consider a broader range of essential human predispositions in modeling behavior (1996), I am less so with respect to her attacks on traditional scientific epistemology (1995), although acknowledging that her efforts have encouraged us to focus more on what scientists actually do.

40. Thus I desire strongly that my children vote in national elections when they come of age, because I believe that high voter participation contributes to a healthy democracy and because healthy democracies contribute to healthy international relations. I vote, and I want them to vote, because it is the behavior I would wish others to follow. But I will not encourage such behavior through the fiction that their action (or mine) has any measurable probability of affecting specific electoral outcomes. I do not see these positions as in conflict.

nent to human behavior, we need, however, to be as precise as we can about its nature and the domains within which it is likely to apply.

Arming people with an inaccurate model of human behavior is like giving them a bad map. With confidence in one's guidance they may try for some time to navigate by it, but as deconfirming evidence and evidence of uncharted shoals accumulate, they will eventually discard or modify it. How long this will take is uncertain, and in the meantime, much damage can accrue. In a related manner, a discipline cannot ultimately survive as a scientific enterprise if it is not prepared to confront the predictions of its models with evidence and if it is unwilling to modify them when they consistently fail to perform well.

Science, which can be thought of as the pursuit of rational judgments, has a defensible record as a progressive endeavor, albeit one pursued by humans with their attendant frailties. In progressive disciplines such as the natural sciences, more accurate models do eventually triumph over less accurate models in the war for intellectual shelf space in the minds of both scientists and nonscientists.[41] We should have confidence that the same will ultimately be true in our own areas of inquiry.

The use of the plural (*people*) in my daughter's question and in my response is significant. My answer did not mean that there might not be some individuals who would do anything for money or that a given individual at some time in his or her life in some domains might not fit this description. It leaves open the likelihood that, in the aggregate, willingness to engage in certain behaviors may alter as a consequence of changes in monetary or other material incentives (there is much evidence in support of this proposition). It does, however, make a statement about baseline levels of behavior and, in turn, about what is a reasonable inductive prediction (based on experimental and field data) of what one could expect from the typical human being in social groupings she is likely to encounter. In particular, given the widespread media coverage of deviant behavior to which she is exposed, she needed to be reminded that in fact the likelihood that other conspecifics will launch unprovoked harmful attacks on her is low—not zero—but low. Chapter 5 will argue, contra Lorenz (1966), that such probabilities are low not principally because of a thin veneer of civilization imparted to us by socialization and enculturation, although these processes are important, but because, as humans, most of us possess, as do other animals, strong hardwired predispositions restraining intraspecific violence.

---

41. But it may take some time. Lane (1996, 125) points out that the influence of Freudian (psychoanalytic) treatments of mental illness did not wane until the National Institute of Mental Health refused to fund therapies that could not be shown to work better than other less expensive treatments.

Neither the economic nor the sociological/anthropological tradition within social science has seriously addressed these questions, the economic because of lack of interest in explaining or denial of the importance or reality of these behavioral anomalies; and the sociological/ anthropological because of belief that one can fully account for them by appeal to the aggressively nonbiological concept of culture. For different reasons, neither of these conflicting positions is satisfactory. We need to move beyond simply opposing one to the other from behind the fortresses of established disciplinary traditions.

Limits of Microeconomic Theory as a Predictive Enterprise

Emphasis so far has been on the failures of rational choice theory in the realm of strategic interaction: the purview of game theory. Consideration of the explanatory successes of microeconomic theory in general can enable us to make some of the same points. Competitive markets in their pure form disguise intricate interdependencies among people by confronting decision makers with prices, rather than the actions or likely actions of other individuals. The predictive power of microeconomic theory derives largely from assumptions that, everything else equal, people prefer more to less goods, and less to more bads, and that these categories are not entirely subjective. In the right domains these assumptions allow good predictions of human behavior in the absence of data on the past actions of the particular individual(s) involved. If there are five lines at a tollbooth, and one is much shorter than the others, I can predict pretty accurately that the next arrival will join it, even though I have never met the driver of the car in question. I can also predict, although this is a more complex problem, that if I double the toll on the bridge, fewer people will drive over it and more will take the roundabout route that avoids the charge. The power of the theory arises because of the existence in groups of at least a few decision makers who will change their behavior in response to changes in material incentives. Its apparently axiomatic foundations derive from the universality of sophisticated foraging algorithms among humans, a result of millions of years of evolutionary history. These algorithms facilitate optimization in games against nature, and competitive markets turn interactions among humans into what appear to be games against nature, because prices confront the individual as parametric.

The assumptions of the theory, however, provide no characterization of the scope of its applicability. They do not tell us within which domains we will see violations of the prediction that people will choose more over less. We can only find that out empirically. Nor does theory by itself explain what the quantitative dimensions of individual response will be. In the second problem just presented, I can predict that fewer people will take the bridge (direction of change), but I cannot predict how many fewer. To do so I need to employ statistical or econometric methodology bringing to bear data on past behavior of drivers under various circumstances. In either event, the underlying determinants of *how many* fewer, such as individual preferences, are assumed. They are primitives of the system.

To take another example, if I consider two items in my house, a high value, easily carried item, such as a camera, for which there is a well-developed resale market, and a large, difficult to transport item, such as a sofa, for which secondary markets are thinner, I can predict with good accuracy that it is more likely that the first item will be stolen. The prediction is based on the assumption that thieves, like other humans, are likely to be good economists. *But microeconomic theory per se does not permit me to predict what the overall probability of theft of either item will be.* It may predict the response of thieves to changes in incentives but does not predict the level of criminality. To go beyond this I will need data.

Consider, for example, the following dichotomous choice: steal if punishment is low and/or there is no probability of detection; otherwise do not. Researchers in the economics of criminal behavior have argued, and evidence supports them, that increases in the severity of punishment and/or the probability of detection will reduce the frequency of a specifically targeted behavior. But the more fundamental question, which the standard economic model does not explain, is why the baseline propensity to steal, with a zero likelihood of punishment, is not 100 percent (Field 1979c).[42] The fact that the baseline is not 100 percent reveals that a lot of people, in this domain, are choosing less over more.

This question is closely related to experimental "puzzles" already encountered: why don't 100 percent of experimental subjects defect in single play PD experiments, why do subjects persist in making voluntary contributions to public goods, why don't players always take what is put on the table in the first stage of a centipede game, and why don't subjects in

---

42. The English jurist Sir Henry Maine observed: "men do sometimes obey rules for fear of the punishment which will be inflicted if they are violated, but compared with the mass of men in the community this class is but small—probably it is substantially confined to what are called the criminal classes— and for one man who refrains from stealing or murdering because he fears the penalty there must be hundreds or thousands who refrain without a thought on the subject" (1888, 50). Maine considered the teaching of parents, religious education, and custom as "explanations" for this fact; he did not explore evolutionary influences. Much more recently, Jon Elster observes: "As is often the case in the social sciences, we may be able to explain the slope of a relationship but not its intercept" (1999a, 28). This book asks, in a sense, whether we must accept this as inevitable.

dictator games keep 100 percent of the money? Manipulation of cooperation and voluntary contribution rates through variation in experimental treatments is consistent with the hypothesis that *some* people at *some* points in their life in *some* circumstances will change behavior in response to a small change in material incentives. The fact that baseline rates are what they are, on the other hand, shows that not everyone, at every point in the life cycle, in all domains of decision making is inclined to take more over less.[43] In studies of strategic interaction, such as those involving the voluntary provision of public goods, Nash equilibrium analysis assumes the contrary.

Of course, my daughter—she with the interest in appropriate models of human motivation—basically knew this. Most people know intuitively that there is in the realm of human interaction (and in their own decision making) both kindness and viciousness, both restraint and aggression, both self-regarding and other-regarding behavior; that it is sometimes difficult to tell the difference; and that behavior can be at times totally impervious and at other times exquisitely sensitive to changes in material incentives.[44] She understood that the predispositions underlying human behavior were more variegated than the "granite of self interest" George Stigler viewed as undergirding social science and in particular the palace of economics (1975, 237).[45]

To add complexity, other-regarding behavior is not necessarily morally praiseworthy, as in instances of selfless cruelty, where humans viciously risk and give their lives in order to wreak havoc on group enemies (Holmes 1990). And self-interest may be socially desirable, where it short-circuits such zealous behavior or leads to the breakup of a producer cartel. One must keep in mind that altruism corresponds only to a subset of other-regarding behavior. At the individual level, malice, envy, and jealousy are all part of the human panoply of emotions, are not generally viewed as praiseworthy, yet may well motivate other-regarding behavior.

Nevertheless, the view I advocated to my daughter, with its indication that we needed a human geology more complex than Stigler's, seems somehow quaint, old fashioned, at variance with and lacking the vigor and strength of the hardheaded and unidimensional vision advanced in some

---

43. Successes in predicting changes in behavior in response to changes in incentives have been repeatedly used in the political science literature, as in economics, to draw attention away from failure to account for *levels* (see Green and Shapiro 1994, chaps. 3–5; 1996, 251, 252).

44. In a famous experiment, Lepper, Greene, and Nisbett (1973) showed that external rewards can sometimes reduce the frequency of behavior otherwise intrinsically motivated.

45. Stigler uses these words to characterize Smith's *The Wealth of Nations* ([1776] 1937), widely viewed as the founding treatise in economics.

economics writing, in political science by advocates of realpolitik or the "new realism," and in evolutionary writing emphasizing selection at the level of the individual organism alone. This latter view of human nature, however, has a problem from a scientific standpoint. It fails the test Friedman, and Karl Popper before him, set for it.

The standard economic model does reasonably well in predicting, in the aggregate,[46] the direction of change in behavior in response to a change in a particular direction in material incentives. This is true in models of strategic interaction and in models of nonstrategic interaction in which prices confront individuals as parametric, as they do in competitive markets. In a great many instances, however, the standard economic model leaves baseline behavioral levels essentially unexplained.[47] Thus changing the temptations for defection can reduce the amount of voluntary contributions to public goods. But such manipulations do not drive the rate to zero. Nash equilibrium analysis predicts that people will *never* cooperate in single play PD games, that they will *never* voluntarily provide public goods, that they will *never* move beyond the first stage of a centipede game, and that they will *always* keep all of the money in dictator games.

In a commentary on an article summarizing experimental results on the voluntary provision of public goods, a Scandinavian biologist indicated his own presumably Bayesian belief that the data did not invalidate for him the assumption of strict behavioral egoism (Stenseth 1989, 722). He recognized, however, that others might see things differently and that the matter was uncertain. Nevertheless, in the presence of such uncertainty, he argued, *it was safer to assume that individuals were essentially selfish:* if we were wrong, he maintained, the cost was nil, whereas great potential damage would result if we made the reverse error. What were these costs? Presumably the breakdown of social order from within and/or

---

46. In general, economics, like most of the social sciences, aspires to actuarial (aleatory) but not clinical (epistemic) prediction (Dawes 1994, 79; Beach, Barnes, and Christensen-Szalanski 1986). Using standard price theory economists will predict that some individuals will curtail their cigarette consumption if a $2/pack tax is imposed. They will perhaps even predict, based on econometric estimates of the price elasticity of demand, the total amount of the cutback. But they will not usually predict *which* particular individuals will cut back. On the other hand, within the analysis of strategic interactions (game theory), some conclusions are so broad and universal (players will *always* defect in a single play PD game) that they imply (clinical) predictions of individual level behavior. Nash was disappointed by the *specific* behavior of Alchian and Williams in the first PD experiment.

47. "Economics as a positive science is a body of tentatively accepted generalizations about economic phenomena that can be used to predict the consequences of changes in circumstances" (Friedman 1953, 39).

the overrunning by more hardheaded and less deluded groups of societies made vulnerable by such beliefs. His loss function defined over Type I and Type II errors on this issue is implicit in the attitudes of many social scientists, particularly economists and others attracted by the apparent predictive power of rational choice theory.

But the assumption that there is no cost of assuming strict egoism when the hypothesis is wrong is questionable. The assumption leads inexorably to the conclusion that giving up the first strike option is not rational: the Nash equilibrium prediction, and its normative counsel to decision makers, is to defect. Relatively few people are aware that John von Neumann and Bertrand Russell both advocated a nuclear first strike against the Soviet Union in the early 1950s (see chap. 4). Suppose von Neumann's and Russell's argument had prevailed. Would this outcome have been without cost? It is at least a matter for debate.

When we realize how easy it is for others to end our lives (by failing to give up the first strike), or when we feel murderous impulses ourselves, we may suddenly appreciate how truly fraught with potential danger is the world. When we realize how infrequently we must concern ourselves with these dangers, we cannot but be struck by how remarkably safe the world is. These dual observations are apparently inconsistent: the world cannot at the same time be both more dangerous and safer than it appears. It is one of our jobs as behavioral scientists to illuminate and resolve this paradox.

Romanticism and cynicism define two polar views of essential human nature. The first is associated, to some degree unjustly (see Wrong 1994, 90–99), with Rousseau's idealized vision of a state of nature inhabited by noble savages, happy, but with virtually no intercourse with each other save that necessary for reproduction. The second is associated with Thomas Hobbes and his vision of a world prior to Leviathan in which life was not only solitary but also nasty, brutish, and short. Each can be refuted on the basis of experimental and observational data, including anthropological studies of hunter-gatherer societies. Each invokes a demonstrably inaccurate view of human nature and the range of political cultures it enables, and the adoption of either can be dangerous to health and welfare. The former view might be problematic, for example, if one were strolling through a high crime area, or a war zone at night, particularly if one could not be identified as a member of an "in-group" controlling the region. But the latter view can be equally damaging as a prescriptive guide, because it leads inexorably, as it did for von Neumann and Russell, to the logic of first strike. Even before the Neolithic revolution, our tool use enhanced already existing asymmetries between our ability to end the life of other humans and our ability to forestall the end of life in others through means other than refraining from harming them. Technological progress leading ultimately to nuclear, chemical, and biological weapons has only amplified this asymmetry.

The assumption of strict egoism, with its implication of Nash equilibrium outcomes, is inconsistent with a large body of empirical and observational evidence. It leaves us with no coherent account of how cooperation beyond kin groupings emerged and leaves largely unexplained the origin of the coexistence, often peaceful, of powerful sovereign nations. Initial forbearance (cooperation in what might well be a one-shot PD) is the foundation without which a range of altruistic and increasingly mutualistic behaviors cannot develop. It is upon that rudimentary foundation that complex social organization is built.

My daughter did not need me to tell her that there were individuals who would steal from her or otherwise do her harm when it was in their individual interest to do so. The news media do an effective job of making her aware of this. And were she to take a course in price theory, the normative relevance of the individual benefit/cost calculation would be drilled into her, with perhaps little regard to the domain of its applicability.

But she perhaps needed to be reminded of another truth, one also consistent with her knowledge and experience. And that is the truth about baseline levels of human behavior. *Not everyone* will steal or stab her in the back under such circumstances; indeed, if one takes a random sample of ten individuals, it is quite likely that none of them will. Her concerns that doors be locked, however, are not without foundation. If one takes a large enough sample, the probability rises of encountering individuals who practice first strike for reasons of both opportunism and prudence. Such individuals are sometimes referred to as sociopaths.[48] It is because of the risk of encountering individuals of this type, generally greater in the absence of established social organization, that a willingness to forego first strike is biologically altruistic when manifested in low frequency environments.

---

48. Sociopaths are estimated by criminologists to comprise between 3 and 4 percent of the male population and less than 1 percent of the female population and to account for roughly 20 percent of those incarcerated. Personality attributes include "egocentrism, an inability to form lasting personal commitments, and a marked degree of impulsivity. Underlying a superficial veneer of sociability and charm, sociopaths are characterized by a deficit of the social emotions (love, shame, guilt, empathy, or remorse). On the other hand, they are not intellectually handicapped, and are often able to deceive and manipulate others through elaborate scams and ruses, or by committing crimes that rely on the trust and cooperation of others" (Mealey 1995, 523). Would it be unfair to define *Homo economicus* as a sociopath without the charm?

The Dark Side of Cooperation and the Significance of Political Culture

Variation in the development of distinctive political cultures can dramatically affect the manifestation of tendencies toward restraint, particularly as directed toward out-groups. Thus risk of harm may increase not only as the number of individuals encountered grows but also as does the number of cohesive groups of individuals. Contacting a variety of different cultures, regrettably, increases the probability one could find oneself, for reasons unrelated to behavior, defined as an individual who does not warrant such restraint. There is, in other words, a dark side to the apparently virtuous circle whereby mutual forbearance leads to cooperation with its attendant benefits. Evidence from throughout human history and from studies of chimpanzees, our closest relatives,[49] suggests that growing strength of within group reciprocity is sometimes paired with an increasing propensity, particularly among males, to deny forbearance to nongroup members, making critical (in humans) the political definition of what in fact are the boundaries of relevant groups (Weart 1998, 235–36).

Humans throughout history have been prepared to risk and/or give their lives in support of or solidarity with a group or faction extending considerably beyond immediate kin and have frequently done so in a wantonly cruel fashion. The ease with which hostility can be directed against out-groups stems from the same underlying inclination that Fehr and Gächter document in their investigation of how internal order is sustained: a willingness to punish those, including third parties, who in a real or imagined fashion, violate norms of behavior. In these instances self-interest, or concern with interests of immediate family, could operate as a check on such behavior. That it fails often to do so is testimony again to the fact that there are other essential predispositions underlying human behavior.[50]

By *essential*, I mean so commonly exhibited as to warrant inclusion in a human ethogram. This does not, however, mean strictly universal. That is, I do not mean that the predisposition is driven entirely by genetic fac-

49. An organized unprovoked attack by a group of chimpanzee males on a member of a different group was first witnessed by a member of Jane Goodall's research team in Gombe National Park in Tanzania in January 1974. Her team concluded that the attack was most likely ultimately fatal. The episode led to a radical rethinking of assumptions about essential characteristics of chimp behavior. To date, *Homo sapiens sapiens* and *Pan troglodytes* (the "common" chimpanzee) are the only species in which such behavior has been observed. It has not been reported for bonobos (*Pan paniscus*). For discussion of ethological research on the behavior of members of the two *Pan* species, our closest living relatives, see chapter 5.

50. Ethnocentrism—preference for people "like us"—is a real phenomenon, but contrary to what has been frequently argued, in-group definitions are not governed principally by identifiable racial or ethnic characteristics. See Brewer 1982; Vail 1989; Peters 1998.

tors or that genetic influences have necessarily evolved to fixation. Even if a propensity to play cooperate in one-shot PDs with non-kin is an *almost* universal human predisposition, not all will share it or have it evoked by experience to the same degree, and within groups, such "deviants" have a high potential to be differentially advantaged (the political implications of this are discussed subsequently). Given that reality, how selection pressures ever permitted those who generally cooperate in one-shot PDs to become statistically if not always politically dominant within human populations is one of the central puzzles of social and natural science, at least as important as the study of how complex organization is sustained. In order to resolve that puzzle we must consider the possibility that natural selection among our ancestors occurred not only at the level of the individual organism but also above it. Doing so permits us to consider the possibility of a broader range of behavioral predispositions and evaluate the relative importance of each in a way that is not biased from the outset against certain conclusions.

Genocide

How pessimistic should we be about a propensity for violent group-energized attacks on those viewed as "the other"? First of all, as we recognize the widely recorded instances of xenophobic behavior by humans organized in groups, we should also acknowledge its paler complement in the historical record. These are instances in which humans, often at great risk to themselves, aided members of out-group(s), simply because they too were conspecifics. The most carefully documented instances of such behavior took place in the context of the most extreme xenophobic behavior on record: the unprovoked war against the Jews waged by the Third Reich between 1933 and 1945, in most severe form between 1941 and 1945. In 1953, after the Holocaust, the Israeli government established the Yad Vashem foundation to honor the memory of the six million who perished, but also, as stipulated in the founding legislation, to recognize the actions of the "Righteous among the Nations": non-Jews who, without expectation in advance of monetary reward, risked their lives to save Jews from death or deportation to death camps. Awards have been made to those both living and dead only when a variety of criteria have been satisfied and after careful investigation by a commission headed by a justice of the Israeli Supreme Court.

The efforts of Raoul Wallenberg and Oskar Schindler are perhaps best known, but there are others: approximately sixteen thousand men and women have been honored to date. In many of these instances, careful investigation permits us with considerable confidence to reject a desire for reward, fame, or approbation as motives for such behavior. Indeed, a number of individuals, sought out so that the Yad Vashem Medal might be bestowed on them, declined the honor. The Danes, as individuals and as a nation, for example, succeeded in saving the lives of all but a few of their Jewish compatriots, in marked contrast to what happened in other nations. After the war, Danish war veterans as a group refused to accept individual Yad Vashem Awards (Monroe 1996, 142). They did, in their view, only what others would have done in their place, and others, they felt, had done much more. This is a common sentiment expressed by those honored for heroism. But while acknowledging their efforts, we must discount the truth-value reflected in their humility. Were it truer, we would not so honor these individuals.

If the behavior of these honored individuals was exceptional, however, so too, in the broad sweep of history, was that of the Nazis who elicited it. As shocking, in some senses, as the sheer magnitude of the crimes committed is the evidence of the tens of thousands who willingly participated in them. Nevertheless, organized genocide on this scale was not and is not the historical norm, one reason why German Jews, twelve thousand of whom died serving their country in World War I, could not believe anything of this nature would actually happen to them. The behavior of the Third Reich and those who supported it, precisely because of its exceptional and horrific character, requires that we recognize the power, extent, and pervasiveness of normal[51] human predispositions against intraspecific violence of this nature. Similarly, it is because of the abnormal character of his or her predispositions and behavior that we stigmatize the individual actions of a sociopathic killer, no matter how intelligent and no matter how rational he or she may be in forming beliefs or pursuing aims.

While the behaviors of Yad Vashem honorees, or winners of Carnegie Hero Awards are often taken as archetypal examples of altruism, the more empirically significant form in originating and sustaining complex social organization is the more quotidian restraint on first strike. Restricting our understanding of altruism to affirmative acts of assistance leads to an improper circumscription of a phenomenon that has much broader manifestation. A predisposition toward such restraint has, as far as we can infer, always been an essentially human predisposition, just as it is among lions, wolves, and many other animals capable of harming each other.[52] We speak of the competitive environment as being a "dog-eat-dog" world,

---

51. I use the term in its statistical sense of referring to the central tendency of a distribution.

52. The emphasis is on restraint on intraspecific harm. Lions and wolves are predator species that earn their protein by hunting down, attacking, killing, and eating members of other species, including, according to Ridley (1999, 33), close relatives: lions eat leopards, and wolves eat coyotes.

but in fact dogs do not eat other dogs, and wolves do not eat other wolves. Chapter 5 considers the argument of a broad stream of writers, including Lorenz, who have maintained that although such patterns of hardwired intraspecific restraint may well characterize animals, comparable mechanisms are lacking in humans.

The Nazi program of extermination directed against Jews is an exceptional event, yet the more general and widespread phenomenon of "civilized" war might seem to argue in favor of Lorenz's view. But the phenomenon of war is not simply an illustration of humankind's inherently violent and aggressive tendencies. War gives rise to extremes of both cooperation and conflict. Some of the most impressive (because they are rare) examples of affirmative altruism toward non-kin take place in situations of organized conflict, such as instances in which a soldier throws himself on a grenade to save his buddies. *Absent a PD solution module, organized war would be impossible. So too, for that matter, would peace.*

Evolutionary history has endowed us, like other animals, with extraordinary drives facilitating self-preservation and a powerful learning technology permitting us efficiently to act in pursuit of their satisfaction. But such capabilities cannot account for initial interactions characterized by mutual forbearance of first strike. These propensities are complemented by others that underlie and enable the complex social and economic organization we today take for granted. This is not to argue that altruistic behavior toward non-kin is necessarily praiseworthy from a moral standpoint (although it may be and often is). Nor is it to suggest that psychological design determines behavior: rather, it embodies developmental programs whose phenotypic expression may vary depending upon environmental cues.

Our understanding of essential features of human nature is clouded by our existence within established social groupings. That is why experimental evidence, in which researchers can control otherwise uncontrollable features of the environment, is particularly important in isolating irreducible human predispositions. Such evidence, in conjunction with a wide range of field data, requires us to chart a careful path between romantic idealism, a view that might deny the existence of backstabbers, and the narrow cynicism of one strain of individualist models carried to their logical conclusion, suggesting that we are all, all the time, backstabbers if it pays us to do so and that every person we encounter should be treated as a potential backstabber or, in the limit, a sociopath.

Economists are generally reluctant to accept or adopt the language of abnormal psychology, and thus to describe sociopaths as "deviant" personalities. But is it simply a matter of luck or happenstance that so few individuals happen to have this particular preference ordering? Are we to attribute this entirely to the consequences of effective socialization among the rest of the population? These are issues that have remained essentially unaddressed by those adhering to the intermediate position described in note 8 of the prologue.

Humans have aggressive, cruel, and sometimes vicious impulses, to be sure, and are quite capable of acting on them in ways that seem obviously to increase the fitness of the actor and reduce that of the target—the opposite of altruistic in an evolutionary sense. The puzzle is why actions based on such impulses are so frequently absent, among individuals as well as among interacting groups or nations.

This is a problem economists sometimes dismiss with a nod to the invisible hand or the civilizing role of trade, the doux commerce thesis (Smith [1776] 1937; Hirschman 1982). But the twin and related traditions, when examined closely, are simply vehicles for marveling at and celebrating the reasonableness of acting cooperatively within a group when others are, particularly where there is expectation that, if provoked by defection, cooperators will match like with like, even directing punishment toward third party violators. When one is a marginal invader and (inductively) extrapolates native behavior based on observed frequencies, doing in Rome as the Romans do may well appear to be the reasonable, rational, self-serving course to pursue. In the limiting condition, were one certain all other players were irrevocably committed, or in other ways driven to Tit-for-Tat, the behavior of the rational invader, no matter how egoistic and otherwise prone to first strike, would be observationally indistinguishable from that of the rest of the population. This remarkable and somewhat counterintuitive result does not, however, provide us with a good account of the origin of such behavior.

Hobbes, the State of Nature, and Democratic Peace

Hobbes began by assuming that the most important shared attribute of humans, their common denominator, is their *ability to kill each other* ([1651] 1909, chap. 13). His analysis is thus congruent with the emphasis of many twentieth century writers such as Sigmund Freud and Konrad Lorenz on a "thin veneer of civilization" standing between us and an apocalypse in which we would tear each other apart (on the similarities between Freud's and Hobbes's views of human nature, see Montagu 1956, 38).

There are, however, two weak points, related to each other, in Hobbes's analysis. The first involves contract. Without an external enforcer, he argues, contracts are cheap talk, because each person, having made an agreement, can and will benefit from violating it ([1651] 1909, chap. 14). Leviathan solves the problem of the one-shot PD by allowing people within the scope of its embrace to play cooperative game theory, that is, to enter into enforceable contracts. But the solution is a deus ex machina and finesses the question of how the grandest contract of them all—the social contract—could be entered into without some other external enforcer, one logically prior to the existence of Leviathan.

The second issue concerns the actual character of the state of nature. Hobbes's picture of it is not pretty: it involves a state of perennial violence, or threat of violence, that divides humans into small kin groupings—families—"the concord of which depends on natural lust."

> In such condition there is no place for industry, because the fruit thereof is uncertain: and consequently no culture of the earth; no navigation, nor use of the commodities that may be imported by sea; no commodious building; no instruments of moving and removing such things as require much force; no knowledge of the face of the earth; no account of time; no arts; no letters; no society; and which is worst of all, continual fear, and danger of violent death; and the life of man, solitary, poor, nasty, brutish, and short. ([1651] 1909, chap. 13)

The state of nature was one suggested to Hobbes by conditions in England during its civil war and one that resonates with our contemplation of late twentieth century Somalia or Bosnia.

I do not wish to diminish how unpleasant and anxiety provoking life in any of these environments is or was. But here is the truly tough question for Hobbes: if the state of nature is *unimaginably* horrible, why did it not lead to the extinction of the human race?[53] (Lorenz solved this problem implicitly by hypothesizing that "civilization" was invented in the nanosecond after humans became truly dangerous to each other by discovering tools.) And if the state of nature can and does persist for more than a nanosecond, what human predispositions make this possible? Might these predispositions involve a more extensive repertoire of human motivations than those allowed by Hobbes—and might relaxation of the assumptions we make about human nature also help resolve the first issue:

---

53. In fact, in some passages, Hobbes's description of the state of nature is not one of unmitigated violence: "if there be no power erected, or not great enough for our security, every man will and may lawfully rely on his own strength and art for caution against other men. And in all places where men have lived by small families, to rob and spoil one another has been a trade, and so far from being reputed against the law of nature that the greater spoils they gained, the greater was their honour, and men observed no other laws but the laws of honour; that is *to abstain from cruelty, leaving to men their lives and instruments of husbandry* ([1651] 1909, chap. 17; my italics).

how does a social contract get established in the absence of an external enforcer?

Standard game theoretic analysis actually provides a less than airtight justification for the necessity of a Hobbesian state as a means of *preserving* order. If one can establish an environment of indefinitely repeated interaction, and can coordinate on a cooperative equilibrium, such an equilibrium might be self-enforcing (see Ellickson 1991), particularly if the number of parties is small and exit from continuing interaction is difficult.

One can't, however, jump to the conclusion that states are necessarily superfluous. Theory remains silent on how transition from one shot to repeated interaction might take place, why it leads to one rather than another of the multiple equilibria that could ensue in environments of indefinitely repeated interaction, and what guarantees the inability of individuals simply to exit from indefinite interaction, thus avoiding the penalties for defection that are essential in allowing the equilibrium to be self-enforcing.[54]

There is a related question based on the evidence discussed earlier. If humans possess predispositions to play cooperate in one-shot PDs, predispositions with an important genetic component, then our ability to coexist in an environment sufficiently peaceful to allow the species to persist does not inhere fundamentally in Leviathan. The strongest proof of this can be found in the realm of international relations. Hobbes himself agreed that sovereign states operated within a state of nature. How have we survived in the absence of a world state?

The observation of international relations thus gives us insight into the problems that the organized state, according to Hobbes, was intended to solve. If we take this project seriously, we must begin to be more realistic about the actual character of a state of nature. Historical and contemporary evidence indicates that, in spite of periodic and sometimes horrific outbreaks of interstate violence, international relations do not degenerate into a spate of conflicts so terrible that the species is extinguished. Given the availability today of nuclear, chemical, and biological weapons, it appears likely that that *could* happen. But it hasn't. In other words, sovereign states are not constantly at war with each other, and we do not literally experience an international *war of all against all*.

One can argue that a non-war equilibrium among *states* is self-enforcing based on the material interests of individual countries, due to an indefinite horizon of interaction. But several familiar difficulties present

---

54. The relatively small number of nations—less than 200—makes it easier collectively to monitor behavior and, through threat of punishment, deter defection.

themselves. With nuclear weapons, a superpower has the capability of effectively destroying a counterparty, rendering the horizon of interaction a matter of choice rather than an environmental given. Second, environments of indefinitely repeated interaction support multiple equilibria: why this one? Finally, and this is related to the second problem, we return to the issue of origin: how did this environment of repeated, relatively peaceful coexistence ever come about?

To be sure, international tranquillity is periodically rent with outbreaks of war. But armed conflict is not typical of interactions among sovereign states. There is, in addition, persuasive evidence that the path taken by individual states in achieving complex social organization has important influences on the degree and targets of interstate conflict. Neither of these empirical regularities is fully explicable within the Hobbesian framework.

The final section of this chapter considers international relations as providing an additional range of field observation inconsistent in many ways with the predictions of the standard economic model and relevant in evaluating Hobbes's proposed solution to the PD. Much field observation of behavior of individuals within nations is confounded not only by the existence of social norms that may result in the punishment by private parties of defection, but also by the existence of formal governmental structures and enforcement mechanisms. If one is dismissive of the power of social norms, one can argue that individuals are restrained from potentially self-serving but socially damaging acts by the anticipation of third party retribution through the formal agency of the state. The study of international relations involves the interactions of powerful sovereign actors unconstrained by a supranational world government with effective police power.

Within the field of international relations, generally domiciled in political science departments, the doux commerce thesis draws support from the coupling of two propositions, one well established and the other less so. The less firmly established claim is that countries or groups with highly developed national and international commercial cultures are less likely to go to war with each other. Harold Nicolson, for example, an experienced British diplomat, contrasted the behavior of Britain and other democracies during the interwar period with that of fascist and communist regimes. The former, he suggested, reflected the virtues of the merchant class, "moderation, fair dealing, reasonableness, credit, compromise," in contrast with the first move(r) aggression and deception characteristic of the warrior mentality (Nicolson 1963, 132, 144). Note, however, that Nicolson's argument couples the doux commerce argument with an assumed correlation between commercial culture and democratic political regime.

Qualitative observations of the sort made by Nicolson do not support the inference, often drawn, that the establishment of or strengthening of commercial relations between nations will reduce or eliminate the probability of war between them. Indeed, systematic studies cast considerable doubt on this proposition (Barbieri 1996; although see Oneal and Russett 1999). In contrast, empirical evidence strongly supports the view that war between two nations can be avoided by assuring that a firmly rooted democratic political system prevails in each. Thus in rereading Nicolson's observation, we must ask whether Britain's diplomatic style was driven by its democratic political system or by its flourishing commercial culture.

Evidence suggests the former. A recent book, building on a well-established literature in political science and based on an exhaustive reading of history and a detailed consideration of ambiguous cases, concludes with little qualification that "well established democracies have never waged war on each other" (Weart 1998, 13).[55] The more firmly established proposition is that democratic states simply *do not go to war with each other*. Note, remarkably, that this proposition is advanced as something far stronger than simply a probabilistic statement, highly unusual in social science. In an influential article published in 1988, Jack Levy maintained that this regularity was "as close as anything we have to an empirical law in international relations" (Levy 1988, 662).[56]

Democratic governments are only marginally less prone to war: they have a high propensity to join preexisting conflicts (partly because they are much better than other forms of government at maintaining leagues or alliances), they will respond to attack, and they will sometimes attack non-

---

55. Weart defines a democracy as a political system in which at least two-thirds of adult males are enfranchised, a "well established" democracy as one marked by the toleration of dissent (no exile, imprisonment, or execution for political opposition) for a period of three years or more, and a war as cross-border violence organized by political units resulting in two hundred or more deaths in organized combat (Weart 1998, 13, 293–95). To the degree that results are driven by differences in political culture, not just differences in formal institutions, Weart's three-year criterion suggests the possibility of relatively rapid transformations of political culture, even after decades of stasis, a position consistent with Kuran's. This book builds upon a well-developed body of literature in political science. The idea of the democratic peace is not new. Kant suggested the hypothesis in 1785, although he was wrong in maintaining that democratic peoples were necessarily less belligerent. Weart's contributions include extending the scope of inquiry to classical Greece and medieval Italy (most other studies focus only on modern democracies) and establishing that oligarchic republics (those in which less than a third of adult males were enfranchised) rarely went to war with each other, reinforcing the view that political regimes make grants of first move(r) altruism to other regimes they view as "like us" and making a convincing case that republics, and only republics, have been capable of forming durable, peaceful leagues.

56. This regularity continues to attract an extraordinary degree of attention from political scientists; see in particular recent issues of the *Journal of Conflict Resolution* or the *Journal of Peace Research*.

democratic regimes. They thereby end up engaging in war almost as frequently as autocracies (Raknerud and Hegre 1997, 387). But they do not go to war with each other.

The empirical regularity that underlies this conclusion stands as a challenge to the dominant realist, neorealist, or realpolitik approach in political science, which maintains that international relations are, and argues normatively that they should be, governed strictly by considerations of national advantage, just as Nash's model of human behavior presumes that decisions are and should be governed solely by considerations of individual advantage. If the neorealist approach is correct, we should not see correlations between the regime character of state dyads and the propensity for armed conflict between them. But we do.

The realpolitik or neorealist approach to international relations finesses an important problem. Most interstate relations have about them a strategic structure of gains and losses similar to those faced by experimental subjects in PD games. The biggest gains to "national interest" come when a belligerent stance is matched with a conciliatory response, the biggest losses when a conciliatory stance is met with a belligerent response.[57] Mutual conciliation is a Pareto efficient solution. But since, regardless of the position adopted by one's counterparty, belligerence is the individually superior stance, belligerence is the dominant strategy and a defect—defect pairing is, as before, the unique Nash equilibrium. It does no good to object that belligerence is not necessarily a dominant strategy if interactions are repeated. *We must explain transitions from single play interactions to those where repeated interactions may be presumed.*

War is in fact a relatively rare event in international relations. If neorealism is truly correct, then it would also be true that international diplomacy is epiphenomenal: cheap talk, without any real consequence for outcomes. Studies of diplomatic history, such as that leading up to World War I, World War II, and most other significant international conflict, suggest otherwise. Indeed, it is because humans possess both PD solution modules that enable them to abide by agreements in the absence of an external enforcer and foraging modules that might incline them to violate those agreements that diplomatic skills have value.

Henry Kissinger, the twentieth century's foremost advocate and practitioner of realpolitik, argued repeatedly that the character of regimes was

---

57. If one argues, instead, that the biggest losses for both parties occur when a belligerent stance is met with a belligerent response, then the game becomes the related one of chicken, or, as Maynard-Smith described it, hawk-dove. The issue of how to characterize the game is ultimately philosophical. Is it better, under threat, to surrender one's sovereignty and live like a slave or to fight to the death in a potentially unsuccessful attempt to preserve liberty? The issue is discussed in greater detail in chapter 4.

irrelevant to international diplomacy: what mattered were hardheaded calculations of national interest. In practice, however, his comments show that he recognized the empirical likelihood that regime character influenced international behavior. With regard to the Soviet Union, for example, he observed that their rulers "had prevailed in a system that ruthlessly weeds out the timid and the scrupulous" and that this domestic history made them disinclined to conciliation abroad (Kissinger 1982, 245). Similarly, Nicolo Machiavelli, who praised treachery and deceit among princes, conceded as an empirical matter that republics had a higher propensity to bargain honestly (Weart 1998, 79) and would be less likely unilaterally to abrogate a treaty. In both the history of classical Greece and that of Italian city-states, there is evidence that republics, which had learned how to reconcile competing interests domestically, attempted to apply this same model to their international diplomacy.

The explanation for this phenomenon of peace among democracies needs to be developed against a larger backdrop. From an evolutionary standpoint, the most important challenge is not to explain why there is so much conflict between individuals beyond the level of immediate kin groups but why there is so little; the same challenge applies to behavior between states (on this point, see Zahavi and Zahavi 1997, 16).

Evidence from more than two millennia of recorded history is consistent with the view that an established (more than three-year-old) democratic political culture in two regimes prevents conflict between them. The phenomenon of democratic peace illustrates two characteristics of the human predisposition to make grants of restraint on first strike: such grants are not restricted to kin, but they can, with higher probability, be restricted to those deemed worthy of equal treatment because they are "like us." It also reminds us of what is not largely determined by genetic factors in human affairs, that is not simply a predictable consequence of species typical behavioral propensities. Regime choice is, ultimately, a collective decision that can go and has gone in different directions and has important consequences.

Moreover, the in-group/out-group demarcation, so central to ethnocentrism, is only partly—some argue minimally—explicable with reference to identifiable intergroup differences in physical characteristics. Such differences are neither a necessary nor a sufficient condition for strife. There are many instances of bitter divisions among populations that are ethnically and racially indistinguishable (e.g., some of the conflicts in the remains of Yugoslavia) and other instances in which in-groups encompass a racially and ethnically diverse population (e.g., current day Switzerland). Cultural, ethnic, religious, or racial uniformity has never provided insurance against violent intra- or intergroup conflict. More frequently than not, politics and history have determined national or cultural identity, rather than the reverse. This view is supported by experiments in social psychology demonstrating that even when subjects are assigned to groups randomly, they can very quickly be made to believe that members of the other group are inferior and less deserving of rewards (Brown 1986, chap. 5). The criterion of differentiation can be as inconsequential as whether members of "their" group are (supposedly) more inclined to overestimate or underestimate the number of dots appearing on a computer screen in a given time interval (Tajfel and Billig 1974).

What gives political culture and structure, then, such apparent power to influence the probability of violence among state dyads? Suppose we grant that natural selection above the level of the individual organism has endowed most humans with a predisposition most of the time to play cooperate in one-shot PDs. Such tendencies must still be evoked by environmental cues and can be attenuated in their absence or in the presence of different ones. For both environmental and genetic reasons, those with higher predispositions to practice first strike will persist in every group in a minority status. Moreover, as the analysis of chapter 2 indicates, such individuals will, within each group, be differentially advantaged. In nondemocratic societies, one aspect of differential advantage, aside from greater reproductive success, is a greater probability of exercising political power (this likelihood is reflected in Kissinger's remarks). Thus in nondemocratic societies ruthless individuals (those lacking aversion to first strike, those who win by intimidation and are used to doing so domestically) can more easily lead societies into aggressive wars not necessarily reflecting the predispositions of the majority of the population. They do so in part because they may misread a conciliatory negotiating stance on the part of another regime as evidence of exploitable weakness, in particular an unwillingness to bear the costs of conflict if attacked or otherwise provoked.

Democracies are somewhat less likely than autocracies to launch aggressive war, even against nondemocratic societies. Democratic forms of government require leaders to be responsive to the will (predispositions) of the majority. An unprovoked attack during the Cold War by the United States and Britain on the Soviets, a nondemocratic society, would, however, not have violated the democratic peace regularity, was not beyond the realm of possibility, and could have been sold to the U.S. public had the enemy been sufficiently demonized. Game theoretic analysis (read Nash equilibrium analysis) supported it, as did the nation's most prominent game theorist.

Nevertheless, in the early 1950s, advocates of first strike against the Soviets faced an uphill struggle to persuade citizens that aggressive war was consistent with democratic principles. One advocate urged the United

States to overcome its aversions and become comfortable with being an "aggressor for peace" (see chap. 4). In contrast, the doctrine of massive retaliation was easily salable within the United States, Britain, and other democratic countries, *even though both elements of the strategy are widely recognized as irrational from the standpoint of an egoistic actor.*[58] Democracies, like the humans whose will their leaders reflect, tend to be prototypical Tit-for-Tat players, universally when interacting with other democracies and frequently in interacting with others. They make grants of restraint on first strike to those they believe merit such treatment, especially other democracies. They apparently take the existence of an established democratic system in a counterparty as an observable cue that leaders are "like us," which means not necessarily that they are ethnically or racially similar but rather that they will be held accountable by those they rule, and are more likely to interpret a conciliatory negotiating stance as reflecting a desire to avoid war (the lose-lose Nash equilibrium) as opposed to a sign of weakness and an invitation to go for the big gains by talking and acting belligerently. The democratic nature of a political regime is a readable signal to another democracy that the dyad will be able to work out differences through negotiation and avoid resort to force.

Similarly, for the same reason that completely self-regarding invaders of a society of Tit-for-Tat players will find it prudent to act in an observationally equivalent fashion, autocracies, even when their leaders possess much stronger penchants for aggressive war, may be dissuaded from belligerent moves when they perceive themselves to be in an environment of Tit-for-Tat players. This was the underlying basis of the post–World War II doctrine of containment.

Political scientists have long assumed that the same kind of analytical tools can be used to understand interactions among nations as is used to understand interactions among individuals, and as we have seen, there is considerable merit to this view. Certainly game theoretic concepts such as the Prisoner's Dilemma are useful in understanding options faced by states as well as individuals. And certainly the standard economic model and its neorealist sibling in political science face isomorphic difficulties in explaining actual outcomes of individual interactions and international relations.

Some object that the analogy fails because states are not unitary

---

58. Although the United States has never officially forsworn the first use of nuclear weapons, it is generally assumed that such use would take place only in the context of a severe unprovoked threat to the national interest. The strategy of massive retaliation is a reactive stance that requires one to give up the advantages that might obtain from an offensive first strike. von Neumann did not think this was rational. Second, deterrence requires forming an intention to retaliate, a threat to perform an action it would not be in one's material interest to undertake in the event deterrence failed.

actors. The concept of the unitary actor is an abstraction at the level of states, and understanding the different accountabilities faced by leaders in democracies as compared with autocracies gives insight, for example, into why regime character affects outcomes. But the objection is less compelling once one begins to adopt a modular approach to cognition. For the concept of the unitary actor is also something of an abstraction at the level of the individual. Just as opposing points of view coexist in polities, so do sometimes opposing predispositions coexist within individuals.

As members of established social groups, for example, we are each of us, as a matter of fact, both invader and native, coolly assessing the scene from the standpoint of hard nosed game theory, as if human-human interactions were strictly a foraging problem and part of the background blur that makes cooperation (forgoing first strike) the generally reasonable thing to do. This duality implies that inconsistent behavioral propensities supporting these two roles coexist within individuals, although natural selection has heavily influenced the domain specific probabilities that these propensities will be expressed. We (at least westerners) are largely unaware of this contradictory coexistence because of what psychologists call the *fundamental attribution error* (Jones and Nisbett 1972). We attribute our own behavior too much to situational factors—we are simply rationally responding to costs, benefits, and opportunities—while explaining the behavior of others too much with reference to dispositional factors or personality traits—behavioral regularities resistant or less responsive to such factors.

This bias may be particularly helpful for those steeped in individualistic traditions (see Wilson 1999, 284). By suggesting a higher predictability and a lesser reliance on rational calculation in the behavior of others than we attribute to ourselves it may make it easier for us to preserve the view that we, at least, are Nash optimizers, while at the same time allowing us to reconcile this view with the incorporation of empirical data on the past behavior of counterparties in making our decisions (Kreps et al. 1982). But it is also a reminder that introspection is a poor guide to understanding how much our responses in particular situations may actually be constrained by behavioral predispositions, tendencies that have been evolutionarily favored and that are central to the understanding of complex social organization.

The consequence of restraint on first strike, the control of direct unprovoked aggression, is never entirely complete because of the persistence at low frequencies of deviant propensities, or low probability propensities within particular individuals. But it is still remarkably complete, helping, in conjunction with very small numbers of police or their equivalent, to create the security of persons and security of property that are, within states, preconditions for reciprocity, whether it be in the more primitive nonsimultaneous form identified by anthropologists as generalized reciprocity or its more modern manifestation in market exchange. Restraint on first strike also facilitates the emergence of coexistence among sovereign nations, even though it may be possible to account for the *preservation* of peace through collective security as reflecting the rationally pursued interests of particular states.

Sociologists and anthropologists attribute restraint almost exclusively to enculturation and/or the effect of socialization. Many political theorists attribute it to the institution of formal government, although that can be only part of the answer, since at the microlevel people seem capable of establishing workable rules in its absence (Ellickson 1991) and powerful nations manage more frequently than not to avoid conflict even in the absence of world government. Rational choice theorists emphasize how the pursuit of material interest can contribute to the maintenance of reciprocal relations.

My argument is that explanation of these phenomena, which must account also for their emergence, is to be found not just in self-interest narrowly defined, but in a complex of human behavioral propensities selected for over thousands of generations prior to the arrival of *Homo sapiens sapiens* and evident in the behavior, neurobiology, and cognitive mechanisms of humans today. This model can be empirically validated and shown to be consistent with evolutionary theory, in contrast to the standard economic model, particularly in its application to strategic interactions, which is based on a priori assumptions buttressed by a flawed reading of evolutionary theory and evidence.

Some version of this model of human behavior, steering a course between romantic idealism and cynicism, is what children should and for the most part do carry into the world as they update and modify its predictions on the basis of personal experience; knowledge about the external world obtained through the study of history and current events; and perspectives on human interaction gained through art, literature, and other forms of fiction. We are doing both science and humanity a disservice if we give people a choice between the seriously incomplete standard economic model, justified by improper appeals to evolutionary theory and data, which if carried to its logical conclusion leaves virtually no room for altruistic inclinations, and different assumptions about human behavioral predispositions based only on blind faith. Presuppositions about human nature of the latter sort are vulnerable *irrespective of their truth content* absent some kind of scientific foundation.

Virtually all known ethical systems contain some version of the categorical imperative (although, regrettably, the fine print reveals that such rules have almost always been intended to apply only to within group, not out of group members). These imperatives are intended both as a normative/prescriptive guide to behavior among those who merit equal treatment (the relevant in-group) and as an implicit positive description of general tendencies in human behavioral propensities within the group. Because these characterizations are so similar across groups, however, we can conclude that they reflect essential features of human nature reflected in the experimental results with which this chapter began. This is so even though these descriptions in each instance claim to be applicable only within a particular group, and are often contrasted with the purported barbaric, uncivilized ways of outsiders. *Behavioral science should aim for an accurate characterization of essential human predispositions, and the respective domains in which they are likely to be stronger or weaker, a characterization that must lie at the foundation of any social scientific model with aspirations to improved predictive power.*

CHAPTER 2

Multilevel Selection and Restraint on Harm

Skepticism about the existence of any type of "true" altruism beyond that displayed toward kin draws powerful support from a widespread belief among social scientists and others that such predispositions, had they arisen initially at low frequencies in a population, could not have withstood the disadvantageous force of natural selection operating on individual organisms. Organisms exhibiting such traits or practicing such strategies, it is thought, would necessarily have faced reproductive fitness penalties leading to the extinguishing of whatever genetic predisposers influenced the behavior.

This view frequently appeals to Darwin for support, but the appeal is unwarranted. What may appear on the face of it to be simply inconsistent with the theory of natural selection is not. No reputable biologist disputes the proposition that it is possible for a trait imposing a fitness disadvantage on the actor but benefiting one or more conspecifics to increase in frequency in global populations. This can involve not only predispositions to sacrifice for offspring but also, under the right conditions, to behave altruistically in ways that benefit non-kin and are disadvantageous to the actor. The debate among biologists has not been around the theoretical possibility of group level selection. It has concerned the nature and empirical likelihood of mechanisms allowing such traits to increase in frequency, and important changes in the character of consensus thinking on these issues have occurred in the past decade (see, e.g., Maynard-Smith and Price 1973, 15; Wilson and Sober 1994; Sober and Wilson 1998).

Altruistic behavior, defined in evolutionary terms as behavior that reduces the probability that the organism exhibiting it will survive and propagate in a manner that increases survivability and propagation likelihoods of at least one other conspecific, cannot *by definition* withstand the force of natural selection operating only at the level of the individual organism. Debate about the conditions under which traits predisposing to altruism might originate and increase in frequency has consequently been an important issue for biology. Accounting for altruistic behavior, or explaining why apparently altruistic behavior is not in fact so, has also been a central concern for social science since its origins and consequently for economics as a social science. It is critical, therefore, that we understand what biology, and in particular the theory of natural selection, does and does not tell us about this issue.

A relatively uncontroversial avenue through which altruistic traits may survive favors sacrifice for kin. The theory of kin selection is based on the concept of inclusive fitness (Hamilton 1964), which considers the impact on gene propagation of selection at all levels, not just that of the individual organism. Behavior that benefits three children, or three siblings, at the expense of the actor's survival, will not necessarily reduce inclusive fitness, since although the actor suffers, even to the point of death, the propagation of genes predisposing to such behavior will be enhanced by the increased survival probabilities of progeny or kin. Benefits are weighted by the number of benefited conspecifics and their genetic propinquity and measured against reproductive costs to the actor. If the overall (inclusive) benefit-cost ratio is favorable, then natural selection will favor genes predisposing to such behavior, even if the behavior damages the life prospects of the actor manifesting it. The theory of kin selection is broadly accepted and has provided important insights into the behavior of both human and nonhuman animal species.[1]

But altruism toward kin does not exhaust the range of behavior damaging to individual fitness that we must account for. For example, parents of adoptive children often exhibit behavior remarkably similar to behavior toward biological offspring, an observation that has been made with respect to humans and other primates (Wilson 1978, 151).[2] Individuals give anonymously to charities, and there are well-documented examples in war and elsewhere of individuals sacrificing themselves to save the lives of others in their group or otherwise acting as good Samaritans (Frank 1988,

---

1. Inclusive fitness is a gene's eye perspective that considers the impact of behavioral tendencies on the subsequent global frequency of genes that predispose to them. It takes into consideration the fitness benefits that behavior may confer on kin or other conspecifics. Standard textbook usage (e.g., Strickberger 1996, 603) interprets inclusive fitness to include mechanisms favoring kin selection but to exclude mechanisms that may benefit non-kin. Hamilton (1975), the originator of the concept, grants that the terms are commonly used in this sense but observes that inclusive fitness in principle includes the effects of selection at all levels. Thus the suggestion that inclusive fitness theory is an alternative to multilevel selection models is unwarranted. In fact, kin selection is an instance of group level selection.

2. When families contain both adopted and biological children, parents, on average, do favor their biological children (Buss 1999, 196–204). However, the baseline level of adoption is not zero. Substantial numbers of humans are clearly willing to sacrifice their own material welfare to raise children who are known not to be theirs biologically.

chap. 11).[3] And, we must consider what is the more empirically important form of altruism toward non-kin: failure to harm, or a willingness to forgo the option of first strike.

We are faced with a conundrum: the apparent inability of models based on natural selection to account for predispositions underlying the experimental and field data referenced in chapter 1. In a range of publications culminating in their 1998 book *Unto Others,* Elliott Sober and David Sloan Wilson (1998; see also Wilson and Sober 1994) provide an accessible articulation of what is the only viable mechanism capable of resolving it. Their solution, building on a theoretical and empirical literature that begins with Charles Darwin (see Wade 1978; Sober and Wilson 1998, 56), is not to dispute the proposition that the forces of individual selection operate against the survival of altruistic behavior, and that genes predisposing to such behavior will be selected against if this is the only force operating on their survival probabilities. Rather, their analysis is based on the proposition that multilevel selection—selection at the group as well as the individual level—is both logically possible and empirically important. Their argument is consistent with Hamilton's concept of inclusive fitness but emphasizes the operation of selection at levels above that of the family or kin groups. It incorporates the insights reflected in the Price equations (Price 1970, 1972; see the subsequent discussion in this chapter) and provides a more empirically plausible account of the operation of group selection than did earlier explorations such as that of Sewall Wright (1945).

Group Selection Theory: Intellectual Background

Wright recognized the fitness disadvantage experienced by altruists within each group. But he suggested that if groups were small enough and isolated enough altruism might *by chance,* that is, through the mechanism of genetic drift, evolve to fixation within some groups, and that such groups could then outcompete others by persisting longer and colonizing new territories by contributing more dispersers. The Wright approach to group selection involves differential extinction of separate groups.

---

3. The *U.S. Infantry Manual* advises a GI confronted with a live grenade in a trench to cover it with his body. By allowing himself to be killed a soldier can save the lives of several other soldiers, so the behavior is clearly adaptive from the standpoint of the squad. It is equally clear that such behavior is not adaptive for the individual, particularly if others are prepared to step in. Not moving first is a weakly dominant strategy, and the Nash equilibrium is for no one to move and for everyone to die. Of the 207 Medals of Honor awarded during the Vietnam War, 63 went to soldiers who threw themselves on exploding devices (Blake 1978, 53–58). Similarly, Secret Service agents are trained to take a bullet for their president. These instances show how training or enculturation can strengthen otherwise weak predispositions.

The conditions necessary for this model to operate continue to be viewed by evolutionary biologists, including Sober and Wilson, as unlikely to obtain. Evolution to fixation is considered improbable in the first place, since it relies on small numbers of similarly altruistic individuals finding themselves by chance in the same group. Second, if there is enough dispersion to permit the colonization of new territories, there is also likely enough dispersion to permit dispersing nonaltruists from other groups to invade existing altruist groups (Maynard-Smith 1964; Wade 1978).

Sober and Wilson's model, in contrast, does not require evolution to fixation within some groups or a high degree of geographical isolation and differential extinction rates: only a positive covariance between altruist gene frequency and group growth rates combined with periodic dispersal into the general population followed by group re-formation (see the discussion that follows).

Although appeals to group selection were common in the 1940s and 1950s among biologists, ethologists, and some social scientists, the concept came under withering attack in the 1960s by a more self-consciously analytical generation of biologists (e.g., Williams 1966). In the light of these attacks, and, at least initially, in the absence of empirically plausible theoretical models explaining how group selection could operate, the predominant position among biologists from the late 1960s through the early 1990s was that these processes were empirically unimportant in the evolution of human and other species.[4] The position is still held by many, although it is now generally articulated with more qualification. To the degree that the concept of inclusive fitness has been embraced, the supraindividual levels at which it can operate have typically been assumed to extend no higher than family or kin groups.

The consensus position was based in part on the argument that a

---

4. Kavka provides an excellent summary of conventional wisdom on this subject in the mid-1980s. He begins by describing conditions that, he understood from the biological literature, would have had to obtain for group selection to operate: small groups, so that altruism could become fixed in some groups by random variation; and isolated groups, so that free riding nonaltruists could not frequently join altruistic groups. Finally, he summarizes, selection pressures would have had to be severe, so that group selection did not proceed at a very much slower rate than individual selection. The first two assumptions are those embodied in Sewall Wright's analysis. Having laid these conditions out, Kavka then concludes, "Since these restrictive conditions are not often satisfied in nature, sociobiologists downplay the importance of group selection in explaining altruism" (Kavka 1986, 58). Pointing to the unlikelihood that altruistic traits could evolve to fixation in individual demes is also central in Maynard-Smith's 1964 downplaying of the empirical importance of group selection. In the Sober and Wilson analysis, however, although isolation for part of the life cycle is necessary, isolation is not permanent, and indeed cannot be permanent, since periodic mixing through migration and/or exogamy is essential to prevent the otherwise inexorable triumph of nonaltruists within each group.

number of animal behaviors previously "explained" on the grounds that they benefited (were adaptive for) a group could now be shown to be favored by the forces of individual level selection alone and were therefore not "altruistic" at all (Williams 1966). Because the conditions necessary for group selection were assumed unlikely to have obtained, it was argued that natural selection could not have favored truly altruistic predispositions except (the one widely admitted exception) in circumstances where the benefit to kin, weighted by numbers and genetic propinquity, outweighed the potential or actual harm to the organism undertaking the behavior. If behavioral predispositions benefited a group of non-kin, it was because they benefited these individuals *and* the actor (in other words, the behavior was mutualistic, not altruistic). The apparent coup de grâce in the argument against group selection was the more systematic demonstration that traits that provided benefit to a group, provided they were initially widespread, could be sustained (protected from invasion by other strategies) by individual level frequency dependent selection alone (Maynard-Smith and Price 1973).

To the degree that arguments dismissing the empirical importance of group level adaptation were applied to human behavior, evolutionary biologists took a position contrary to traditional midcentury structural-functional arguments in sociology and anthropology that sometimes explained the origin and persistence of group beneficial traits (behavioral propensities perhaps damaging to individuals but beneficial to the group) by appeal to the "evolutionary" argument that such behavior benefited the group. What seemed obvious to a generation of sociologists and anthropologists through the 1940s and 1950s, and to many evolutionary biologists (Wynne-Edwards [1962] 1967) and ethologists (Lorenz 1966), was rejected as wishful thinking that failed to recognize that in natural selection all that ultimately matters is the inclusive fitness of organisms and, in the limit, individual genes (Williams 1966; Dawkins 1976).[5]

The rejection of group level selection was hailed as a victory over decades of loose argument in which "evolutionary" analysis "explained" individual and group features with reference to adaptation at different levels. In a number of respects the controversy mirrored that surrounding the critique of the traditional sociological/anthropological tradition by economic or rational choice theorists. It is true that structural-functional analysis at the level of the group often said little about, or simply did not consider, how such adaptations, practiced by individuals, originated and how they persisted in the face of the weight of individual level selection

---

5. Sober and Wilson quote a colleague's advice from a "very distinguished evolutionary biologist" as late as the 1980s: "There are three ideas that you do not evoke in biology—Lamarckism, the phlogiston theory, and group selection" (1998, 40).

pressures. But, as we shall see in chapters 3 and 4, evolutionary analyses limiting selection to the level of the individual organism also often have little to say about the issue of origin, just as do rational choice models whose conclusions such evolutionary analyses reinforce.

The individual level selection program, in the hands of its most enthusiastic proponents, has attempted with great vigor to eliminate altruistic behavioral predispositions as a relevant empirical category by showing how behavior previously attributed to these predispositions could in fact be favored by individual level selection. The effort parallels and mirrors in its conclusions the efforts of rational choice theory. To the degree that a trait is favored by individual level selection, it cannot be altruistic. Nevertheless, both experimental and field evidence suggest that the category of biologically altruistic behavioral predispositions remains significant, in human as well as in nonhuman species (Frank 1988; Sober and Wilson 1998; deWaal 1982, 1996; Axelrod 1984, 91).

The research program based exclusively on the study of individual level selection has not adequately accounted for the ability of such traits to establish themselves in populations initially lacking them. At some point in our evolutionary past, such traits were absent, whereas now they appear to be widespread. We lack a coherent historical account of that transition, just as in the rational choice/game theory literature, we lack a coherent account of transition from one-shot to repeated PD games.

Species in which an altruistic predisposition such as restraint on intraspecific violence may be widespread will frequently be observed in situations in which the behaviors are sustained and reinforced by frequency dependent selection operating at the individual level alone. In such instances we will have difficulty identifying altruistic or irrational predispositions from field data alone because, if continued interaction may reasonably be presumed, observed behavior is theoretically consistent with their absence. That is why experimental studies of human subjects that control for such factors as concern with reputation or anticipation of subsequent encounters are so important in isolating essential predispositions. The results of such studies (see chap. 1) indicate that we are simply not justified in defining away the category of other-regarding behavior, of which altruistic action is an important component, or in predicting that we will eventually be able to do so.

The Modern Group Selection Argument

Instead, Sober and Wilson argue, the focus should be on providing a rigorous theoretical account that acknowledges that, by definition, the practice of altruistic behavior reduces the relative fitness of those organisms exhibiting it but that also explains how such behavior can survive and persist, increasing and/or maintaining its frequency in global populations. Note that while individual organisms can, by this definition, be altruistic, genes cannot, and the possibility that predispositions toward such behavior can spread continues to depend on the ability of such behaviors to affect gene frequencies in subsequent generations.

The central argument depends on organisms separating or being separated into groups for part of a life cycle, or perhaps for a period of several generations, and then reentering a global population before again reassorting into groups. Genetic recombination, outcrossing,[6] and infrequent mutation are sufficient to produce variability in individuals. In small groups, average group predispositions toward altruistic behavior will not be identical, even where initial assortment into groups is done randomly (Cavalli-Sforza, Menozzi, and Piazza 1994, 13). Within each group, altruists will lose out in the competition for resources and in particular in the competition to pass on their genes to the next generation. Consequently, their share of each group will fall (or at best stay even in the unlikely event altruists completely dominate a group) throughout the period of time that the group has a distinct existence. This point, that altruists, and the genes predisposing toward such behavior, will be evolutionarily disadvantaged from the standpoint of selection at the individual (within group) level, is the central core of the attack on group level structural-functional explanations, and Sober and Wilson do not take issue with it. *But, and here is the critical proposition, because the behavior of altruists differentially benefits groups in which their frequencies may be relatively higher, the proportion of altruists in the global population may rise in cases where the forces of group selection are stronger than the forces of individual selection.*

Examples of circumstances favorable to group level selection include the life cycle relationships between parasites and other disease vectors and their hosts. Suppose groups of a polymorphic virus with more and less virulent versions invade a number of host organisms, let us say rabbits. Among the rabbits, chance variation will result in varying mixtures of the two forms within each of them. Within each host, the more virulent versions enjoy a fitness advantage and increases in frequency. But organisms

---

6. *Genetic recombination* refers to reproductive process in diploid species. Pairs of chromosomes trade segments before the final random assignment by meiotic division of one or the other of each recombined pair to produce germ cells (sperm or eggs). The latter process is sometimes referred to as outcrossing: the random selection of a single set of chromosomes from the mother (one from each recombined pair) and a single set of chromosomes from the father (one from each recombined pair) to produce a zygote.

infected with high frequencies of the more virulent strain die quickly, before they can infect many other hosts. In contrast, hosts infected with less virulent mixtures live longer, more successfully spreading the disease. The longer living hosts therefore exercise a greater weight in determining the frequencies of the two versions in subsequent time periods, and each of their "votes" carries higher proportions of the less virulent strain. Paradoxically, the less virulent strain will be decreasing in frequency within every host, yet increasing over time within the global population.

In fact, such a scenario has been documented among rabbits in Australia in the early 1950s when confronted with the myxoma virus introduced by the government to control their exploding population. Initially mortality was very high, but gradually it declined, suggesting that the rabbits were acquiring resistance. Subsequent testing revealed two outcomes, one of which was surprising. First, the rabbits had indeed, on average, become more resistant to myxoma, which would be expected from individual level selection operating through differential mortality within the rabbit population. The surprising and unexpected conclusion applied to the viral population. The virus itself had become on average less virulent, as measured by extracting blood from rabbits in the wild and comparing samples so obtained with original viral samples stored in a laboratory. This outcome would not be expected if natural selection were operating only at the level of the individual virus, as it was indeed within each host (Lewontin 1970). The initial interpretation of this episode as reflecting the operation of group selection was controversial; most evolutionary biologists, including George Williams, now accept it (Williams and Nesse 1991, 8). The mechanism is essential, indeed, to the burgeoning field of Darwinian medicine.

Wright's analysis of group selection relied on the evolution to fixation of altruistic traits within some groups, combined with interdemic (intergroup) competition. The Sober and Wilson analysis does not require evolution to fixation in any group but emphasizes the necessity of periodic recombining of or migration between groups—called *trait groups* by Wilson—in order for group selection to occur. Altruists from the faster growing, more altruistic groups must periodically disperse throughout the global population (for discussion, see Wade 1978). Absent such a mechanism, the forces of individual selection will eventually triumph, and the selection against altruistic behavior within groups will drive such behavioral propensities to extinction, as those emphasizing the forces of individual level selection have repeatedly emphasized.

The possibility that altruists may be declining in frequency within every group and yet rising in frequency in the global population—an apparent contradiction—can be more easily understood with reference to the Simpson paradox.[7] A compelling example of this was an investigation at the University of California at Berkeley in the 1970s of alleged discrimination against women in admissions to graduate study. Aggregate data showed that admission rates for women were lower than for men. But when administrators looked at the data department by department they found no evidence of discrimination: in each department women were being admitted at approximately the same rate as men.

The explanation for the paradox was that the distribution of applicants by department was not the same for the two sexes. In particular, women were applying disproportionately to departments in which it was more difficult for an applicant of either sex to gain admission. This covariance meant that the averages of the departmental admission rates, roughly equivalent for men and women, differed from the global average admission rates, in which women did less well than men. What was true at the level of each individual group (department)—roughly equal admission rates—was not true for the entire population of applicants (Dawes 1988, 297).

Similarly, in considering the fate of altruists, what is true for each individual group (altruists are losing out) may not be true for the global population, *because groups in which altruists are differentially concentrated may grow more rapidly.* The argument, at first glance, seems akin to the story of the retailer who lost money on every sale but made it up on volume. Upon careful examination, however, the Simpson paradox is not based on such an inherently contradictory claim.

Consider another concrete example: the forces determining the male-female ratio in sexually reproducing organisms. Suppose some females in a population develop a tendency to produce more female than male offspring. The forces of natural selection operating on individual organisms within the group will tend to drive the ratio back toward approximate equality. Females who give birth to more females than males will lose out to females who give birth to balanced numbers of males and females because the latter type of female will have more grandchildren. Why?

In the second generation, males will be scarce, and the second type of female will have produced relatively more of them. These scarce males will disproportionately impregnate daughters of both types of females, giving the second type of female more grandchildren, and passing on genes predisposing to roughly equal numbers of male and female children. Traits predisposing to having a higher ratio of female offspring will decline in subsequent generations, until the sex ratio returns to balance. This is the fun-

---

7. The paradox exists when a population divided into groups exhibits a population average that differs from the average of the group averages. See Simpson 1951.

damental evolutionary explanation for the approximately equal sex ratio observed in our own species (Fisher 1930; Maynard-Smith 1993, 12). It is an archetypal case of frequency dependent selection and operates irrespective of whether a fraction of males never mate. It is an example of frequency dependent selection because the fitness of a particular gene depends on its own frequency and the frequency of other genes in the population.

On the other hand, consider again the introduction by mutation or genetic recombination of a tendency within some females to produce a higher proportion of female offspring. Assume now that the population is randomly sorted into a number of smaller groups, or demes. Groups that happen to possess a higher frequency of females with this trait will, for obvious reasons, grow faster, and thus, provided this covariance is sufficiently strong, it is *theoretically possible* for group selection to produce populations with an unbalanced (female dominated) sex ratio. The operation of group selection also requires that the groups periodically break up and disperse into a general population and then reassort into smaller groups. Otherwise the frequency dependent selection described previously will inexorably, within each isolated group, return the sex ratio to balance.

No mammalian species has a significantly unbalanced sex ratio. But many arthropod species do (Hamilton 1967; 1975, 136), providing strong empirical confirmation of the operation, in some contexts, of group level selection.[8] Cases of female biased sex ratios are typical of small invertebrates who occupy habitats for several generations before dispersing more widely—thus providing the mixing of group progeny that is essential to prevent the inexorable forces of frequency dependent selection within each group from eliminating the group-positive[9] trait (Sober and Wilson 1998, 41).

The Price Equations

More generally, consider a species whose population periodically divides itself into a large number n of groups. Some of the individuals in the population possess a certain trait, whose frequency in each group i is, at the beginning of the analysis, p_i. Each group i begins with size q_i. Organisms interact and receive payoffs that affect relative fitness and contribution to the next generation. After this process, the size of group i is $q_i{}'$, and the

---

8. Arthropods are members of the invertebrate phylum that includes insects, spiders, and crustaceans.

9. I use the term *group-positive* to refer to a trait that, when prevalent in a group, permits it to grow more rapidly. Similarly, the term *individual-negative* refers to a trait that decreases the relative fitness of the organism within the group.

gene frequency is p_i'. If the gene is group positive and individual negative (altruistic), then $q_i' > q_i$ and $p_i' < p_i$: all groups will grow in size (but possibly at different rates), and in all groups the frequency of the trait will drop. Depending on the covariance between group size and gene frequency, however, it is possible for the global gene frequency to rise even though it drops within each group.

Here is why. The global frequency of the gene P initially is equal to the average frequency in each group p plus a covariance term that reflects the degree to which larger groups also contain higher frequencies of the gene. More formally, if the average of the group gene frequencies

$$p = \left(\sum_{i=1}^{n} p_i\right)/n$$

and average group size

$$q = \left(\sum_{i=1}^{n} q_i\right)/n$$

and the covariance of p_i with q_i

$$\mathrm{cov}(p_i, q_i) = \frac{1}{n} \sum_{i=1}^{n} (p_i - p)(q_i - q),$$

then the initial global gene frequency

$$P = p + \mathrm{cov}(p_i, q_i)/q.$$

Global gene frequency equals the average group gene frequency p plus the covariance between group size and gene frequency divided by the average group size (q). If the covariance between group size and gene frequency is 0, the initial global gene frequency P will be identical to the average group gene frequency p.

Now interaction takes place within the groups, and the various organisms receive payoffs in the form of differential evolutionary fitness that is reflected in the number of their progeny. After one generation, the new global frequency

$$P' = p' + \mathrm{cov}(p_i', q_i')/q'.$$

If the measure s_i of a particular group's benefit, and thus growth factor

$$s_i = q_i'/q_i,$$

then the change in global gene frequency can be decomposed into two terms, the first reflecting the effect of within group selection and the second the effect of between group selection.

$$\Delta P = P' - P = \sum_{i=1}^{n} ((p_i' - p_i)(q_i'/\sum_{i}^{n} q_i')) + \text{cov}(s_i, p_i)/s.$$

The first term is a weighted average of the changes in group gene frequencies ($p_i' - p_i$), with the weights ($q_i'/\Sigma q_i'$) reflecting the ex post size of the groups. Under the assumptions that the trait in question is group positive and individual negative, this term must be negative, reflecting the effect of within group selection. The second term, on the other hand, reflecting the effect of between group selection, may be positive. In this term s is a weighted average of the group growth coefficients, the weights ($q_i/\Sigma q_i$) reflecting the initial sizes of the groups:

$$s = \sum_{i=1}^{n} s_i (q_i / \sum_{i=1}^{n} q_i),$$

and cov (s_i, p_i) is a weighted covariance, with the weights based on initial group sizes.[10]

This decomposition clearly separates the effect of within group selection (the first term) from that of between group selection (the second term). As the evolutionary biologist Steven Frank describes them, the Price equations are "an exact complete description of evolutionary change under all conditions" (Frank 1998, 13). If the gene is an altruistic one, the first term will be negative because in no group will the new gene frequency p_i' exceed the initial frequency p_i. But if there is a sufficiently large covariance between the group growth coefficients s_i and the initial gene frequencies p_i within the group, then the global frequency P of the gene may increase even if the frequency falls within every particular group. Hamilton's model of kin selection (1964) can be interpreted as a special case of this more general model.

Observed evolution toward lower virulence in pathogens, along with unbalanced sex ratios in certain arthropod species, provides strong prima facie evidence of the operation of group selection in nonhuman populations. Another design that would seem to have required selection above

---

10. In calculating a weighted covariance, the means for both variables are also calculated as weighted averages, using the original sizes of the groups (q_i) as weights. Thus the mean used for the group gene frequencies p_i is not the arithmetic average of the group means p but rather the weighted average, using group sizes q_i as weights. This yields the global population gene frequency P as the appropriate mean.

the level of the individual is the system of sexual reproduction itself that prevails among mammals and many other plants and animals.[11] John Maynard-Smith has emphasized that in order to outcompete partheno-genetic organisms (those that produced by mitotic asexual reproduction), sexually reproducing organisms would have had to have possessed a twofold competitive advantage, because 100 percent of gene endowment can be passed on through the former mechanism, as opposed to only 50 percent in diploid species (those that receive half their genetic complement from their mother and half from their father). Biologists have argued that a system of sexual reproduction provides the possibility of a greater reservoir of variability, but as Maynard-Smith observes, the advantages of greater plasticity (phenotypic variation) due to genetic recombination in sexually reproducing organisms appear to accrue at the group or species level, not at the individual level (1993, 202–4).

Why would maintaining a greater reservoir of variability be beneficial to a species? Bacteria and viruses have life cycles orders of magnitude shorter than those of humans. Consequently, their rate of evolution is much faster, as evident in the moving target represented by the AIDS virus, or the rapid development and epidemic spread of new variants of flu. A large reservoir of variability means that a species maintains a more diversified portfolio of possibilities should a new pathogen attack. This is not the same as saying that sexual reproduction increases the directional rate of evolution through provision of a larger pool of variability. In constantly reshuffling genes in response to new disease attacks, organisms are running as fast as they can just to stand still: thus the reference to the Red Queen (from Lewis Carroll's *Alice in Wonderland*) in the title of Matt Ridley's 1993 treatment of the topic.

But explanation of the evolutionary advantage enjoyed by sexually reproducing species, and its resistance to invasion by other strategies, is not the same as an account of the origin itself of this peculiar system of reproduction. Ridley and the biologists whose work he cites write sometimes as if they believe they have solved that challenge without appealing, implicitly or explicitly, to group selection in any form. But the literature Ridley summarizes offers an astute analysis of the *maintenance* of the system. It is a functional analysis, not necessarily wrong, but on the other hand not necessarily providing much insight into phylogeny. Maynard-Smith's concern remains: upon first appearance, a sexually reproducing variant of a species would have had to possess a twofold reproductive advantage over its parthenogenetically reproducing cousin in order to evolve without group selection, and the advantages of a greater reservoir

---

11. This interpretation remains controversial.

of genetic variability would have accrued at the group or even the species level, not at the individual level. Some group selection would appear to have been necessary to allow sexually reproducing organisms to gain a foothold, even though today such selection may play no role in the maintenance of the system.

The intense effort to avoid appeal to selection above the level of the individual organism (except for kin selection) misconstrues the message of a gene-centered view of evolution. We seek to identify those mechanisms that have permitted genes predisposing to certain behaviors or designs— those that have survived—to have persisted and spread. Genes increase in frequency because they control or regulate designs or strategies that foster survival and propagation within a selection environment determined by other genes in the same organism, other living organisms of the same and other species, and inanimate features of the natural environment.

When, in spite of repeated efforts to find plausible explanations for selection at the level of the individual organism or below, none is forthcoming, consideration of a group level mechanism is appropriate. Evident in Ridley 1993 are the passion with which some scholars and writers are determined to avoid multilevel selection models, and their faith that it will be possible to do so. In light of the evident widespread preference for individual level selection models, mirroring the appeal of rational choice approaches in the social sciences, I critically examine proposed individual level explanations for the origin of reciprocal relations among non-kin, such as that of Trivers, in chapters 3 and 4.

Ideology and Levels of Selection

With a few notable exceptions, in particular work by Gary Becker (1976, 284, 294), Jack Hirshleifer (1977, 25; 1982, 30–33), and Paul Samuelson (1993), models of group selection have received little attention and are little known within the economics profession.[12] Each of these authors favorably considers group selection as a plausible explanation for some of the behavioral predispositions at issue here. But aside from these important contributions, there is very little on group selection in more than a century of economic discourse.

In contrast, such models, and the theoretical possibility of multilevel selection, are well known among evolutionary biologists. Nevertheless,

---

12. A search of the JSTOR archive, scanning the texts of thirteen major economic journals from 1890 to 1994, picked up only ten hits for the term *group selection*. Four of these were to works of the previously mentioned three authors, and a fifth was to an *American Economic Review* piece by E. O. Wilson. The other hits involved use of the words *group selection* in different contexts.

throughout the late 1960s, 1970s, and 1980s, group selection explanations served repeatedly among biologists as objects of derision, as examples of intellectual error, to be disdained just as thoroughly, but for different reasons, as creationist fallacies.[13] The enthusiasm with which these approaches were rejected went beyond what can readily be accounted for on the basis of defects in their earlier formulations, and reflected an attitude of at the same time condescension and righteous triumphalism of those fighting the good fight to vanquish the forces of obscurantism and ignorance.

Part of the distaste for such models seems to have been driven by a preference for methodological individualism combined with a belief that group selection approaches necessarily entailed its rejection. This view is false. Among biologists who have seriously entertained selection above family or kin units, and those who have not, there is no longer much disagreement that what matters ultimately for natural selection are environmental effects on gene frequency operating over time on phenotypic expression. Thus debate about the empirical importance of multilevel selection is not necessarily debate about the relevance of a "gene's eye" view of the world.

That perspective actually poses a greater challenge to the rational choice emphasis on the individual organism as the only relevant unit of analysis than it does to the evolutionary model of group selection developed in this chapter. Again, that is because there is nothing to preclude genes adopting "devious" strategies that disadvantage their carriers but result in higher frequencies of such genes in the future. This is exactly what happened in the evolution toward less virulence of the myxoma virus.

An example of rhetorical overkill is found in the work of Richard Dawkins, a writer whose writings have in other contexts been unfairly criticized.

> As for group selection itself, my prejudice is that it has soaked up more theoretical ingenuity than its biological interest warrants. I am

---

13. Equally controversial have been explanations invoking genetic drift. Drift can affect traits with relatively little reproductive significance: for example, variations in coloration providing little differential camouflage. Such traits are *selectively neutral*. Drift can occur in populations, initially identical in gene frequency, that have become separated. If the resulting groups are small, chance differences in the survival of particular organisms may cause a divergence in coloration among descendants of the two parts of the original population. Random drift from this source may be augmented because in small samples heterozygous individuals will not contribute alleles on a strict 50:50 basis. Drift can also be used to account for the evolution to fixation of a trait that is selectively disadvantageous, as did Wright in his model of group selection. Biologists are urged (e.g., Mayr 1983, 326) to adopt drift explanations only after all possible selectionist explanations have been explored and rejected. See also Gigerenzer et al. 1989 (154–57).

informed by the editor of a leading mathematics journal that he is continually plagued by ingenious papers purporting to have squared the circle. Something about the fact that this has proved to be impossible is seen as an irresistible challenge by a certain type of intellectual dilettante. Perpetual motion machines have a similar fascination for some amateur inventors. *The case of group selection is hardly analogous: it has never been proved impossible and never could be.* Nevertheless, I hope I may be forgiven for wondering whether part of group selection's enduring romantic appeal stems from the authoritative hammering the theory has received ever since Wynne-Edwards ([1962] 1967) did us the valuable service of bringing it into the open. Anti-group selection has been embraced by the establishment as orthodox, and, as Maynard-Smith (1976) notes, "It is in the nature of science that once a position becomes orthodox it should be subjected to criticism . . ." This is, no doubt, healthy, but Maynard-Smith dryly goes on: "It does not follow that, because a position is orthodox, it is wrong." (Dawkins 1982, 115; my italics)

Dawkins has in this passage turned his considerable rhetorical skills, skills frequently deployed against creationists or, with more restraint, against punctuationists such as Stephen Jay Gould, against group selection. The rhetoric here is slippery, however, and casual readers are invited to draw precisely the analogy between efforts to demonstrate perpetual motion and defenses of the possibility of group level selection. If the case of group selection is "hardly analogous," why are the cases so carefully juxtaposed? And, one might respond to Maynard-Smith, simply because the claim that group selection is biologically unimportant is or was orthodox does not imply that it is or was correct.

Earlier in the book from which this passage is drawn Dawkins discusses "how we painfully struggled back, harassed by sniping from a Jesuitically sophisticated and dedicated neo-group selectionist rearguard, until we finally regained Darwin's ground" (Dawkins 1982, 6). Again, this is slippery rhetoric, since Darwin explicitly recognized the possibility of selection at the group level as part of the explanation for certain features of human behavior. Evolutionary theorists commonly, and with some justification, portray themselves as heroic warriors against the obscurantism reflected in various attempts to reinstate creationist alternatives to the theory of evolution. It has been easy for some to don the same rhetorical garb in countering an idea that, as Dawkins states, has never proved impossible and never could be, because it is not inconsistent with evolutionary theory and indeed the gene's eye view that Dawkins advances. Whether or not it is a plausible explanation for a human behavioral propensity depends, in part, on how it stacks up against alternate explanations of the phenomenon. These are scientific, not ideological, questions.

The same kind of remarks that Dawkins makes about papers on group selection might easily be applied to the enormous outpouring of work devoted to explaining the existence of nondefection behavior by strictly egoistic players in Prisoner's Dilemmas. That extraordinary effort within economics, political science, and psychology has illuminated much about the mechanisms sustaining mutuality and reciprocity when games are iterated. But it has come up dry with respect to why people would play cooperate in a one-shot PD or even why people would "coordinate" on a cooperative equilibrium in an indefinitely iterated game. This has not been for want of effort.

In contrast, evolutionary theory provides a coherent account of how natural selection may benefit genes predisposing to certain behaviors through selection at levels other than the individual organism—and thus an evolutionarily consistent rationale for the persistence of a widespread, although not universal, tendency within humans to practice restraint on first strike. Organisms so predisposed may play cooperate in a one-shot PD, particularly if they are armed with an ability to forecast "trustworthiness" from verbal and nonverbal cues (see chap. 5).[14] What is important in these debates is the logical consistency of arguments and their evidential foundation, not the amount of effort that may or not have been devoted to addressing the problem.

In his controversial 1975 book *Sociobiology* Edward O. (E. O.) Wilson identified the explanation of altruistic behavior as the central problem in evolutionary biology (Wilson 1975, 20).[15] It is also, arguably, the central

---

14. The ability to make such forecasts in the one-shot simultaneous play game does not change the strict dominance of the defect strategy. But it might reduce somewhat the expected disadvantage of irrationally playing cooperate. A two stage sequential move variant of the one-shot PD, sometimes called the game of trust (Güth and Kliemt 1994), is suggested by some to be a more realistic way of modeling the "original state" (Mantzavinos 2001, 133–34). In the first stage player 1 must either cooperate or defect. If player 1 defects, the game is over. If he cooperates, player 2 can either cooperate or defect. Player 1 does best if both cooperate but does worst if he cooperates and player 2 defects, a profile that, in turn, yields the highest payoff to player 2. Realizing that a rational player 2 will defect, player 1 does so initially, leaving them both with lower payoffs than could be obtained under the cooperate-cooperate profile. Like the fixed and known duration simultaneous play game, this variant allows forecasts of counterparty behavior to become relevant in deciding how best to play. If you can accurately predict that your counterparty will irrationally play cooperate in the second stage, it can be rational for you to play cooperate in the first. But if you are rational, and assume your counterparty is as well, you will never get to the second stage, any more than you will in the centipede game, to which this is closely related.

15. By 1983, on the other hand, Wilson was of the opinion that the problem had largely been solved, due to theoretical and empirical work by Hamilton, Trivers, and Maynard-

problem in modern social science. Although Wilson did not give much emphasis to group level selection (beyond kin selection) in his 1975 work, the consensus in evolutionary biology has changed in the last quarter century, and E. O. Wilson, Williams, and others are today more circumspect in their evaluation of its empirical importance. E. O. Wilson is quoted, relatively favorably, in the cover copy of Sober and D. S. Wilson 1998, and George Williams, whose 1966 book launched the attack on group selection, now recognizes evidence of unbalanced sex ratios as indicative of its operation (Williams 1992, 49).

Economists are largely unaware of these changes in the intellectual landscape—in some cases even unaware that group selection is a possibility within the framework of evolutionary theory. It is time to consider the import of the sophisticated restatement of the logic of multilevel selection as well as the biological evidence in support of it. Too often economists and rational choice theorists appealing to evolutionary theory have simply used it as a convenient means, when challenged, to provide a rationale for assuming strict behavioral egoism. The argument has been that assuming maximization of material self-interest as the key human motivation is justified by evolutionary theory and evidence: over eons, natural selection must have culled out all those who were not individual maximizers. Armen Alchian's 1950 *Journal of Political Economy* article, which derived profit maximization as a consequence of differential firm extinction, is often cited in support of this kind of reasoning.

As the preceding discussion makes clear, this is too simplistic a reading of the theory and evidence of evolution and their import for social science. Whereas Alchian's argument may have some plausibility with respect to business firms, its applicability to individuals is questionable if the mechanisms of natural selection that have operated in human evolution differ from those we posit affect companies. Dawkins is right that a gene-centered view, and the related concept of inclusive fitness, implies that the traditional opposition between selection at the level of the individual organism and at the group level poses alternatives poorly. But the question that always underlay that debate with respect to humans remains: what are our essential behavioral predispositions? Are we essentially social, as Aristotle insisted, or is war of all against all (outside possibly of family units) the default in the absence of government, as Hobbes suggested?

Smith (Lumsden and Wilson 1983, 49). Whereas the Hamilton work stands up well as an explanation of altruism toward kin, subject to the predictive imperfections he himself recognized, the Trivers model is much less than it seems as an explanation of origin of altruism toward non-kin. And Maynard-Smith's concept of an evolutionarily stable strategy, although useful in understanding stability, was not intended to explain origin. See chapter 3.

Although eschewing the Leviathan explanation of social order, economists have tended to embrace the Hobbesian assumptions about underlying human behavioral predispositions. Rational choice theorists have traditionally accounted for social order by identifying individual level forces that sustain it once established, believing incorrectly that in so doing they have thus adequately accounted for origin.

In a celebrated passage in *The Wealth of Nations* Adam Smith observed that we do not depend on the benevolence of the butcher, the brewer, or the baker for our sustenance ([1776] 1937, 14). This passage, and the metaphor of the invisible hand of which it was part, describes mechanisms that sustain and maintain complex social organization. For Smith, origin was less of a concern in his second book. Unlike many modern rational choice theorists, he was quite comfortable assuming a range of human motivation (behavioral predispositions) extending beyond strict egoism, a range he had detailed in his earlier work *The Theory of Moral Sentiments* (1759 [1976]).

In that work he described how mutuality could be fostered by "love, gratitude, from friendship, and esteem," in which case society "flourishes and is happy." In the immediately following passage, anticipating the conclusions of modern day game theorists and his emphasis in *The Wealth of Nations,* he also detailed how, in environments of indefinitely repeated interaction, mutuality could be sustained as the consequence of purely self-regarding motivations.

> Society may subsist, among different men, as among different merchants, from a sense of its utility, without any mutual love or affection; and though no man should owe any obligation, or be bound in gratitude to any others, it may still be upheld by a mercenary exchange of good offices according to an agreed valuation. (Smith 1759 [1976], 85–86)

The Wealth of Nations addressed how interest maintains order, not what gives rise to it. If we take seriously the likelihood that group selection was important sometime in our evolutionary history, we need to rethink foundational assumptions of economics, sociology, and the other social sciences. And, in ways that may not be immediately apparent, allowing for its likelihood can have a substantial impact on the tenor of conclusions arising from sociobiology/evolutionary psychology research. The implications of group selection cannot simply be pasted on to a set of positions developed under the understanding that its operation was impossible or unlikely.

I argue, in that spirit, that the behavioral assumptions incorporated in the standard economic model are at best incomplete and that the Aristotelian position—that we have essential predispositions facilitating sociability beyond kin based groups—has more empirical validity. I begin with the claim that humans possess a widespread tendency to practice restraint on first strike and that the success of this trait cannot be accounted for by selection at the level of the individual organism alone. Ockham's razor, however, counsels that we should prefer simpler explanations to more complicated ones, and certainly models of individual level selection are simpler than the group selection mechanisms detailed earlier. Chapters 3 and 4 therefore extend the discussion of whether there are satisfactory explanations of the origin of these predispositions consistent with the operation of selection at the level of the individual organism alone.

Differential Role for Group Selection in Altruism toward Kin and Non-kin

Before leaving Sober and Wilson and the intellectual battles they chronicle, it is worth reflecting on the different intellectual fates of arguments regarding altruism toward kin and non-kin. Whereas the Hamilton kin selection mechanism is broadly accepted, arguments about altruism toward non-kin remain controversial. Like Hamilton, Sober and Wilson interpret the kin selection mechanism as an instance of group selection. They then proceed as if the phylogenies of altruism toward kin and altruism toward non-kin are similar in all fundamental respects and as if what is necessary to persuade skeptics of the role of group selection in each is the same. Here I think they are mistaken.

Certain behaviors expressed toward non-kin are indubitably altruistic (and not rational for egoistic self-interested agents) upon first appearance at low frequency. When established at high frequency, however, they may well be mutualistic (in the interest of both the actor and the group) as Adam Smith intuited. Such behaviors, established at high frequencies in a population, will comprise evolutionarily stable strategies in the sense that they are resistant to invasion by any other strategy. They will then be sustained by frequency dependent selection, a mechanism that requires none of the apparatus associated with group selection.[16]

---

16. Sober and Wilson have, I believe, erred in trying to interpret the frequency dependent models of equilibrium maintenance developed by Maynard-Smith and Price as instances of group level selection, where the group is any pair of interacting individuals. In thinking about altruism toward non-kin, the role of group level selection is in accounting for a particular evolutionary trajectory, not, primarily, in maintenance of an equilibrium once established.

Once we admit the possibility of frequency dependent selection, a strategy's altruistic character can depend in part on the frequency with which that and other strategies are expressed among other members of the relevant population. A trait that is indubitably altruistic at low frequency will, by definition, be driven to extinction by within group individual level selection. The same strategy, present at high enough frequencies, however, may enter a basin of attraction for an end state equilibrium in which it persists at high frequency, an equilibrium that will return to the end state if shocked by a minor perturbation.[17] The phylogeny of the strategy can therefore entail a historical role for group selection in counteracting the negative within group selection encountered upon first appearance and allowing the strategy to attain a high enough frequency such that it can enter a basin of attraction in which group selection is no longer necessary for its maintenance.

We are therefore able to distinguish between behavioral predispositions that require group level selection to increase in frequency in the first place *and to be sustained at high frequencies* and those that require group selection to spread upon initial appearance, but at high enough penetration *no longer require it.* We thus differentiate between a role for group selection in determining the evolutionary trajectory that drives a trait from initial appearance to high frequency or in the limit fixation and its role in maintaining a high frequency equilibrium once established. In particular one can distinguish among traits initially altruistic between those whose ultimate within group fitness is frequency dependent and those whose within group fitness is not frequency dependent. Traits in the latter category (e.g., sacrifice for kin) are altruistic at the beginning, middle, and end of their trajectory. Traits in the former category (those involved in what is commonly called reciprocal altruism) can, at the end state of their evolutionary trajectory, no longer be characterized as altruistic (they have become mutualistic), because they no longer impose a within group fitness disadvantage.

Consider two archetypal examples: (*a*) a behavioral predisposition to sacrifice one's own fitness in order to improve the survival of offspring and (*b*) a package of traits involving refraining from first strike, retaliating if attacked, and punishing first strikes on third parties. Upon first appearance at low frequencies in a population, both impose a within group fitness disadvantage on the actor but benefit at least one conspecific. Both, upon

---

17. I do not mean to suggest that there is some final goal toward which evolutionary trajectories move. The terminology is intended more formally to draw a distinction between the study of evolutionary trajectories, which addresses origin, and maintenance of equilibrium, which addresses stability.

initial appearance, are thus altruistic from a genetic standpoint. Both will therefore require group selection (or the far more unlikely process of genetic drift) if they are to evolve to higher frequencies.

But the willingness to sacrifice for offspring retains its within group fitness disadvantage throughout its evolution to what we will assume is close to fixation. It was altruistic upon first appearance and remains unambiguously so today. Frequency dependent selection within the group plays no role in its maintenance: the fitness disadvantage is completely independent of whether the other parent or other parents possess the trait.

Now consider the package of traits that underlies behavior toward non-kin. These traits are subject to within group frequency dependent selection. Although the predispositions impose a fitness disadvantage and are thus altruistic upon first appearance at low frequencies, the disadvantage will decline as within group frequency rises. These traits initially require between group selection if they are to rise in frequency. But above a certain frequency, group selection may no longer be necessary to sustain them, because the traits, if exhibited within a group with a high enough frequency, no longer possess an individual level within group fitness disadvantage. They still benefit the group, but they no longer disadvantage the individual.

Whereas the kin selection mechanism—which involves group level selection at the level of the family unit—has been relatively uncontroversial among evolutionary biologists,[18] the same has not been true for group selection explanations of altruistic behavior toward non-kin. The initial Maynard-Smith and Price work (1973) investigating restraints on intraspecific harm and subsequent development of the concept of an evolutionarily stable strategy (ESS) explored the implications of frequency dependent selection in equilibrium maintenance. In their analysis group selection played no role. They analyzed the operation of the end state of a long evolutionary trajectory, one in whose early stages group level selection may well, however, have played an important role. Their great insight was to understand and explain how strategies that might benefit a group— such as refraining from first strike—could be sustained in the absence of any selection at the group level. Initially, a number of theorists—perhaps even Maynard-Smith and Price themselves—believed mistakenly that this conclusion provided the explanation for the persistence *and* the emergence of altruistic behavior as the consequence of individual selection forces

---

18. Its interpretation as an instance of group level selection has not been widely advertised (perhaps due to the group selection controversies) or seriously disputed (it has, after all, been proposed by the originator of the mechanism).

alone.[19] But this is an error—again, the inverse genetic fallacy—that arises from confusing the explanation of forces that sustain an equilibrium with those responsible for the trajectory that led to it.

In many ways analogous have been developments in iterated game theory. The "folk theorem" indicates, assuming indefinitely repeated interaction and sufficiently low discount rates, that a package of traits such as (*b*) can be sustained by rational choice provided it is once established, but the theorem leaves unanswered how that equilibrium from among a multiplicity is selected (Fudenberg and Tirole 1991, chap. 5).

Within the language of the Price equations (see the preceding discussion), we can posit that for traits subject to frequency dependent selection, there is, within each group, some critical level θ, $0 < \theta < 1$, such that if $p_i > \theta$, then $p_i' > p_i$. This is a statement about the replicator dynamic—and indicates that if the within group frequency of the altruistic trait is above θ, then the trait is no longer truly altruistic, since its frequency will grow or remain stable even within the group as a consequence of frequency dependent selection. Once global frequency $P > \theta$, group selection will no longer be necessary to prevent P from falling or to enable it to grow.[20]

Suppose one has a large population with pairs randomly interacting to play one-shot PDs. The fitness payoffs are as follows: cooperate-cooperate: 3,3; defect-defect: 1,1; cooperate-defect: 0,5; defect-cooperate: 5,0. Consider now the effect of frequency dependent selection on the fitness of cooperators and defectors. Let p = the frequency of cooperators.

Fitness of Defectors: $W_d = 1(1 - p) + 5(p)$,
Fitness of Cooperators: $W_c = 0(1 - p) + 3(p)$.

The fitness of both cooperators and defectors will rise with an increase in the frequency of cooperators. But since the fitness of defectors

---

19. Dawkins, for example, wrote the following comment: "there is a common misconception that cooperation within a group at a given level of organization must come about through selection between groups. . . . ESS theory provides a more parsimonious alternative" (1980, 360; cited in Sober and Wilson 1998, 79). According to Maynard-Smith (1993), it is Dawkins who suffers from the misconception: ESS does not provide such an alternative because it addresses the stability of an outcome, not its origin.

20. In his 1975 work, E. O. Wilson is acutely aware of the problem: "Granted a mechanism for sustaining reciprocal altruism, we are still left with the problem of how the behavior gets started." He goes on to talk about a critical frequency above which altruist genes will spread as a result of frequency dependent selection, but is unable to explain how that critical frequency is attained initially, saying that this remains "unknown" (Wilson 1975, 120). It is simply not possible within an individual selectionist framework to provide such an account.

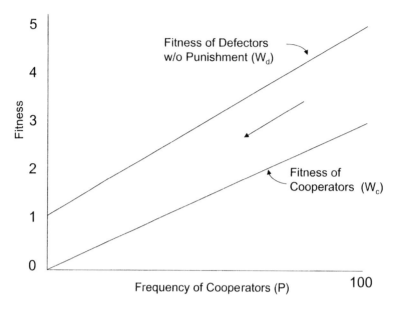

Fig. 1

is greater at any frequency, as can be seen in figure 1, cooperators can never gain a foothold, and defectors will dominate the population.

Now posit a slightly different strategy among the cooperators: call it cooperate*. In addition to cooperating in any pairing, they scan the horizon and (at some cost to themselves) punish any defectors they see as well as any who fail to punish. One of these punishments is a minor annoyance (and imposes a minor fitness cost), but the total punishment costs received and fitness costs imposed will vary with the frequency of cooperators* and defectors in the population. The following equations assume that the cost to the punishee is triple that to the punisher, but the asymmetry is not critical to the analysis. Let p = the frequency of cooperators* and W_{d*} the fitness of defectors, now vulnerable to punishment.

Fitness of Defectors: $W_{d*} = 1(1 - p) + 5(p) - 3(p)$,
Fitness of Cooperators*: $W_{c*} = 0(1 - p) + 3(p) - 1(1 - p)$.

At low frequencies of cooperators* (high frequencies of defectors) the punishment tendency imposes substantial additional fitness costs on a cooperator* and is only a minor annoyance to a defector. But above a crossover point, calculable by equating W_{d*} and W_{c*}, the fitness of coop-

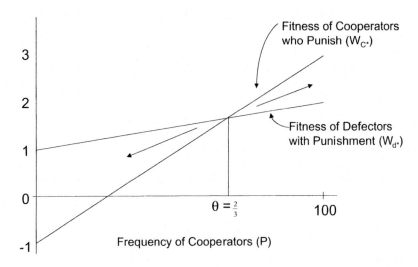

Fig. 2

erators* rises above that of defectors, and at any frequency above that θ (in this case, 2/3), cooperation will evolve to fixation and be resistant to any invasion of (a small number) of defectors (see fig. 2).

Below θ, individual selection alone will consign cooperators* to extinction. Suppose, however, that group selection enables cooperators* to grow initially above θ. If one then studies the mechanics of equilibrium maintenance in the end state, one will see no evidence of currently operating group level selection, even though the historical operation of such selection would be critical in providing an account of the phylogeny of the behavior. Explanation of origin may require different assumptions about levels of selection as compared with explanation of maintenance.

In more complex models, P may not necessarily increase to 1 (evolve to fixation); there may be some τ, $\theta < \tau < 1$, at which $p_i' = p_i$. There will then exist a polymorphous equilibrium in which some actors with selfish predispositions, a minority, survive.

It would be overly optimistic to expect this formulation to resolve the contentious and continuing disputes about the role of group selection. But it has the advantage of drawing attention to the distinctions between the modeling of evolutionary dynamics and the modeling of evolutionary stability. The most widely accepted examples of group selection—unbalanced sex ratios in arthropods, the evolution of virulence in pathogens, the willingness of parents to sacrifice for offspring (see Sober and Wilson 1998, chap. 2)—all involve cases in which group selection is necessary not only to account for the historical evolutionary trajectory but also to maintain the equilibrium end state. Within groups, $p_i' < p_i$ always holds. The special conditions that Sober and Wilson enumerate as hallmarks of group selection—separation into groups or demes for part of a life cycle, or for several life cycles, combined with pooling of offspring and their re-formation in new or modified groups, in the context of a positive covariance between p_i and group growth rates, are clearly identifiable in each of these cases. In the second instance, for example, pathogens inhabit a host, within which they will replicate until the host dies and the offspring are pooled into the general population and subsequently compete in infecting new hosts. In the last instance offspring are raised in small separated family groups before dispersing into the general population and ultimately re-forming in family groups.

When, in contrast, we examine predispositions controlling intra-specific violence, the existence of such conditions today is not so apparent. Beyond families, humans are no longer organized in tightly knit groups with little interaction among them for sustained periods (although these conditions may have prevailed earlier in our evolutionary history). And, if we begin by considering restraint on first strike to be an altruistic act, it quickly becomes clear that, within complex social organizations, such behavior is not necessarily altruistic in the sense that it imposes a fitness disadvantage on the actor. Indeed, if a willingness to punish third party defectors is widespread, it may be first strike that imposes the negative fitness consequence. First-degree murder is currently punishable by death in a number of U.S. jurisdictions.

Those skeptical of the evolutionary importance of group selection, such as Maynard-Smith or Williams in their earlier work, hold up with pride models elucidating how group beneficial but no longer altruistic (i.e., mutualistic) predispositions are maintained in the absence of any group level selection. Proponents of group selection insist correctly in asking how such (originally altruistic) predispositions could ever have survived upon first appearance at low frequencies in a population. The proposed resolution of these two positions is this. For a class of predispositions, in particular those involving altruistic behavior toward non-kin, frequencies rose initially through a process of group selection. The population is assumed to have divided into small groups (say, thirty to one hundred individuals) such that random assortment permitted some variation in the average phenotype of each group.[21] As the result of a positive covariance of group growth rates with the frequency of the altruistic predisposition within each group, P increased, even though with initial frequencies in

---

21. Group selection requires such variation, which will be larger the smaller the size of the group; assortative mating or an ability to recognize other altruists is not required for the model, although it will tend to strengthen the effect of group selection.

each group below θ, $p_i' < p_i$ within each group. As global frequencies rose, first one and then several groups began crossing the threshold, with $p_i > θ$, and consequently $p_i' > p_i$. In groups with frequencies of the gene(s) above this critical level, there ceased to be a within group fitness penalty for the altruistic strategy: the strategy ceased to be strictly altruistic from a biological standpoint, although it continued to benefit the group. When the global population P attained this critical level, group selection no longer was necessary to prevent P from declining or to allow it to rise: like protective tariffs, it could now decline or fall by the wayside, and the predispositions originally altruistic—think industries no longer infant—could survive on their own as the result of frequency dependent selection at the individual level.

Proponents of group selection, such as Sober and Wilson, have gone too far in suggesting that the neglect of group selection is always the result of what they call the "averaging fallacy": the tendency to look only at the overall effect of a behavioral tendency on genes predisposing to it without concern for the respective roles of group and individual level selection. The observation that a "cooperative" or group beneficial strategy can be sustained in equilibrium in the absence of group selection is simply not an instance of this "fallacy." Group selection may play little or no role in the maintenance of this equilibrium (even though it may have played an essential role in evolution to the equilibrium).

If we expand the strategy space, a population of cooperators* is not necessarily evolutionarily stable (see chap. 3). It could, for example, be invaded by those who refrained from third party punishment, which would make it vulnerable to invasion by defectors.[22] Nevertheless, the formulation proposed here has the advantage of preserving the intuition that there is something different about the mechanisms involved in kin selection—interpreted by Sober and Wilson (and Hamilton) as an instance of group selection—and those underlying reciprocity toward non-kin (both required group selection in their origination, whereas only the former exhibits it in its maintenance). It helps us appreciate the logic of the advice to Robert Trivers that he entitle his 1971 article "A Theory of Reciprocal Selfishness" (see chap. 3). And it helps us understand why Robert Frank is continually reduced to describing one and the same action as both selfish and altruistic (chap. 4)—the action may be altruistic in a biological sense in an asocial state, but gradually becomes consistent with selfishness (mutualistic) as global population frequencies of conspecifics following this strategy surpass θ.

---

22. Indeed, one would need to posit individuals who also punished those who didn't punish those who didn't punish, etc., in an infinite regress, to have a monomorphic population entirely proof from invasion.

CHAPTER 3

Reciprocal Altruism, Norms, and Evolutionary Game Theory

In complex social settings where people have established reputations they care about and where they may anticipate repeat engagements with their counterparties, most people most of the time play cooperate when finding themselves in PD-like situations. They do so without even thinking about whether this is the "smart" thing to do. In many instances such behavior turns out, ex post, to benefit the actor. Indeed, the very fact that such behavior later appears to have been "smart" or "intelligent" sometimes feeds skepticism that there is anything altruistic about the behavioral motivators that may underlie it.

Grounds for such skepticism weaken, however, when we move to the laboratory and control experimentally for the expected amount of repetition. The altruistic origins of reciprocal behavior now become more discernible. In a one-shot PD, cooperation is always altruistic and can never be rational. Things are a bit more complex in a fixed and known duration game, in which the altruism of cooperative or contingently cooperative strategies may be frequency dependent.[1] *Assuming counterparties are also rational,* however, such strategies, as in the single play game, can never be rational. Alchian and Williams, both sophisticated students of rational choice, knew that their game was of fixed duration but began their one-hundred-play interaction with rather different views of what was the "smart" thing to do. The explanatory challenge from an evolutionary standpoint remains one of accounting for how predispositions, such as that manifested by Williams on his first play, or by subjects who play cooperate in a one-shot PD, could have survived in an environment where they were not already widespread.

A coherent explanation is that at critical points in our long evolution-

---

1. Another illustration of the concept: we may characterize as courageous advocacy of an idea or a view that, although shared by few, we believe to be true. The attribution of courage to the act of advocacy is *inversely frequency dependent.* In the limit, we attribute no courage at all to the advocacy of a view we believe to be true when such a view is already widely shared. Kuran's analysis of the phenomenon of preference falsification also makes use of this mechanism.

ary history, group selection permitted such predispositions to gain a foothold in populations, evolving through replicator dynamics not necessarily to the point of fixation but to a point of predominance within a polymorphous equilibrium *that no longer depended on group selection for its maintenance.* Thus, while much reciprocal interaction in modern society can be "rationalized" as mutually beneficial, supported by the cognitive modules we associate with logic, mathematical reasoning, and foraging behavior, a different set of modules favored by group selection remains in the background, a legacy of our evolutionary trajectory and a backstop in the event environments of repeated interaction cannot, or can no longer, be reasonably assumed.

This chapter addresses the model of reciprocal altruism developed by Robert Trivers, the concept of social norms as commonly used in traditional sociology and anthropology, the definition of an evolutionarily stable strategy (ESS) as reflected in the work of John Maynard-Smith, and the experimental/theoretical contribution of Robert Axelrod. I conclude with a brief discussion of the similarities and differences between evolutionary and economic models. Chapter 4 takes up the influential work of Robert Frank, one of the most ambitious recent attempts to blend economic and evolutionary analysis.

The Trivers Model of Reciprocal Altruism

Among evolutionary biologists and psychologists the paradigmatic account of the origin and persistence of altruism toward non-kin is that provided by Robert Trivers's theory of reciprocal altruism (Trivers 1971; for a recent textbook treatment see Buss 1999, 253–55). Trivers's model explicitly eschews appeal to group level selection, but although it provides a plausible account of persistence (as does the standard game theoretic model assuming repeated and indefinite interaction that underlies it), it lacks an explanation consistent with individual level selection for the making of initial grants, a precondition for establishment of a relationship of generalized reciprocity among previously unacquainted individuals. In other words, it does not adequately address the problem of origin.

Trivers posits a drowning man who will die with .5 probability if no rescue is attempted. A rescuer can save the man with a .05 probability that both will die. Clearly, propensities to behave altruistically in such instances will be selected against by individual level selection, since those who do not rescue will have a slightly higher probability of survival and procreation. "Were this an isolated event, it is clear that the rescuer should not bother to save the drowning man. But if the drowning man reciprocates at some future time, and if the survival chances are then exactly reversed, it will have been to the benefit of each participant to have risked his life for the other" (Trivers 1971, 36). True enough, but here Trivers falls prey, as do others, to the inverse genetic fallacy. Marveling at the mechanisms that sustain mutuality in an environment of repeated interaction, he believes that in identifying these he has identified the mechanism responsible for origin.

At the hypothetical first such encounter between unrelated and previously unacquainted individuals, the situation of attempting to rescue is analogous to refraining from first strike, even though the former is an act of commission and the latter one of omission. In both cases the action benefits the recipient at some risk to the grantor. And in both instances we have behavior that would be disadvantaged by individual level selection. Similarly, the explanation for why the initial recipient does not "cheat" (fail to reciprocate when the tables are turned) is that "Selection will discriminate against the cheater if cheating has later adverse affects [*sic*] on his life which outweigh the benefit of not reciprocating." Again, a defensible position—but one that represents a description of mechanisms that sustain an equilibrium, not those that may have been necessary to establish it.

Explaining cooperation in one-shot Prisoner's Dilemmas always poses a problem for rational choice models or evolutionary analyses based on individual level selection. The play of cooperate is unambiguously altruistic and irrational, yet the cooperate-cooperate profile is the best of the three efficient outcomes for the players considered jointly. If one can transition to an environment in which repeated interaction, particularly indefinitely repeated interaction, can more reasonably be assumed, then interest, along with altruistic inclinations, can work together to sustain intercourse. But *assuming* one is in such an environment is not an adequate explanation of transition from one-time encounters.

In discussing the Trivers model, Ken Binmore comes to the same conclusion. "Reciprocal altruism is about how equilibria in the Game of Life are *sustained*" (1998a, 185; his italics). The Trivers analysis is therefore mistakenly interpreted as an account of origin. But what does Binmore have to tell us about origin? As we saw in chapter 1 (n. 9), rather little. He insists, and rightly so, that we define the term *rational* precisely and having done so convincingly rejects argument after argument designed to demonstrate that it is somehow "rational" to play cooperate in a one-shot PD game. He therefore reasons that "It is impossible for reciprocity to emerge in a one-shot game" and insists that we only concern ourselves in analyzing the "Game of Life" with games that are *indefinitely repeated:* "If our Game of Life really were the one-shot Prisoner's Dilemma, we should never have evolved as social animals" (1998a, 10, 263). But since this assumption of indefinite interaction is a large part of the description of what needs to be explained, this is no more a solution to the problem of origin than is the approach adopted by Trivers. In fact it is the same "solution," except that Binmore is more explicit about what he has and has not assumed.[2]

Once mutual relations and more complex social organization have been established, they can be sustained both by evolutionary mechanisms operating at the individual level and by the sort of cost-benefit calculations emphasized by economists: both point in the same direction. Yet absent that achievement, any expectation of reciprocity by the first rescuer must be a matter of blind faith, and so must it be by the second.

Trivers indicates that one of the preconditions of his analysis of the emergence of reciprocal altruism among humans is "life in small, mutually dependent, stable, social groups" (1971, 45); his assumption is that this was a feature of Pleistocene existence. I would add that it probably also was of hominoid and anthropoid ancestors. But if groups of these forerunners extended in membership beyond immediate kin, we must inquire how continuing interaction could have emerged without the benefit of a propensity to play cooperate in one-shot interactions with non-kin, altruistic behavior that, by definition, would have been selected against by individual level selection.

If one strips away the biological examples, Trivers's analysis is simply an evolutionary variant of the myriad attempts by economists and political scientists to explain the origin of cooperation without abandoning the egoistic assumptions common in rational choice theory. One is continually left with the puzzle of how one gets from the "asocial" to the "social" state. Trivers dismisses any possible role for group selection as "not consistent

2. Within the framework of canonical game theory, the outcome we can interpret as consistent with reciprocal inclinations (cooperate-cooperate) cannot emerge in a one-shot PD game. But that is different from concluding that it cannot do so in actuality. Binmore casts doubt on many of the experimental results that show such emergence by arguing that subjects initially do not fully understand the game and that when thrust into unfamiliar experimental situations they carry over behavior that is the result of previous interactions in nonexperimental situations. With repetition and learning, he argues, they will eventually come to play according to Nash predictions. As we have seen, his view is not consistent with the sequence of plays in the very first PD pairing, that between the hardly naive Armen Alchian and John Williams. Is Binmore prepared to argue that he can successfully "debias" subjects who persist in playing cooperate in a single shot PD by pairing them with a succession of anonymous partners, so that they eventually "learn" the "correct" play? His position on these issues is completely consistent with his view that "insofar as true altruism is meaningful in a biological context, it is discussed under the heading of kin selection" (1998a, 185). How does he know that truly altruistic acts, including passive altruism (failure to harm), let alone the admittedly rarer active assistance of Yad Vashem honorees, are restricted to that which can be accounted for under the heading of kin selection?

with the known workings of natural selection" (1971, 44). Although the statement is made with reference to the explanation of warning calls in birds, it is clearly intended to have more general applicability and as such is far too strong. Again, with respect to human reciprocal altruism, "no concept of group advantage is necessary to explain the function of human altruistic behavior" (48). Insofar as the statement refers to the maintenance of reciprocal relations once established, it can be true, although one might object that the behavior is now mutualistic, not altruistic. Explanation of maintenance is distinct from an account of origin, which requires unambiguously altruistic behavior.

Why does the first rescue take place? One might argue that the rescue was made in error, that the rescuer mistook the drowning man for a close relative. But there is no suggestion in the 1971 article that this is a feature of the Trivers model. Were it to be a feature, one could surely argue that organisms less prone to such errors would have advantages in individual level competition, particularly where the process involves species that can be dangerous to each other, such as early hominids. And we are still left with the question of why the individual rescued does not simply "take the money and run" but rather is now differentially predisposed to reciprocate, should the tables be turned.

The common hypothetical example used to illustrate the emergence of reciprocal altruism is of a bird afflicted with a disease-bearing tick. The bird can groom all parts of its body but its head. Clearly the species as a whole will be better off if propensities to groom conspecifics spread. Seeking to avoid appeal to group level selection, the Trivers model posits the spread of Tit-for-Tat playing birds, "after a few of them had gained a toehold." How could such behavior ever gain a toehold, given the disadvantages to the individual who first practiced it?

The theory downplays the obstacles necessary for reciprocity to emerge by emphasizing that the cost to the grantor must be less than the benefit to the grantee. This is an example of the same strategy we will observe in the next section with respect to social norms. The emergence of altruism is made contingent on initial behaviors whose fitness cost is so relatively small that we are tempted to ignore it. Once that step has been granted, of course, a chain of conclusions follows. And of course, once the reciprocal relation has been established, this condition will hold trivially, as it does for almost everything else the organism does. In reciprocity sustained by mutual interest, the cost of expending energy will in almost all instances be less than the benefit enjoyed. Once established, the reciprocal relation becomes just an indirect means of obtaining the benefit, in the same way the United States uses foreign trade as a "machine" for turning grain into oil.

But if the reciprocity is just an indirect means of obtaining a benefit more valued than the cost expended, why do we call it reciprocal *altruism?* Why not *reciprocal selfishness,* wording suggested to but rejected by Trivers when he originally wrote the article (see also Hardin 1977, 14, in which the author proposes the term *coupled egoism*)? Ambiguity arises because, once we are in the realm of iterated games, the altruistic character of contingently cooperative strategies depends on their frequency and that of other strategies in the general population.

We cannot simultaneously describe an action as both altruistic and selfish, yet we find ourselves repeatedly drawn into this bind. The problem is that we are used to thinking of the character of an action, altruistic or not, as determinable through consideration of the action or strategy in isolation. For some types of behavior, for example, sacrifice for kin, no difficulty arises from this habit of thought. But in considering relations among non-kin, it leads us into contradiction, because whether or not an action or strategy is altruistic may depend not only on the description of the strategy itself, but also on an environment composed of other organisms and the strategies they are playing.

The frequency dependent and thus ambiguously altruistic character of cooperative behavior among non-kin is reflected in E. O. Wilson's distinction between the "hard core" altruism of parental sacrifice for children and the soft core altruism of reciprocity (i.e., where there is expectation of reward) (Wilson 1978, chap. 7). A lack of precision remains, however, in Wilson's formulation: what exactly does the distinction between hard and soft mean in this case? The biological definition of altruism is quite precise, and a behavior in a particular context either does or does not satisfy it. Focusing on the frequency dependence of the altruistic character of a behavior can help resolve the ambiguity.

Two armed men with fingers on triggers, each carrying quantities of cash, confront each other. In one sense, restraint on first strike is cheap: not pulling the trigger requires less energy than pulling it, and the benefit to the counterparty is large. On the other hand, if a delayed squeeze means the counterparty gets off a shot first, the cost of the grant may be fatal. Restraint is altruistic in low frequency environments, mutualistic where frequencies of similar strategies are high. Tooby and Cosmides's tentative exploration of the problem (1996) does not adequately address the evolutionary hurdle faced by strategies of restraint, in part because it persists in understanding altruism to be limited to affirmative acts, not crediting the more empirically important form of failure to harm.[3] The most empirically

---

3. Their observation about how relatively easy it is for evolution to produce means of disrupting another organism's existence, as opposed to actively benefiting it, only adds to the strength of this argument (Tooby and Cosmides 1996, 124–25).

important behavior in the category of cooperative plays in situations appropriately modeled as PDs may simply be not attacking.

The Trivers theory is therefore less than it may initially appear to be. The idea that "I'll scratch your back if you'll scratch mine" seems at one level to be an account not only of why such cooperation is individually rational, and would be favored by individual level selection once widely established in a population, but also why it would be favored by the forces of individual level selection upon initial appearance in small numbers. But if matters were so simple there would be no issue or dilemma faced by players in a two stage Prisoner's Dilemma in which the choice at stage 1 is for player 1 to groom or not groom player 2 and at stage 2 for player 2 to groom or not groom player 1.[4] The players would have no difficulty in reaching the Pareto efficient outcome best for them jointly.

The problem, as economists repeatedly emphasize, is that of free riding. It pays player 2 to allow himself the luxury of being scratched (or groomed) without then expending the energy of reciprocating. Knowing this, it is not rational for player 1 to groom, and it is unlikely either will get groomed unless player 1 is willing to make a grant of first move(r) altruism and player 2 irrationally reciprocates. Both parties are of course worse off if there is no mutuality, but that is the essence of a Prisoner's Dilemma in the first place.

It is hard to see how Trivers has overcome this difficulty. Emphasizing that the cost of granting the favor to the grantor must be less than the benefit to the grantee seems to lower the bar for such behavior to originate. But a cost is a cost, and at the individual level, selection should favor organisms that do not waste energy, even in activities that seem to cost little. Trivers seems to be saying that we are more likely to see reciprocal behavior develop when each organism faces the following choice: if I pay $1 you will get $10, as opposed to a structure where each animal says, if I pay $10, you will get $1. But this is really a statement about a condition that obtains once the reciprocity equilibrium has been established. This condition must apply to any established relation of reciprocity sustained by individual level rationality or selection. It certainly applies in market exchange, where goods and services move from lower valued to higher valued locations. No organism will thrive by spending $10 in energy to provide itself with $1 of benefits, whether it does so directly for itself or indi-

---

4. This sequential move version of the PD is sometimes refered to as the game of trust. Formally, if the first player chooses not to groom, the game ends. If she grooms, then the game moves to the second stage, where the second player has a choice of grooming or not grooming. Grooming is an instance of first move(r) altruism because it provides the second player with the option of earning the highest return, at the cost of exposing the first player to the risk of the worst return.

rectly through some form of reciprocal relationship such as trade or non-simultaneous exchange.

Perhaps we should understand Trivers's argument as an attempt to explain where, among different possible loci, we are most likely to see reciprocal relations originate. Here there may be some traction. *If* people or organisms are going to sacrifice in favor of others, it is plausible that they are more likely, on average, to do so under circumstances where the costs to them are relatively low and the benefits to the target relatively high. Thus we would predict that "heroes" would be more likely to risk their own lives to save that of a drowning person than to obtain an additional pencil for someone in need of a writing instrument to complete a crossword puzzle. Indeed, we could imagine the recipient of such "largesse" in the latter case berating the donor for his or her foolhardiness.

But the fundamental problem on the table is not how to account for the differential geographical or situational incidence of such acts. *It is to explain why any such behavior occurs.* Nash equilibrium analysis predicts that no one should cooperate in a one-shot or fixed and known duration PD, that voluntary contributions to public goods should be zero. The irreducible fact is that in the initial rescue attempt, the rescuer expends $1 to get nothing. It does no good to point out that perhaps he will get $10 down the road. Since this individual is illustrating *by his very action* the possibility that a drowning person might expect with some positive probability to be rescued by someone for whom the now water challenged individual has *provided no prior favors,* and since logic and the analysis of individual level selection lead to the conclusion that it is in the interest of the rescued party to accept the rescue and then not to reciprocate, it is hard to see how the rational rescuer can make any reasonable conclusion other than that the cost and risk of the rescue are a pure grant, unlikely to change in any way the subjective probability that he will be rescued were he similarly distressed in the future. And, to switch back to an evolutionary perspective, it is hard to see how such grant making behavior could be favored by the forces of individual level selection upon initial appearance at low frequencies.

We are back to the "Yossarian" problem. Yossarian doesn't want to fly bombing missions because of his reasonable concern that he might be killed. When asked what would be the consequence if everyone felt that way, his reply is that he'd be a damn fool to feel any differently.[5]

Zoologists have objected to Trivers's theory on the grounds that reciprocal altruism is rare in the animal kingdom: vampire bats, which share

---

5. The reference is to the protagonist in Joseph Heller's novel *Catch 22* ([1961] 1995).

regurgitated blood among each other, are a prime but exceptional example. This objection arises in part because of the implicit restriction of "reciprocal altruism" to behaviors involving affirmative assistance. If we take into account the more widespread phenomenon of failure to harm, the existence in many animal species of restraints on intraspecific violence indicates that the phenomenon is more important than has been recognized, even in nonhuman species.

What makes human behavior distinctive in this regard is the coupling of failure to harm altruism with an important, albeit weaker, predisposition to make affirmative grants to non-kin, rare elsewhere in the animal kingdom. The development of both types of altruism required the evolutionary favoring of a whole range of specialized brain subsystems that permit the systematic rejection of the counsel of logic and mathematical reasoning. Some of these subsystems, particularly those restraining intraspecific violence, most probably predate the evolution of an expanded cerebral cortex that now allows us to be decent logicians and mathematicians.[6]

Grants of first move(r) altruism, retaliation when costs have already been sunk, punishing third party defectors: none of these can easily be shown to have a rational foundation when practiced in asocial environments (in economic terms, those lacking the expectation of indefinitely repeated interaction; in evolutionary terms, those lacking high frequencies of similarly predisposed organisms). Yet, when attacked by someone they have never seen before and are unlikely to see again, many people reject the counsel of reason and respond in kind, even though the ex ante willingness to strike back has clearly failed to deter the initial attack and the retaliation may invite another round of aggression. Rapists, muggers, and military strategists may try to subdue their counterparty with an overwhelming show of force. In doing so, they appeal to their victims' *rationality* to get them to submit. The response of the individual under attack reflects the outcome of a war between the counsel of different cognitive modules.

---

6. Both paleontological evidence charting the growth of cranial capacity and the fact that our closest animal relatives have smaller skulls and lack these latter capabilities suggest that they are of relatively recent evolutionary origin (no chimpanzee has come close to solving Fermat's Last Theorem). At the same time, both of our chimpanzee relatives—*Pan troglodytes* and *Pan paniscus*—live socially in troops of between thirty and one hundred, making it very likely that our common ancestor six million years ago did so as well. Thus the inference that the predispositions enabling our social existence predate the refinement of cognitive abilities we generally see as underlying rational choice by humans. See chapter 5 for further discussion.

The behaviors listed at the start of the last paragraph generally impose a fitness cost on the individual conducting them, although they may benefit others. They are either unambiguously altruistic in a biological sense or are likely to be altruistic in environments where manifested at low frequency. Consequently, evolutionary mechanisms cannot allow them to spread if the possibility of multilevel selection is excluded. Trivers's apparent individual level selection solution to one of the most vexing problems in evolutionary biology—and social science—is a mirage.

Reciprocal Altruism and International Law

The solution proposed here is that natural selection operating at the group as well as the individual level has endowed most of us with predispositions to act, in certain domains, in biologically altruistic ways, predispositions mirrored in certain universal features of human culture. Whereas most social scientists accept at least parts of this argument insofar as it applies to relations among kin, skepticism reigns in regard to its applicability to relations among non-kin. The difference is partly attributable, I have suggested, to the frequency dependence of the altruistic character of cooperative behavior in the latter case, a dependence that is poorly understood.

Consider another "Prisoner's Dilemma." What should an army do with captured soldiers? Prisoners of war are expensive to feed and guard, and if allowed to escape represent additions to an enemy force that may contribute in the future to harming one's own soldiers. Failure to execute represents a grant of first move(r) altruism with potential fatal consequences for the grantor. The commander faced with this life and death choice is in a situation remarkably analogous to Trivers's man on the riverbank. At some small cost to himself and his troops (risk that the captured soldiers will escape and wreak violence on the releaser's forces, costs of feeding and guarding captives) he may confer a large benefit (life) on the POWs. One can argue that it is efficient for all armies not to execute, but the first commander to adopt such a policy has no reason, from a strictly self-interest standpoint, for supposing that others will reciprocate.

The conventional wisdom has been that a more liberal attitude toward POWs reflects the gradual progress of civilization and culture. But given the logic that apparently favors execution, we need to ask how conventions regarding the "humane" treatment of POWs and the "humane" conduct of war ever became established. Sir Henry Maine's classic 1888 treatment of the subject is still worth reading. He observes that it cannot be because a world government legislated these rules (thus the Hobbesian solution cannot apply). Legislatures, he points out, are relatively modern and in any event played little role in the evolution of international law.

> In truth, far the most influential cause of the extension of particular laws and of particular systems of law over new areas was the approval of them by literate classes, by clergymen and lawyers, and the acquiescence of the rest of the community in the opinions of these classes. When then we are asked by what legislative authority International Law came to be adopted so as to make it binding on particular communities, we should rejoin that the same question must first be put respecting the extension of Roman Law and of every other system of law which, before the era of legislatures, gave proof of possessing the same power of propagation. (Maine 1888, 19)

Rules mandating the humane treatment of captured soldiers appear to have achieved a similar resonance among opinion leaders in different states. The question now becomes whether this was just coincidental. Aware of these remarkable commonalities, jurists often mystified them with reference to *natural* law, by which they usually meant that the shared mentalities that led to the widespread resonance of "appropriate" rules were of divine origin.

If our modern sensibilities lead us to reject divine inspiration as the explanation for this resonance, the phenomenon perceptive observers such as Maine were addressing is nevertheless one that needs explanation. My argument is that differential receptivity to norms that are more or less universal in human cultures is influenced by hardwired predispositions in much the same way as receptivity to learning language is hardwired (see chap. 5). The basic predispositions that give rise to holding rather than executing prisoners are those that give rise to cooperative behavior in one-shot PDs.

The anthropologist Robin Fox argues similarly, in discussing ritualized restraints on violence.

> These rules and regulations . . . are the labels that speaking men use for the kinds of behaviors that nonspeaking men would have indulged in anyway. . . . even nonlanguage men did not fight without rules. . . . These may not have been explicit, but they existed; and when he came to speak and to symbolize he gave them expression. In other words, the rules of fighting are as natural as the fighting itself. (Fox 1989, 145)

In most instances war is not unrestrained, goalless violence. And when it does involve the mobilization of aggressive impulses in support of attacks on out-groups, one can argue that the predispositions appealed to are closely related to those involved in the maintenance of social order through the punishment of those violating internal rules.[7]

If these arguments are correct, we should not necessarily see a linear trend over time favoring more humane treatment. And in fact, we lack clear evidence that the Geneva conventions, for example, have been associated with a reduction in the frequency with which prisoners of war are killed or mistreated. POWs were slaughtered prior to its passage and continue to be slaughtered, even by signatories, subsequent to it (Schaller, Scharf, and Schulzinger 1998, 77). These events are today generally perceived as atrocities, except perhaps by those who perform them, but the record preconvention was not one of unmitigated barbarity, any more than postconvention has been marked by its absence. In many respects, the twentieth century has been not only bloodier than, but at least as marked by atrocities as, the nineteenth, particularly if we begin the nineteenth century in 1815 and end it in 1914. Maine quotes the Swiss jurist Vattel, writing well before the first Geneva convention, that "what struck him most in the wars of his day was their extreme gentleness" (1888, 24).

In suggesting that conventions regarding the treatment of prisoners represent the codification of a "natural law" in the sense that they are consistent with and reinforce hardwired predispositions, one must proceed with caution. Many practices such as toleration of slavery have been rationalized and defended over the years using similar language. The argument here is simply that a human willingness to ascribe to and act in accordance with certain more or less universal "norms"—codifying norms in the language of chapter 1—has a biological determinant, in the sense that we are differentially prepared to accept, live by, or promulgate such behavioral rules. This argument is anticipated by Aristotle, who, as Dennis Wrong observes, "carefully distinguished between 'natural' social relations and those created by 'law and custom,' devoting considerable effort, notably in his discussion of slavery, to deciding which was which" (Wrong 1994, 2).

The outcome of that "considerable effort," nevertheless, was that Aristotle ended up endorsing slavery as natural, indicating how delicately this kind of argument must be used. Toleration of slavery is today widely viewed as culturally variable, and there is overwhelming evidence to suggest that its practice is diminished in comparison to its prevalence as recently as two centuries ago. Involuntary servitude does, it is true, persist in parts of Asia and Africa. But it is not legally recognized, and few would claim that the overall incidence of slavery is near what it was in the heyday of the Atlantic slave trade and legally sanctioned systems in North and South America.

---

7. Genocide can be thought of as the metastasis of these tendencies.

Social Norms

Historical evidence of gallantry in war and the informal development of conventions governing treatment of prisoners, even amid the chaos and organized violence of armed conflict, offer observational evidence in favor of the existence of a hardwired PD solution module. War involves extremes of both cooperation and conflict: its conduct would not be possible in the absence of such a module, nor would be the ability to wage peace.

Influential traditions in sociology, anthropology, and certain branches of psychology and political theory, however, maintain that human behavioral predispositions toward cooperation are the exclusive product of culture: we are born into the world as "savages," and it takes the combined efforts of such institutions as family, school, and religion to impart a veneer of civilization to our innate asocial and violent impulses. But how, if we are essentially as so described, did complex organization, which at least the latter two of these institutions presuppose, ever come into existence?

Altruistic behaviors, whether they be forgoing the advantage of first strike or more affirmative action, such as risking one's life to defend a group or save a drowning man, are definitionally at risk from the forces of individual selection and are not rational, as that term has been defined here. Recognizing this, traditional sociologists and anthropologists developed the concept of social norms to explain how "society" rewarded and punished certain behaviors in general depending on whether they were group positive or group negative. James Coleman, for example, equates culture with social norms that "mandate action that is not in one's own interest, or proscribe behavior that is" (DiMaggio 1995, 29; Coleman 1990). Thus, the explanation for why people might act in a way that did not necessarily benefit them individually is that they are encouraged to do so or constrained to do so by social norms.

Norms do not have an ethereal existence, independent of the individuals whose behavior they regulate. This is true both of universal norms and those more culturally variable. But whereas culturally variable norms support behavior that many might privately want changed (see Kuran 1995), universal or codifying norms are not affected by this tension. They can be seen as articulated descriptions of behavioral predispositions widely manifested. But how did such predispositions survive the forces of natural selection and become widespread?

Whether or not adherence to norms imposes a fitness disadvantage from selection forces at the individual level depends on the frequency of such adherence in the population. If frequency is low, then adherence to a promulgated norm is altruistic. Since adherence to norms, upon initial articulation or promulgation, is likely disadvantaged by the same evolutionary forces that militate against more life-threatening altruistic behavior in the first place, sociologists and anthropologists who appeal to them are no closer to an explanation of how such behavior originated than is Trivers.

A number of authors, including Sober and Wilson (1998, 143–45), distinguish between primary altruistic behaviors, such as risking one's life to defuse a threat that jeopardizes an entire group, and secondary behaviors that may reinforce or support such efforts. Primary behaviors, understood to be those that often involve a significant decrease in the probability of an individual's survival or procreation, can be favored in the aggregate if the between group selection in favor of them more than counterbalances the within group selection against them (see chap. 2). The latter, however, may represent a very substantial barrier that group selection must overcome if altruism is to emerge and persist. At low frequency, adhering to secondary norms, however, would also involve a negative impact on relative fitness at the individual level, albeit one that is generally smaller. In economic language, adherence to social norms, regardless of whether they are primary or secondary, is likely to involve some reduction in the relative welfare of the individual undertaking it.

A decision to shun a transgressor against a third party, for example, may preclude what might otherwise have been profitable opportunities for exchange. Supporting the widow and children of a dead "hero" in accord with a group norm will involve some individual sacrifice of resources. From an evolutionary perspective emphasizing individual level selection alone, social norms can never be the complete explanation for the origin and persistence of primary behaviors for two reasons: first, because although they may reduce somewhat they are unlikely in practice to eliminate entirely the disadvantage associated with such behaviors; and second, because the individual evolutionary incentives that militate against behaving in accord with norms would have obstructed their spread or evolution to higher frequency. One should not minimize the degree to which adherence to secondary as well as primary norms will be evolutionarily disadvantaged, if such adherence is practiced in an environment in which a predisposition to do so is low. Particularly at low frequency, adherence to norms is altruistic behavior writ small. As economists have noted, behaviors that promote public goods are themselves public goods.

Positing norms that punish those who don't punish (or punish those who don't reward) is not a solution to the problem of origin, since adherence to secondary norms must also overcome the initial incentives against adhering to them. Proceeding down this route invites an infinite regress (norms to punish those who do not punish those who do not punish . . .). Secondary or even tertiary norms can be descriptively relevant for understanding how end state equilibria are sustained by frequency dependent selection, but positing them does not effectively deal with the problem of origination within a framework that limits selection to the level of the individual organism alone (Boyd and Richerson 1985, 229–30).

In general, the pursuit of such explanations is reflective of a particular strategy to resolve the conflict between, on the one hand, defining altruistic action as behavior that benefits another conspecific at the expense of the actor and, on the other hand, insisting that the origin and persistence of propensities favoring such behavior be favored only by individual level selection. The strategy involves making more costly altruistic behaviors depend on behaviors with smaller fitness costs until one has reached a behavior whose fitness cost seems so small that a bit of intellectual sleight of hand makes it apparently disappear. This is precisely the mechanism Binmore attempts to use in justifying the transition from one-shot games to games involving indefinite repetition (1994, 120, 124–25). But no matter how small the fitness cost, if the behavior is indeed altruistic, it cannot, by definition, be favored by individual level selection.

The most significant benefit that an organism can give another may simply be not to attack it. This confers large fitness benefits on the receiver but may expose the acting organism to substantial risk. Unless one can get beyond that, it is not worth talking about the logic of sacrificing for the group, let alone norms that might support such behavior. The analysis of secondary norms presupposes cohesive and persistent groups whose existence is logically prior as an object of explanation. The elucidation of mechanisms that sustain complex social organization once established is not the same as the provision of a coherent account of origin.

Kuran's work (1995) discusses how maladaptive (inefficient) norms may solidify and persist and how individuals who suffer from them may find it rational to participate in the perpetuation of their own oppression. His definition of rationality, broader than that used in defining the standard economic model, distinguishes between the utility individuals get from speaking their minds and the disutility they get from articulating an unpopular position. Critical to his analysis is the idea that expected public opinion may differ from average (true) private opinion, that the former will typically be estimated from past observations, and thus that past history can produce a lock-in on norms that a majority of the affected populace might actually like changed.

Kuran's analysis is a significant contribution to our understanding of the mechanisms whereby cultural and institutional variation originates and persists. My analysis in this book is principally directed at a subset of norms, those common to all known human societies. In his language they can be understood as those in which there is in fact no divergence between private and public opinion. My explanation both for this lack of divergence and for the universality of these norms is that we are differentially prepared—hardwired—to find these norms reasonable or appealing. Unlike the particular pattern of cultural and institutional variation, which can be seen in part as the result of accidents within the time span of recorded history, the existence of universal norms appeals to historical forces at a much earlier phase: those that determined the evolutionary trajectory giving rise to the human genotype.

The *origin* of the fundamental behavior that codifying social norms are designed to account for, behavior that presupposes a willingness of individuals to abide by them even when so doing does not advance their material and/or reproductive interest, cannot be fully accounted for either within the standard economic model as the outcome of the interactions of purely egoistic agents or, within an evolutionary framework, as the result of selection at the level of the individual organism alone. Nevertheless, the phenomena that the concept of norms attempts to illuminate/explain are, indeed, real and important.

A number of scholars, some of whose work is described in this and the next chapter, have attempted to bridge the divide between sociology and economics by considering the implications of evolutionary processes. But, following the conventional wisdom in biology, and almost to an individual, these thinkers have taken it as a given that natural selection can take place only at the level of the individual organism. The assumption clearly makes it impossible for any form of hardwired altruistic predispositions to evolve from initial appearance at low frequency.

The analysis developed in this book offers an opportunity to preserve the principle of methodological individualism and at the same time account for some of the phenomena that sociologists, anthropologists, and experimentalists have documented and explored. *But it does so at the cost of rejecting strictly self-regarding egoistic preferences.* It is a sociobiological model, but one capable of accounting for a range of behavior anomalous within the rational choice tradition. It is also a methodologically individualist model. *Adhering to methodological individualism, in other words, does not require assuming that individuals are strictly individualistic.*

Accounting for Universal Human Norms

If norms are not the explanation for human altruism and the complex social organization it permits, what do they represent? *To the degree they are more or less universal, they are simply words we give to the codification and reinforcement of essential human tendencies.* Why would one need words for them, beyond describing them, if the tendencies are essential?

For three reasons. First, the predispositions may not have evolved to fixation (deviant tendencies may subsist at stable levels). Second, these programmed tendencies may need to be evoked by environmental cues and run the risk of being extinguished or weakened in their absence—or in the presence of different ones. Finally, even though powerful predispositions may override the counsel of reason and logic on a systematic and predictable basis, individual humans are free to choose and to overrule in the opposite direction. Thus sexual relations among children reared together and murder within established groups both indubitably occur, although the rates are minuscule in comparison with the opportunities presented for such behavior. That these actions sometimes do occur is neither evidence against the existence of powerful innate predispositions militating against them nor evidence confirming the role of cultural norms as the exclusive explanation for why such "deviance" is not more widespread.

On the other hand, as Edgerton reminds us vividly in *Sick Societies* (1992), some norms do vary cross-culturally (as does the content, but not the deep structural grammar, of language). That variation has been widely documented by anthropologists and catalogued in the Human Relations Area Files (see Sober and Wilson 1998, chap. 5). Norms differ, and these differences have consequences because norms may be both maladaptive and persisting. This variation occurs within limits, nevertheless, reflecting evolutionary pressures that have placed a premium on addressing recurring environmental challenges over millions of years. As obvious examples of these limits, no society has a norm sanctioning matricide by young children or mandating that men drive on the right, women on the left (Field 1984).

From an evolutionary perspective, the central task is explaining what is universal about human norms.[8] These include, inter alia, articulated standards of obligations toward kin; restraints on harming other members of one's group; and in general, some version of the categorical imperative regulating reciprocal relations among non-kin.[9] We can take this subset of norms as codifying what is *essentially* human. Since these norms are universal, they play *no role* in accounting for cultural variation.

---

8. Similarly, the evolutionary challenge in linguistics is to explain what is universal about human language acquisition, not the particulars of different languages.

9. For example, a version of the golden rule is common to the normative belief systems of virtually all cultures. A few instances: Kant's categorical imperative is presaged in Christian ethics ("In everything, do to others what you would have them do to you"—Matt. 7:12) and, in reverse chronological order, in writings by the Jewish spiritual leader Hillel, the Greek philosophers Aristotle and Plato, and the Chinese philosopher Confucius (Poundstone 1992, 123). On support for ethical universals among anthropologists, see Edgerton 1992 (35). Clyde Kluckholm, a cultural relativist for much of his career, endorsed the idea of cultural universals in 1955 (Kluckholm 1955).

The explanation of norms that do vary, and consequently may have independent consequences, is an important but subsidiary issue, the principal subject matters of cultural anthropology and the comparative and historical study of political, legal, and economic systems. It is possible that such variation has been influenced by specialized algorithms: hardwired rules that do not determine behavior or culture but canalize learning in certain directions depending on the particular environmental conditions encountered. Because I endorse the possibility of persisting maladaptive (inefficient) institutions, however, I think this mechanism, which seeks a microlevel cognitive foundation for the conclusions of structural functionalism, is weaker than its proponents suggest (see Lumsden and Wilson 1981). Instead, we need explicitly to acknowledge accidents of history in determining cultural variation.

Within evolutionarily determined limits, an idiosyncratic component of culture remains, even after taking account of what can be attributed to hardwired behavioral predispositions or differential learning receptivities interacting with regional environments. The causes of such idiosyncrasies are historical and case specific (path dependent), and consequences for social and economic performance can be real. For norms that are universal, however, reflecting common human behavioral propensities, we need to adopt a somewhat different strategy. Their explanation is also historical, but in a more explicitly Darwinian sense, and the relevant periods of historical time are orders of magnitude longer.

The characteristics of this universal component of human culture reflected in universal norms have been determined by the same influences that wrote the rules of universal grammar or delineated the universal blueprint of the human anatomy. Over thousands of generations of prehistory, natural selection favored designs that led organisms based on them to experience greater reproductive success, because such designs were well suited to deal with recurrent features of the natural environment. The impact of current environmental conditions on design is vanishingly small, although, because there is also some continuity between contemporary conditions and those of human prehistory, much of our design continues to be adaptive.

My claim is that a tendency to practice first move(r) altruism toward humans outside of the immediate kin group is part of universal human culture, and that it evolved because groups with high frequencies of individuals with such propensities tended to grow more rapidly. They did so because they were more successful at coordinated foraging as well as coordinated defense (preemptive or otherwise) against other groups and because such groups suffered less from internal conflict. All of these factors contributed to greater reproductive success relative to other groups.

Within each group, however, individuals with propensities to display this behavior lost out, in the sense that their relative fitness within each group was lower.[10] The inexorable tendency for such within group selection to eliminate the propensity within each and every group was defeated by intergroup migration or population exchange combined with periodic group combination and splintering. Hamilton (1975) suggested that conditions likely prevalent in the middle to late Pleistocene were particularly favorable for the operation of group level selection. These conditions included small groups, partly isolated from each other, that tended, nevertheless, to practice exogamy (exchanging mates with neighboring groups). The importance of continuing genetic exchange, even after the exit from Africa 100,000–120,000 years ago, is consistent with morphological similarities in *Homo erectus* fossils from Asia and Africa.

Evolutionary Game Theory

It is tempting to take for granted the social environment that provides the background to everyday life and, in ways sometimes unrecognized, conditions expectations of the behaviors of others. It is fallacious, however, to conclude that because certain behaviors are rational for egoistic actors *conditional on that background,* it therefore follows that the collective behavior that ensues must have been predictable ex ante as the result of rational action of strictly egoistic individuals. This kind of reasoning unjustifiably mixes normative and descriptive game theory, to use Reinhard Selten's (1998) terminology. According to Selten, normative theory, which aims to deduce a guide to best strategy, as well, in principle, as a description/prediction of human behavior, treats empirical evidence as *irrelevant* (his italics). For descriptive game theory, on the other hand, *only* empirical evidence is relevant.[11] Selten argues that we must practice a strict methodological dualism, making a sharp distinction between normative and descriptive theory (22). His position on this issue is notable given his theoretical contributions to game theory. Normative game theory can help us understand the structure of social dilemmas we face but often fails as a guide to how we should act or as a very good descriptive prediction of how people do act.

John Maynard-Smith and George Price are responsible for launching

---

10. Thus Chagnon's finding that humans who have killed (and thus might be presumed to be less frequent granters of first move(r) altruism) enjoy higher reproductive success and have higher prestige does not necessarily mean such tendencies dominate among humans because they have been evolutionarily favored, even though such individuals may be relatively advantaged within each group (Chagnon 1988).

11. Selten is a bit redundant here, since evidence by its nature must be empirical.

the field of evolutionary game theory, an approach that enables us, when applying it to human behavior, to bypass debate about whether or not an action is rational. In a seminal 1973 article exploring the regulation of intraspecific conflict among animals, they introduced the concept of an evolutionarily stable strategy (ESS). Maynard-Smith and Price defined an ESS as a strategy that, given that it predominates within a population, cannot be successfully invaded by any mutant strategy. Stated another way, the best counter to an ESS must be itself: no other strategy can do better, because if that were possible, the ESS would be invadable and therefore no longer evolutionarily stable. An ESS is therefore a Nash equilibrium, often polymorphic, involving more than one strategy in stable proportions (Binmore 1998a, 279).[12] Their analysis helps us understand how group beneficial strategies may sustain themselves once established through frequency dependent selection. The paper, however, was intended to offer an alternative to group selection explanations of the evolution of restraints on intraspecific harm.

The word *evolution* in the last sentence is critical, because it implies a trajectory, driven by a replicator dynamic, that over time transforms the proportions of gene frequencies in a population as natural selection differentially rewards different phenotypes. The ESS concept actually says very little about that trajectory and the extent to which the replicator dynamic is driven solely by selection at the individual level. What the paper and the subsequent development of the ESS concept actually show is that individual level selection alone can sustain an end state equilibrium characterized by such restraint, not that individual level selection would necessarily have led to it. The idea behind frequency dependent selection is that the fitness of a particular strategy may depend on the strategies followed by other members of the population.

It is important to understand the differences between frequency dependent selection and group selection, of which the Hamilton kin selection mechanism is an instance. *The former has nothing necessarily to do with the latter.* Hamiltonian kin selection, for example, both originates as the consequence of and is sustained by group level selection and depends not at all on frequency dependent selection. The inclusive fitness enhancing effects of a gene suddenly appearing that predisposes to sacrifice for offspring will be independent of the number of similarly motivated conspecifics in the local or global population. Provided the benefits to kin weighted by genetic propinquity are greater than the costs to the actor,

---

12. Although all ESS are Nash, not every Nash equilibrium is ESS. Because ESS is a stronger, more restrictive criterion, it is considered, in technical terms, an equilibrium refinement.

such a gene will tend to evolve toward fixation, as we may assume it has in humans and other mammals. It will then also be sustained (protected by invasion from genes less prone to induce sacrifice by parents) by group level selection, so long as parents tend to raise their own offspring.

In contrast, frequency dependent selection doesn't require the subdivision of a population into separate groups (here family units) for part of a life cycle. It doesn't depend on a covariance between group growth rates and the frequency of genes in particular demes, or subpopulations. Instead, the effect on fitness is a function of the proportion of strategies in the entire population, in which pairs of organisms are assumed to be repeatedly selected at random for interaction.

A population in which all but a small minority practice Tit-for-Tat, and in which members must interact with each other more than once over an indeterminate planning horizon, and in which the discounting of the future is not too great, is proof to immediate invasion by a strategy of continuous defect.[13] From an economic perspective, we might in this instance speak of complex social organization being sustained by frequency dependent selection.

On the other hand, since a given structure may have multiple equilibria, showing that a strategy profile involving some cooperation may be a Nash equilibrium or, to use the stronger criterion, an evolutionarily stable strategy, does not adequately address the problem of origination. Writing in 1993, Maynard-Smith states clearly that the analysis of an ESS, which centers on the effect of frequency dependent selection, provides little insight into origins or generally what we understand when we use the word evolution. *It is concerned with explaining the stability of evolutionary environments once established* (Maynard-Smith 1993, 11–12).

Although the point is recognized,[14] the concept of an ESS continues to be used, sometimes rather casually, in two different senses. Dixit and Skeath, for example, offer the Maynard-Smith definition and then go on to say, "This is a static test, but often a more dynamic criterion is applied: starting from any mixture of phenotypes, a particular phenotype is evolutionary stable if the population evolves to a state in which this phenotype dominates" (1999, 321). The latter definition is more restrictive, since it implies a unique equilibrium end state, irrespective of starting point. May-

---

13. Tit-for-Tat is not, however, strictly speaking, ESS. It can first be invaded by less retaliatory strategies, such as All Cooperate, which then render the population vulnerable to continuous defect.

14. For example, Weibull: "as with Nash equilibrium, the evolutionary stability property does not explain *how* a population arrives at such a strategy. Instead it asks whether, once reached, a strategy is robust to evolutionary pressures" (1995, 33); or Fudenberg and Levine: "an ESS . . . is a static concept that was inspired by, but not derived from, considerations of evolutionary dynamics" (1998, 52). See also Hirshleifer and Martinez-Coll 1988 (368).

nard-Smith takes pains to emphasize the possibility of multiple ESS, whereas the dynamic criterion suggested by Dixit and Skeath excludes that possibility. To quote Dixit and Skeath again: "The eventual outcome of the population dynamics, *or* a strategy that, when used by all players cannot be upset by any successful invasion of another, will be an evolutionary stable strategy" (322; my italics). The sometimes unrecognized conflation of Maynard-Smith's original ESS idea with the more restrictive dynamic definition is again testimony to the power of the inverse genetic fallacy.

Evolution is a historical process, one in which selection at the individual level is always a potent force. Altruistic behavior, *by definition,* will be disadvantaged by selection pressures at this level. Any explanation of the emergence of cooperation must provide an account of how such forces are overcome. The Hamilton kin selection mechanism does so: it accounts both for the replicator dynamics that lead to evolution toward fixation and the mechanisms that sustain and protect this equilibrium once established from less sacrificing invaders. The Maynard-Smith–Price analysis does not provide such an account. The replicator dynamics that lead to widespread behaviors that favor groups require group level selection early in their evolutionary trajectory, even if they do not, once established at high frequencies in populations, require it for maintenance. At that point, frequency dependent selection at the individual level alone can be enough to sustain the equilibrium.

The Axelrod Computer Tournaments

Two of the most striking contributions to debates about the conditions under which cooperation can emerge have been the computer tournaments organized by Robert Axelrod (1984). His tournaments personalized the issues in a way they had not been since the initial Alchian-Williams pairing three decades earlier. Subjects were, once again, not "naive" college students but sophisticated students of human interaction, a number of whom were encouraged to examine and consider their own behavior and, in most instances, make their approach public. The results of these tournaments have been widely viewed as evidence that cooperation can be expected to evolve as the result of the interactions of purely self-interested agents. As in the case of Trivers's analysis or the concept of an evolutionarily stable strategy, I will argue that such an interpretation is not warranted. The play of Tit-for-Tat in the first tournament cannot be defended as rational under the assumption that one's fellow contestants are also rational. And the evidence in the second tournament that sophisticated contestants will coordinate around one of a number of rational choice equilibria does not in and of itself provide insight into why this particular one was selected.

Axelrod invited game theorists and other social and behavioral scientists familiar with the Prisoner's Dilemma to submit strategies for a multiplayer PD tournament. In the first of these contests each strategy was paired with itself, a random strategy, and each of the other submitted strategies, with each strategy pair playing a round of two hundred (these rules were preannounced). Strategies could take into account the record of prior plays in a given round in determining responses and were scored according to the total number of points earned in all of these pairings, with 3 points each for mutual cooperation, a 5/0 split where one defected and one cooperated, and 1 point each if both defected. Payoffs were not discounted: a point earned later in a series was worth as much as one earned earlier. Thus a record of mutual continuous cooperation throughout two hundred plays of a pairing earned 600 points for each of the strategies, while a strategy that cooperated for two hundred plays while its counterparty played defect for two hundred plays would earn 0, with the counterparty earning 1,000. Axelrod then averaged scores earned by each strategy in each of its pairings, creating a grand tournament score, which he used to rank strategies and determine the winner of the contest.

How should a rational player have selected a strategy, assuming all other players were rational? Consider how Nash might have reasoned. The grand score was to be determined as the result of scores earned in pairings with every other strategy and itself. A potential submitter could at random choose any one pairing to begin with. Since the play was of fixed duration (two hundred moves), it is clear that game theory prescribes defection on the last play. Since we "know" what will happen on the last play, defection on the next to last play is also the "correct" approach to take. And so forth, like a row of dominoes, backward induction operates until one reaches the conclusion that defection on the first (and all subsequent plays) is the correct course of action. If one assumes one's counterparty reasons similarly, one reaches the stable, unique, no regret Nash equilibrium profile of ALLD-ALLD, where ALLD stands for a strategy of defecting at each and every stage of the game. Having reasoned this way about the first pairing, one can reason similarly for the second and all subsequent possible pairings. ALLD is the only defensible strategy for a rational player in this tournament, assuming all submitters were also rational.

ALLD Is the Only Rational Strategy in the First Tournament

This conclusion can be tested by considering alternatives. For example, why couldn't TFT by all also be Nash, that is, the best response to itself in each pairing? Obviously, there are some responses, such as continuous cooperation, that are just as good a response to TFT as itself. But does there exist an unambiguously better choice? If the answer to this question is affirmative, TFT by all cannot be Nash. And the answer is affirmative, for the simple reason that a strategy of cooperating on all but the last play would always yield a higher payoff, giving one an extra 2 points on the last stage, and imposing a cost of 3 points on one's counterparty, in comparison to the alternative of playing cooperate.

Would it be better to begin defecting earlier against TFT? The answer is no. For example, if one began defecting on the second to last play, the gain of 2 on the penultimate play (5 as opposed to 3) is just compensated for by the loss on the last play (1 as opposed to 3).

TFT by all cannot be Nash, because TFT is not the best response to itself. However, if one believes one is playing against a TFT player, it is the strategy of cooperating on all but the last play, not the Nash mandated play of ALLD, that is to be recommended to the rational player (see Dixit and Skeath, 1999, 258-62). In the context of the Axelrod first tournament structure, this would mean cooperating through the first one hundred ninety-nine stages of the game and then defecting. Although ALLD is Nash in the first tournament, it is not strictly dominant.

Could cooperating on all but the last play by all be Nash? Player 1 could reason that *if* she could predict that player 2 (and all others) would play TFT, it would be rational to cooperate on all but the last play. And player 2 could reason that *if* he could predict that player 1 (and all others) would play TFT, it would be rational to cooperate on all but the last play. But we cannot describe a strategy profile based on this logic as Nash, because each player would be reasoning asymmetrically about their own rationality and that of their counterpart(ies). Obviously, both sets of assumptions could not be true, since each is reasoning that the others are, for whatever reasons, irrational, affected by behavioral *dispositions,* not just the structure of the situation.

Nash required that expectations of the play of counterparties be formed using a deductive methodology premised on the assumption that people chose so as to maximize their material self interest, given the payoff structure of the game *and* the assumption that their counterparty reasoned and chose similarly. Estimates of counterparty behavior based on a statistical methodology could have no place in the analysis: indeed, the assumption that such methodology was irrelevant was in part what distinguished decision theory from game theory. The use of an empirical, inductive strategy in forming expectations of counterparty play is therefore inconsistent with the Nash solution concept.

The issue of how one forms expectations of counterparty behavior is irrelevant in games, such as the one shot PD, where one strategy is strictly or strongly dominant. But it can be important in games with a pure strategy equilibrium comprised of strategies that are not strictly dominant. The two player fixed and known duration game, or its multiparty variant in the first Axelrod tournament, are examples of such games. ALLD is not the best response to all possible strategic choices of one's counterparty, but it is the only strategy that can be defended as rational under the assumption that other players are also rational.

Another way to understand these points is to suppose one is considering "invading" an Axelrod first (Axelrod I) tournament one predicts to be dominated by TFT players. Can one earn a higher tournament score by submitting ALLD? Even though a continuous defect (ALLD) invader wins or ties each of its individual pairings with a Tit-for-Tat, its aggregate score is pitiful. In each pairing with a TFT, ALLD gains on the first play compared to a cooperative strategy (it earns 5 rather than 3) but loses in stages two through two hundred, in which it earns 1, rather than the 3 it could have received by playing cooperate. Although each of the TFT players loses in its pairing with continuous defect, it has many opportunities for "tying" at higher score levels in its plays with other TFTs.

Thus, in a population of ninety-nine Tit-for-Tat players and one continuous defector, with each strategy paired against itself and all others, continuous defect earns 200 against itself and 204 against each of the other ninety-nine Tit-for-Tat players. By contrast, each Tit-for-Tat player earns 199 against the one continuous defector but 600 against each of the other Tit-for-Tat players, including itself. One ALLD invader of a population of ninety-nine TFT players therefore earns 20,963 fitness points, vs. 59,599 for each of the TFT players. ALLD is clearly not the best response in this case, though it does boast the superior win/tie/loss record.

But of course the strategy space may be more complex than just these alternatives. A number of writers have emphasized that, where the duration of interaction is indefinite, TFT can first be replaced by less retributive but equally "good" strategies, such as All Cooperate, which then makes the population vulnerable to invasion by ALLD. But in the fixed and known duration structure of the first tournament, the vulnerability of TFT is even greater. It can *immediately* be invaded by the strategy of cooperate until the last play. Such an invading strategy earns 60,196 points: 602 against each of the other ninety-nine TFT players, plus 598 against itself. Each of the TFT players, in contrast, earns 59,997—600 against each of the other 98 TFTs and itself, and 597 against the invader. In sum: in the first tournament, TFT is *not* Nash, it is *not* ESS, and it cannot be defended as rational under the assumption that all other players are rational. On the other hand, even though ALLD by all is Nash, the best response to TFT is cooperate until the last play, not ALLD.

Like the Alchian-Williams pairing, both Axelrod tournaments offer empirical evidence on how smart people actually play. What they do not do is provide insight into how environments characterized by one-shot PDs could have evolved into the repeated play environment assumed in either. In a tournament in which the pairings consisted of single play games, the play of cooperate (the initial move of a Tit-for-Tat player in a repeated game) would clearly be neither Nash nor ESS. A population of ninety-nine cooperators invaded by one defector would eventually be overrun by defectors. The defector would earn 1 in its pairing with itself and 5 in its pairing with each of the other ninety-nine cooperators, for a total of 496 fitness points. Each of the cooperators would earn 0 in its pairing with the defector, and 3 in each of its pairings with itself and the other 98 cooperators, for a total of 298 fitness points. Assuming frequencies in subsequent generations are related to these fitness scores, the cooperators would soon be gone.

A tournament involving single play games, in which defection is the unique Nash equilibrium *and* strictly dominant in each of the pairings, illustrates the very significant hurdles that need to be overcome for iterated interaction to become common. This observation illustrates a general proposition: if a game has a dominant strategy, as does the one-shot PD, that strategy (defect) will also be the unique ESS (Dixit and Skeath 1999, 326). The relevance of this observation for the subject of this book is this: *Something other than a propensity to choose rationally must lie behind the ability of humans to transcend the Hobbesian dilemma.*

Returning now to the fixed and known duration environment, once one abandons the Nash prescribed methodology for forecasting counterparty behavior, the choice of strategy becomes heavily influenced by estimates of what one believes others will do. That is what made the tournament, one without great interest in theory, so interesting in practice. Since the success of a strategy in the first tournament was frequency dependent, choosing a winning submission depended in part on forecasting the universe of other submissions.

What convinced Anatol Rapaport (the winner of both tournaments) that this universe would contain a high enough proportion of strategies involving cooperation to allow TFT to be a superior strategy? Most likely his observations as an experimentalist in his studies of two player fixed and known duration games. As he and his coauthor wrote acerbically in 1965, "The predominance of the [continuous cooperate] lock-ins in the favorable conditions shows that our subjects are not sufficiently sophisticated game-theoreticians to have figured out that [continuous defect] is the only strategically defensible strategy. Apparently this lack of strategic sophistication allows many of them to find the commonsense solution, namely the tacit collusion, and so to win money instead of losing it" (Rapaport and Chammah 1965, 66). His evidently superior forecasting ability encourages us to reflect again on the likelihood that a rational forecast of human behavior, including our own, is one that is reached empirically, allowing for behavior that may not always meet John Nash's definition of rational choice.[15]

Axelrod II: The Second Tournament and Model Massaging

In the follow-up tournament, each submitted strategy was paired with itself and every other strategy five times, with the length of each round chosen from a probability distribution consistent with a median game length of 200. After the entries had been submitted, Axelrod selected the five game lengths—identical for each pairing—to be 63, 77, 151, 156, and 308. I have stressed in the previous section that TFT, or indeed any strategy involving even the slightest degree of cooperation, could not be Nash in the first tournament. This observation is relevant in considering why Axelrod changed the rules between the first and second competitions. He states that he made this change to eliminate "end game effects." Maynard-Smith, in summarizing Axelrod's work, explains that this modification "avoids the complication that programs may have special rules for the last game" (1982, 168). But what was wrong with allowing strategists to consider special rules for the last games or stages?

Axelrod seems to have been concerned with the widely known result just elaborated: in two player fixed and known duration games, continuous defect was the only Nash equilibrium, and the only defensible strategy for a rational player, if players are assumed to choose rationally. He points out, for example, that if interactions are indefinitely repeated then cooperation may emerge, implying that it cannot emerge as the result of rational choice except under this circumstance (1984, 10–11).

Theory specified that in order to permit a rational choice cooperative equilibrium in such a pairing, subjects could not know the exact end of the interaction. As Binmore describes it, "the famous folk theorem of game theory . . . says that almost any outcome of the static game that gets repeated can be sustained as a Nash equilibrium of the repeated game provided that the players never have reason to think that any particular repetition is likely to be the last" (1998a, 280). All of the theoretical work in Axelrod's appendix pertains to the two person game, indefinitely repeated. The fact that cooperation emerged in the first tournament appears to

---

15. The defining feature of a rational expectation in John Muth's sense is that it uses all available information in forming a forecast. In macroeconomics, rational expectations are often contrasted with those that are adaptive. Adaptive expectations may, however, sometimes be justified as rational, particularly where there is uncertainty about, for example, the credibility of a monetary authority's commitment. The Nash approach views prior evidence of human behavioral predispositions, above and beyond the almost axiomatic presumption that they are strictly egoistic, as irrelevant (see also Selten 1998).

have been retrospectively perceived as something of an embarrassment. One cannot help thinking, therefore, that at some level the modification in the rules for the second tournament was at least partly intended to bring the empirical (descriptive) results into conformity with what Axelrod saw as a conflict between his data and the theoretical (normative) conclusion that an indefinite number of plays was a necessary condition for cooperative behavior to be sustained by rational players in two player games. If theory tells one that cooperative behavior cannot emerge among rational players with a fixed number of plays, but evidence (from the first round) shows that such behavior does manifest itself when strategies designed by humans are paired with each other, why would one then lower the bar, making it easier, according to theory, for cooperative behavior to emerge?

I do not have an exact name for what Axelrod has done. The more common problem when data are inconsistent with favored theories is to ignore or massage the data. To his credit, of course, Axelrod did none of that, but there does seem to be a bit of "model massaging" here—massaging the tournament design to eliminate an apparent contradiction between theory and data. Would not the results have been even more striking had the tournament continued with fixed game length? A well-developed experimental literature going back to Flood and Dresher showed that human subjects, sophisticated and otherwise, were quite willing to play strategies that simply could not be defended as rational. Why be concerned about adding to it?

How important was it for Axelrod to show that the emergence of cooperation was the result of *rational* choice? On the one hand, "There is no need to assume that the players are rational. They need not be trying to maximize their rewards. Their strategies may simply reflect standard operating procedures, rules of thumb, instincts, habits, or imitation. . . . The actions that players take are not necessarily even conscious choices" (1984, 18). At the same time, he talks several times in his first chapter about the bearing of his work on "the emergence of cooperation among egoists without central authority" (24; see also 6); these words echo the title of his 1981 *American Political Science Review* article. Thus, he does seem determined to reach the positive and normative conclusion that "egoists" do and "should" practice some form of Tit-for-Tat.[16]

A final note: Axelrod places considerable emphasis on the requirement that a strategy, in order to be effective, "must be able to take into

---

16. As Jonathan Baron has noted, "When we study performance in laboratory games . . . we must be aware of the fact that repeated games may not actually involve social dilemmas at all" (1988, 402). So long as two player games are of fixed and known duration, however, they do. Axelrod's modification of the rules between the first and second tournaments was designed to turn an interaction apparently involving a social dilemma into one that did not,

account the history of the interaction as it has developed so far" (1984, 30). This conclusion is stronger than is warranted. Tit-for-Tat, as the winner, is certainly an effective strategy. But this rule, requiring only four or five lines of programming, cooperates on the first play and then simply echoes whatever the opponent did on the previous play. The "look back" horizon is at best one play. Tit-for-Tat did better than other, often complex strategies that tried to exploit knowledge of a round's entire past history (34–35). A more defensible conclusion from these tournaments would be that a strategy, in order to be effective, "must take into account what happened on the previous play." This is an interesting conclusion in itself, relevant perhaps to research that has emphasized the surprising power of simple forecasting heuristics compared to more complex alternatives (Gigerenzer and Todd 1999).

Axelrod's Simulations

In the latter chapters of his book Axelrod reports on his simulations of successive rounds of the second tournament, with a replicator dynamic such that the frequency of each strategy in subsequent rounds was dependent on its success in the previous round. The evolutionary[17] ambitions of this modeling are reflected in his comments:

> The idea is that the more successful strategies are more likely to be submitted in the next round, and the less successful strategies are less likely to be submitted again. To make this precise, we can say that the number of copies (or offspring) of a given entry will be proportional to that entry's tournament score. We simply have to interpret the average payoff received by an individual as proportional to the individual's expected number of offspring. (1984, 49)

He finds that TFT players tend to increase in frequency, which is not surprising, given that the second tournament had initially attracted a high frequency of conditionally cooperative strategies.

But this is not an explanation of the origin of cooperation because it accounts neither for the distribution of initial submissions nor for the repeated nature of interaction built into the tournament structure. Hamilton's theory of kin selection was a major step forward because it offered an evolutionary account of the *origin* of altruistic behavior toward kin. It

---

partially eliminating the conflict that his empirical results otherwise seemed to pose to normative theory.

17. He described his approach as ecological, since he did not allow for mutations (new strategies) to appear.

explained how organisms with a higher propensity to sacrifice for their children (or kin) could successfully invade a population in which such propensities were lower or absent, even though such traits might adversely affect the survival of the organisms exhibiting them. The Trivers model and most of the work in economics and political science on iterated (repeated) games, on the other hand, are expositions of maintenance. Without accounting for transition from single to repeated play, or, within the context of indefinitely repeated interaction, for the selection of one among a number of possible equilibria, we do not have a coherent account of the origin of cooperative or altruistic behavior toward non-kin.

Hamilton, who coauthored a chapter of Axelrod's 1984 book, sometimes failed fully to appreciate the strength of his own theory vs. the explanations advanced for altruistic behavior toward non-kin by Trivers and others. A commentary (with a different coauthor) on work regarding the voluntary provision of public goods begins discussion of the argument of a target article as follows: "[the authors say that] according to EI [egoistic incentive] theory, people will always choose the selfish strategy in social dilemmas. This is not true if kinship is involved or if there are repeated interactions" (Houston and Hamilton 1989, 709).

This is not quite accurate. Egoistic incentive theory, strictly speaking, predicts that parents will selfishly choose not to sacrifice for their children. The parent who does practice such sacrifice is being unselfish, even if the genes that may predispose to such behavior are not. Second, the parallel treatment of the theory of kin selection on the one hand and the elucidation of mechanisms sustaining cooperation pursued by egoistic individuals locked into a series of repeated interactions of unknown duration, on the other hand, obscures the different achievements of these models.

Evolutionary Models Are Not Identical to Economic Models

Economic and game theoretic ideas have influenced the work of Trivers and Maynard-Smith, just as evolutionary concepts influenced Axelrod's work. Generally speaking, an economic model can be translated into evolutionary language, although the converse is not necessarily so easily done, since an evolutionary framework makes no assumptions about whether organisms maximize utility or even pursue purposive action.

The economic framework of utility maximization provides, of course, a large tent in which all variety of motivational goals may be posited. Pure altruists, for example, "solve" the single play Prisoner's Dilemma without difficulty, since for them, cooperate is a strictly dominant strategy. Common usage, however, restricts microeconomic models to those in which agents efficiently advance their own material interest. Thus the action of the soldier who throws his body on a grenade to save the lives of his buddies is generally evaluated by economists as being objectively irrational, as is the action of an experimental subject who rejects a positive offer in an ultimatum game, apparently preferring nothing to something.

Some will argue that if this is what the dead man or the subject wanted, and so it is, as they have revealed by their actions, then it is ipso facto rational. But many analysts within the rational choice tradition are wary about proceeding down this route, because it vitiates claims economics might have to making predictions about behavior independently of empirically derived knowledge of human behavioral propensities. Why would we, usually posthumously, award Medals of Honor to soldiers who cover explosives with their bodies if we thought such actions were basically selfish? I have adopted the convention of restricting economic models to those that posit an efficient pursuit of an actor's material welfare, because I believe this is a reasonable characterization of much contemporary practice within the profession.

Models in evolutionary biology avoid discussions of motivation and what rationality means, and they put much less focus on instrumental means-ends choices by individual actors. Models in evolutionary biology are as relevant for worms or viruses as they are for primates. Economic models are not, because they focus on rational choice. Rational choice models are not relevant for worms, unless one is willing to grant the concepts of consciousness and purposive action much wider purview than has been traditional.

Game theory has been used both in evolutionary biology and in economics, but what the theory models is somewhat different in the two cases. In evolutionary biology, there is no consideration of motives and no consideration of conscious thought or choice, or intentionality. Individual variation produces propensities toward different behaviors that are acted upon by the forces of natural selection; the benefits or payoffs come in the form of increases in fitness. Altruism is simply behavior that increases the fitness of others and reduces that of the actor. In game theoretic models in economics, the emphasis is on rational choice; the payoffs are usually in the form of material benefits that may but will not necessarily increase the spread of the organism's genes in future generations. In economic models motives may matter in determining whether an action will be characterized as altruistic. And assumptions that agents act in ways contrary to their individual interest will often be attacked ab initio on the grounds that such behavior is not consistent with rationality. Thus the model builder may be discouraged from positing such behavior.

Within an evolutionary framework there are no implicit restrictions on what behavioral predispositions may be posited. Rather, the intellectual discipline comes in requiring that one develop a plausible model of how a particular trait, and the gene(s) that may predispose to it, survives the forces of selection operating on it upon first appearance at low frequencies in a population. In practice, in recent years, evolutionary analysis has focused almost exclusively on individual level selection and on the maintenance of equilibria. Evolutionary mechanisms have therefore often been appealed to as reinforcement for the assumption of strict egoism in economics. But the Darwinian framework provides space for the operation of natural selection at more than one level and consequently for the survival of a range of essential human predispositions broader than those upon which the standard economic model is premised.

From the standpoint of evolutionary biology, the forces of natural selection may be indifferent between behaviors that enable an organism to survive and continue to procreate and behaviors that prevent that outcome but permit survival of and procreation by two children. The important distinctions between economic and evolutionary models have, however, often been blurred by the use of a restricted set of the latter to justify the standard version of the former. Such a rhetorical strategy has elided important differences in their structure. *In particular, evolutionary theory is concerned with genotypical influence on phenotype and the feedback through natural selection on gene frequencies in the future.* Economic theory, however, is concerned with decision making by the organism as an entity and, in its standard or canonical form, rules out behavior that might benefit genes predisposing to it, if such behavior is not in the material interest of the organism.

Restricting the operation of natural selection to the individual level closely aligns the results of evolutionary models with those of the standard economic model, since organisms that efficiently pursue their material welfare, choose life over death, and, ceteris paribus, choose more wealth over less, will find their relative fitness increased by individual level selection. In particular, neither approach is consistent with or is likely to predict biologically altruistic behavior. But the range of mechanisms through which natural selection can operate is broader than that so allowed.

The majority of humans end up fathering or mothering children and sacrifice enormously for their well-being. Since what is here selfish from the standpoint of the gene is altruistic from the standpoint of the acting organism, and thus altruistic from the standpoint of the rational actor, we must conclude that the majority of humans at least sometime during their life cycle practice altruistic behavior toward others and have the emotional experience of so doing. It cannot, then, be an emotionally alien experience to humans or an inessential component of their behavioral makeup for them to be empathetic. Indeed, growing evidence indicates that children as young as a few days old cry when they hear other infants crying but not when they hear other noise or a tape recording of their own distress (Hoffman 1981, 129–30). Most rational choice theorists do not argue the point, making an exception with respect to behavior toward kin in their assumption that humans act in all domains so as efficiently to maximize their material welfare. But the line tends to be drawn, in one way or another, with respect to relations among non-kin.

For biologists, explanation of altruism toward kin is a central and largely resolved issue. As in the social sciences, controversies have surrounded the understanding of behavior among non-kin, mirroring the denial of the relevance of altruistic inclinations in understanding such behavior implicit in the standard economic model. The predictive/explanatory difficulties this entails can be appreciated, simply, as a chain of reasoning that leads to a conclusion at variance with observational and experimental evidence.

1. *Behavioral Assumption:* Individuals efficiently maximize their material self-interest. This reflects the essential feature of the standard economic model and specifies an externally observable goal—maximize material self-interest—and assumptions about how this goal is pursued—efficiently, that is, making decisions based on all available information using rational rules.

2. *Scientific Justification:* Argument from natural selection. Those humans who in the past did not have such predispositions were culled out; therefore this model accurately characterizes essential human behavioral predispositions. The argument from natural selection is used to endow proposition 1 with the quality of an axiom: an accepted fact so unquestioned that it may serve as a foundation for proof of more fundamental claims.

3. *Normative Conclusion/Descriptive Prediction:* Mutual defection in single play PD games; continuous defection in Prisoner's Dilemma games of fixed and known duration. Many implications for social organization, or the lack thereof, may be derived from this prediction.

4. *Inconsistency between Theory Prediction and Data:* Prediction is inconsistent, and not in minor ways, with experimental and observational data.

Something is wrong. But if the justification 2 for the behavioral assumption 1 is correct, the reasoning seems airtight. The proposed solution involves recognizing that the justification (step 2) is invalid. Evolutionary theory and evidence do not, in and of themselves, exclude the possibility of selection for some traits at levels other than that of the organism. If this possibility is recognized, then 2 is no longer an automatic justification for 1. And if 1 is modified to allow the possibility that humans are born with predispositions to practice first move(r) altruism, a trait favored at least initially at the group but not the organismic level, a trait that can be weakened, strengthened, or modified by environmental experiences but one that nevertheless defines baseline practice and expectations, then predictions of theory are no longer necessarily at odds with experimental and observational data. This modification is the essential first step in laying the foundations for a behavioral science with improved predicted power.

This view is controversial, and a natural question is to ask whether there are other options. These options have been explored exhaustively. The Trivers approach, as we have seen, does not solve the problem of altruistic behavior directed at non-kin but merely extends a long tradition of identifying conditions that may sustain reciprocity once established. Axelrod's tournaments begin with an environment of iterated games, which assumes one of the biggest hurdles on the way to complex organization has already been overcome. As Maynard-Smith himself observes, the concept of an evolutionarily stable strategy (ESS) addresses issues of stability, not origin. Appeal to norms does not solve the problem because adherence to them, at least initially, faces the same negative individual level selection as the underlying behavior.

The widely disseminated view that the problem of altruism toward non-kin has been solved without the necessity of appealing to evolutionary trajectories involving group level selection represents a misconception. It has been "solved" by focusing on end state equilibria in which the behavior has become mutualistic.

Much as we might like to insist on a strict separation of science and politics, the two in practice are interrelated.[18] But as scientists, social or natural, we should do our best in reaching conclusions to leave the possible political implications of our findings behind. The alternative of ruling multilevel selection out of order leaves the reasoning sequence 1–4 intact, along with its unfortunate outcome: a contradiction between theory prediction and experimental/observational data. That is, failure to move in

---

18. Views about the Prisoner's Dilemma are sometimes mapped onto political ideologies, with "belief" in cooperation being a "liberal" position and "belief" in deception a conservative position (Poundstone 1992). But it is hard to see the logical necessity of this correlation. The question is one of coherence and consistency with data, and the conclusions with regard to essential human behavioral propensities in this book could provide foundation for "classical liberal" views of the natural order and the limited role of government.

this direction leaves in place, particularly in economics and political science, an *empirically invalidated* model.[19]

Evolutionary biologists' treatment of the empirical importance of group level selection may have been misleading and unfair, but it has never involved the denial of the possibility of multilevel selection. On the other hand, the standard economic model, which reflects an organism level perspective, is inconsistent both with a gene's eye view of the world and with the possibility that natural selection may operate on different levels to increase gene frequency in subsequent generations.

Resistance to entertaining the possibility of group selection seems to stem partly from fear that to open the floodgates even a crack will unleash a torrent of romantic, naive, and *empirically unjustified* models of human nature that, if allowed to influence political discourse, will have devastating consequences. In some instances this appears to be wound up in a belief that opposition to group selection models indirectly defends the standard economic model and whatever political implications are seen flowing from it. Whatever the merits of this type of reasoning, this view fails to appreciate that support for the economic approach does not flow automatically from success of the gene's eye view. Consider this passage from Ridley's *The Red Queen.*

> Within a few years of [George] Williams' book, Wynne-Edwards was effectively defeated, and almost all biologists agreed that no creature could ever evolve the ability to help its species at the expense of itself. . . . Williams knew full well that individual animals often cooperate and that human society is not a ruthless free-for-all. But he also saw that cooperation is almost always between close relatives . . . or that it is practiced where it directly or eventually benefits the individual. (Ridley 1993, 36)

Note the familiar problem with the final part of the passage. Once established, a group of contingently cooperative players prepared to punish violations, including those against third parties, and punish those who fail to punish those who fail to punish, and so on, can be evolutionarily stable: the meanest, most selfish agent invading that population will find it strictly rational to behave in a manner indistinguishable from the other members of the population. In the limit, such behavior can be viewed as completely consistent with self-interest: it has been drained of altruistic content by the

---

19. Surely Kuhn and Lakatos never intended to suggest that empirical tests of scientific theories were without relevance. Lakatos objected to Popper's notion of the crucial or decisive experiment. He argued that theories are not in fact rejected based on limited failures of prediction: they are rejected only when something better comes along (Lakatos 1970, 101). My argument is (*a*) the failures of prediction are not isolated and (*b*) there is an alternative, whose elements this book spells out.

increase in frequency of similarly inclined individuals. But the observation that cooperation tends to be practiced where it directly or indirectly benefits the individual tells us nothing about the origin of such behavior or about how predispositions to play cooperate could survive the individual level forces of selection arrayed against them upon first appearance in a population.

Genes are the ultimate repository and locus of the raw material upon which selection operates, and there is nothing in evolutionary theory or practice that prevents a gene pursuing a particularly "devious" strategy whereby it predisposes an individual to jeopardize its own survival in a way that benefits other individual organisms in the actor's group, so long as that strategy results in an increase in that gene's frequency in subsequent generations. When reproduction (passing on genes) and an organism's survival are in conflict, reproduction wins, and when a behavioral trait puts an individual at risk but benefits its group in a way that increases the inclusive fitness of the gene so predisposing, the organism bears the risk and the gene reaps the benefit. Organisms are not selected for; designs are (Tooby and Cosmides 1990, 394). Selection at the group level may be less important today than it was in the evolutionary past, but there is nothing in the gene's eye view that precludes such "strategies."

Some sociobiologists and evolutionary psychologists continue to insist on denying at the outset, almost on a priori grounds, the possibility that group level selection operates or has ever operated in an empirically significant fashion in evolutionary history. In certain areas of inquiry, the study of vision, for example, such a restriction has little effect, but in others it is crippling—like trying to walk across a tightrope having first shot oneself in the foot. If persisted in it will likely generate a series of pathologies, different from but no less deleterious than those that have beset rational choice theory in economics and political science. It is an uphill battle in many cases to persuade social scientists to consider biological influences on behavior. The logic and evidence are such that those of us interested in such persuasion should abandon knee-jerk opposition to the possibility of group level selection. Failing to do so will just make the climb harder, aside from leading to repeated contradictions.

Skeptics typically conflate sociobiology with rational choice models with a gene's eye perspective. This is too broad brush. It is not the gene's eye view of the world that is especially wanting.[20] Nor is it sociobiology or

---

20. Sober has argued that selection operates on organism traits and that there is rarely a one to one relationship between particular genes and traits. Moreover, he points to the case of heterozygous superiority as a counterexample to a gene's eye view. Genes for sickle cell anemia are fatal in homozygous form, but in malarial environments, the heterozygous form has fitness superiority compared to normal homozygotes (Sober 1984). See Sterelny and Griffiths 1999 (61–70) for responses to Sober's criticisms and an attempt to chart a middle ground (1999, chap. 5).

evolutionary psychology per se, provided we are less dogmatic about the possibility of group selection and open to the possibility of persisting mal-adaptive behavior. Rather it is the standard economic model, which is based on the assumptions that people are rational and that rationality means the efficient pursuit of the actor's material self-interest and the belief that these assumptions are equally applicable across all domains. It claims too much, a charge that has been levied at all three of these approaches but is particularly relevant here. We need an empirical and evolutionarily informed program for identifying essential human behavioral propensities beyond those emphasized by the standard model and the domains in which they are most likely to manifest themselves. We need these baseline or base rate data, and we need to agree on their relevance, in order to construct a behavioral science with improved predictive capabilities.

To sum up thus far, I am making four claims. First, that the behavioral propensities that manifest themselves in altruistic behavior are empirically relevant, extend to behavior toward non-kin, and should be understood to include the passive altruism reflected in failure to harm. Second, that an evolutionary approach emphasizing group or multilevel selection provides a coherent framework for understanding how such traits might have become established in populations and that existing "explanations" for such behavior do not. Third, that economic models are not necessarily the same as evolutionary models in their implications. In particular, the justification by appeal to evolutionary theory for the standard economic behavioral assumptions is invalid. Finally, that attempts to account for the origin of altruistic behavioral propensities toward non-kin through evolutionary models restricted to individual level selection or, what turns out to be the equivalent, economic models where agents efficiently pursue their own individual self-interest represent journeys down similar intellectual culs-de-sac. This last point is illustrated and expanded upon in chapter 4.

CHAPTER 4

Deconstructing Frank

Robert Frank's widely cited 1988 book *Passions within Reason* represents a heartfelt plea, particularly to social scientists, to recognize the category of altruistic behavior as empirically relevant. For skeptics, it provides an accessible summary of evidence of such behavior. What follows, however, is critical of Frank's second key objective—his attempted explanation of this phenomenon—and is designed to illustrate further the limitations of an economic/evolutionary approach that, from the outset, limits selection to the level of the individual organism.

We should applaud Frank's attempt to understand a range of behavior that many economists have downplayed, ignored, or even suggested does not exist. He has taken seriously the problem of altruism in a way some more ideologically committed have not. To read this work critically is to take it seriously.[1] Nevertheless, his analysis is riddled with inconsistencies and contradictions. Not acknowledging in a consistent fashion the limitations of a strictly economic approach, or an evolutionary approach limiting selection to the level of the individual organism, vitiates an analysis that tries to integrate the two approaches.

By deconstructing the analysis we can illustrate the pitfalls of trying to explain the origin of altruistic behavior within a model that focuses, from an evolutionary standpoint, on the forces of individual level selection alone. Not bringing this issue to the surface leaves one group of scholars secure in knowledge of "flaws" in argument such as this, unable quite to specify them, yet confident, because there is so little "theoretical" foundation for the persistence of altruism, that in fact it does not persist. This is an untenable position because, as Frank and others show, and as is self-evident to many nonacademics, there is a substantial body of experimen-

---

1. Although often referenced, the book has received remarkably little critical attention. A recent exception is Reder 1999 (326–30). For an example of continued uncritical acceptance, see Sterelny and Griffiths 1999. These authors, astute critics and expositors of the biological literatures, describe *Passions within Reason* as "probably the best book yet on the possible evolutionary significance of a wider range of emotions" (304). Ignored by those convinced altruism is empirically unimportant, Frank's book has been embraced by those who see it as reconciling the standard economic model with other-regarding behavior.

tal and observational evidence for such behavior. Of perhaps equal concern, not undertaking this critique leaves another group confident that there are available good individual selectionist explanations of such behavior.

Frank implicitly criticizes economists for their skepticism about the empirical relevance of altruistic behavior. He is right to do so. The problem, as in the Trivers model, is the commitment to explain it within an evolutionary framework that precludes the operation of natural selection above the level of the individual organism. Because Frank restricts himself to an evolutionary past in which only individual level selection can have occurred, he must ultimately accept the logic of the pop Darwinism view of evolution: natural selection has necessarily eliminated any other-regarding behavioral predispositions. To account for the emergence of the behavior he wishes to explain, he finds himself forced, as was Trivers, to develop his theory based on rational calculation by self-interested agents. The recurring problem is that, for such an agent, altruistic behavior, were it to be practiced in a population where it manifests itself initially at low frequencies, would be fitness reducing for an individual organism and thus, according to the definition used in this book, irrational.

In spite of its evolutionary trappings, Frank's account is at its core narrowly economic and consistent with the assumptions of the standard economic model. Behavior results from constrained maximization of utility functions devoid of arguments reflecting the utility of others. But the issue goes beyond the possible need to add additional arguments to utility functions or modify the way they may enter. There may be limits within which the metaphor of constrained maximization itself is useful in modeling human behavior. A fully evolutionary framework can help us understand these bounds. *Passions within Reason* goes half the distance, but the effort produces an analysis that is muddled and contradictory.

The centerpiece of the theory is a treatment of the strategic role of emotions. By permitting us credibly to commit to threats or promises it might not in the future be in our interest to deliver on, Frank argues, passionate behavior allows us to "solve" problems, like nuclear deterrence, that would otherwise be insoluble. But he never satisfactorily explains whether emotional behavior is ultimately under the control of reason, and thus can be considered truly strategic, or whether it is not. If emotions are truly under the control of reason, then a tendency to exhibit emotional behavior cannot serve its appointed role of giving credibility to commitments or threats. Normative game theory is premised on the proposition that one's counterparty is also rational, in the sense that Nash understood the term. If reason controls the passions, a rational player would see through emotional display as a ruse and would, anticipating similar reasoning on the part of the counterparty, not bother to use it in the first place.

If emotions are not under the control of reason, on the other hand, one has difficulty explaining how passionate people would continue to experience positive selection pressure once repeated interaction had been established and reason (and individual level selection) alone was sufficient to maintain a cooperative equilibrium. Rational actors would, one can argue, shun potential counterparties prone to exhibit such behavior in favor of those whose behavior was viewed as less volatile and more predictable. Passionate individuals would have a hard time surviving, unless we were to posit a species typical preference for dealing with passionate as opposed to purely reasonable people. Perhaps we are indeed so predisposed. But then we are back to the problem of origin. The analysis does not explain how such a self-harming and thus irrational tendency could have survived upon first appearance if selection occurs only at the individual level. Frank's treatment of the role of a reputation for displaying emotional behavior as a guarantor of threats or commitments is inadequately developed.

If we understand emotional behavior to reflect behavioral predispositions contrary to what would be counseled by reason narrowly and precisely defined, an expression of cognitive modularity (see chap. 5), then Frank's intuition that such tendencies are relevant to developing a more comprehensive empirically based social science is probably correct. But his analysis does not get below the surface of the issues raised by this intuition.

The cover copy for the book includes these observations.

> In thousands of studies of family, school, business and politics, behavioral scientists have claimed that altruism is irrelevant, and that "passion," our feeling for our families, lovers, friends, even our good will for the world in general, is illogical. It seems a simple matter of time before social commitment disappears in the wake of personal gain. . . . this book shows why passionate behavior may be reasonable.

The first sentence is an accurate characterization of trends in late twentieth century social science. While increasing numbers of economists, like Frank, have tried to wander away from Stigler's palace, their outflow has been matched by new recruits from political science, sociology, and anthropology, dazzled by the magnificence of the structure and its "granite" foundations. So the problem of the dismissal of altruism is real.

What of the second sentence? Throughout the book Frank uses a number of synonyms for *rational,* such as *reasonable* or *prudent,* in apparent hope of avoiding the criticism that he is characterizing behavior as at the same time both rational and irrational. Is Frank arguing that reasonable behavior is necessarily rational?[2] If apparently irrational actions—the play of conditional cooperation in a fixed and known duration PD game—end up serving my material interest, is he suggesting that we call such behavior reasonable but not rational? In discussing a rational man, does he mean to appeal to the individualistic approach of the eighteenth century *homme éclairé*—we might call him enlightenment man—or that of twentieth century economic man, *Homo economicus?* If the former, is Frank arguing that since passionate behavior may be "reasonable," it is therefore rational? But if that is true, how can we define passionate behavior as the negation of the counsel of reason?

The introduction of *Passions within Reason* begins to explain what the author intends: "In this book, I make use of an idea from economics to suggest how noble human tendencies might not only have survived the ruthless pressures of the material world, but actually have been nurtured by them" (Frank 1988, ix). To achieve this goal, Frank must somehow explain the withstanding by altruistic behavioral propensities of the forces of individual level selection *at the point where they first emerge at low frequencies.* He understands well the obstacle: "Biologists tell us that behavior is shaped ultimately by material rewards, that the relentless pressures of natural selection will cull out any organism that foregoes opportunities for personal gain" (ix).

Frank appears here to distance himself from this pop Darwinist view, but in limiting himself to an individual selectionist framework, he must ultimately accept it. He mischaracterizes Darwin, however, and biologists in general, as counseling a framework in which selection can take place only at the individual level. Darwin recognized the possibility of selection at the group level. He appealed to it parsimoniously, and so should we. But when an account of the origin of well-documented and widespread behavioral predispositions stubbornly refuses to yield to models based on individual level selection alone, group selection models offer a viable alternative.

By choosing to operate within a framework that explicitly precludes selection above the level of the individual, Frank stacks the cards against himself and lays the groundwork for the difficulties that follow. He finds himself over and over again trying to conclude that behavior he defines as irrational is in fact rational. According to the law of contradiction in logic, a reasoning process that, based on the same evidence, leads to contradic-

---

2. The first definition given for *reasonable* in some dictionaries is *rational;* in most they are listed as synonyms.

tory conclusions is flawed, because a statement about the world cannot be both true and false (Dawes 1988, 9). The quagmires into which Frank descends might have been avoided had he abandoned the concern with whether or not behavior is rational and instead worked within an evolutionary framework allowing group as well as individual level selection.

Frank argues in the introduction (he is not the first; the idea goes back at least to Schelling 1960 and can be found also in Hirshleifer 1987) that it is rational to threaten to behave irrationally in order to deter theft or aggression, because such threats may deter such harm, thus benefiting the actor materially: "Being predisposed to respond irrationally serves much better here than being guided only by material self interest" (Frank 1988, x). The underpinnings of this critical argument are not, however, fully explored. Did natural selection favor propensities to practice "irrational" behavior at the point where they first emerged at low frequencies? If so, how can this have been if selection operated only at the level of the individual organism? Or is this a statement about what works well for an egoistic "invader" confronting baseline human behavioral propensities whose origin is simply assumed? This latter claim is sustainable, since frequency dependent selection can, under such conditions, favor the behavior, which can then also be viewed as rational.

We are led inexorably to the following contradiction. If being predisposed to respond irrationally serves "much better," then does that not, by definition, make such behavior rational (rational behavior is that which efficiently advances the material welfare of the agent)? Yet one cannot claim that a behavior is both irrational and rational and still have the terms retain meaning. Sooner or later, for example, threats to retaliate may have to be exercised, even when doing so *can be stigmatized and will be stigmatized by Frank as irrational* because the harm has already been incurred (costs are sunk) and retaliation invites an additional round of retaliation.

This is precisely the issue that concerned the game theorist Reinhard Selten in 1965 when he developed the idea of subgame perfect rationality and its associated equilibrium concept. Selten rejected the idea, implicit in Schelling and Frank, that one could consider rational a strategy involving a threat to behave irrationally if a certain outcome was reached at a yet to be played stage of a multistage game. For a strategy to be considered rational, Selten suggested, it must be rational for each of the component subgames. Since a commitment to retaliation after failed deterrence is not rational, neither is the entire strategy of which it forms part. Selten, however, was not concerned with whether, descriptively, such an announced strategy actually *worked* to deter aggression; his interest was whether one could term it rational.

Rather than continuing down a road that leads ultimately to unresolvable semantic and philosophic controversy, it is far better in my view to recast the entire argument—not just part of it—in evolutionary language. One can then explore whether, or under what conditions, a behavioral propensity to retaliate against cheaters or those who appear untrustworthy *even where this is contrary to one's material interest* serves to increase inclusive fitness. Whether such behavior satisfies Selten's or anyone else's definition of individual rationality is beside the point in such analyses.

As has been pointed out, one must guard against concluding that because a behavior can be viewed as rational for a strictly egotistical invader of a population of conditionally cooperative players, and no other invading strategy can do better, it therefore follows that the resulting cooperation has been explained as the consequence of egoistic rational choice or selection only at the individual level. One has accounted for the *maintenance* of an equilibrium—in particular its resistance to invasion by those who might essay defection—but one has not accounted for its origin. In such circumstances, there will be more than one equilibrium that can be sustained by frequency dependent selection. Others will not necessarily involve the cooperative outcomes just described. Through what dynamic evolutionary process has this particular equilibrium been "selected"?

In any event, before trying to model cheating and the problem of detecting it, one must address an "irrational" behavioral predisposition that is logically prior: the practice of first move(r) altruism. The willingness to refrain from cheating (or killing) those who have not previously violated one's trust, even when doing so may be contrary to one's material interest, is a manifestation of first move(r) altruism. Combining this predisposition with the one Frank explicitly recognizes, a willingness to retaliate in response to defection (including defection against third parties), one has, essentially, an organism that practices Tit-for-Tat.

A rational agent—one interested in efficiently advancing its material welfare—would not adopt cooperative or conditionally cooperative strategies except under certain conditions. Conditionally cooperative strategies presuppose that one has already transitioned from single play, in which cooperation is unambiguously altruistic and irrational, to repeated play. In a two player fixed and known duration PD, one has to believe one's counterparty irrational to do other than defect continuously. In two player PDs of indefinite duration, TFT can be defended, assuming others rationally play it as well. It leads to a Nash equilibrium, although not one that is unique. Similarly, in the multiplayer context of the first Axelrod tournament, one would have to have some reason for believing that the frequency of such strategies in the rest of the population would be high in order to rationalize abandoning ALLD. Binmore argues that "no compelling reasons exist for supposing that Nature will necessarily select a neighborly strategy like Tit-for-Tat. Nasty strategies that begin by playing *hawk* have at least as much right to a place on Nature's agenda" (1994, 175).

But perhaps Binmore is wrong. Like Trivers and Frank, he is committed to an individual selectionist framework, and he finesses the transition from an environment of single play PD games to one in which indefinite repetition can be assumed or expected. If, as I am arguing, predispositions to practice first move(r) altruism, favored by selection above the level of the individual organism, are essential in providing a coherent evolutionary account of that transition, then, upon "arrival" in an environment of indefinite repetition, one can interpret these predispositions as facilitating coordination on a conditionally cooperative strategy. Hardwired biases, a legacy of the transition, may, along with historical patterns of interaction, serve the function of a focal point in coordinating on one of a number of possible Nash equilibria (Schelling 1960, 54–58). In such an equilibrium, the guidance of "reason" and a nonrational PD solution module are no longer in conflict. The resulting equilibrium, but not the evolutionary trajectory that led to it, can then be viewed as undergirded by rational choice.

Frank continues: "We will see that the modern presumption of a severe penalty for behaving morally is utterly without foundation" (Frank 1988, xi). This confuses the observation that there is often little penalty for and in fact there may be benefits from operating "morally" within an *established social grouping* with the problem of origination: how such behavior could have survived upon initial appearance at low frequencies. If one assumes, as does Frank, an evolutionary environment in which selection operates only at the individual level, predispositions to behave "morally" can never establish themselves. If groups with a higher frequency of "moral" actors grow more rapidly, and if these groups periodically disperse and re-form, then it is possible for predispositions to "moral" behavior, such as the practice of first move(r) altruism, to survive the penalty they experience at the individual level. And once organisms with such predispositions come to predominate, once $P > \theta$ within a group, to use the language of chapter 2, it may be strictly "rational" for the meanest and most unscrupulous invader to behave as if he or she were strictly moral.

But this is not Frank's argument. If the presumption of a "severe" penalty is "utterly without foundation," does the same hold for a "mild" penalty? He continues: "We have always known that society as a whole is better off when people respect the legitimate interests of others. What has not been clear, least of all to modern behavioral scientists, is that moral behavior often confers material benefits on the very individuals who practice it." True enough. Students of the one-shot PD have long understood that cooperate-cooperate is the most jointly desirable of the three Pareto efficient outcomes; that egoism militates against the achievement of this outcome has always been the central core of the dilemma. We also know that, having invaded a population of conditionally cooperative players, practicing cooperation (behaving morally) confers material benefits on the invader, although there is no longer much that is "moral" about such behavior.

Frank's problem, like that of Trivers, is that he believes that in elucidating mechanisms of maintenance, he has shed light on origin. Upon first appearance, moral or cooperative behavior cannot easily survive the forces of individual level selection arrayed against it, if it is practiced in the presence of other rational actors interested in efficiently advancing their material welfare. At the point of first appearance, the issue is whether amoral behavior confers larger benefits, so that those operating morally suffer a reduction in relative fitness at the individual level.

What we call moral behavior is likely to be altruistic at low frequencies but mutualistic at high. The nub of the problem is transition. In evolutionary biology, altruism is defined as behavior that increases the individual level fitness of other organisms at the expense of the acting organism. Thus what Frank says *cannot be true* if he is addressing the problem of origin. Frank combines the correct empirical observation that altruistic behavior persists with the incorrect belief that only behavior that increases fitness at the level of the individual organism can persist to conclude,[3] by implication, that altruistic behavior must have increased fitness at the individual level if and when it appeared initially at low frequencies in a population.

Hatfields, McCoys, and Margaret Thatcher

The main text of Frank's book (chap. 1) begins with a description of the feud between the Hatfields and McCoys, a classic conflict involving a bloody thirty-six-year-long cycle of vengeance and retribution. A striking empirical claim is immediately advanced: "The McCoys, or the Hatfields, could have ended the violence at any moment by not retaliating for the most recent attack. At each juncture it was clear that to retaliate would produce still another round of bloodshed" (Frank 1988, 2). The conclusion, although intuitively plausible, is neither self-evident nor deducible

---

3. The assumption is incorrect because behavioral tendencies that disadvantage an organism exhibiting them may persist and grow in population frequency if they benefit genes predisposing to them.

using the standard a priori assumptions of economic analysis and game theory.

Frank has just described an episode in which Hatfields attempted to end the dispute once and for all by killing all the remaining members of the main McCoy family. The raid was not entirely successful. How can one conclude normatively, given the apparent intent of this raid, that failure to retaliate would have caused the bloodshed to end? Could one not equally well have argued that failure to retaliate would only have encouraged further aggression and persuaded the Hatfields that the likely costs of completing their agenda were likely to be lower rather than higher?

When one individual, or one group, is intent on destroying another, as was true with the German attempt to annihilate the Jewish people, or the Palestinian commitment to destroy the state of Israel, or the Serbian drive to extirpate Moslems in the Balkans in the 1990s,[4] it is not at all clear that failure to retaliate even when such action involves costs both now and in the future is the key to cessation of violence. The argument that this *is* the key forms the centerpiece of pacifist philosophy, and within the logic of a strictly economic/game theoretic framework, there is a powerful kernel of truth here. Pacifism stresses the irrationality of responding to violence with violence. Opponents of pacifism stress the irrationality of failing to follow through on a policy of deterrence, since absent a willingness and credible commitment to follow through, deterrence is worthless. How else to deter future attacks than to indicate to the attackers what will be the cost of such adventurism? Certainly, such arguments must have prevailed among both the McCoys and the Hatfields, just as they have prevailed among the Palestinians and the Israelis and, until very recently, among Catholics and Protestants in Northern Ireland.

But can a priori economic theory, *unnourished by empirical data on human behavioral propensities,* support at one and the same time both pacifism and the theory of deterrence? The answer is that it cannot. Allowing a role for such data, and partially converting a strictly game theoretic issue into a decision theoretic problem, is a step toward making progress beyond this apparent impasse. It can help, for example, explain coordination on a cooperative equilibrium in an indefinitely repeated game. But it is only a step, because in some contexts, such as the fixed and known duration PD game, or the problem faced by the proposer in a one shot ultimatum game, treating the problem as decision theoretic requires an asymmetry in the degree of rationality attributed to each of the two players.

Economic rationality as Nash understood it, or evolutionary

---

4. I do not necessarily mean to equate the severity or moral status of the intentions of actors in each of these instances.

processes in a model where selection is restricted to the individual level, can no more explain the origin of the second pillar of Tit-for-Tat, a propensity to retaliate in response to defection, than it can the first: refraining from aggression until attacked. Indeed, a rational choice model reflecting psychological egoism, which assumes that agents will and should act efficiently to advance their material welfare, suggests that if it is in one's interest to attack another, one should do so right away, irrespective of past or present behavior of the target of one's attack. Thus one of the most famous pacifists of the twentieth century, the philosopher Bertrand Russell, as well as one of the originators of game theory, John von Neumann, both advocated first strike against the Soviets in the early 1950s. "If you say why not bomb them tomorrow, I say why not today? If you say today at five o'clock, I say why not one o'clock?" The quote is attributed to von Neumann in an obituary published in 1957 (Blair 1957, cited in Poundstone 1992, 143).

Did advocates of first strike consider superpower relations a Prisoner's Dilemma, or did they actually think of themselves as playing the related game of chicken? The question has broader implications. Evolutionary game theorists such as Maynard-Smith have analyzed frequency dependent selection in environments in which organisms interact according to the payoffs of the game of chicken, a variant of which Maynard-Smith called hawk-dove. Some seem to have seen in these analyses an account of the origin of complex social organization.

Chicken is commonly illustrated by the scene in the James Dean film *Rebel without a Cause,* in which two adolescents drive cars as fast as they can toward a cliff (one could also imagine them being driven straight toward each other). The first to swerve loses. A game of chicken is not, however, a Prisoner's Dilemma. In particular, it has two (not one) pure strategy equilibria, and consequently does not share with the PD the feature that defect (don't swerve) is a dominant strategy. If both parties choose not to swerve, the very worst outcome for each results (death). If one knows for certain one's counterparty won't swerve, the rational choice is to swerve. The assumption reflected in the assumed payoffs in the game is that both parties prefer living to dying—to swerve if the other guy doesn't—although they much prefer the outcome where the other guy blinks.

My emphasis in this work—shared by Axelrod, Kavka (1986, 110–11), and many others, including, implicitly, Hobbes—is that PD, not chicken, is the appropriate metaphor for the asocial state. It is the relevant vehicle for thinking about whether altruism, including the altruism reflected in restraint on first strike, can survive a world in which natural selection operates only at the individual level.

One can argue that superpower relations, even though they take place in the absence of an overarching Leviathan, do not reflect the conditions of the original state because such relations are already embedded in a pattern of continuing interaction, making possible self-enforcing cooperative equilibria. Nevertheless, nuclear weapons and other weapons of mass destruction, which raise the possibility of total annihilation of a foe, severely call into question the necessary applicability of the assumption of continued interaction.

Was von Neumann thinking PD when he thought about superpower relations, or was he thinking chicken? William Poundstone, von Neumann's biographer, clearly thought the former descriptor appropriate, inasmuch as he titled his book after the game. To see superpower relations as a PD is to see first strike (defect) as the dominant strategy for both parties: *preferable irrespective of the action of the other party.*

There may be merit in thinking about superpower relations as a sequential rather than a simultaneous move PD. Either player has the option of moving first, but once the move has occurred, the counterparty has an opportunity to respond. To attack first and achieve domination without retaliation is most preferred. But least preferred is the reverse scenario, with mutual incineration preferred to that possibility. Is there any evidence that advocates of first strike had such preferences? Did they really prefer an exchange of nuclear attacks in which they and/or their families were no longer living to being overrun but perhaps ending up alive under communism? Apparently so. A common refrain of first strike advocates in the 1950s was "Better dead than red." These words imply a very precise preference ordering.

If that sentiment is taken seriously, nuclear conflagration (the defect-defect outcome) was preferred to the cooperate-defect outcome (our behavior listed first), although the most preferred outcome was of course defect-cooperate. The worst case imaginable was for us to fail to attack, give up the advantage of the offense, and be attacked and overrun by the enemy (cooperate-defect). Most preferred was the plan of action recommended by von Neumann and Russell: we attack at one o'clock (it is now 12:59), and the enemy is either too devastated, too demoralized, or too rational to strike back (defect-cooperate). But if for whatever reason these calculations turn out to be wrong, and attack does provoke retaliation, nuclear exchange (defect-defect) is still preferable to the prospect of being on the receiving end of an unprovoked attack (cooperate-defect). Finally, since the Nash algorithm assumes one's counterparty is also reasoning in a similar rational manner, one must conclude that a Soviet attack is imminent. Prudence, therefore, along with less noble sentiments, reinforces this conclusion: *push the button now.*

If the alternative of rolling over and surrendering after a first strike (cooperate-defect) is in fact preferred by policymakers to the defect-defect outcome, even though defect-cooperate is preferred to both, then we should characterize superpower relations as a game of chicken. Some policymakers may have so preferred. It is likely that both Kennedy and Khrushchev did so in the Cuban missile crisis. *But not advocates of first strike.* In October 1962 von Neumann had been dead for five years. But we can speculate what his advice would have been. We know that he advocated first strike in 1950. Before he died in 1957 he told the Harvard philosopher Hilary Putnam he was "absolutely certain 1) that there would be a nuclear war and 2) that everyone would die from it" (Putnam 1979, 114).

Where could that absolute certainty have come from? I speculate that it was from the mathematical certainty that defect was a dominant strategy in a one-shot PD, an analysis related to von Neumann's advocacy of first strike. If the question was only when, he wanted to get in the first lick. The idea that hardwired restraints on intraspecific harm stood in the way of nuclear holocaust would have been dismissed by von Neumann as laughable—and perhaps also by many social and behavioral scientists today. But if such a position is laughable, you must ask yourself this: would you have been with von Neumann and Russell in advocating first strike against the Soviets in 1950? Would you, in 1962, have been with Curtis LeMay in criticizing Kennedy's blockade strategy as analogous to Chamberlain's actions at Munich in 1938? And if not, why not?

Neither the Soviets nor the Americans ended up pursuing the course of action recommended by von Neumann. Instead, a policy of mutual assured destruction (MAD) emerged on both sides. At the end of his book Frank discusses the logic of this strategy, which is based on the premise that neither party will attack because the other side will retain sufficient force to launch a devastating reprisal. The apparently straightforward argument here is that while first strike might be rational if the counterparty lacked the capability to retaliate, the situation changes if that condition no longer obtains. But this interpretation misses a subtlety of the von Neumann analysis. His reasoning did not so much count on the absence of a Soviet *ability* to retaliate to our first strike as on the *absence of a will* to do so.

If we follow Selten we are led to conclude that to deter by threat of retaliation and to be deterred from launching a first strike by threat of retaliation are both irrational stances, because once a first strike has been launched by one's counterparty there is nothing left to deter, and retaliation invites yet another round of attacks, with devastation to both sides (Frank 1988, 243). Following through this chain of reasoning regarding the implications of a noncredible threat of retaliation, one can, by assuming one's counterparty is rational, forecast no retaliation and therefore conclude that it is rational to launch a first strike! A key question in nuclear strategy is therefore whether we rely on the Nash algorithm, refined by Selten, for forecasting counterparty behavior or also allow some input from an inductive/empirical methodology for which there is little or no room within the Nash framework.[5] Why? Because as an empirical matter an actor might be willing irrationally to forego first strike if he or she had some grounds for believing the counterparty would irrationally do the same and in particular if the actor believed the counterparty might irrationally retaliate if attacked.

I don't mean to suggest that von Neumann discounted entirely the possibility of retaliation. However, he did not, as did others, view his proposed course of action as recklessly endangering the security of the United States (in fact he believed failure to follow his counsel would have that effect). I do mean to argue that his chain of reasoning was partially premised on the likelihood that the Soviets, if perhaps foolish in delaying their own strike, would nevertheless be rational in the Nash/Selten sense following our attack on them.

The unsettling implications of this logic underlay the Doomsday machine in the film *Dr. Strangelove* and concerns on the part of both U.S. and Soviet nuclear strategists that military personnel might not be capable "irrationally" of pulling the nuclear retaliatory trigger after an initial strike. Repeated *publicized* drills among silo crews in which personnel never knew whether they were dealing with a drill or the real thing were, and are, essential in creating the equivalent of human/mechanical Doomsday machines and making sure their existence was, and is, known to adversaries.[6]

---

5. Dixit and Skeath's analytic narrative of the Cuban missile crisis fudges a bit in suggesting that there was, from the standpoint of subgame perfect rational choice theory, no difficulty in assuming that the United States would carry through on its implied threat of nuclear war if the Soviets had not backed down (Dixit and Skeath 1999, chap. 13). According to the logic of backward induction, the United States would not have done so, and the Soviets, realizing this, should have faced no incentive to agree to withdraw the missiles. Dixit and Skeath speak of making incredible threats credible by creating a situation characterized by "controlled lack of control" (451), and they integrate Graham Allison's emphasis on how bureaucratic politics created an environment where neither leader completely controlled the situation (Allison 1971). It was the Soviet knowledge that this might be so that made the U.S. threat credible. This logic is similar to that used by Richard Nixon when he argued that he wanted his counterparties to think he was a little bit crazy. Thus he wanted to be rationally irrational. But if our thinking is to be precise, and we wish to use the term *rational* in a consistent fashion, we must reject this kind of argument as embodying a contradiction.

6. The Doomsday machine was wired to launch a devastating reprisal if the Soviet Union was attacked. It could not be countermanded. A key element of the script emphasized the Soviets' error in keeping their machine *secret*. In the real world, the design of both U.S. and Soviet (now Russian) launch sites has been driven by two powerful and to some degree opposed imperatives. First, make it impossible for "Lone Rangers" to go ahead and imple-

Frank seems at the same time to say that MAD made and makes sense even though it is not based on assuming strict rationality among players (it does not satisfy the criteria for subgame perfect rationality),[7] whereas the conflict between the Hatfields and the McCoys did not make sense, because actors failed to operate according to the counsel of strict rationality. He can't have it both ways. He cannot dignify pacifism in response to aggression as rational, stigmatizing retaliation as irrational, while at the same time appearing to dignify MAD as rational and opposition to it as irrational. With no more and no less legitimacy, the labels in each of these cases can be reversed. In the absence of additional assumptions about, or empirical evidence pertaining to, human behavioral propensities, rational choice models, by themselves, provide a poor means of predicting outcomes in these cases or, for that matter, of providing useful normative guidance. As Rapaport and Chammah observed, "Once the limits of two-person zero-sum games are transcended, game theory, while remaining a powerful tool for analyzing the logical structure of conflicts of interest, loses its prescriptive power. In this realm, strategically rationalizable courses of action are frequently intuitively unacceptable and vice versa" (1965, 23).

One can as easily use such models to justify a unilateral cease-fire, what Frank seems retrospectively to counsel for the Hatfield-McCoy conflict, or even unilateral disarmament, as to argue the contrary position. Rational choice models unenriched by data on human behavioral propensities are unable to provide guidance as to which type of action is more likely to reduce violence as opposed to encouraging more of it.

I belabor this point because it is the first major proposition advanced by Frank and because the problems with it illustrate the incomplete and contradictory nature of his analysis. The subtitle of *Passions within Reason* is *The Strategic Use of Emotions.* It is indeed common for evolutionary

---

ment the von Neumann/Nash/Russell strategy. This is done through dual key systems with locks positioned at sufficient distance (beyond arms' reach) so that one person cannot turn them both simultaneously. At least two authorized individuals must agree that codes received represent a valid launch order. The second imperative is to train personnel so that, upon receipt of such orders, they will have no more hesitation in turning their key than does a Secret Service agent in interposing her body between a bullet and the president, in spite of the fact that reflection might suggest the irrationality of the action of the Secret Service agent, or that of the missile technician who obliterates multiple enemy cities, given that deterrence has evidently failed. The compromises involved in trying to reconcile these conflicting imperatives do not make for pretty reading or encourage sound sleep. See Leslie 1996 (chap. 1).

7. Again, this is Selten's (1965) language. So long as there is a decision point after the aggressive attack, the threat of retaliation is not credible if each player believes the other to be rational, since at that point deterrence has failed and mutual assured destruction is disastrous for both parties.

biologists to talk about strategies adopted by organisms, even those lack-ing consciousness or intentionality. Economic (normative) game theory models, however, involve conscious choice informed by reason. But the essence of truly emotional behavior is that it represents a short-circuiting of the behavioral guide provided by reason, narrowly and precisely defined. Thus it is a contradiction to interpret the use of emotions as strategic, if that implies that they are chosen rationally. One can, within an evolutionary framework, explore whether organisms with emotional repertoires end up with fitness advantages, but this brings us to the ques-tion of whether, within such a framework, selection is operating only at the level of the individual organism.

If one has been attacked and is told by the attacker to surrender at the risk of further attack, why, from the standpoint of the Nash reasoning algorithms, should the damage one has just incurred, assuming it has not damaged retaliatory capabilities, affect the decision on whether or not to initiate military operations against the other actor? After all, bygones are bygones: the costs are already sunk, and no action can restore the damage. What is the point of sending millions more to their death? *On the other hand,* if one concludes that it is rational now to harm the attacker, because one had previously threatened to do so under these conditions, why was it not rational to do so before the attack, when one would have had the advantage of the offense?

The entire theory of deterrence is based on the proposition that we will *irrationally* forgo the offensive advantage of first strike, that we will *irrationally* retaliate if we are hit by such a strike, and that we can expect our counterparty *irrationally* to act according to the same logic. Mutual assured destruction, a version of Tit-for-Tat, albeit with very large stakes, is premised on the idea that humans possess some sort of specialized neu-robiological subsystems that will predispose us to overrule the counsels of pure reason when confronted with problems of this sort. More concretely, it is premised on the proposition that policymakers will overrule the coun-sel of John von Neumann and Bertrand Russell.

Either there is a separate category of behavior that is not driven by the dictates of reason (emotional behavior), or there is not. If there is a separate category, then emotional behavior is not rational, and rational behavior is not emotional. If there is not a separate category, then Frank's entire discussion of the problem of mimicry (people pretending to be emo-tional when they are not) is irrelevant. Mimicry would be of no value because those attempting it would be perceived to be pretending to be will-ing to act in ways that no one would find credible. If emotional behavior is actually under the control of reason, then it cannot serve to make other-wise noncredible commitments or threats credible.

Whether or not MAD (or, for that matter, Tit-for-Tat) is truly mad (if madness be the absence of rationality) is, from an evolutionary standpoint, beside the point. Genetic factors that predispose toward certain types of behavior, including emotional behavior, may have engendered feedback loops that caused action inclinations underlying them to spread and persist. If they have spread and persisted, and if we understand how that could have occurred, that is all we need to reconcile natural selection and the theory of evolution with a positive, empirically based description of essential human behavioral tendencies.

The theory and practice of deterrence make no sense unless one assumes that humans possess baseline predispositions to behave in fundamentally irrational ways. If we assume all actors are "rational" (concerned only about their own material welfare), each should feel free to launch a first strike without fear of retaliation, secure in the knowledge that an attacked counterparty would realize the irrationality of striking back. Since attack could permit territorial aggrandizement or other political gains, each should attack right away: failure to move first, with its attendant advantages, will be irrational when there is no threat of retaliation. It is in part because an actor assumes his counterparty is not rational and will not accept the argument that bygones are bygones, costs are sunk, and so on, that he does not launch a first strike. Of course the counterparty refrains from first strike because she makes the same calculation. Such behavior may appear intuitively to be in some sense reasonable, but from within the framework of game theoretical analysis, we cannot avoid the conclusion that deterrence works only because each party assumes the other is fundamentally irrational and is prepared to act in a similarly irrational fashion.

In addition to John von Neumann and Bertrand Russell, a number of other military and civilian opinion leaders in both Britain and the United States argued for a first strike against the Soviet Union shortly after its acquisition of the atomic bomb. Those arguing for obliteration of the country President Reagan would subsequently stigmatize as the "evil empire" included Winston Churchill, Douglas MacArthur, and Francis P. Matthews, secretary of the Navy under Truman. Matthews's language was the most florid. He argued that the United States had to overcome whatever unease its democratic heritage might induce and get comfortable with the idea of being "aggressors for peace."

But Russell's stance is the most surprising. Known as a lifelong pacifist and for his work as the first leader of the Campaign for Nuclear Disarmament, throughout the middle 1950s Russell denied his early support for a "preventive war" against the Soviet Union. In a 1959 BBC interview he was confronted with evidence of his earlier advocacy and forced to acknowledge it. When pressed as to why he had so long denied this advocacy, he claimed he had "completely forgotten" his earlier position (Poundstone 1992, 4, 141–64, 195–96).[8]

It is not clear how close the United States came to becoming an "aggressor for peace." Curtis LeMay, commander of the air squadron that delivered nuclear bombs to Hiroshima and Nagasaki and subsequently director of the U.S. Strategic Air Command and an influential military leader throughout the 1950s and into the early 1960s, was widely viewed as favoring such action.[9] Undoubtedly there were similar discussions about the desirability of first strikes on the Soviet side. In the event, cooler, presumably less rational (!) minds prevailed, and the formally irrational MAD strategy took hold on both sides. But why? Why did the latter strategy, which involved mutual grants of first move(r) altruism, prevail, whereas von Neumann's and Russell's quintessentially rational approach did not?

One consideration commonly adduced to explain U.S. hesitation involves the question of whether we came close to having the technical capacity for a first strike that would effectively have obliterated the Soviet Union's ability to inflict damaging retaliation. Advocacy of first strike is sometimes defended on the grounds that there was a brief window in the early 1950s, after the Soviets had the atomic bomb but before they had the hydrogen bomb, during which the United States had that capability. There are historical grounds for questioning whether this was true: the number of operational warheads during this period on either side was small and, to each party, uncertain. If it in fact was true that we had this

---

8. It is an interesting footnote in intellectual history that Russell, at the turn of the century, declared that the theory of evolution, in contrast with mathematical logic, had no significant implications for philosophy (Sterelny and Griffiths 1999, 3). Consistent with his strong support for the centrality of mathematical logic, he questioned the indispensability of causal reasoning, necessary if we are going to allow data on past or baseline behavior to be used in forecasting how humans will act. He compared the law of causality to the British monarchy, both surviving because they are "erroneously supposed to do no harm" (Russell 1918, 180; cited in Sperber 1995, xvi). Consideration of first strike has periodically resurfaced in discussions of U.S. military strategy. Kennedy's secretary of defense, Robert McNamara, examined the option briefly before rejecting it as infeasible, and during the first Reagan administration there was much talk that nuclear war was winnable (Fitzgerald 2000, 92, 150).

9. At a meeting of the Executive Committee of the National Security Council during the Cuban missile crisis in 1962, LeMay basically accused Kennedy of cowardice for his failure to accept plans for aerial bombardment followed by full scale invasion of Cuba: "This blockade and political action, I see leading right into war. . . . I don't see any other solution . . . This is almost as bad as the appeasement at Munich." Kennedy responded, "I appreciate your views. These are unsatisfactory alternatives. The obvious argument for the blockade was [that] what we want to do is to avoid, if we can, nuclear war by escalation or imbalance" (May and Zelikow 1997, 178, 186).

capability, so that we can completely discount the risk that a retaliatory capability would have survived our first strike, we need to ask why the United States did not overcome its scruples as a democratic state and embark on this course of action.

Actually, we need to ask this question even if one makes the contrary assumption, that the limited number of warheads made the United States unable to neutralize the counterparty's retaliatory capability. It was still arguably "rational" to strike first, since the Nash/Selten solution concept counsels assuming one's counterparty is rational and a rational opponent would, having experienced a first strike, have no interest in retaliating (damage has already been done, deterrence failed, what is the point of killing ten million of the enemy just to show you were not bluffing?). An equally powerful line of reasoning reinforces the argument for first strike: whether or not one's counterparty is evil incarnate, *it will perform the same reasoning, and conclude it should attack first.* There will be von Neumanns and Russells on the other side. Therefore, both parties, concluding rationally that attack is imminent, or hoping to get the jump on a less timely (and more foolish) counterparty, launch aggressive war that they may "rationalize" as defensive.[10] The Nash equilibrium is reached in a no regret conflagration, whose logic is captured beautifully by Stanley Kubrick and screenwriter Terry Southern in the closing images of *Dr. Strangelove,* as a wildly happy, indeed ecstatic, U.S. Air Force pilot sits astride a U.S. bomb, waving his cowboy hat as he and his payload fall away from a B-52.

One of the central characters in the screenplay, Jack D. Ripper, is widely believed to have been modeled on Curtis LeMay. The film has been interpreted as reflecting the monumental irrationality, indeed madness, of certain types of strategic thinking, but as I have tried to indicate, a different perspective can suggest the contrary, if one defines madness as the absence of rationality, narrowly and precisely defined.

The same kind of logic that could lead one to conclude that a first strike entailed no risk of retaliation led Yale Brozen, a student of industrial organization, to conclude that one need not worry about the threat of retaliation (for cheating) as a mechanism that might maintain price cartels: "such action would be as irrational and as unlikely as predatory pricing" (Brozen 1982, 136). This type of reasoning, which involves denying the existence or likelihood of a phenomenon for which there is substantial empirical evidence, based on the predictions of a model whose behavioral

---

10. There is, of course, no need truly to "rationalize" first strike: within a Nash universe it is, as von Neumann saw, the epitome of rationality. The fact that even Hitler felt compelled to rationalize his aggressive actions as defensive is testimony to a widely shared human predisposition not to accept the von Neumann conclusions.

assumptions are supported by an incomplete understanding of evolutionary theory, is paradigmatic of a style of economic argument one finds
difficult, sometimes, to credit as scientific. In terms of the decision theoretic character of the problem, the issue in many instances again comes
down to whether the theoretical algorithm or an alternate empirical/induc-
tive methodology gives the better forecasts of counterparty behavior.
Reliance on models premised on the Nash algorithm (enriched by the Selten equilibrium "refinement") leaves unanswered the puzzling empirical
questions of why we do not live in a war of all against all and how it is that
complex social organization, including felonious behavior like cartel formation in the United States (Wiley 1988), as well as that we may value
more positively, ever arises and persists.

Frank continues his discussion of the Hatfield-McCoy conflict by
asking, "What prompts such behavior? Surely not a clear-headed assessment of self-interest. If a rational action is one that promotes the actor's
interest, it is manifestly irrational to retaliate in the face of such devastating costs" (Frank 1988, 2). Here Frank unequivocally embraces the *irrationality* of following through on threats central to a deterrence strategy,
an endorsement that some, indeed Frank himself later in the book, are less
willing to accept. Obviously, many European Jews, using Frank's
Hatfield-McCoy prescription and having witnessed wanton violence such
as occurred on Kristallnacht, made these calculations as they were shipped
by Germans to concentration camps where they met their demise. Those
who participated in the Warsaw uprising reasoned differently. The judgment of whether or not their actions were rational is a philosophical one
that the tools of economics cannot and have not answered. What Frank
takes as obvious is not at all obvious.

We know from historical (nonexperimental) evidence that sometimes
people retaliate even though the costs are high and the chances of their survival almost nil. We know from such evidence that countries often refrain
from attacking their neighbors, even when their neighbors are weak and
there might be gains from so doing. The apparently inconceivable idea
that the United States might engage in hostilities with Canada has figured
as a comic theme in a number of recent films such as the scatalogical but
intermittently funny *South Park: Bigger, Longer, and Uncut* (1999). (Of
course armed forces of the United States *have* invaded Canada twice, most
recently during the War of 1812.) We know from the evidence of history
that strategic bombing rarely weakens the willingness of enemies to resist.
We know from the evidence of history that people will sometimes fight and
die to defend their country.

We also know from the evidence of history that people will sometimes vote (see chap. 1).[11] We know that people will sometimes make anony-mous donations to charity, or leave tips at restaurants they will never revisit, or donate blood for the benefit of others they will never meet (more than nine million people in the United States do so annually) (Hunt 1990, 13; data are from the American Red Cross). We know from experimental evidence that people will sometimes return wallets full of money that they find in the street, or play cooperate in single play PD games, or retaliate at cost to themselves against third party rule violators. Perhaps most impor-tant, we know that people and states will often refrain from first strike, even when doing so exposes them to risk. *None of these behaviors can, con-sidered in isolation, be defended as rational according to the strong definition set forth in the prologue.*

Frank effectively makes the case that people engage in irrational behavior that can be beneficial to a group. But he also argues correctly that such behavior may, if it is sufficiently widely practiced, also be beneficial to the individuals who make up the group. If the behavior is beneficial to the individual, though, how can it be characterized as irra-tional? I suggested a resolution of this conundrum in chapter 2 by propos-ing that the altruistic character of an action can be frequency dependent and that by appealing to group selection we can explain how a behavior, altruistic at low frequency, may increase in frequency to the point that it becomes mutualistic. This is a solution, however, that Frank rules out of bounds ab initio.

Frank's first chapter continues by noting that social and natural sci-entists have invested a great deal of time and resources in attempting to account for seemingly irrational behavior, usually by trying to identify some overlooked source of gain to the agent, certainly a true statement. He mentions two examples of such arguments and his tone implies skepti-cism about each. The first is the treatment of kin selection by evolutionary biologists. His reservations are based not on an objection to its logic but rather on doubts as to whether the evidence for altruism can all be slotted into this category. This is an entirely reasonable concern, since a great deal of altruistic behavior is not directed toward close kin.

The second reference is to IRS tax compliance philosophy: "Or, econ-omists will explain that it makes sense for the Internal Revenue Service to spend $10,000 to prosecute someone who owes $100 in taxes, because it therefore encourages broader compliance with the tax laws." The tone

---

11. As Morris Fiorina puts it, "There have been any number of minor debates—is the probability of a tied election 10^{-15} or 10^{-12} and so forth—but the bottom line remains: no individual's impact on the election outcome is sufficiently great that his or her expected benefit from voting exceeds his or her cost" (Fiorina 1990, 334). Note that the existence of an informed electorate is as much of a paradox for a rational choice theorist.

suggests that Frank views this as obviously silly. But if he thinks MAD is a defensible strategy for a rational actor to pursue, he should certainly approve of what the IRS does. The IRS is behaving irrationally to make its threats credible and increase compliance rates, which helps it achieve its mission. This is another case of behavior that can be rejected as irrational on narrow cost-benefit terms (why should we spend $10,000 of taxpayer money to recover $100?) or defended for its deterrence effect, just as the Israelis defended retaliatory raids for Palestinian rocket attacks. If, on the other hand, Frank is skeptical of the rational foundation of deterrence theory, does he believe that economic theory implies that pacifism is an appropriate policy? Or does his skepticism drive him to advocate first strikes?

The text proceeds to discuss conflicts, such as the Falkland Islands war between Argentina and England.

> Both sides knew perfectly well that the windswept, desolate islands were of virtually no economic or strategic significance. At one point in history it might have made sense for the British to defend them anyway, as means of deterring aggression against other more valuable parts of a far-flung empire. But today, of course, there is no empire to protect. For much less than the British spent in the conflict, they could have given each Falklander a Scottish castle and a generous pension. (Frank 1988, 3)

One can add that for the combined Union and Confederate costs of the Civil War, all slaves could have been purchased at market prices and provided with forty acres and a mule. In fact, in the 1830s in the British Caribbean, government revenues were pledged to service bonds issued to free slaves by buying them from their owners at market prices. So what is the point? Is Frank saying that Margaret Thatcher was irrational to pursue this conflict? He clearly implies that deterrence might have been rational if Britain had still controlled Canada. But earlier he has argued, in discussing the Hatfields and McCoys, that retaliation to aggression is never rational, since the costs have already been incurred (bygones are bygones) and retaliation just invites more death and destruction.

Apparently Thatcher's actions were not motivated by reason, because the beginning sentence of the next paragraph reads as follows: "Many actions, purposely taken with full knowledge of their consequences, are irrational." Frank notes that such behavior is often attributed to passions overcoming reasoned pursuit of self interest and that normatively, it is often claimed, one of our main challenges as humans is to control our passions to avoid such outcomes. He then says, "My claim, on the contrary, is that passions often serve our needs very well" (Frank 1988, 4). But if passionate behavior is truly perceived as purposive, it cannot have the effects Frank claims for it, for it cannot increase a counterparty's subjective belief that you may, in the future, irrationally retaliate for attack. If such behavior serves our needs "very well," it surely does so better than other strategies and therefore must be rational. Yet Frank has just characterized such behavior as irrational. He goes on to talk about how "The apparent contradiction arises . . . because we face important problems that simply cannot be solved by rational action. The common feature of these problems is that to solve them we must commit ourselves to behave in ways that may later prove contrary to our interests."

Thus nuclear antagonists feel compelled to build Doomsday machines or their equivalent, and humans feel compelled to threaten to behave emotionally if challenged or attacked. The "important problems" with which Frank is concerned are strategic: they involve interactions with other parties with decision-making capability. What exactly, however, does it mean for *one* party to "solve" a problem? Does it mean to act in a fashion that Frank views as socially desirable? Does it mean, precisely, to arrive at a Pareto efficient outcome of a game? Not all of the efficient outcomes are as jointly desirable as others. In 1938 Hitler solved his problem by seizing Czechoslovakia. Neville Chamberlain "solved" his problem by not retaliating. Pareto efficient outcome: within the scope of available possibilities, neither party could be made better off without making the other worse off. It was, however, a better "solution" for Hitler than it was for Chamberlain or the Czechs. During the Cold War, on the other hand, the United States and the Soviet Union "solved" their problem by spending hundreds of billions of dollars on arms that most military personnel had no intention of ever using, because they expected deterrence to work. Pareto inefficient outcome. Nevertheless personnel were "fully prepared" to use them had deterrence failed, even though they knew that to do so would be irrational.

Committing to be irrational cannot serve one's interest if one has no intention of retaliating if first attacked and if this is so perceived. But if one intends to retaliate after attack, then the overall strategy cannot be subgame perfect rational. How then can such behavior be truly purposive? If the terms *rational* and *irrational* are to have meaning, we cannot simultaneously characterize behaviors as, at one and the same time, both (this was the essence of the issue that bothered Selten). Again, the advantage of an evolutionary approach is evident. If one allows multilevel selection, one can argue that behavior that reduces the fitness of an individual organism may nevertheless increase in populations if it increases the inclusive fitness of the genes that predispose toward it.

Frank goes on to analyze deterrence explicitly. An individual who has a reputation for striking back, even at great cost, may not be tested because of the fear of such retaliation. It is, of course, this logic that underlies the argument that a large standing army, along with air and naval forces, is the surest way to prevent these military capabilities from being used. The strategy of Mutual Assured Deterrence (MAD) was associated with the absence of nuclear war between the United States and the Soviet Union during the four decades of the Cold War. One can argue that by spending so much for arms, both the United States and the Soviet Union signaled their willingness to behave irrationally—reducing consumption levels to build more and more bombs and delivery systems. Thus, according to this logic, the other side had fewer doubts that their opponent would respond to a first strike with devastating retaliation, even though the injury of a first strike could not be undone and even though retaliation would result in tens of millions of additional deaths. Of course, one can ask, from a strictly decision theoretic standpoint, why evidence that one's counterparty is behaving irrationally should increase the precision of one's estimate of his or her future behavior.

Large military forces can be accumulated not only by those who wish to deter aggression but also by those who see war, as did Carl von Clausewitz, as a continuation of political intercourse by other means (Clausewitz 1873, chap. 1). There were those on both sides of the Cold War who believed that their counterparty intended to acquire a first strike capability and use its threat or actuality as a vehicle for territorial aggrandizement or world domination. This fear led to arguments on both sides in favor of preemptive attacks to remove options from the accumulator, arguments that dovetailed with perhaps less morally defensible aspirations for domination or territorial gain. These mutually reinforcing arguments remind us that in Prisoner's Dilemmas, both prudence—action designed to protect against catastrophic loss—and avarice—action intended to reap the largest possible gain—counsel defection.

MAD may have prevented the defect-defect outcome, but in doing so it established a hair trigger, and hair raising, international environment, in which the slightest miscalculation, data processing error, or failure in the chain of command could have unleashed untold destruction. Why did MAD, this formally irrational strategy, succeed in preventing mutual destruction? Perhaps we were lucky. But a contributing factor was assuredly that the game of deterrence played itself out within the context of a configuration of human reasoning and behavioral propensities that implicitly guided the choices of key players. That configuration is not adequately reflected in the typical assumptions of normative game theory or in the standard economic model embodying a strong version of rationality.

There are other historical examples: certainly mid–twentieth century Germany, where deterrence failed, or perhaps was not seriously attempted, and the obvious attractiveness and rationality of aggressive war prevailed. Taking a broad view, however, what is puzzling from the standpoint of a strictly rational approach is not how much war there is but how little. Again, without introducing empirical evidence on human behavioral propensities and, ideally, accounting for these propensities within a consistent evolutionary framework, rational choice models in and of themselves cannot take us very far in helping us deal with the vexing problems of deterrence, armament, and disarmament.[12] Nor can they take us very far in understanding the origin of complex social organization, with which these issues are formally analogous.

Unfairness, Ultimatums, and Bargaining Games

From the standpoint of a nation or ruler, the most effective deployment of military power may well be where it can be used as a tool for intimidation, and military and political objectives can be obtained with little or no damage to one's forces. There is an old Jack Benny joke in which the comedian describes being held up by a mugger who announces, "Your money or your life!" Benny replies, very slowly, "I'm thinking." The humor arises because we see the conflict between the apparently rational response (hand over the money) and our knowledge that some people will, as does Benny, hesitate or, in the extreme, infuriated by this demand, fight or throw the money into the river.

Such "irrational" behavior is highlighted in ultimatum game experiments involving a slightly less extreme story line. In these games, a "proposer" offers a division of a fixed sum. If the counterparty accepts the division, the money is split as proposed. Otherwise, neither gets anything. The subgame perfect Nash equilibrium for a game involving $10, with a minimum denomination offer of $ 0.01, is for the proposer to demand $9.99 and the counterparty to accept $ 0.01. Most experimental subjects, however, reject such demands, and therefore most who demand $9.99 end up with nothing.

Earlier, with regard to the Falklands war, Frank argued, "Many actions, purposely taken with full knowledge of their consequences, are irrational." Is rejecting a positive offer in an ultimatum game an example of such action? Frank seems ambivalent. On the one hand, those who

---

12. As Rapaport and Chammah concluded in 1965, "it is typical of arguments in support of a particular style of play in Prisoner's Dilemma that the features of the game which support the argument can be turned around to support the opposing argument" (212).

reject such offers seem clearly to prefer nothing to something—a clear violation of a strong version of rationality. On the other hand, Frank repeatedly emphasizes the individual benefits (consequences) that may result from walking away. He argues that a person known to "dislike" an unfair bargain can "Credibly threaten to walk away from one, even when it is in her narrow interest to accept it. By virtue of being known to have this preference she becomes a more effective negotiator." The individual interest argument is valid, however, only if negotiation or play of the game continues, that is, if the interaction is repeated. Yet rejection is observed experimentally *in single play games where anonymity is assured.* Some individuals, finding themselves in Mr. Benny's situation, instead of handing over the money, will make unprintable suggestions to the mugger, possibly contributing to the loss of their life. The behavior observed in ultimatum games cannot simply be a result of rational calculation based on the expectation of repeated interaction.

Those who believe that these results are the consequence of measurement errors or peculiarities of the experimental design pursue two lines of argument. The first is to argue that the stakes are too small to get people's attention. The repetition of the experiments in third world countries such as Indonesia casts doubt on this view (Cameron 1999). It is possible that the minimum offer (but not dollar amount) typically necessary to elicit assent might fall as a percentage of the stake as the stakes increased. On the other hand, a risk averse proposer may be inclined to offer a more even split to reduce the probability of ending up with nothing. Does anyone really believe that if $10 million were involved, the Nash/Selten prediction would be realized? The subgame perfect equilibrium offer is still $0.01 for you (and $9,999,999.99 for me). Would you accept such an offer? And supposing you were offered $2 million knowing that your proposer would, if you accepted, get $8 million, would you accept, or would the prospect of envy lead you to reject it? Or is your rejection based on a more simplistic distaste for unequal division? How much difference would anonymity make, and if it makes a difference, why should it make a difference? How drastically would your behavior change if you were told you were playing against a computer, and again, why should it matter at all? It is unlikely that raising the stakes by several orders of magnitude would eliminate the anomaly in games played with other humans.

The second route is to say that the experimental environment is unfamiliar and people need time to learn how to play the game. The ultimatum game is so transparent this seems on the face of it unlikely. What is there to learn? There is some evidence that repetition may cause a drift in the direction of the theoretical prediction. But although the anomaly may be reduced, it is not eliminated.

Other parts of Frank's analysis suggest that rejecting a positive offer *is* one of those "irrational" actions, taken with full knowledge of their consequences. At times, he appears to second the view, advanced by behavioral economists such as Thaler, that such behavior is the result of a taste for "fairness" that is widespread in human populations. The fairness approach presumably implies that this taste is so powerful that it can override a desire for individual gain. But Frank does not abandon the instrumental argument that cultivating a reputation for fairness is helpful in achieving ends: in fact, as we have seen, it is central. If the latter position is advanced, then there is no other-regarding aspect to these actions. Talk about fairness is a sham: rejections of offers are simply strategic choices made in games known to be iterated.

From a game theoretic standpoint, there are indeed several problems with the fairness as instrument argument. If actors are rational, why would they even bother to talk about, or listen to talk about, fairness? If on the other hand subjects are bringing to these games heuristics that work well in day-to-day life, not fully absorbing the fact that the games are one shot, one has a related problem. Bargaining advantage through reputation cultivation comes from a credible willingness to walk away, *irrespective of the character of the offer.* One could equally well argue that being known as someone who loves *unfair* bargains, particularly where they benefit *that person,* and is prepared to walk away unless the deal provides disproportionate benefits *to her* will be at a great advantage in negotiating, provided of course that repeated interactions are expected and people keep track of reputations.

The purpose of running single play games with anonymity is to control experimentally for iteration and reputation effects. If that control has been successful, then we are picking up the consequences of predispositions that are hardwired and/or the effect of socialization/enculturation. I am inclined to think that the hardwired component is more important than those who advance the fairness interpretation suggest. A taste for fairness paints a very positive face on the rejection behavior, but it seems clear that knee-jerk reactions of anger and the prospect of envy—two emotions not thought to be reinforced by socialization/enculturation—are intimately entwined in these results. A more plausible view is that we are hardwired with biological Doomsday machines, machines that can be triggered if we are offered what we view as an insultingly small share of a resource to be divided. Positing an innate and—by Nash's definition—irrational concern with fairness is consistent with this behavior but may not be the best characterization of it.

We know from experimental evidence that people will walk away from deals that provide them some benefit but not as much as the offerer.

We do not know, however, if people will also walk away from deals in which they are offered disproportionate benefits. Since proposers do not normally propose to take *less* than a 50 percent share in ultimatum gains, one would need to use confederates posing as experimental subjects to explore this possibility, or else query subjects as to how they would act were such an offer to be made. Would most subjects simply take the money and run? Finding that a significant fraction would also walk away from such offers would strengthen the fairness argument. Finding that they do not would support the Doomsday machine interpretation.

It might appear that in interpreting rejections in terms of hardwired Doomsday machines, I am embracing the Frank/Hirshleifer view of the strategic role of emotions. The critical difference in our views concerns the understanding of the term *strategic*. If the term characterizes conscious, deliberate choice in situations involving human interaction, then their analysis appears to involve a contradiction. My objection is that if the emotions are truly strategic in the sense that they are consciously chosen, they cannot fulfill their assigned role of making commitments credible or guaranteeing threats. Frank states clearly at several points that such actions are irrational, but then repeatedly backtracks, suggesting that they are sort of rational.

On the other hand, if emotional responses are human Doomsday machines, they can unambiguously be viewed as irrational from a Nash/Selten standpoint. If they reflect hardwired "knee-jerk" reactions (they are often characterized as such), then they are not undertaken as the result of calculation and with an orientation to the possibility of future benefit. They are not usefully interpreted as the consequence of constrained maximization of a utility function. They cannot then be viewed as strategic in the sense in which economists typically use the term.

If a propensity to undertake such action imposes a fitness cost on the individual, which it clearly does in an asocial state, since something is better than nothing, then the predispositions underlying such behavior cannot have been favored by individual level selection upon initial appearance at low frequencies in a population. Thus, if these predispositions are real and important, as the experimental and observational data suggest they are, I conclude that they must have been favored at some point by selection at a higher level.

The Symmetric Bargaining Problem

The (asymmetric) ultimatum game needs to be carefully distinguished from the symmetric bargaining problem, in which two individuals must independently propose the share they will take of a fixed resource, with the knowledge that if the shares exceed 100 percent, neither will get anything. Brian Skyrms has developed an intriguing argument that a propensity to propose a 50 percent share for self is likely to emerge as the result of frequency dependent but individual level selection in human populations. Such a process will lead to outcomes of equal division, seeming to reflect a taste for fairness but actually the result of the simple fact that organisms that take 50 percent are likely to do better over the long run and come to exhibit high frequencies within populations. The behavior that gives rise to these results is not altruistic or other regarding, although it has been interpreted as such. Thus equal division in these problems, commonly understood as the consequence of a cultural focal point (Dixit and Skeath 1999, 212), may actually have an underlying biological foundation, but not one that required group selection to evolve.

Here is Skyrms's argument. In the symmetrical bargaining problem there exists a multiplicity of informed rational choice Nash equilibria, ranging from a 50/50 split to a 99/1 split and including all possible combinations of divisions that sum to 100 percent. Each is a Nash equilibrium because, conditional on the other's demand, neither player could have done better by making a different demand and in fact would have done worse. For example, consider a 90/10 split. As the second party, I examine retrospectively the advantages of having asked for 11 percent and realize under that scenario I would have gotten nothing. If I consider having asked for 9 percent, I realize I would have gotten less than the 10 percent I did. Using similar logic, the first individual has no regrets about not having demanded 91 percent, because she realizes she would then have received nothing. She also has no regrets about not having asked for 89 percent, since 90 is preferable to 89.

Skyrms's insight is that a genetic predisposition to demand 50 percent in such circumstances can evolve as a consequence of the same type of frequency dependent selection whereby Fisher explained the rough constancy of mammalian sex ratios (see chap. 2). Begin, for example, with a society in which everyone demanded 70 percent, in which no one would get anything. A mutant invader that demanded 30 percent or less would do better than the group average and would begin to spread. As the numbers of such individuals increased, mutants who demanded 35 percent could begin to establish a foothold, and so forth, until, through a continuing process of frequency dependent selection, the population would stabilize, composed of those who demanded 50 percent. Demanding 50 percent, therefore, is an evolutionarily stable strategy, in the sense in which Maynard-Smith and Price (1973) first intended it. Indeed, as Skyrms (1996) notes, it is the *unique* ESS of the symmetric bargaining game, even though it is only one of an infinite number of Nash equilibria in the two person game (11).[13]

In this instance, evolutionary game theory permits us to select, from among a multiplicity of informed rational choice Nash equilibria, the one such equilibrium that is evolutionarily stable. The replicator dynamic is such that one will reach this equilibrium irrespective of the starting point. A notable aspect of Skyrms's analysis is that the explanation of the emergence of equal division in the symmetric bargaining problem need not involve other-regarding behavior and need not appeal to selection above the level of the individual.

The behavior observed in asymmetric bargaining (ultimatum) games, however, is different: something else is involved. The interplay between this "something else" and a concern for individual wealth maximization is, to be sure, subtle and complex.[14] The ultimatum (and the dictator) game results reflect behavior that, unlike that in the symmetric bargaining game, cannot, upon initial appearance at low frequency, have been favored by the forces of individual level selection. Most people, asked if they want $2, will accept. Offered $2 but told that if they accept, the offerer will get $8, and if they reject, neither will get anything, many people reject. In economic terms, such behavior cannot be viewed as rational.

Irrational Play in PD and
Ultimatum Games: Implications

The evidence from single play PD games reveals a normatively irrational behavioral propensity to play cooperate. This corresponds in nonexperimental situations to giving up the advantage of the first move in what might or might not end up as a game with more than one stage. The ultimatum game results reveal a normatively irrational willingness to retaliate against those who have not made such grants (offering an "unfair" bargain is interpreted here as an aggressive move, analogous to a failure to make a grant of first move(r) altruism). The Fehr and Gächter results show that people are prepared, irrationally, to retaliate against those who violate social rules, a propensity that can be interpreted itself as a social

---

13. There are a number of complications, including the possibility of polymorphous equilibria that are inefficient in the sense that they involve a lower average payoff than does equal division but that, once established, are strictly stable. The seriousness of the problem depends in part on how divisible the good is, that is, the "granularity" of the problem.

14. Were that not the case, one would see no differences in the results of ultimatum and dictator games (where the proposer simply offers a division, keeping his or her share in any case, while the acceptor has the choice of taking or not taking what is offered) (Roth 1995b, 328). In fact, the average demand by the proposer in dictator games is larger, although it is still well below 100 percent.

rule. In order to explain the origin and development of complex social organization, we need these predispositions.

Once a network of complex and multiple relations of reciprocity among non-kin has been established in a manner that participants view as reliably predictable, these practices become, for the marginal invader interested in efficiently advancing her material welfare, increasingly rational, provided we accept as rational the use of empirical algorithms for predicting the behavior of counterparties. Retaliation for defection becomes increasingly unnecessary, and as this happens, cooperation becomes increasingly drained of its altruistic content. The devotion of constant vigilance to monitoring those around one for signs of hostile intent (defection) can begin to take on the appearance of irrationality, earning its devotees such labels as *paranoid.* Paranoid behavior can be and generally is viewed as irrational because once we accept an empirical (inductive) methodology for forecasting counterparty behavior, the expected benefits of detecting the rare defection are more than outweighed by the costs of constant vigilance. Yet from the standpoint of the Nash algorithm, tightly embedded in most normative game theory, one can ask why the "paranoid personality" is not exhibiting rationality in its highest order, refusing to fall for the scandal of induction in making predictions about what others intend for him or her. Is not eternal vigilance the price of freedom?[15]

Although in many instances a statistical methodology offers help in determining, for practical purposes, a normatively rational action, it does not do so in all. Just as insurance companies are unwilling to insure against hazards unless they have a broad and relevant statistical basis upon which to base actuarial prediction, humans are sometimes faced with circumstances for which experience has not prepared them and in which they lack a database from which reliably predictive forecasts of counterparty behavior may be made. From the standpoint of the empirical algorithm, the least predictable and for that matter perhaps most interesting human behavior occurs at the point where it is no longer clear, or has not become clear, whether or not one is in a relationship whose continuance is reliably predictable. At such points one enters a twilight zone where the character of

---

15. Paranoids cannot always be described as irrational, even using this empirical argument. The first U.S. secretary of defense, James Forrestal, was hospitalized at Walter Reed after his doctors diagnosed him as delusional: he was persuaded he was being followed everywhere by Israeli secret agents. It turned out subsequently that he *was* being followed everywhere by Israeli secret agents, who were concerned about his possible pro-Palestinian leanings. Forrestal, who subsequently jumped to his death from a window of the hospital, was clearly disturbed, but his mental state was most likely not improved by the fact that no one would believe him (Sagan 1977, 181).

certain behaviors wavers uncertainly from being rational to being irrational or vice versa. Cooperative acts regain some of their original altruistic character, because they now, again, expose the practitioner to real risk
of harm. Attention to the behavior of others that might normally be
viewed as excessive becomes prudent. In this crepuscular zone, one may
feel compelled to make good on threats to retaliate, damaging the retaliator without garnering obvious benefits. But of what good is preserving a
reputation for being tough if your counterparty has signaled that the relationship is over? Or is it? These moments, fraught with ambiguity and relatively rare in an individual's lifetime, provide glimpses into the evolutionary challenges of explaining the origin of the behavior that underlies
complex social organization.

The single play ultimatum game, like the single play PD game, is particularly important in understanding essential human tendencies because
it illuminates in harsh relief predispositions that are strictly irrational,
according to the Nash algorithm, simply because the experimental design
has eliminated any possible role for reputation or calculations based on a
presumption that the relation will continue. If situations are in flux, of
course, as they are in most psychological thrillers, then all bets are off as to
what is normatively correct. The empirical forecasting methodology is
most likely highly inaccurate, because of lack of adequate historical data
for the particular individuals involved, and Nash algorithm predictions
based on deduction may not be any better. The ability to fall back on
knowledge of essential human tendencies, knowledge that from a decision
theoretic standpoint can be viewed as base rate data, may be all one has to
rely on. At this point, since defection is strictly dominant in a one-shot PD,
the relevant question becomes whether that empirical methodology turns
out to be relevant in forecasting one's own behavior.

What, then, should we tell our students (or our children)? That in a
great many (but not all) environments they are likely to encounter, virtue
will indeed be rewarded and one will lose by being unvirtuous. On the
other hand, in single play interactions, where social structures are fluid,
breaking down, or not yet established; where continuing interactions cannot be, or can no longer be, reliably predicted; where past behavior
embodied in reputations is no guide to the future; and where considerations about the value of investing in reputation may be nugatory, no such
guarantee applies, and the normatively "correct" play is to defect. Nevertheless, even in such fluid circumstances, a great many humans will cooperate (this is a descriptive statement), and because they do, being virtuous
may turn out to be less damaging to one's health and wealth than might
otherwise be predicted. Children (and adults) must be prepared to under-

stand the implications of the regularity and predictability of routine social existence, at the same time they are prepared, if necessary, to confront true social dilemmas in situations of great fluidity.

If the decision is a matter of life and death, it is not surprising that some prudent individuals may feel drawn to a solution that exposes them to least risk; it is indeed a behavior that would be favored by the forces of individual level selection. What is surprising is that so many people are not. Nonconsequentialist ethical systems—those that, unlike utilitarianism, sever a link between an action's rightness and its consequences—codify norms that reinforce playing cooperate in such circumstances. But they do not explain the origin of the underlying behavioral propensity that, since it cannot have been favored by individual level selection, must have been favored by selection at a higher level. That behavioral propensity, in turn, helps account for why organized and predictable social structures are the empirically dominant environment for humans. They help explain why, above and beyond our interactions within a kin group, we do not live in a continual war of all against all and, perhaps, why the Cold War did not turn hot.

Making grants of first move(r) altruism is, as is reflected in the terms used, altruistic from an evolutionary standpoint and not likely to be encouraged by selection at the individual level alone. It is harder at first to interpret the act of retaliation as altruistic: it will almost surely reduce the fitness of the practitioner from the standpoint of individual level selection, but it is hard to see how it increases the fitness of the person on the receiving end. The solution is to understand that the true beneficiary of the action is not necessarily the individual(s) at whom the action is directed but rather all other members of one's group, who, because of one's willingness, and that of others, to punish defectors, find themselves less at risk from deviant behavior.

Emotional Lability as a Doomsday Machine

We now come back to the core of Frank's argument: "Being known to experience certain emotions enables us to make commitments that would otherwise not be credible. The clear irony here is that this ability, which springs from a failure to pursue self-interest, confers genuine advantages. Granted, following through on these commitments will always involve avoidable losses. . . . The problem, however, is that being unable to make credible commitments will often be even more costly. Confronted with the commitment problem, an opportunistic person fares poorly" (1988, 5). Thus Frank appears to embrace the interpretation of a publicly known susceptibility to emotional display as a human Doomsday machine, resolving the problem of subgame imperfection associated with noncredible threats or commitments. The ability to make credible commitments means the ability to telegraph likelihood that in the future one may behave irrationally, for example, by refusing to walk out on a commitment even when it subsequently becomes advantageous to do so.

The subtitle of the book, *The Strategic Use of Emotions,* is an indication of how central to it is the idea that the display of emotional lability (changeableness or unpredictability) is as important for individuals as were publicized attack drills for U.S. and Soviet nuclear missile crews. This idea is key to Frank's understanding of how other-regarding behavior originates and is sustained, and it seems to betoken a catholic approach to human cognition and choice, one open to the implications of modularity. On page 6, for example, he states that we are born with certain tastes and drives and that "rational assessment is only one of many forces that can arouse the feelings that govern behavior directly." This position raises the possibility that functionally specialized neurobiological subsystems might, in certain cases, overrule the counsel of our general reasoning ability. Frank suggests that emotions and feelings reflect the operation of such variegated behavioral impellers, apparently reflecting a willingness to abandon the restriction that the only behavioral predispositions that may be presumed are those reflecting the operation of rational choice directed at efficiently serving material self-interest.

He goes on to quote Jerome Kagan: "Construction of a persuasive rational basis for behaving morally has been the problem on which most moral philosophers have stubbed their toes. I believe they will continue to do so until they recognize what Chinese philosophers have known for a long time: namely feeling, not logic, sustains the superego" (Kagan 1984, xiv, cited in Frank 1988, 12). But no sooner has Frank laid the groundwork for an acceptance of views such as Kagan's than he backpedals: "The emotions may indeed sustain the superego. But as the commitment model will make clear, it may well be the logic of self interest that ultimately sustains these emotions." Here Frank recommits himself to the rational choice framework in general and that of normative game theory in particular and, at the same time, signals his intention to integrate traditional economic analysis with an evolutionary approach. This will lead him again and again to argue, untenably, that one and the same behavior is at the same time irrational and rational. He underlies his intent several pages later in writing that "what I hope to show here is that [the presence of emotions] is in perfect harmony with the underlying requirements of a coherent theory of rational behavior" (16).

We are back at square one in terms of method. The attempted marriage of economic and evolutionary approaches underestimates the differences between them and assumes that they are necessarily of the same species and thus likely to produce viable offspring. This is a misconception! To the degree that standard rational choice models, which emphasize individuals acting efficiently to improve their own material welfare, are translated into evolutionary language, by definition they must involve models in which selection operates only at the level of the individual organism. This restriction makes such models incapable of accounting for the origin and persistence of altruistic behavioral predispositions toward those other than kin.

Again, all concern with the issue of credibility presupposes a solution to the more fundamental problems of social organization, so that there is a reliably predictable likelihood of repeat interactions. Emotions as signals of credible commitment cannot be the explanation for the origin of cooperation because origination involves moving from an absence of social organization, in which structures of interaction cannot reliably be predicted to persist, to a situation where they can. Credibility or reputation can only be an asset within the subsequent state: within the context of relatively established social structures. Trivers's initial rescuer must act because of some innate predisposition, not out of any necessary expectation of future gains from interaction based on prior learning.

Frank's Treatment of Evolutionary Theory

In chapter 2 of *Passions within Reason* Frank attributes the strongest foundation for the self-interest model to Darwin, whom he incorrectly identifies as emphasizing individual level selection alone. As Frank notes, "If human nature, too, was shaped by the forces of natural selection, the apparently inescapable conclusion is that people's behavior must be fundamentally selfish" (1988, 24). It is never clear, however, whether Frank means that this conclusion is only "apparently" inescapable or that it is *in fact* inescapable. If natural selection is indeed allowed to operate only at the level of the individual organism, then the latter conclusion obtains, which would appear to contradict Frank's view that other-regarding behavior is an empirically important behavioral category. Although familiar with work in evolutionary biology, Frank does not proceed along the one route that would permit him to avoid this contradiction. That route is the one Darwin himself suggested, a route that involves the possibility of natural selection operating at multiple levels.

Frank goes on to discuss Hamilton's concept of inclusive fitness, pointing out that its limitation (as generally implemented) is a failure to account for altruistic behavior toward non-kin. Even if hunter-gatherer societies were closely related, one still should not expect to see group positive behavior based on such models. Second cousins share only 1/32 of their genes; they are on this basis close to indistinguishable from total strangers (1988, 27). This is an important point for those who believe that kin selection alone solves the problem of explaining human altruism in relatively small groups.

Frank continues by discussing Trivers's theory of reciprocal altruism in which A scratches B's back in the hope and expectation that B will scratch A's back. That this often happens is beside the point. It does not explain why those who accept grooming but do not reciprocate do not come to dominate a group: they will clearly be favored by individual level selection (Hamilton 1975, 150). Frank argues that Trivers's model cannot explain "hard core altruism," and Frank is right. He goes on to discuss Tit-for-Tat and the PD problem and is perceptive in understanding some of the limitations of Axelrod's work, in particular the implicit assumption that counterparties have no choice but to interact with each other repeatedly (Frank 1988, 32).

Frank indicates awareness of the possibility of group selection (Frank 1988, 37–39) but rejects its likelihood, apparently because he views these ideas as out of favor within the evolutionary biology community. His position on this issue is strictly conventional, and one can find innumerable examples of similar argument elsewhere. He does not discuss the import of biological evidence on female-male sex ratios in arthropods; or the evolution of virulence in microorganisms; or the work of Price, Steven Frank, Wade, Sober and Wilson, and others who have effected a theoretical and empirical defense of its possibility. Much of this work was available when *Passions within Reason* was published, although its implications had not been as forcefully and widely articulated as is true today.

As scholars we are only human, and it is perhaps understandable when we are loathe to challenge majority opinion, particularly in an area outside of our area of training. But respect for intellectual authority has the potential to get us into serious trouble. The problem with rejecting out of hand the multilevel selection route, aside from the fact that the reasons given for so doing are weak (logic and evidence are generally sounder than argument from authority), is that doing so gives rise to analysis that is internally contradictory. In any event, although Frank quotes E. O. Wilson in support of the antigroup selectionist consensus, Wilson is now more equivocal, describing the 1998 Sober and D. S. Wilson book as "important and original," containing "the definitive contemporary statement on higher level selection and the emergence of cooperation" (quoted on cover). And although economists are fond of quoting E. O. Wilson in defense of their "hard-headed" approach, he does not return the compliment. Indeed, in his 1998 book, *Consilience,* he is openly disdainful of what economists have contributed to our understanding of evolution.[16]

Finally, Frank considers whether "Cultural Conditioning"—socialization or the inculcation of norms—can account for self-sacrificing behavior. His most important observation is that adherence to norms is not advantaged by the forces of individual selection (1988, 40). Thus the problem posed by adherence to norms is the same as the problem posed by any form of altruistic behavior (as I have noted in chap. 3, adherence to norms is altruism writ small).

Frank observes that norms may "restrict our baser impulses as well as encourage those considered more noble." For example, he indicates that norms may restrain the "irrational" pursuit of vengeance, noting that the maxim *an eye for an eye, a tooth for a tooth* was intended to restrain rather than encourage the pursuit of vengeance (Tit-for-Tat requires matching injury for injury, not exceeding it) (39). But Frank needs to be careful. By suggesting that "excessive" vengeance is irrational, he implies that retaliation calibrated to the dimensions of the injury *is* rational. Proportionality (let the punishment fit the crime)—a key consideration in calibrating U.S. retaliation against terrorist attacks—may work best empirically, but defending the policy as more "rational" than a policy of no retaliation or one embodying tenfold escalation is fraught with difficulty.

If the purpose of threatened retaliation is deterrence, any level of ex post retaliation once deterrence has failed is not rational, according to the narrow and precise definition implicit in the Nash/Selten method for analyzing situations of strategic interaction. Frank intermittently embraces this position, most obviously in his opening castigation of the folly of the behavior of the Hatfields and McCoys. So which is it? Is retaliation according to the *lex talionis*—an eye for an eye—rational, or is it not? In order to push our understanding forward, we must adopt a clear definition and adhere to it consistently. This Frank does not do.

Chapter 2 provides an intelligent overview of explanations of altruistic behavior other than his own. Most of his positions here are similar to mine, with the important exception of his summary rejection of the multiselection route. In chapter 3, Frank reaffirms his objective: "My task . . . is to make use of a simple idea from economics to sketch an alterna-

---

16. "The enterprise within the social sciences best poised to bridge the gap with the natural sciences, the one that most resembles them in style and self confidence, is economics. The discipline, fortified with mathematical models, garlanded annually by its own Nobel Memorial Prize in Economic Science, and rewarded with power in business and government, deserves the title often given to it, Queen of the Social Sciences. But its similarity to 'real' science is often superficial and has been purchased at a steep intellectual price" (E. O. Wilson 1998, 212–13).

tive individual selectionist avenue along which altruism and other forms of apparently self-serving behavior might have emerged" (Frank 1988, 45). As we have seen, this simple idea is not so simple after all, and his quest is quixotic, for the simple reason that behavioral propensities cannot simultaneously reduce individual level fitness and increase it. Once contingent cooperators have become established in a population, and repeated interactions can be assumed, cooperation by an invader is no longer altruistic but becomes, if we resolve the issue of how we know, or how we forecast, the strategies of counterparties, self-serving. But that does not mean that a population-wide pattern of cooperation has emerged out of the behavior of egoists. These confusions are reaffirmed at the end of chapter 3, when Frank talks about how "the fact that trustworthy persons do receive a material payoff is of course what sustains the trait within the individual selectionist framework" (69). True enough, but demonstrating what sustains group cooperation is not the same as explaining its origin.

Reputations and Induction

Frank goes on to explain how considerations of reputation may make it rational for people to be moral. For example: "Someone who is caught cheating on one occasion creates the presumption he may do so again" (Frank 1988, 71). Descriptively, it is clear that the ability of individuals to keep track of others' reputations, and to update these reputations inductively based on repeat performance, helps sustain social relations in established settings. From a game theoretic perspective it may also be viewed as facilitating coordination on a particular rational choice equilibrium when there may be others (Greif 1989; Klein 1997). But there are two difficulties in appealing to this mechanism as explanation for the origin of cooperation among non-kin. First, for obvious reasons, it cannot be used in accounting for transition from one-shot to repeated interaction. Second, we have introduced a role for an empirical/inductive methodology for forecasting counterparty behavior. This runs contrary to an important methodological principle in canonical game theory.

David Hume argued in *An Enquiry Concerning Human Understanding* (1741) that induction was deductively invalid, and his arguments have never been effectively refuted. In exploring a deductive rather than an inductive methodology for forecasting behavior, Nash in a sense followed Hume's logic. Although I believe there is good reason to study reputational mechanisms from a descriptive standpoint, and that there are practical reasons to make use of them in many instances of day-to-day life, one can argue, as implicitly did Nash and other economists who follow him, that it is normatively irrational to base decisions on them in a world whose structure may be changing and, more fundamentally, that inductive inferences are at best speculations. This is a prospect that keeps actuaries and insurance company executives, as well as philosophers, up at night (Pinker 1997, 351).

But if we stick with the Nash algorithm, our practical problems are more severe and our forecasts of behavior much worse. Reputational data must now be deemed of no value for this purpose. Using the Nash algorithm, which implies that dispositions, as opposed to situations, have no influence on human behavior, one has no way of rejecting the possibility that the counterparty who has never cheated is simply trying to build up a stock of reputational capital, with the anticipation of cashing in at some future date. And that date is not predictable, based on logic alone.

Such strategies may be low frequency, but they are not zero frequency. Exactly this type of behavior has recently been observed on eBay, the Internet based electronic trading system. Transactors are requested to post their evaluations of buyers or sellers after a deal is consummated. Anyone with more than four negative postings is denied access to the system. But some cases of fraud have involved individuals who conducted an initial series of transactions, earning exemplary reviews, and then went in for the big score, stiffing a number of counterparties who had relied on the previous unsullied reputation of the seller before sending off their certified checks for merchandise that was never delivered.

Empirically, of course, many people do refrain from cheating when they could get away with it and try to associate with those who behave in a similar fashion. The overall success of eBay and its policies confirms this view. So we come back to the decision theoretic question. Should we or should we not make any use of data on reputation in deciding with whom we should transact? Should we dismiss the possibility that the concept of disposition or personality is predictively relevant and reason deductively that anyone building up a favorable reputation is simply doing so with an eye to exploiting those who might be foolish enough to base their decisions on it?

I have suggested earlier that an action may fail the criterion of rationality either because it is premised on beliefs not arrived at rationally or because, conditional on these beliefs, it does not "best" serve the desires or preferences of the actor. Questions surrounding the rationality of basing decisions on a reputational mechanism concern the appropriateness of different algorithms in forming expectations of human behavior, in particular, whether or not the use of statistical algorithms involving prior behavioral data leads to an expectation that is rational in the Muth sense.

Lester Telser follows in the Nash tradition, arguing that it is not.

"Reliability is not an inherent personality trait. A person is reliable if and only if it is more advantageous to him than being unreliable. . . . Someone is honest only if honesty, or the appearance of honesty, pays more than dishonesty" (Telser 1980, 28–29). Telser is simply reaffirming Hume's proposition that all induction is speculative, particularly where it is applied to human relations. At a more down to earth level, he is trying once again to draw a clear line of demarcation between games against nature, for which most recognize data tabulation and collection and algorithms for statistical inference as relevant and useful, and games against humans, where only mathematics and logic (not statistics) are deemed relevant and useful (Williams 1954, 207). In terms of the "fundamental attribution error," he is denying the relevance of "disposition": situation is all that is relevant for predicting behavior. And he is endorsing the basic behaviorist position reflected in social learning theory: individuals do not have general personality traits but react as they do because of the specifics of a particular situation in a way that does not carry over to other situations.[17]

Telser would probably not take the same position were he trying to forecast whether or not a particular aircraft engine will break down over the next week. He would not say, "Reliability is not an inherent engine trait. An engine is reliable if and only if it is more advantageous to it than being unreliable." Telser would agree that we would then be faced with a decision theoretic problem and presumably would agree that prior breakdown records for different individual engines are relevant, as well as overall base rate data on frequency of breakdowns for engines of this design and this vintage. Now imagine he is trying to decide which horse is likely reliably to perform over a long trek. Would he use the same methodology? Now he wishes to forecast the behavior of several chimpanzees. Would he argue, "Reliability is not a trait inherent in an individual chimpanzee. A chimpanzee is reliable if and only if it is more advantageous to it than being unreliable"? Finally, he is dealing with a group of humans. For Telser, by the time we get to humans, decision theory, which relies on an empirical/statistical methodology, is now without relevance; only game theory along the lines Nash laid down is appropriate.

As we saw in chapter 1, in a one-shot PD, forecasts of counterparty

---

17. Because my argument is principally concerned with species typical predispositions, I have generally not addressed issues surrounding the heritability of individual differences. Since my argument involves selection, however, there would have to be a heritable component of such inclinations. Studies of identical and fraternal twins suggest that approximately 50 percent of the variance in altruistic inclinations can be attributed to genetic differences among individuals. The same is true for a number of other personality traits (see Hunt 1990, 54–56; Hauser 2000, 110–11).

play are simply irrelevant in choosing rationally one's best strategy, although practically speaking, one could imagine that such a forecast might influence one's willingness to play irrationally. In a two player fixed and known duration game, a forecast that the counterparty would play irrationally could lead one rationally to alter one's strategy. In games of indefinite duration, where cooperative play can possibly be justified as rational but where there are multiple equilibria, such estimates are also critical in estimating whether or not one is likely to be able to coordinate on a cooperative equilibrium.

Even though game theory is predisposed against admitting the value of empirically based forecasts of human behavior for normative theory, we can see how it begins to creep in in some of the more complex analyses. Admitting data on base rates and individual reliability is equivalent to acknowledging that the distinction between games played against nature and games against humans is not hard and fast. Games against humans are, after all, to some degree games against nature, because humans are biological organisms designed and structured as the result of natural selection operating over a long evolutionary history. To that degree, tools of decision theory can be relevant in making decisions involving strategic interaction among humans or, for an external observer, in simply trying to predict behavior.

If we accept the Telser/Nash view, we must conclude that it is impossible to extract any predictively relevant information from human past behavior, either individually or in the aggregate. Econometrically, we are saying that lagged values of past behavior add no additional power in forecasting behavior, when they are included along with right hand variables measuring current conditions. In fact we do base our predictions of counterparty behavior in part on base rate data and individual past reliability, and we generally find it worth doing so. Indeed, one of the few robust findings from the field of clinical psychology is that past overt behavior is one of the best predictors of future behavior—far superior to clinicians' "trained intuition," which adds almost no value (Dawes 1994, 5, 26). Is it or is it not silly to give prisoners time off for good behavior? To argue that considerations of reputation—our own and others—are relevant in making strategic decisions is to admit a role for empirical data on human behavior game theorists are generally reluctant to consider, for it casts doubt on the predictive power of the purely analytic methods offered.

With respect to predictions involving groups of humans, I am arguing that base rate data are relevant and are in part what we are attempting to extract in the search for essential human predispositions. The incorporation of reputation, or the use of data on frequency of past behavior in forecasting future behavior, is a species of causal inference based on the observation of contiguity and succession (correlation). We observe that past overt behavior is one of the best predictors of future behavior and infer a causal mechanism based on personality structure, or "inherent personality traits," or species typical predispositions to explain these regularities. We have no logical basis for doing so, but we end up with better forecasts if we admit such data. As Daniel Sperber nicely puts it, "Causal beliefs are both indispensable to human understanding and unfounded" (1995, xvi). The canonical game theoretic approach, with its emphasis on deductive logic, can pride itself on its cleanness, on its avoidance of logically unfounded reasoning. But to paraphrase E. O. Wilson, this elegance is purchased at a high price when the tools are applied to domains of strategic interaction, to which they are thought to be particularly appropriate. That price is the quality of forecasts of counterparty behavior. And, in many instances, the quality of forecasts of our own.

Even admitting an empirical/inductive methodology, there may be, as noted, some circumstances where it will perform less well. Decision theory emphasizes that one should place different weights on base rate data under different circumstances (Koehler 1996). Perhaps exceptional cases surrounded the observed past behavior and it will not be repeated. Perhaps the circumstances now are exceptional. Where data on past behavior exist, and I would argue that such data are always going to be of some use, it is still a leap of faith for us to reason that the future will display the same regularities as the past, that the characteristics of a population will roughly reflect those of a sample, that our prior observation of similar circumstances gives us grounds for forecasting behaviors that have not yet occurred. But it is a useful leap.

Presentist Bias and the Function of Anger

Frank goes on to discuss experimental research that shows that we have a preference for immediate rewards that goes beyond what traditional discounting can account for (this is sometimes referred to as *hyperbolic discounting*). Faced with a choice of $100 twenty-eight days from now and $120 thirty-one days from now, most subjects will choose the latter. But faced with a choice of $100 now or $120 in three days, most will choose the $100 (Frank 1988, 77). This behavior is not rational from a decision theoretic standpoint and represents a behavioral predisposition driven by some neurobiological subsystem that short-circuits the counsel of logic. The predisposition is interesting, may have been favored by individual level selection, and may have a role in understanding the ability of altruism to establish itself. But if so, Frank has not put his finger on it.

He uses these results to provide an explanation for why "merely prudent" people may cheat, even when they have a strong probability of being caught. Such an individual has difficulty in adequately crediting the great gains from not cheating (which will come in the future) and balancing them against the immediate benefits. Whether or not this argument has psychological merit, it has little relevance to the question of the emergence of altruism. Decisions about whether or not to cheat are relevant only after fundamental social problems have been solved and the agent is operating in an environment predominated by noncheaters playing Tit-for-Tat where repeated interaction can be assumed. The more basic evolutionary question is how the environment became populated in the first place by those who will not cheat unless first cheated. If one has not satisfactorily explained why people refrain from cheating when it would pay them to cheat, does it make a great deal of sense to try to explain, as does Frank here, why people may cheat when it *doesn't* pay them to?

Frank also suggests that this presentist bias may cause us to refrain from getting angry when we are wronged because the costs are now and the reputational rewards are in the future, whereas a propensity to anger helps us avoid this pitfall. "Anger helps shift the relevant future payoffs into the present" (Frank 1988, 83). But Nash/Selten rationality tells us it is perfectly rational not to get angry, because retaliation once deterrence has failed is irrational! Frank is arguing that a tendency to anger will trump the rational behavior (let bygones be bygones) that fails to deter aggression. Instead, anger produces an irrational propensity toward retaliation that may deter it. Perhaps so, but one cannot then turn around and argue that getting angry is in fact rational.

Frank spends considerable time earlier in the book discussing the ultimatum games and the evidence that people will refuse "unfair" bargains. Now he has reversed course entirely. Our willingness to place disproportionate weight on gains that will occur in the very near future helps us understand why some people will accept unfair bargains. But from the standpoint of rational choice theory we have no need of behavioral data to explain why people accept these bargains. It is strictly rational to do so, because something is always better than nothing.

The discussion of the role of hyperbolic discounting is regrettably emblematic of the type of armchair theorizing that is commonplace within the rational choice tradition. And it bears some of the hallmarks of the heuristics and biases research program discussed in greater detail in chapter 6, in particular a willingness to "explain" an apparent deviation from normatively counseled behavior with reference to a menu of heuristics without developing a coherent predictive framework explaining when some rather than others will apply. Thus it becomes sometimes difficult to know whether we are dealing with an essential human predisposition or one that is introduced adventitiously in an ex post fashion to account for troublesome behavior. In Frank's book it is impossible sometimes even to figure out what is the "troublesome" behavior. Is it a propensity to accept "unfair" bargains or a propensity to refuse them?

There are clearly important questions about the evolutionary role played by a propensity to anger. Successful implementation of Tit-for-Tat involves a number of different types of self-control problems. I understand a self-control problem to be one where, through an effort of will, we must consciously override the counsel of one behavioral impeller and accept that of another. In some cases such problems involve directing behavior toward that counseled by one's faculties for making rational choices; in other cases they involve directing behavior away from such behavior.

If one is playing Tit-for-Tat one should get angry only after one has been wronged and then only for a limited duration, particularly when the counterparty then plays cooperate (apologizes, makes amends, etc.). One type of control problem involves that identified by Frank: forcing oneself to respond to a slight with anger, even though this imposes costs now and even though Nash/Selten rationality counsels that bygones are bygones, retaliation won't undo the slight, and so on. Another type of control issue involves refraining from becoming angry when one has not been wronged, even though doing so might permit an immediate advantage or provide defense against another acting in this fashion. Controlling anger is critical to the practice of first move(r) altruism. Someone who attacks another who has just entered the room because she does not like his looks is not practicing first move(r) altruism and is not laying the foundation for a cooperative relationship. Finally, there is a control problem in limiting the anger to a period of "one play": achieving proportionality in the response and not permitting the emotion to fester and feed on itself after amends have been made, thus forestalling the possibility of reestablishing cooperation. Frank's exploration of the role of anger in implementing a Tit-for-Tat strategy and the several control problems that present themselves, situations where different behavioral impellers are providing sharply contradictory advice, only scratches the surface of this complex emotion and the challenges posed by its function, possible use, and control.

In exploring the high human preference for short term rewards Frank has identified an interesting human behavioral predisposition, one at variance with the predictions of decision theoretic models based on rational choice. But he has not shown why it is relevant to the emergence of cooperation. He concludes this section with this observation: "In cases where reputational considerations weigh in favor of action, the angry person will be more likely to behave prudently than the merely prudent person who feels no anger." Frank, I believe, is sensitive to the charge that he is in several places describing the same behavior as both rational and not rational. He tries here to avoid the criticism by substituting the word *prudent* for *rational.* The problem is not finessed. Does he mean to suggest that it is possible for a prudent action not to be rational? Or for a rational action not to be prudent?

One can equally well argue that the "merely prudent person who feels no anger" may behave more prudently than the congenitally angry person who flies off the handle when one comes in wearing a red shirt. As indicated previously, the analysis of the role of anger in implementing a Tit-for-Tat strategy poses real challenges, only some of which does Frank address. Anger is a volatile emotion, difficult to trigger in some, difficult to bring under control in others, sometimes both. Acting under the influence of anger is not acting prudently, if by prudently we mean *engaged in behavior consistent with the counsel of reason.* Anger almost certainly plays a role in a complex of behaviors that together have been evolutionarily adaptive. But the evolutionary advantage of a propensity to anger cannot be considered out of context. In certain contexts, anger may be group positive and individual level negative, in others the reverse.

If anger is not simply dissembling, it is by definition not prudent. Aristotle did not counsel against ever being angry. In the *Nichomachean Ethics* he argued that the key was to be angry with the right person, to the right degree, at the right time, for the right purpose, and in the right way (1959, 96–97). What one does with anger—how much one yields to its siren song—may be strategic, but its reality as a behavioral impeller is not. Does *prudently* mean *rationally?* If so, we are back to describing behavior as at one and the same time rational and irrational.

Frank summarizes (chap. 6) a variety of psychological and physiological research making a convincing case that many visible signs of emotions are linked involuntarily to the emotions themselves. But again, what he does with this evidence is problematic. "If for example, trustworthiness and a tendency to blush go together, and if being known to be trustworthy is advantageous, selection pressures can clearly affect both the tendency to blush and the emotion that triggers it" (Frank 1988, 133). True enough, but if selection occurs only at the level of the individual organism, it will operate against both tendencies. A signal that one is trusting and trustworthy makes one an ideal mark for a deceiver. If group selection is allowed, on the other hand, matters are different. If groups high in those inclined to trust (or to trust once) grow more rapidly and periodically recombine in the general population, and particularly if this tendency is reinforced by assortative "mating," then forces of natural selection, understood to mean those operating both at the individual and at the group level, can favor the spread of such propensities. The effect of both tendencies on inclusive fitness will be positive, even though the within group effect is negative.

Those of us who are trustworthy—who carry out our commitments even when it would be to our immediate advantage to do otherwise—may like to think that it incidentally provides us material benefit. In an environment with sufficient structure—reliably predictive information on behavioral propensities of others, required repeated interaction—being trustworthy or speaking honestly may be defended as a rational choice. But at that point an individual choice (e.g., by an invader) to be trustworthy no longer has much altruistic character.

In a less predictable environment, or one characterized by lower frequencies of cooperators or conditional cooperators, no such conclusion follows. In such circumstances, those of us who are trustworthy when we could cease to be and benefit ourselves must remain content with the oft-stated observation that virtue is its own reward. The healthy young man who stands by his dying spouse for seven long years as she withers away as the result of an incurable illness has honored his marital vows to stick by a spouse in sickness and in health but has passed up opportunities to remarry and father offspring. A society with a high percentage of trustworthy people of this type may grow stronger and larger, but it is not because the behavior increases the relative fitness of trustworthy individuals, taking into consideration the forces of individual level selection alone.

Frank's book is written, as is Sober and Wilson's, very much from the standpoint of the "good" people of society. But unlike Sober and Wilson, who confront the advantages enjoyed by "cheaters" head-on, Frank's treatment is often asymmetrical. Anger, he argues, helps us overcome the presentist bias that would otherwise cause us rationally to accept positive (but "unfair") offers in ultimatum games. But why shouldn't a bias toward the present also prevent "bad" people, who care nothing for fairness, from rejecting somewhat profitable deals in order to establish reputations as tough bargainers? If the use of emotions is strategic, Why can't "bad" people also use them to overcome this bias? And if they can, why should the net effect of these behavioral predispositions be to make a society fairer?

We also see an asymmetrical treatment in Frank's comments on the role of love in marriage: "The worry that people will leave relationships because it may later become rational for them to do so is largely erased if it is not rational assessment that binds them in the first place" (Frank 1988, 196). Why should this be so? Take the case of a young, wealthy, handsome man who proposes to a poor, rather plain looking woman past the age of childbearing. Surely the woman, even if she goes through with the marriage, must worry that, since the behavior of her spouse in the first place has been so flaky by evolutionary standards, he will be more likely to stray or leave, even if she manages to create a warm home environment for him. I come back to a point made earlier with regard to nuclear strategy: why should evidence that one's counterparty has behaved irrationally in the past increase the precision of one's estimate of his or her behavior in the future?

Frank is certainly right that some elements of marital relationships defy calculation just as many do not, and that people can look for rationalizations for what they have done. But if the emotions are strategic, as the title of the book suggests, then they involve following the dictates of reason. If we are to use them to account for behavior that cannot be rationalized then we must give up the effort to interpret true emotions in strategic terms.

Frank's confusion is vividly illustrated in his comment that "again and again . . . we have seen that the most adaptive behaviors will not spring directly from the quest for material advantage." He insists, correctly, in calling our attention to altruistic behavior toward non-kin. Since the forces of natural selection have not eliminated such behavior, he implicitly reasons (correctly) that it has been adaptive. Critics will point out (as I have) that such behavior imposes an (individual level) evolutionary disadvantage on those who practice it, at least upon first appearance. Frank attempts to work his way out of this box by persuading us that behavior that by definition cannot be favored by the forces of individual selection somehow is. It is an intellectual cul-de-sac that cannot be exited until one begins seriously to consider the interaction of group level and individual level selection.

Frank's argument, again, is akin to the main *Dr. Strangelove* theme, with human emotions playing the role of the Doomsday machine. Being known as someone often under the sway of emotions, making one prone to behavior apparently not under the control of reason, enables commitments or threats that would otherwise lack credibility to possess it. But if emotions are truly not under the control of reason then they belong nowhere within a discussion of strategy, which presumes conscious calculation of choice based on the existing situation and the likely behavior of one's counterparty(ies). Evolutionary game theorists sometimes talk about the "strategies" of lower animals or plants that clearly lack consciousness: it's an "as if" kind of usage designed to characterize the outcome of natural selection. But there is little in Frank's book to suggest that this is what he has in mind with respect to humans: the discussion is at its heart choice theoretic. Frank describes behavior as "seemingly" irrational. If the terms *rational* and *irrational* are to have any meaning, one must be the negation of the other. They cannot overlap.

If a reputation for emotional behavior is cultivated, and known to be so, it ceases to guarantee commitments and threats, because counterparties understand that such behavior can, ultimately, be turned on or off at will. If people know the Doomsday machine can be turned on or off, it serves no purpose. On the other hand, if people know that the emotional side of a person is truly beyond the control of reason, then they may be reluctant to enter into relationships with this individual in the first place, viewing the individual's behavior as too unstable and consequently too unpredictable. Frank's analysis of the role of emotions in human interactions is therefore at best incomplete.

The Formal Model

Let us conclude by examining the formal model appearing in an appendix that apparently underlies *Passions within Reason.* Frank first analyzes a large population playing one-shot PDs in random pairings with each other. Hypothetically varying the frequency of cooperators from 0 to 100 percent, he shows that the fitness of both defectors and cooperators rises the more cooperators there are in the population (see chap. 2 in this volume, fig. 1). Unfortunately, the fitness of defectors will be higher than that of cooperators at any frequency, so the dynamics are such that cooperators will go extinct regardless of starting frequency. They cannot invade a population of defectors and cannot survive at first appearance at low frequency.

Frank then considers what would happen if cooperators were able costlessly to emit a signal identifying themselves as cooperators and also to detect such signals with unfailing accuracy. By choosing selectively, cooperators can now interact only with other cooperators, leaving defectors to interact only with other defectors. Under these circumstances, cooperators will have higher fitness at any frequency, and cooperators will therefore evolve to fixation within the population.

Frank does not appreciate that, having explicitly eschewed any role for group selection, he has nevertheless posited a set of assumptions that creates an environment, indeed the most favorable sort of environment, for its operation. In this case the groups are none other than the cooperating dyads. Frank's assumptions make them like the demes in Sewall Wright's analysis, in this case completely immune from invasion.

What is required, however, to move from the first set of assumptions to the second? The *evolution* of such a system in the absence of any group selection would require a most improbable set of coincidences: first, the simultaneous appearance of at least two conspecifics predisposed to cooperation; second, the simultaneous appearance in both of them of an ability to emit a nonfalsifiable signal of sympathy; and third, a foolproof ability in both of these conspecifics to detect such a signal. If one of the abilities appeared in a defector and the other in a cooperator, cooperation would be dead on arrival. These individuals would, moreover, in a large population, have to locate each other immediately, avoiding costly interactions with other (defection prone) conspecifics. In comparison, the assumptions Sober and Wilson require to enable some kind of evolution by group selection seem modest.

The existence of signal emission and detection equipment, once in place, could help explain how cooperative outcomes are sustained, and Frank's experimental work has provided important evidence of their operation. Frank spends considerable time exploring the "rationale" of turning off the signal detection equipment (if it is costly) if the frequency of cooperators rises above a certain level, creating a fitness chart with discontinuities at one end of the frequency range, and the likelihood that cooperators will not evolve to fixation but will attain a polymorphous equilibrium, turning on signal detection only if frequency drops below a certain level. But the fundamental *evolutionary* problem, unaddressed, is the origin of this apparatus in the first place.

Nothing in *Passions within Reason* overcomes the fact that in the absence of an established social structure of repeated interactions, or in the absence of this signal emission and detection equipment, or in the absence of a population with a high frequency of individuals similarly predisposed, behaving "nicely" puts one at a disadvantage from the standpoint of the forces of individual selection. In interactions among humans, "nice" people bear potential handicaps. If the dominance of nice people is so great in an established group that these handicaps vanish, then the behavior in question is no longer nice, merely prudent. Groups that have large numbers of trustworthy individuals, on the other hand, may grow faster or stronger, and consequently, assuming periodic group mixing, cooperative or conditionally cooperative inclinations may grow or become stabilized in a larger population. In evolutionary terms, one cannot account for the phenomena that interest and concern Frank without allowing a role for group level selection.

Frank has summarized a great deal of experimental evidence showing the many failures of the rational actor model accurately to predict behavior. He criticizes the rational choice model in saying that "Its hard-nosed if unhappy conclusion is that over the millennia, selfish people have gradually driven out all others" (Frank 1988, 257). Frank states that this logic is wrong but does not successfully explain why, because he has restricted his evolutionary framework to one that accommodates individual level selection alone. How did all those unselfish people who, in the past millennia, have been driven out, ever get established in empirically important numbers in the first place? Frank sees the problem, but his solution will not persuade those skeptical of his views because it leads to so many internal contradictions.

To his great credit, six years after the publication of *Passions within Reason,* Frank acknowledged in print the relevance of the group selection mechanism. Here is what he said in commenting on a 1994 target article by Wilson and Sober in *Behavioral and Brain Sciences.*[18]

> [They] have persuaded me not only that [my mechanism whereby "genuine" altruism toward non-kin might evolve by natural selection] can be viewed equally as group-selectionist in their terms, but also that there is an advantage in doing so. As a committed individual selectionist, I confess that I was *very* reluctant to reach this conclusion. I hope that my attempt to explain my change of heart will caution other individual selectionists against dismissing [their] argument prematurely. (Frank 1994, 620)

This acknowledgment is, regrettably, little known, and its implications are not widely appreciated. *Passions within Reason,* along with work by Trivers and Axelrod, continues to be cited by many as evidence that one can account for altruistic behavior and the origin of complex social organization using a strictly individual level selectionist approach or, from a social science perspective, as reflecting the outcome of rational choice.[19]

---

18. This format of intellectual exchange is one that economics and other social sciences might well consider emulating. A "target" article is made available on-line. A prequalified set of scholars then has the option of sending in commentary. All of this is published along with a combined bibliography. Since most of the players in a field contribute, one can easily get a good overview of new and breaking developments and how they are received. In the social sciences, in contrast, when a controversial work appears, one can often only ascertain its initial reception through a series of conversations in which scholars sometimes tell you what they think of a work but often preface these comments by noting that, of course, they would not say this in print. The *Behavioral and Brain Sciences* format evidently does not limit critical commentary but does discipline its quality. No one wishes to appear a fool in print, for example, by commenting on work not actually read. Yet the norms are such that most of the major contributors in a field apparently feel a responsibility to make their views known, rather than allow the absence of a commentary to be interpreted itself in a way they do not wish.

19. See Green and Shapiro 1994 (chap. 4) for a thorough and effective critique of attempts to square the empirical reality of positive voter turnout with the predictions of rational choice theory. In *An Economic Theory of Democracy* (1957), Downs predicted very low turnouts except in "close" elections where voters might believe they could influence the outcome. But although "low" turnout in the 30–40 percent range in elections considered not to be close is of concern to some political scientists, the numbers remain far too high to be consistent with Downs's analysis. Riker and Ordeshock in 1968 tried to square theory with evi-

The foraging algorithms at the heart of what we study in economics are powerful indeed. But in situations of social or strategic interaction, their guidance can be short-circuited or blocked by the operation of others. We need to recognize the implications of the modular structure of our mental organs, evidence for which is detailed in chapter 5. Trying to construct a foundation for altruistic or cooperative behaviors on the basis of rational choice mechanisms alone leads us not to a Stiglerian palace underpinned by granite. Rather, it is like trying to build a house on quicksand.

---

dence by adding a sense of civic duty to utility functions. But this is just the sort of ex post emendation that leads to criticism from purists as ad hoc. Again, we can use the word rational to mean what we want, but proceeding down this route rapidly leads to models that lack out-of-sample predictive capability and are therefore difficult to refute.

CHAPTER 5

Altruism, Rule Violators, and the Case for Modularity

Pioneering social theorists such as Thomas Hobbes, John Locke, and Jean-Jacques Rousseau explored the emergence of complex social organization in ways that left little place for knowledge known or discoverable about human prehistory that might contribute to evolutionarily informed expectations about fundamental behavioral propensities. Hobbes, Locke, and Rousseau, in spite of their empiricist contributions, made *assumptions* about these base rates—in some cases quite different ones. But the validity of what was assumed was taken, particularly by Hobbes and Locke, as largely self-evident. These philosophers contributed to establishing a tradition of social contract theorizing that is to this day largely a prioristic.

Rousseau, to his credit, did try to exploit medical knowledge, data on comparative anatomy, early anthropological studies of primitive people, and observations on animal behavior in developing his theory (see Wrong 1994, 17). Our base of scientific knowledge is now, however, much improved compared to what existed in the seventeenth and eighteenth centuries, and our assumptions about human prehistory need no longer be premised almost entirely on speculation. Advances in ethology, paleontology, and molecular biology today permit a range of reasonably definite inferences about our origins and development in the millions of years prior to the Neolithic revolution. First, the overwhelming weight of paleontological evidence, genetic analyses, and behavioral studies of our closest animal relatives, in particular chimpanzees (*Pan troglodytes*) and bonobos (*Pan paniscus*), is that we are descended from animals "that had lived for millions of years in hierarchically structured communities with strong mutual attachments" that extended beyond kin (de Waal 1996, 167).

Many scholars have been and remain ambivalent about the core presumption of ethology: that we can learn something useful about human cognition and behavior through the study of other animals.[1] Skepticism

---

1. Leslie White commented a half century ago: "Because human behavior is symbolic behavior and since the behavior of infra-human species is nonsymbolic, it follows that we can learn nothing about human behavior from observations upon or experiments with lower animals" (White 1949).

derives in part from a hard won twentieth century consensus that variance in capabilities within human "races" dwarfs any that may exist among them and that it is scientifically indefensible to rank human groups on any sort of evolutionary continuum (e.g., Montagu 1956). This important consensus has had the side effect, however, of widening the gulf between what are typically viewed as essential human characteristics and those possessed by animals, further than can be justified by the evidence. In a desire to inter irrevocably views that African pygmies or Australian aborigines were somehow closer to animal forebears than were other humans, scientific evidence on human-animal continuity has been downplayed. There is no reason in principle, however, why a nonracist anthropology cannot be consistent with a more balanced recognition of the facts of human evolution.

The central fact is, as Darwin gingerly suggested in *The Origin of Species* (1859) and finally explored more exhaustively in *The Descent of Man* (1871), that we are descended from animals. Today, in contrast with the nineteenth century, or even the mid–twentieth century, we can be quite explicit about the line of descent. The accumulating evidence is overwhelming that we are one of three surviving chimpanzee species who share over 98 percent of our DNA, should probably be classified in the same genus, and are descended from a common ancestor who lived roughly six million years ago. The study of our closest relatives can, as can the study of our own behavior, tell us something about the morphological and behavioral characteristics of that ancestor, although we must, as Darwin himself warned, be careful about assuming the common ancestor was like any particular extant species (1871, 199).

Nevertheless, fossil evidence going back to *Australopithecus* shows apelike features in known hominid ancestors, suggesting that existing chimpanzee species, assuming they have not evolved as rapidly as humans, may bear important similarities to that ancestor. In an influential paper in 1978, Adrienne Zihlman and her colleagues concluded that the bonobo, or pygmy chimpanzee (*Pan paniscus*), is probably morphologically and perhaps behaviorally closest. In any event, traits common to two or more of the surviving species have a strong claim to having been characteristic of the common ancestor, although we can never entirely reject the possibility of different evolutionary paths subsequent to branching leading to similar outcomes. If we are interested in identifying essential behavioral predispositions in humans—those that have been evolutionarily selected for over a long history—evidence on animal behavior and cognition is, subject to these caveats, relevant.

If it is true that as humans we possess behavioral impellers that, within certain domains, override the counsel of logic and mathematical reasoning as interpreted by normative game theory, predisposing us, for example, to play cooperate in one-shot PDs, the hardwiring that induces them has almost certainly been in our genetic heritage for a long time. Chimpanzees and bonobos as well as humans all exhibit social organization that would be impossible without such predispositions, and there is a strong likelihood this was also true of our common ancestor.

In considering first move(r) altruism or restraint on first strike, therefore, we should focus on an evolutionary period extending over millions of years, not on some relatively recent period in which fully modern humans assembled to agree on a social contract, before which time life was demonstrably more solitary, poorer, nastier, more brutish, and shorter. For first move(r) altruism, at least in the form of failure to harm, we are dealing with an environment of evolutionary adaptation that extends back not 500 or 50,000 generations but 150,000 or 200,000, most likely more.

Lorenz's Account of the Control of Intraspecific Violence

Such restraints, particularly toward members of the same species, are, after all, common among animals, many of which are believed, based on fossil records, to have changed much less than have we since the time of a shared ancestor. In *On Aggression,* Konrad Lorenz observed that even "full time" predators like lions and wolves had evolved powerful behavioral inhibitors that restricted intraspecific violence (Lorenz 1966, 129–30, 241). How did Lorenz account for these inhibitors? Through appeal to group selection, a mechanism he adduced frequently and with abandon, one of the reasons he, along with Wynne-Edwards, was one of the targets of the individual selectionist revolution. Although I take issue with much of the thrust of Lorenz's analysis of restraint in humans (see the discussion that follows) it is hard to see how he could not have been correct with respect to the role of group selection in the evolution of those behavioral inhibitors among animals.

Absent a satisfactory explanation of hardwired restraints on intraspecific violence, we cannot move to game theoretic environments in which indefinitely repeated interactions are assumed. Wolves are heavily armed predators who earn their calories by killing other animals. Conspecifics are potential sources of protein. Failure to attack members of one's own species cannot be explained as the consequence of the possibility they might fight back, since that expectation does not inhibit attacks on non-conspecifics, particularly where they may be smaller and weaker. And yet wolves generally refrain from attacking other wolves, regardless of size.

Among predator species, smaller and weaker members of the same species represent a potentially lucrative source of calories as well as potential competitors for other forms of food, both plant and animal. So why do animals not avail themselves more frequently of these opportunities for self-advancement? Much of the explanation can be found through consideration of the Hamilton kin selection mechanism. Sexually reproducing organisms with a high propensity to attack and/or eat reproductively mature members of the opposite sex of their own species might live long and well fed lives, compared with those that did not. But for obvious reasons they would be unlikely to pass on their genes. Thus a propensity to refrain from attacks on opposite sex conspecifics would, overall, face positive selection: such propensities would increase inclusive fitness. Note that this is a consequence of a group level selection factor that overwhelms the (negative) individual level selection factor, with the group here identified as a male-female dyad. A case can be made that group level selection played a role in the evolution of the system of sexual reproduction itself (see chap. 2), and the evolution of hardwired restraints on attacks on opposite sex conspecifics was likely part of this package.

The second important question is why, once we have propensities facilitating fertilization and gestation, parents do not more frequently attack and/or consume their offspring, who represent, again, ready stores of calories as well as potential competitors for other food sources. This is not a trivial issue, given the rates of infanticide and sometimes cannibalism reported for many species relatively close to us evolutionarily (de Waal and Lanting 1997, 118). Again, the answer is straightforward: animals averse to consuming their young would be more likely to pass on genes predisposing to such behavior simply because their offspring would be more likely to reach maturity and procreate, thus resulting in the spread of such dispositions in subsequent generations. An exception, which accounts for much of the preceding data, is the tendency observed in some animals for males to kill offspring not their own when they mate with a new female (Hrdy 1979). In general, however, restraint on the killing and/or consumption of young is favored by group level selection, with the group now including parents and offspring.

Restraint on attacking members of the opposite sex and restraint on consuming one's offspring are both explicable in terms of the Hamilton kin selection mechanism. They involve behavior that disadvantages the organism practicing it but benefits the group, in this case the kin group. As has been imperfectly acknowledged, the Hamilton mechanism operates as a variant of group selection favoring altruism within a trait group here defined as the family.

But this leaves unresolved the question of restraint on attacks on non-kin conspecifics. The metaphors we use to characterize the competitive marketplace and the real world are often influenced by an unsophisticated pop Darwinism, suggesting far higher rates of such activity than in fact obtain. Witness: *It's a dog-eat-dog world* or, with respect to a business competitor, not just *We're going to eat their lunch* (deprive them of caloric sustenance) but also *We're going to eat them for lunch* (deprive them of caloric sustenance, provide us with caloric sustenance, and remove a potential competitor for calories in the future). But it is not literally a dog-eat-dog world, and same species competitors only rarely eat each other for lunch. Why not? Why wasn't it, to extend the argument backward to canine ancestors, a wolf-eat-wolf world?

One cannot start, in explaining restraint on intraspecific violence, by assuming an environment of indefinitely repeated interaction. If the outcome of not defecting in the face of defection at first meeting is that one is dead, and the defect-defect outcome is only marginally superior for the players, restraint on intraspecific violence simply cannot evolve if selection operates only at the individual level. The replicator dynamics point in only one direction: to a Hobbesian world that is nasty, short, and brutish, leavened only by a modicum of restraint in relations with mates and children.

This is why Ken Binmore refuses to be drawn into a discussion of how such restraint might evolve as a result of rational choice, or individual level selection, in an original state characterized as a series of one-shot Prisoner's Dilemmas. Having concluded with justification that it cannot, he is determinedly critical of those who argue otherwise. He is more or less wedded, as are most practicing game theorists, to an individual level view of natural selection, consistent with his emphasis on rationality narrowly and precisely defined. Thus, in order to account for restraint on intraspecific violence and other forms of cooperation, he must begin his analysis by positing an environment of indefinitely repeated interaction. Having made this common assumption, he has established necessary although not sufficient conditions for the maintenance of cooperative behavior. The assumption is only necessary because a variety of equilibria including those involving continuous defection can sustain themselves through the operation of rational choice, giving rise to a large academic enterprise in explaining through simulation or a priori restriction the determination ("selection") of which one of the possible equilibria prevails.

Admitting group level selection in favor of some altruistic tendencies, the most important of which is the negative altruism of failure to harm, is, on the other hand, a plausible vehicle for explaining the transformation of one-shot into iterated games. But it is also the camel's nose under the tent in terms of admitting the possibility that human behavior may be driven by other than self-regarding preferences or that different cognitive modules may drive behavior, possibilities resisted tenaciously by many game theorists for reasons both historical and ideological.

Offspring of both sexes develop into adolescents and eventually into mature adults. What protects them from attacks on other conspecifics? Trivers's theory of reciprocal altruism is of no help in accounting for the origin of such restraint. Without group level selection, the first wolf who fails to attack a ravenous conspecific, giving up the advantage of the offense, is most likely dead meat (see chap. 4). Wolves are collectively better off if they "agree" not to attack each other—that is a Pareto efficient solution—but that is precisely the dilemma reflected in a one-shot or fixed and known duration PD. And we cannot simply dismiss the difficulty on the grounds that a species killing and/or eating one of its own is completely unthinkable.[2]

Lorenz was ultimately concerned with human aggressive impulses and went on to argue that *Homo sapiens* (unlike lions and wolves) had not had enough evolutionary time to develop hardwired restraints on such behavior. Rather than evolving weapons physically integral to our organism, we had "suddenly" discovered the use of tools for hunting. "Overnight" we became very dangerous to each other as well as other animals, lacking the restraints that would have evolved through group selection, he claimed, had those weapons been physically integral. The fact that our weapons were abruptly invented rather than slowly evolved meant, according to Lorenz, that today only a thin veneer of civilization keeps us from tearing each other to shreds. This view was consonant with a wide variety of postwar literature, including Freudian psychology and fictional works such as William Golding's novel *Lord of the Flies* ([1962] 1983).

But Lorenz's analysis is far too broad stroke, and his reliance on "culture" to explain our persistence is unpersuasive. Much as we may credit our efforts as parents, and acknowledge the impact of institutions of socialization (family, church, school), do we really believe that the absence of murderous behavior on the part of the predominant portion of the population is entirely attributable to these efforts? Lorenz mistakes the success of "civilization" in tamping down the practice of "blood vengeance" (as manifested in the Hatfield-McCoy feud referenced by Frank) and insisting that retribution be public for the ultimate cause of restraint on intraspecific murder per se.

---

2. Restraints on intraspecific violence do not preclude murder of adult conspecifics and do not necessarily preclude infanticide, even among some of our close relatives. Some current estimates of infant mortality due to this cause are 37 percent in mountain gorillas, 35 percent in gray langurs, 43 percent in red howler monkeys, and 29 percent in blue monkeys (de Waal and Lanting 1997, 118). For an evolutionary explanation based on sexual selection, see Hrdy 1979.

The practice of blood vengeance in situations lacking strong state power, still evident in some environs today, does not imply a widespread human predisposition to launch unprovoked first strikes against unrelated conspecifics but rather a predisposition to *respond* to such attacks with self-righteous wrath. Such responses are sometimes wildly disproportional to the insult, leading to escalating cycles of violence, and I do not mean to suggest that the norms that sustain this behavior are necessarily adaptive. But from a broader perspective, a secondary and often neglected puzzle is why retaliation is so often restrained. While cycles of violence and retaliation do break out from time to time, and receive extensive media and historical attention, they represent the exception rather than the rule. Absent such restraint, humans would long since have destroyed themselves through undamped volleys of strike and counterstrike. Once started by even a small probability spark, the fires would burn ever more ferociously, consuming everything in their midst.

The successful promulgation of the norm of measured response reflected in the *lex talionis* is likely partly attributable to hardwired predispositions to restrain secondary retaliation, in this case to that which is proportional. The promulgation of such norms by lawgivers can influence behavior, by altering expectations of what others expect, but such cultural developments cannot be the entire explanation of restraint on intraspecific violence.

Lorenz's analysis presupposes an implausible sequence of events. The discovery of the use of tools as weapons, which turned us into such powerful threats not only to other animals but also to each other, would have had to have been followed *almost immediately* by the "invention" of culture, just in time to keep us from hacking ourselves to death. And how did culture control the expression of these vicious tendencies? Through the articulation and promulgation of social norms restraining individually rational but group damaging behavioral tendencies.

But why were these norms initially accepted when first articulated, and why would they have influenced behavior? As we have seen in chapter 3, adherence to norms requires the same short-circuiting of self-interested calculation as would be required to explain any kind of restraint in the first place. Thus, if one is assuming a world in which only individual level selection can occur there is a real problem in accepting his explanation.

I suggest here a more plausible hypothesis that accepts Lorenz's admission of the possibility of selection above the level of the individual in the evolution of restraint among animals, but not his account of the control of intraspecific violence among humans. Like lions and wolves, we possess hardwired inhibitions that powerfully restrain intraspecific violence, predisposing us to retaliation when it occurs but also restraining that retaliation to some degree. These predispositions have an extensive evolutionary lineage, and we and our ancestors have had them for a long time. Cultural restraints on intragroup violence represent a codification— to which we may be particularly receptive—of predispositions that made groups possible, not an entirely independent cause of social organization in the first place.

All of these predispositions are subject to the qualification noted in chapter 1: growing within group solidarity, made possible by these inclinations, may reduce the likelihood that restraint is manifested toward members of "other" groups. Group solidarity requires an aggressive willingness irrationally to retaliate and punish violators of group norms. The growth of solidarity may encourage this biologically favored predisposition to be directed outward. Chimpanzees, for example, will attack and kill unaccompanied members of out-groups—but only if three or more adult males in a group are present (Hauser 2000, 46).

Nevertheless, I view these restraints—on the propensity to strike first and on the possibility of massive, disproportional retaliation—as the most empirically important form of human altruism, the fundamental enablers of complex social organization. The affirmative assistance stressed by the Russian anarchist Peter Kropotkin in *Mutual Aid* (1910) is a weaker impulse, one whose scope is more culturally variable. Yet most discussions of human altruism focus exclusively on affirmative aid, a practice that has obscured the importance in humans of hardwired restraints on first strike, altruistic in an evolutionary sense as much as the actions we celebrate (in their purest form) when we honor heroic behavior.

The progress of civilization has clamped down on blood vengeance within states and reinforced the principle of *lex talionis* in armed conflict among nations. Successful socialization, as proponents of schooling in Massachusetts in the mid–nineteenth century argued, can dramatically reduce the number of police officers per capita needed to maintain social order (Field 1974, 1976a, b). Within the limits posed by hardwired restraints, political culture and institutions have important independent effects on outcomes. Neither control of primary aggression nor that on the proportionality of retaliation is ever complete, although sometimes the "advance" of civilization only displaces a "problem" to a different level. For example, in the Middle Ages, suppression of private justice elevated excesses of retaliation to the public arena, with horrible retribution often meted out by states for trivial violations. That historical reality, in the context of Enlightenment thought, was responsible for the prohibition of cruel and unusual punishments reflected in the Eighth Amendment to the U.S. Constitution.

The basic flavor of blood vengeance can still be observed in the death penalty meted out by states for the crime of murder and in the practice of war by organized states, particularly those that are not democratic, and in locales where organized state power is weak. If blood vengeance was the "way of the jungle," the prehistorical modality, we can infer that in the worst cases it led to an environment of endemic intraspecific violence. But such violence has evidently not been sufficiently severe or widespread to lead to the extinction of the species (for a view suggesting that so far we have just been lucky, see Leslie 1996). Indeed, humans have spread to occupy all continents of the world and to grow in numbers to the point that there are now more than *six billion* of us. Surely this is not the record of a species lacking hardwired restraints on intraspecific violence or rely-ing entirely on cultural forces for its suppression.

Much as we may be depressed and revolted by the carnage of twenti-eth century wars and genocide, it must be kept in perspective. Violence, murder, and war fascinate us, in part because of their abnormality, and lead us to overlook the complementary propensities to restrain the exercise of first strike, to limit retaliation, and to make peace after conflict. We are fascinated by the Middle East, or Northern Ireland, or the Hatfields and the McCoys, which feature apparently endless cycles of strike and coun-terstrike. We overlook the facts that these represent one tail of a statistical distribution, that the vast majority of episodes of intraspecific violence end after one or two cycles. It follows that humans, like primates (de Waal 1989), possess abilities, to some degree hardwired, to limit these escala-tions and make peace (for a description of conflict resolution still worth reading see also Kropotkin 1910, 134).

The pessimistic views of George Orwell about the future of the human race have not yet been borne out. John von Neumann's, Bertrand Rus-sell's, and Curtis LeMay's advocacy of first strike against the Soviets, and that of their counterparts in Moscow, did not, in the event, plunge us into a nuclear holocaust. The world, it is true, is a dangerous place, but it is also true that no other species is as prone to altruistic behavior toward non-kin, not only the extraordinary altruism of Yad Vashem award winners but also the more mundane and more empirically important altruism reflected in the restraint from first strike that preserved the peace in the Cold War and prevented our ancestors from annihilating each other.

The interpretation of our progenitors as killer apes, popularized by writers such as Robert Ardrey in the 1960s and 1970s, is widely rejected today, in part on the basis of analysis indicating that Raymond Dart seri-ously misinterpreted the original fossil evidence associated with his dis-covery of *Australopithecus* in 1924 (Cartmill 1993, chap. 1). A dent in the child's skull quickly interpreted as consequent upon a blow from another conspecific has been shown to fit very well with the jaw of a saber-toothed tiger found in the same cave. The evidence now seems much stronger that the southern ape was hunted by and at great risk from large carnivores, particularly at night. The hypothesis that intelligence, tool use, language, and human cooperation all flowed from the imperatives, once we had descended from the trees, of seeking out and killing large carnivores, a staple of anthropological texts and museum dioramas through the 1970s, is today almost universally discredited. As the work of ethologists has shown, chimpanzees also have a taste for flesh, yet they have not evolved our higher intelligence. Moreover, as regards the putative link between social hunting and superior intelligence, lions developed complex cooperative hunting skills but evolved neither language nor the ability to do differential equations.

The rise to prominence of the hunter hypothesis that, as Mark Cartmill (1993) has shown, had political appeal on both the left and the right, was certainly influenced by ideological factors. The same can be said for its retreat, but reinterpretation of evidence and the development of competing hypotheses have ultimately been more decisive. One can say this precisely because the hypothesis had such appeal across the political spectrum.

Steven Stanley (1996), for example, has fashioned an argument for the origin of human intelligence emphasizing the challenges of overcoming vulnerability to large carnivores. He maintains that climatic changes (triggered by the uplift of the Isthmus of Panama) resulted in a cooling of temperatures in Africa and a shrinkage of the transitional woodlands between savanna and rain forest, the traditional habitat of *Australopithecus*. As the southern apes were forced to the ground in search of food, they became much more vulnerable to predators. Most of them died out, Stanley suggests, but one group began evolving toward *Homo,* acquiring the higher intelligence associated with tool use; the discovery of fire; language capability; the growth in brain size of the human embryo; and, because of limits on the extent to which the width of the female pelvis could expand while still allowing bipedal locomotion, the birth of babies born more helpless and dependent than those of other species.

The latter was both necessitated and made possible by the final abandonment of trees. The imperatives of learning to avoid being eaten by carnivores, rather than our discovery of how to hunt them with weapons, created the evolutionary advantage for higher intelligence, leading to larger brained infants, whose skulls could squeeze through birth canals only if they were born at an earlier stage of fetal development. Tree climbing by mothers was then impossible, since such helpless infants could not be expected to cling to arboreal caregivers (Stanley 1996).

Whether Stanley's views ultimately gain widespread acceptance remains to be seen. I mention them to indicate the availability of evolutionary scenarios different from those suggested by the hunting hypothesis. *Australopithecus* may have caught and eaten small game and might have engaged in violent internecine conflict, although it seems increasingly unlikely, if we accept the interpretation that he lived in constant fear of predators, retreating to the trees each evening. And it remains possible, although uncertain, that *Homo sapiens* exterminated *Homo neanderthalensis* thirty-five thousand years ago (Trinkaus and Shipman 1993). My argument extends only to a claim about hardwired restraints on intraspecific violence and is subject, as noted, to the important qualification, addressed in chapter 1, that increasing within group solidarity (made possible by this propensity in the first place) may weaken its manifestation toward out-group members.

Focusing our attention on our two closest living relatives, we get a mixed report. The warlike and aggressive behavior of common chimpanzees can be contrasted with the more peaceable mechanisms for dispute settlement observable in bonobos; either set of predispositions may have predominated in our common ancestor. In any event, humans, chimps, and bonobos do not live in a war of all against all;[3] nor is there reason to believe that they or any of their ancestors, including their and our shared ancestor, ever did. de Waal argues, based on comparative study of the previously mentioned three ape species as well as rhesus monkeys and stump-tailed macaques, that inborn predispositions facilitating reconciliation after conflict predate not only the common ancestor of the three chimpanzees but also the common ancestor of monkeys and apes, referring to a branching of the lineage that occurred at least thirty million, rather than just six million, years ago (de Waal 1989, 270). Such mechanisms must be prevalent in humans as well.

Of course there is evidence of violent behavioral tendencies along many branches of our family tree. Such behavior has great salience, but it must be kept in perspective. We can choose to focus on the predatory behavior of wolves and lions to confirm Tennyson's view of nature as red in tooth and claw, but in doing so we risk ignoring the inhibitions these animals exhibit toward intraspecific violence. We can choose to focus on chimpanzees' brutal aggression toward members of other chimpanzee groups, but in doing so we ignore the predispositions that enable their intragroup cohesion, cohesion that extends beyond what can be accounted for by kin selection.

Lorenz's analysis complemented other strands of thinking popular at

---

3. In this context I define a war of all against all as an environment in which there are no restraints on *intraspecific* violence save those predicted by the Hamilton kin selection mechanism.

the time he wrote, including Sigmund Freud's analysis in *Civilization and Its Discontents* (1962). The basic thrust of this view was that humans were *essentially* violent and murderous toward each other and only a thin veneer of civilization reined in these impulses and kept them from manifesting themselves in disastrous fashion. There is no point in whitewashing the ethogram either of humans or other animals. But from a historical standpoint, this view begged and begs the question of how "civilization," presumably a relatively recent development, ever had a chance to restrain the behavior of a species, if the analysis were to be fully accepted, that would in an "uncivilized" state surely have torn itself to shreds eons ago. It ignores the fact that advanced and culturally refined groups of humans have often proved the most murderous (some of the most notorious Nazis prided themselves on their love of great opera and fine art).[4] Attributing to "civilization" in the large the restraint of murderous "basic instincts" runs into the same explanatory problems faced by those who appeal, less globally, to "norms" to account for other-regarding behavior among humans (see chap. 3).

Lorenz's comments actually reinforce the likelihood that ancestral progenitors common to humans, apes, and other mammals possessed hardwired inhibitions against intraspecific violence. In some cases the inhibitions he described extended only as far as the individual's group, pack, or pride. But the cohesion and social interaction in these groups are more than can be accounted for by the Hamilton kin selection model. Predispositions toward playing cooperate in one-shot PDs, at least toward members of the same species, must have been part of the genetic endowment of hominid ancestors long before the two-million-year Pleistocene emphasized by Cosmides and Tooby. Other "cognitive adaptations for social exchange," to use their language, may have developed and strengthened during this more recent period, but they did so on foundations already present. For example, their "cheater detection" module was almost certainly characteristic of our primate forebears, at least in rudimentary form, given the sophisticated political life observable today among chimpanzees (de Waal 1982).

Pleistocene adaptations for social exchange developed alongside the explosion of hominid cranial capacity, but they did so on a foundation of other "adaptations for social exchange" already well established, in particular a PD solution module. It is unlikely that that module can be attributed to the development of increased cranial capacity. After all, the smarter hominids became the more "obvious" it should have been that the

---

4. Lorenz argued, unpersuasively, that in the modern world, humans "succumb to barbarism because they have no more time for cultural interests" (1966, 41).

"best" strategy in a one-shot PD game was to defect. So something else must lie behind observed play in this game. As the example of a highly intelligent serial murderer indicates, there is no necessary correlation between cranial capacity and its presumed correlates[5] and restraint on first strike. If increased intelligence was associated with improved abilities to forecast counterparty behavior, we have seen that such abilities become formally relevant only after an environment of repeated interaction has been established.

Because humans exhibit far more reciprocity than chimpanzees or bonobos and probably more so than the common ancestor, it is likely that humans acquired features facilitating reciprocity during the period of rapid cranial expansion (i.e., the last two million years). This may have involved, for example, improved contact management software, for keeping track of who owed whom what. On the other hand, chimpanzees do not do a bad job keeping track of a favor bank. The development of human language is sometimes suggested as critical to understanding human social behavior. I think this is questionable, since human language, requiring the descent of the larynx in comparison to chimpanzee features, is generally believed to be a relatively recent acquisition.

Over an extended historical period both before and during the Pleistocene, humans and their ancestors evolved behavioral impellers enabling social behavior, domain specific adaptations that are different from those dedicated to facilitating optimal foraging. These impellers are based on functionally specialized neurobiological subsystems that are, in their origin, evolutionarily older than our highly developed neocortex. These impellers provide guidance sometimes in conflict with that generated by other faculties, in particular the deductive logic and mathematical reasoning skills we associate so strongly with rationality (the role of skill in statistical inference is more ambiguous here). Behavioral science will advance as we develop a consistent evolutionary accounting of how these systems survived forces of selection at different levels and as we develop, through observational, experimental, neurobiological, and neuroanatomical research, a better understanding of what these different systems are, how they work together, and how they sometimes compete with each other in guiding human action.

What has not proved satisfactory has been the effort by economists and political scientists to develop a unified theory of human behavior based only on a general-purpose reasoning ability devoted to advancing

---

5. Einstein's brain was not particularly large, and, on average, a Neanderthal's cranial capacity was larger than that of *Homo sapiens.* Nevertheless, there is broad agreement that substantial differences in average cranial capacity between species correlate with significant differences in intelligence.

the material well-being of the individual actor. Such an approach does moderately well in understanding foraging behavior and its modern counterparts. It performs much more poorly, however, as an approach to social behavior involving any sort of strategic component. A goal of game theory has been to demonstrate the contrary, yet, as we have seen, such analysis has important deficiencies as a descriptive or predictive theory of human behavior. The need for an alternate approach is driven by, among other observations, the peculiar (from the standpoint of normative game theory) outcomes of single play and fixed duration Prisoner's Dilemma games and the other experimental evidence adduced in chapters 1, 3, and 4. Analogous efforts within an evolutionary framework restricted to selection at the level of the individual organism alone (see discussion of Trivers and Frank in chaps. 3 and 4) have proved similarly unsatisfactory.

What is needed is an empirically based characterization of the human ethogram providing better predictive power than that realized by the standard economic model, derived using a priori reasoning and sometimes defended as universally applicable by a superficial and incomplete understanding of the process of natural selection. This ethogram should reflect not just the variety of innate drives possessed by humans but also an understanding of human cognition as to some degree modular, reflecting the functionally specialized hardwiring that lies behind it.

For all those who have pursued the elusive quarry of an individual level explanation of the origin of cooperative behavior, the methodological prescription proposed here is radical. I have discussed some of the behavioral evidence supporting it. It is important as well that the evidence supporting the proposed view of cognition be marshaled and considered. This issue is relevant not only for economists. Although economists have been profoundly aware of and often taken great pride in how their discipline differs from other social sciences, in particular sociology and anthropology, its assumptions about human cognition and the role of evolution in determining how it now operates are in certain respects quite similar to those common to these other disciplines.

The Standard Social Science Model: A Useful Straw Man

John Tooby and Leda Cosmides have characterized the standard social science model (SSSM) as one that presupposes a fundamental division between biology and the institutional/cultural environment. The SSSM is a straw man, but a useful one. Almost all social scientists have granted that biology endows humans with basic drives toward food and procreation and away from life-threatening situations and that these drives are manifested in physiological and emotional states such as hunger, sexual desire, and fear. Even John Watson, the father of American behaviorism, did allow a role for unconditioned propensities for fear, anger, and love. The thrust of his efforts, however, was to minimize the emphasis on instincts reflected in the work, for example, of William James.

But the modular view of cognition involves considerably more than the proposition that innate drives may be more widespread than behaviorists are comfortable acknowledging. Modularity goes to the heart of common social scientific assumptions regarding the *cognitive means* used by humans to pursue their ends. Thus, whereas a behaviorist psychologist and an economist might differ over whether a drive was truly innate and thus neither conditionable nor extinguishable, both, like many other social scientists, would find congenial the idea that humans pursue the satisfaction of the drive through the use of a general reasoning and learning capability not specialized to particular domains of cognition. For example, the standard social science view has been that, using this general capability, we learn language through imitation and reinforcement, in the same way that a child learns not to touch a stove because it may be hot.

The SSSM can be seen, therefore, as embodying two related propositions. First, whatever biological influences may have operated on essential human predispositions in our prehistory, these have been almost entirely superseded by environmental/cultural factors, thus minimizing the role of innate drives or desires. Second, cognition operates using a general-purpose mechanism. Categories and data structures arise entirely as the result of experience, rather than being partly hardwired at birth, and the same kind of advanced reasoning algorithms are applied to data regardless of their domain (Tooby and Cosmides 1992; Pinker 1997, 44–45).

Tooby and Cosmides' characterization, it should be noted, glides over some important differences in the perspective and approach of economics as compared with other social sciences. The key difference has concerned the role accorded culture. Microeconomics does not fit neatly into the SSSM because of the privileged status it has traditionally granted methodologically individualist models that are at best agnostic about cultural influences on behavior (preferences are to be taken as given; their origin "non disputandum est"). Traditional nineteenth- and twentieth-century sociology and anthropology might be characterized as having taken the view that cultural structures and the social norms they define "non disputandum sunt." Economists, on the other hand, generally remain silent regarding or object to the view that influences on social behavior must be overwhelmingly cultural; the explanatory status of culture or the institutional environment has always been problematic within the discipline.

However, *none of these three disciplines* has been sympathetic to the proposition that the underlying categories and data structures organizing cognition might have a biological, unconditioned foundation or that reasoning algorithms might be specialized to particular domains. Here is where the real similarity with other social sciences lies: most economists, like "most intellectuals [,] think that the human mind must somehow have escaped the evolutionary process" (Pinker 1997, chap. 1). That is, for economists as much as for other social scientists, the mind floats freely in its own realm, untethered to biological or neurobiological substrates. The reasoning abilities it enables are assumed to be general, not specialized to particular domains. Categories into which knowledge is organized are assumed *not* to be prespecified, or differentially favored, at birth. Finally, there is little place within the methodological stance typically adopted for the proposition that evolution, operating over the millions of years of prehistory, has endowed us with functionally specialized cognitive modules that operate independently of our "general reasoning ability" and may trump or augment the guidance of mathematical reasoning, propositional or categorical logic, or standard procedures for statistical inference.

It is a significant leap for economists, almost as much as for other social scientists, to abandon a comfortable Cartesian dichotomy between mind and body and systematically explore evolutionary influences on human behavior and cognition, particularly the proposition that cognition (and consequently behavior) may be influenced by brain subsystems adapted evolutionarily to particular types of situations. Structural functionalists often appealed to evolutionary analogies to explain why certain features of social organization persisted: obviously they did so because they were beneficial to the group; social adaptations that did not meet this criterion did not survive. But, as we have noted, there was, in that tradition, no systematic exploration of how such adaptations could ever have become established, overcoming the obvious selection against them at the individual level.

Economists, on the other hand, have been perfectly happy appealing to Darwin as justification for the assumption that humans are driven by material self-interest advanced by a general-purpose reasoning capability (humans are self-interested and pursue their goals rationally). As we have seen, however, the standard economic model has, using this engine alone, not been able to account for the origin and persistence of altruistic behavior, some form of which underlies most social adaptations.

Evidence for Early Acquisition of First Move(r) Altruism

The chronology of evolutionary branching and the characteristics of common ancestors are critical to my claim that propensities enabling complex social organization *predate* the evolutionary refinement of higher reasoning skills we associate with the more recent growth in cranial capacity—and thus that attainment of such organization is not dependent on or the consequence of the sophisticated cognitive and ratiocinative skills rational choice theorists are prone to emphasize. How are we able, in spite of a gaping hole in the ape fossil record in Africa from about five to fourteen million years ago, to state with confidence that humans and their ancestors have a history of social organization that goes back at least five to ten million years (Cosmides and Tooby 1992, 164)?

The claim is based on a confluence of evidence from different sources. But it begins with our ability to be precise about evolutionary branching and in particular to state that six million years ago we shared a common ancestor with two other surviving chimpanzee species. As indicated, traditional foundations for such a claim, fossilized skulls and skeletons, are not by themselves sufficient to establish chronology at this level of precision. The details of the currently accepted branching chart have been established on the basis of advances in the calculation of differences among species in molecular composition, in particular of DNA, in conjunction with the use of the known fossil record to calibrate these clocks.

Since the early 1950s and the work of Watson and Crick we have known that DNA is the key to understanding an organism's structure and performance. Deoxyribonucleic acid is a large molecule constructed in the form of a twisted ladder. The components of the rails are alternating sugar and phosphate molecules. Attached to each sugar, and forming the rungs, are pairs of nitrogen-containing "base" molecules: adenine (A), cytosine (C), guanine (G), and thymine (T), each pair held together by weak hydrogen bonds. Adenine always pairs with thymine, and cytosine always pairs with guanine. The DNA in each human cell consists of about 3.1 billion base pairs inherited from both parents. Much smaller sequences of mitochondrial DNA, inherited only from one's mother, float in organelles outside of the cell nucleus, the basis for continuing investigation of the long-standing historical controversy regarding the relationship between Thomas Jefferson and Sally Hemmings, as well as developing insights into historical patterns of human migration.

The 3.1 billion base pairs in the human genome, laid end to end, would measure about two meters in length. Every cell in one's body, with the exception of the somatic cells, contains exactly the same information distributed among forty-six chromosomes. Genes are portions of the genome consisting of strings of base pairs marked by start and stop codes. Differentially concentrated among the different chromosomes, they contain sequences of base pairs that code for protein assemblage (exons) interspersed with strings that do not (introns). Genes code not only for structure—how an organism will develop as it grows from a fertilized egg—but also for performance, influencing how the organism will function as it matures.

The key developmental function of DNA is to direct the assemblage of complex proteins from twenty amino acids. This assemblage is carried out with the participation of messenger RNA molecules in protein factories made of RNA and proteins known as ribosomes and is done according to a code "written" in triplets of base pairs (codons) in the organism's functional DNA. The code was deciphered in 1966, thirteen years after Watson and Crick discovered the double helical structure of DNA. Shared by all living things on this planet, it is the strongest evidence that life on earth is descended from a common ancestor, a conclusion reinforced by the similarity of the chemical and physical design of cells throughout the living world and the evidence on chirality (handedness). DNA in all organisms is right handed (coiled up like a right handed double helix), even though there is no principle in chemistry or molecular biology preventing the construction of left handed DNA (Davies 1999, 70–74).

Readers interested in viewing an updated map of the genome and obtaining a sense of how it is being used in commercial and academic research should consult <http://www.celera.com>, the website of the private corporation founded by Dr. Craig Venter, or <http://genome.ucsc.edu>, which provides a window into the complementary work done by the government- and foundation-supported consortium that initiated the sequencing effort. Competition between these two efforts culminated in the joint announcement of completion of a draft sequence in June 2000 and the simultaneous publication of reports by the two groups of preliminary analyses in February 2001 (International Human Genome Sequencing Consortium 2001; Venter et al. 2001).

These analyses indicate that there are between twenty-five thousand and forty thousand human genes, a much lower range than the estimates of one hundred thousand commonly cited as little as a year earlier (thirty thousand appears to be the current consensus estimate). Genes (coding DNA) occupy collectively a small portion of the genome. Of its 200 centimeters, roughly 197 are noncoding (sometimes called "junk" or nonfunctional) DNA—residues of evolutionary history that may have an indirect influence on structure or performance in ways now not well understood. Certain sections are residues of bacteria or retroviruses that attacked human ancestors millions of years ago and have left their genetic signatures. Others are pseudogenes, once functioning genes that accumulated so many mutations as to become noncoding. And perhaps 50 centimeters contain strings of base pairs with, as far as we can now tell, no relevant genetically coded information.

Because most of the coding (as well as noncoding) DNA is the same for all humans—the reason we are all similar in design—more than 199 centimeters of any human's genome are exactly the same as that found in every cell of every other human. And approximately 198 are identical to that found in every cell of every chimpanzee. Minor differences are enough to direct the assemblage of organisms that are in many respects identical, but nevertheless belong to different species. Indeed, all mammals are remarkably similar genetically, a point reinforced by completion of the sequencing of the mouse and human genomes. Of thirty thousand human genes, all but about three hundred have a homologue in the mouse, even though our last common ancestor lived one hundred million years ago, putting some two hundred million years of evolutionary distance between us.

"Functional" or coding DNA comprises between 1.1 and 1.5 percent of the genome, most of which is identical across individuals. The 0.1 percent or less of base pairs (nucleotides) that differ within human populations (approximately 800 per million base pairs according to Venter et al.'s latest estimates) produce polymorphisms that give rise to the genetic component of human variation. It is important to emphasize the overwhelming genetic similarity of all humans and, for that matter, members of closely related species. But there are understandably strong economic incentives to gaining an understanding of genetic influences on individual variation within human populations. Thus a great deal of commercial and academic research is now focused on the less than 0.1 percent of base pairs that may differ.

As the completion of the first draft of the human genome neared in 1998, major resource flows moved to the identification of single nucleotide polymorphisms (SNPs) and the investigation of their correlation with susceptibility to particular diseases. Both diagnosis and treatment stand to benefit. With the ability cheaply to genotype an individual, it will become possible to design drug treatments likely to be most effective and best tolerated by a particular individual. As of June 2000, over 147,000 SNPs had been posted to the website maintained by the National Center for Biotechnology Information <http://www.ncbi.nlm.nih.gov/SNP>. Progress in identifying these has been extraordinarily rapid. The International Human Genome Sequencing Consortium (2001) reported 1.4 million SNPs, Venter et al. (2001) 2.1 million, and the NCBI website, as of December 8, 2000, posted information on over 2.5 million of them. In conjunction with such projects as the genetic study of the entire population of Iceland now being conducted by the firm deCODE genetic <http://www.decode.com> and established research programs on identical and fraternal twins (Hunt 1990, 54–56), it is certain that over the next decade and beyond research will identify more and more genetic correlates not only of disease susceptibility, but also of phenotypic variation, both physical and behavioral.

The full implications of these scientific achievements are only beginning to be digested, but it is hard to imagine that the social and behavioral sciences can remain unaffected by them. A basic understanding of what has and is being accomplished through these efforts is necessary to evaluate claims about heritability of both physical and behavioral traits and because of its bearing on advances in our knowledge of evolutionary history, upon which I now focus.

The writing of evolutionary history consists in determining the branch points at which paths leading to surviving and extinct species diverged. Fossils, which can be dated using evidence on the geological strata in which they are found and techniques based on known decay rates for radioactive isotopes present in accompanying organic material, have traditionally been the primary sources for this history. In the past decade, however, advances in biochemistry have revolutionized evolutionary history. As a consequence, we are now able to fill in some gaps in the fossil record and resolve other long-standing issues by measuring how the DNA in one surviving species differs from that in another.

One technique, DNA hybridization, involves taking samples from two species, splitting them into single strands of DNA by applying heat, and then mixing single strands from each species (Sibley and Ahlquist 1984). The more closely related are the species, the tighter will the strands bond as the mixture cools. One then measures to what temperature one must reheat the combined strands in order to again separate them by causing the mixture to melt. The more closely related the species the more heat is required to separate the DNA hybrid bonds, and the number of degrees by which the melting point of the mixture falls short of the melting point of DNA from a single species is roughly proportional to genetic difference. A one degree centigrade difference is equivalent to about a 1 percent genetic difference.

Paleontological evidence can then be used to calibrate how rapidly the "clock" of molecular change operates. We know from the fossil record that monkeys diverged from apes 25–30 million years ago and now differ in DNA by about 7.3 percent. Gibbons branched out about 22 million years ago. Orangutans diverged from chimps and gorillas between 12 and 16 million years ago and now differ in about 3.6 percent of DNA. Gorillas diverged about 8 million years ago and differ from humans in about 2.3 percent of their base pairs.

The molecular composition of our DNA differs from that of chimpanzees by less than 2 percent and from that of bonobos by slightly less, one of the bases for the current consensus that the early hominid line diverged from that leading to the two chimp species approximately six million years ago, about half the previous estimate (Sibley and Ahlquist 1984). Estimates of genetic difference based on amino acid sequences in proteins, mitochondrial DNA, and globin pseudogene DNA all support this conclusion (Brown 1990, chap. 9; Diamond 1992, 22–24). *We can make these inferences with confidence even though the paleontological record does not provide us with a fossilized skeleton of our common ancestor. Australopithecus afarensis,* the first definite fossilized hominid, appeared about four million years ago.

The evolutionary lines leading to modern day bonobos and chimpanzees split about three million years ago (de Waal and Lanting 1997, 3), with chimpanzees evolving a male dominated, status conscious society characterized by much physical violence, while bonobos evolved in more sexually egalitarian directions, exhibiting little physical violence among themselves. Are bonobos or chimpanzees the more accurate mirror for humans? We cannot say definitively, although bonobos are the only species, with the exception of *Homo sapiens,* to practice face-to-face (ventro-ventral) copulation.

The two species of chimpanzees, *Pan troglodytes* and *Pan paniscus,* the common chimpanzee and bonobo respectively, are our closest living relatives. Jared Diamond (1992) has argued that they belong in the same genus as *Homo sapiens,* basing his position on the proposition that taxonomy ought to be driven by evidence on genetic distance.

Homo sapiens, Pan troglodytes, and *Pan paniscus* each represent a distinct evolutionary pathway from a common ancestral species that lived six million years ago. Traits shared by these three surviving species give us clues as to the social and behavioral characteristics of the common ancestor but may also show similar evolutionary pathways to common outcomes; thus none can necessarily be taken as reflecting characteristics of the common ancestor. Observation of the two *Pan* species does, however, lead to a sharply restricted set of attributes that can be considered uniquely human. It used to be claimed, for example, that humans were the only tool users, the only species with self-awareness (as tested by ability to recognize one's features in a mirror), the only species to engage in face-to-face copulation, and the only species to murder its own. Each of these propositions has now been shown to be false. Claims regarding how unique are the human understanding and use of language continue to be debated, in the face of demonstrated capabilities of chimps, bonobos, and other primates.

The biological laboratory represented by our closest living relatives is shrinking, with the number of wild chimps now estimated to be about 150,000, down from one to two million a century ago. Of these, the number of bonobos is estimated to be only 10,000–25,000, of whom only about 100 are in captivity worldwide, compared to over 1,000 chimpanzees (de Waal and Lanting 1997, 172).[6]

The ethologist Franz de Waal has studied both chimpanzees and bonobos in detail. In his 1982 book *Chimpanzee Politics* he provides compelling evidence of reciprocal altruism among chimpanzees, as well as a Machiavellian male dominated society obsessed with power and status. de Waal's work is not, as it is sometimes portrayed (Dawkins 1998), an overly sentimental portrait of our relatives, although he admits freely to having initially and naively overestimated their cooperative problem solving abilities (de Waal and Lanting 1997, 84). So did Jane Goodall. As is true among our own human relatives, it turns out that there is plenty of evidence of meanness, nastiness, and, in some cases, downright viciousness, including murder, displayed particularly toward nongroup members. Hostility between human groups bears an eerie similarity to that seen in chimps. Chimps patrol territorial boundaries, seek out isolated nongroup members, and kill them (Goodall 1990, chap. 10). But chimps also know how to play Tit-for-Tat, form alliances, and, as a consequence, establish cooperative relations with each other.

Bonobos, originally called pygmy chimps, display much less physical violence toward each other, use sex as a means of defusing potential conflict, and have a distinctive, more female dominated social structure (de Waal and Lanting 1997). They also, as does *Pan troglodytes,* establish and maintain cooperative relations among each other. So, of course, do humans. We can see different aspects of the human ethogram reflected in the two chimp species, for example, face-to-face copulation in bonobos and male dominated groupings permeated with a concern for status, territoriality, and access to females in chimpanzees. But all three surviving species live in groups based on cooperative interaction. Based on this evidence, and paleontological evidence of early hominids and their campsites (Isaac 1983), it is reasonable to extend the history of hominid and prehominid social organization at least back to the point where our evolutionary route diverged from that leading to chimpanzees and bonobos. Genetic tendencies facilitating such behavior were almost certainly widespread in our hominid and hominoid ancestors and most likely already pervasive in the small groupings out of which more complex human societies emerged.

Since there is documented observational evidence of chimpanzees practicing Tit-for-Tat, or reciprocal altruism, it is almost certain that the

---

6. Data on total number of wild chimps from *Wall Street Journal,* February 1, 1999, p. B1. Bonobos have a smaller head but are otherwise about the size of an *Australopithecus.*

basic genetic predispositions and cognitive capabilities enabling social behavior antedate the development of larger cranial capacities that have permitted as an unintended[7] consequence advancements in human capabilities for statistical inference, logic, and the elaboration of complex mathematical and game theory models.

It is putting the cart before the horse to suggest that reciprocal altruism as it is practiced by humans emerged as the result of cogitating agents armed only with highly developed capabilities for logic and lacking any specialized (and evolutionarily prior) genetic predispositions toward such behavior. More likely is it that during the Pleistocene epoch—roughly two million years ago until the end of the last Ice Age and the beginnings of the Neolithic revolution ten thousand years ago—complex social organization moved increasingly beyond that enabled by propensities to make grants of first move(r) altruism involving forgoing of first strike (failure to harm) and began to include a higher frequency of grants providing affirmative assistance to non-kin. While the game theoretical structures of grants involving forbearance and affirmative help are identical, it is the growing importance of the latter that accounts for the greater range and complexity of human reciprocity compared to that observable in chimpanzee and bonobo groups and, most likely, our common ancestor. Adam Smith viewed human exchange as rooted in what he viewed as a natural human propensity to truck and barter, and in the growing frequency of these affirmative grants we may see its origin.

We cannot be certain why cranial capacity expanded so much, but we know that it did, forcing female pelvises to widen about as far as they could without threatening bipedal locomotion and causing human babies to be born at a much less developmentally advanced stage than is true for chimpanzees. There are many candidates for explaining this expansion, sometimes divided into those emphasizing the challenges of dealing with the nonhuman environment, the ecological intelligence hypothesis, and those, the social intelligence hypothesis, that stress the challenges of dealing with conspecifics. Early contenders, such as the imperatives of tool use, are today accorded less credence given the accumulating evidence that such use is not uniquely human and the millions of years over which cranial capacity grew rapidly while tool use remained primitive and unchanging. One must also be skeptical that it is associated with a shift to meat eat-

---

7. Again, I extend the metaphor of considering the operation of natural selection as a designer. There clearly were no designer and no intentionality in the process. My point is that advances in the understanding of logic, arithmetic, and higher mathematics are features of the last several thousand years of human existence, far too short a time for natural selection to have played any role in their development or for their development to have had significant influence on natural selection.

ing: as noted, it is not clear that the cooperative hunting skills displayed by humans are superior to those exhibited, for example, by lions.

Robin Fox has argued that our small brained hominid progenitors stumbled onto the evolutionary advantages of developing transmittable culture, increasing the premium on learning capabilities and the ability to represent ideas or concepts symbolically, which in turn created selection pressures for more CPU and RAM (Fox 1989, 29–30). Others have more specifically emphasized the challenges of interacting with the human, as opposed to the nonhuman, environment, leading to an arms race in which politics, both sexual and nonsexual, placed a premium on evolving, at considerable biological expense, ever larger brains (Ridley 1993, chap. 10). But we need to be specific about the range of skills involved in this arms race. If human survival in interactions with other conspecifics depended on figuring out the Nash equilibrium in one-shot or fixed and known duration PDs, then good logical and mathematical skills would be the key to evolutionary success. Clearly, however, there must be more to it than this.

Whatever the case for linking the growth of cranial capacity to the imperatives of social interaction, development must have occurred within the context of a social "intelligence" based upon a widespread and evolutionarily earlier predisposition to make grants of first move(r) altruism. It is simply implausible that the evolution of bigger brains, making available larger memory as well as language in its human implementation, was a precondition for hominid social organization at the level observable in chimpanzee or bonobo groups. The studies of the two *Pan* species, with their more limited cranial capacities, are evidence in themselves against this view.

Large Brains and Prisoner's Dilemmas

Beyond observing that relatively small brained chimpanzees and bonobos live in cooperative groups extending beyond kin, we can offer several reflections on why an expansion of brain capacity plays an ambiguous role in helping humans "solve" Prisoner's Dilemmas. Learning more about the game does not help us solve it, if by solving we mean arriving at the cooperate-cooperate profile. Being smarter in the sense of being more proficient at mathematical reasoning or formal logic does not help solve it, since these skills drive us toward mutual defection. Possessing language and, hence, the ability to communicate with one's counterparty does not in the least change the normative counsel of defection. Proficiency in statistical inference presupposes the availability of data based on past histories of interaction and becomes relevant only once interaction is expected to extend beyond one play, even if of fixed duration, and we are prepared to entertain the possibility that our counterparty may, irrationally, choose a cooperative or conditionally cooperative strategy. Similarly, the ability, based on facial expression, body language, voice stress, or intonation, to forecast the likelihood of cooperation or defection in advance of play can be quite valuable but only assuming the problem of getting beyond the one-shot PD has been solved.

The cognitive apparatus necessary to form fully "rational" expectations is more sophisticated than that needed to form adaptive expectations and frees problem solving from strict reliance on trial and error methodology or hardwired behavioral heuristics.[8] Human reliance on rational expectations is, however, not unique but rather a matter of degree of sophistication. In the 1920s the German psychologist Wolfgang Köhler documented problem solving by chimpanzees based on planning and foresight, thus providing one of the first challenges to the simple behaviorist model (de Waal and Lanting 1997, 36). The ability to employ more sophisticated expectations formation mechanisms would have made us better foragers or, more generally, better interactors with the natural environment. And it would have made us more successful at playing more complex PD games, given that it was building on an already well-established PD solution module necessary to solve simpler ones.

One of Robert Frank's most striking experimental contributions has been his demonstration that humans are fairly good at predicting who will defect and who will cooperate in single play PD games, provided they are able to talk with their counterparties for half an hour previous to playing, even when players have never met before and confidentiality precludes their ex post knowledge of actual play (Frank 1988, 139–43, 157). Three out of four times, a player correctly predicts cooperation by a counterparty; defection is correctly predicted six out of ten times. Players achieved a mutual cooperation rate of 68 percent in the experiment.

Recent neurobiological research by Antonio Damasio and his colleagues makes a strong case that the ability to make these forecasts is localized in the region of the brain known as the amygdala. Normal subjects consistently and with high agreement identify pictures of faces of individuals they consider trustworthy and those whom they do not. Individuals

---

8. The concept of rational expectations heavily influenced macroeconomic theory in the late 1970s and 1980s, where it was used to argue that costless inflation could be achieved simply by *announcing* a lower growth rate of the money supply. Humans, it was argued, were smart enough to anticipate the long run consequence, rather than be forced to learn through the experience of gradually falling inflation accompanied by high unemployment. The 1982 recession, although not disproof of the basic principle, did raise questions about whether or not it was rational, ex ante, to find credible Paul Volker's October 1979 announcement of a change in monetary regime.

for whom brain scans have identified damage to the amygdala are consistently unable to do so (Adolphs and Damasio 1998; Damasio 1999, 66–67). They are unable to process the nonverbal cues in facial expressions that, in part, enable Frank's subjects to do as well as they do in prediction.

For humans predisposed to play cooperate, the availability of these forecasting abilities reduces somewhat the individual level fitness disadvantage associated with that propensity. By facilitating "assortative mating," it increases the power of group selection to favor predispositions to play such strategies by increasing the variation of altruist frequency between groups. Why this is so can be appreciated by realizing that if there is no variation in such frequency between groups, group selection is powerless.

It would be interesting, in this regard, to try to teach pairs of chimpanzees the game and see how they play. The idea is not completely outlandish. David Premack, for example, has shown that chimps can isolate *cause.* Shown before and after pictures of an apple cut in half or a paper scribbled on, they can identify what object caused the change (Premack 1976). Why shouldn't they be able to learn a PD game? My prediction is that we would see cooperation in 25 to 50 percent of experimental subjects in single play games, rates lower, but not an order of magnitude lower, than those exhibited by human subjects. This similarity of behavior, were it confirmed, would stand in sharp contrast to all sorts of tests calling on the enhanced capabilities of the human neocortex in which human-chimp comparisons would be almost nonsensical.

Although there is no formal difference in the game theoretic structure of altruistic acts that involve failure to harm, as opposed to those that affirmatively provide benefit, the incidence of acts of the latter type is higher in humans than in other species and provides the foundation for the exchange of different goods or services, different not just in their particular identity but in kind. It is the latter that ultimately leads to the development of complex economies. Because of the difficulty of establishing a double coincidence of wants, however, quid pro quo exchange is unusual in primitive human as compared with more advanced societies and was almost certainly unusual in early hominid groups.

Generalized reciprocity can be understood as a series of nonsimultaneous unilateral transfers taking place over time that are, nevertheless, in the long term expected to have some rough balance. The absence of complex simultaneous exchange in hunter-gatherer societies is not the consequence of their possessing different behavioral predispositions. We see more unilateral transfers in such societies (transfers that do not appear to be part of an exchange transaction) not necessarily because their denizens are inherently more altruistic than we are but because they lack the social contrivance of money.

Whereas such transfers among non-kin are never unlimited (thus their interpretation as generalized reciprocity) their occurrence takes place against a backdrop established by first move(r) altruism, initially of the former (forbearance) kind, then of the latter (affirmative help) kind. One needs mutual failure to harm through forgoing of first strike to get the ball rolling. One then needs a first move(r) willing to make a unilateral transfer without knowledge of whether it will be reciprocated or guarantee that it will be.

I do not mean to suggest that humans have evolved to the point where the practice of first move(r) altruism in unstructured situations is automatic or universal. Clearly it is not. Genotypic influences on this predisposition have not necessarily evolved to the point of fixation: polymorphism is likely, and deviant tendencies may persist at low and stable levels. Moreover, in any individual the predisposition toward first move(r) altruism must almost certainly be evoked by environmental cues and can be attenuated in their absence or in the presence of different ones. Socialization, the particular form of cultural norms, and political structure can all influence how these tendencies play out in particular instances.

But only in some instances should we view norms as exerting an independent influence on aggregate behavior. For example, norms forbidding incest between siblings and between parents and children can be viewed as universal and codifying, whereas explicit norms against marriage among first cousins are more likely of the second type, not necessarily adaptive but having relatively more to do with political conflicts involving property inheritance than the prevention of defective children (Betzig 1992; Ridley 1993, 242–43).

Aristotle argued that every organism or thing had both accidental and essential features. Cultural differences represent that which is accidental. What unifies us as humans is the essential. The meaning and interpretation of facial expressions signifying joy, grief, shame, or anger are essential (Ekman and Friesen 1975). The meaning and interpretation of an embrace may be culturally accidental. And although the particular language that we learn is determined by cultural inheritance, the ability to handle a complex language is a genetic trait both unique and essential to humans (Crick 1994, 11).

Language Acquisition

Chimpanzees, bonobos, and humans represent three evolutionary paths from a common ancestor. The brain and other structures of that common ancestor, in turn, reflected hundreds of millions of years of prior evolution. This evolutionary perspective gives credence to the view that humans (and the other chimps) are likely to possess functionally specialized mental organs, some with a longer evolutionary lineage than others. But where is confirmatory evidence based on the study of humans showing that it is meaningful to speak of specialized neurobiological subsystems affecting cognition and behavior?

The most compelling evidence comes from the study of language acquisition and the structure of human grammars. Humans are hardwired at birth with deep structures shared by all human languages. The Skinnerian view that infants *learn* these principles (Skinner 1957) is inconsistent with the disproportionality between the sheer quantity of stimuli infants would have to receive to discriminate, through learning alone, among all potential forms of grammar and the quantity of stimuli they actually receive.[9]

Linguists have by and large accepted the views first advanced by Noam Chomsky in his 1957 book *Syntactic Structures* and forcefully articulated in his 1959 review of Skinner's *Verbal Behavior* (1957). Chomsky argued that the brain possesses functionally specialized subsystems permitting infants to acquire language and imposing deep structural uniformities on all known human grammars. These capabilities operate independently of the influence of local cultural variation. All children, irrespective of their intelligence levels or nationality and regardless of whether they are encouraged to do so, begin to learn language at the same age (seven to eight months), speak whole words by about age one, and by age six speak in complete grammatical sentences. As they acquire language, infants use the same sounds and learn them, within a given language, in the same sequences. English speakers, for example, learn *a* before *i* and *u* and learn *p, b,* and *m* before *t.* Vocabulary acquisition is extraordinarily rapid. By age eighteen, the typical U.S. high school graduate knows about forty-five thousand words, which works out to an average of over twenty-five hundred words a year learned starting at age one. Whereas most human children must be formally taught to read, they do not need such instruction to learn to speak.

Finally, although grammars vary across languages, there are certain deep structural rules, forming a universal human grammar, that are never violated. In a language with both inflectional endings (e.g., indicating plurals and possessives) and derivational endings (that might, e.g., change a verb to a noun), the inflectional ending always follows the derivational ending. For example, the verb form "throw" can become the noun form "throw*er*" by adding the derivational ending *-er.* This can then be inflected using a plural or possessive ending to form "thrower*s*" or "thrower*'s.*" There are approximately five thousand known human languages, one

---

9. This problem is known as the "poverty of the stimulus."

thousand on the island of New Guinea alone (Diamond 1997, 31; Ruhlen 1987). *None of these languages* violates the order in which inflectional and derivational endings are added, and yet there is no reason, from a software engineering standpoint, why this order should be inviolate.

Similarly, no human language forms questions simply by reversing the entire word order of a sentence, and yet that might seem a perfectly natural thing to do were one "designing" a language from scratch. All human languages have a word for *good;* in some *bad* is indicated by *not good,* but in none is the reverse true. In this case *good* is considered unmarked, *bad,* marked. Similarly for the words *deep* and *shallow, wide* and *narrow, many* and *few,* with the first of each pair considered unmarked. In English, because *many* is unmarked, we often say, "How many did you buy . . ." but rarely "How few did you buy?" *All* human languages indicate whether a noun is subject or object either by word order or by inflection. Some rules reflect binary switches: languages go in either of only two directions, but "choice" of one brings with it a set of reliably predictable implications. If standard word order is subject-verb-object (as in English) the language will use *pre*positions and usually place question words at the beginning. If the standard word order in a language is subject-object-verb, it will have question words at the end and use *post*positions. Finally, one might note this intriguing commonality: in all societies, the average duration of a line of poetry is approximately three seconds (Turner and Pöppel 1983). Is this purely accidental?

These conclusions, and many others, suggest that humans are born with a hardwired taxonomic structure for different kinds of words and relations among them (categories of words and rules of universal grammar) that gives us an innate ability to acquire language and that acquisition is not simply the result of learning and imitation (Brown 1991, 78–80; Pinker 1994, 150–51, 233–40; Trefil 1997, 52–54).[10] Studies of the language capabilities of individuals with particular types of brain damage locate this wiring in Broca's area of the frontal lobe and, just behind it, in Wernicke's area on the parietal lobe, both areas that expanded greatly in the last half million years of evolution.[11] Because language is of relatively recent evolutionary lineage, it cannot itself have been a precondition for complex

---

10. Ironically, Chomsky has been skeptical that one can tell a coherent story about how these structures evolved under the pressures of natural selection and has been a leader in rejecting the idea that one can find any precursors of human language ability in our close animal relatives. One need not accept all of his positions to recognize the impact of his scholarship (see Pinker and Bloom 1990).

11. As Lumsden and Wilson put it, "Language is not just the inevitable spinoff of a generalized intelligence. It is the peculiar product of a recently created division of labor among specialized portions of the brain and novel epigenetic rules" (1983, 107).

social organization. The characteristics of human languages and our ability to acquire them are nevertheless relevant for the themes of this book because they provide powerful evidence for the principles both of cognitive modularity and of cross-population universals in human cognition.

These are remarkable discoveries, for they suggest that the appropriate metaphor for our minds at birth is not that of an unformatted hard drive but rather one that has been, at the genetic factory, preformatted and partitioned and has had system and application software, including that appropriate for databases, preinstalled. As Pinker has observed, "Some of the organization of grammar would have to be there from the start, part of the language learning mechanism that allows children to make sense out of the noises they hear from their parents" (1994, 125). Suppose we were to rewrite the preceding sentence to read as follows: "Some of the organization of social relations would have to be there from the start, part of the social relations learning mechanism that allows children to make sense out of the behavior they witness from their parents (and others)." Such a proposition would be just as revolutionary and shocking but, I suggest, no less true.

Infant Cognition

Evidence that humans enter the world with their brains preformatted to organize sensory inputs into predetermined categories and relationships among them is reinforced by research in infant cognition. Some of the following conclusions will appear startling, so a word on methodology is in order. The youngest infants used as subjects for these experiments are three to four months of age. Experimenters first familiarize infants with the initial phenomenon to the point of boredom and measure their baseline visual attention. They then alter a stimulus. If infants pay attention to the new phenomenon by staring at it longer, experimenters interpret this as evidence that the babies are startled or surprised by it. On the other hand, if no departure from the baseline level of attention is registered, experimenters conclude that what the infant sees is consistent with his or her existing mental models of how the world should work. The behavior the researchers attempt to detect is similar to the special visual attention adults pay to apparatus when watching a magician whose feats seem to violate known physical laws. These techniques are used, for example, to determine that infants are surprised by a demonstration of a solid object apparently passing through another solid object (Spelke 1991).

Researchers wish to test very young children, because they are trying to isolate what taxonomic categories and relations among them infants bring with them into the world. Such primitives, it is argued, cannot be attributed to learning along the traditional behaviorist operant conditioning model any more than can be childhood mastery of rules of grammar. Obviously, postnatal learning effects cannot be entirely ruled out. But prior to the age of three or four months, infant behavior is too unstable to make testing using this methodology practical. Moreover, by this age children's stereovision, visual acuity, visual attention, and motion detection have come on-line. On the other hand, subjects are still very young, only barely able to see, let alone reach and touch, and have not yet begun to acquire language.

Extending the frontiers of this kind of research, Kotovsky and Baillargeon (1998) have shown that 2.5-month-old infants have a basic understanding of collision events and that 6.5-month-old infants understand how the size of a moving object affects the trajectory of a struck stationary object. If a medium sized cylinder rolls down a ramp and knocks a toy bug a certain distance, they are surprised if a smaller cylinder knocks the bug farther, but not if a larger cylinder does.

The results from these kinds of experiments are consistent with the hypothesis that infants understand the concept of an object as something whose parts tend to move together. This is no mean feat of visual processing, even for adults. Our eyes tell us we see objects as "a stretch of the visual field with a smooth silhouette, a stretch with a homogeneous color and texture, or a collection of patches with common motion" (Pinker 1997, 317). Interpreting a two-dimensional retinal image in a fashion that permits the inference of objects is of tremendous utility in deciphering the world, since parts of objects tend to move together.

It is clear from experiments by Spelke and Kelman that infants, by this age, possess the concept of an object and that they infer that something is a coherent object based on observation of parts *moving together*. Infants exposed to what looks like a long stick moving up and down, with its middle portion covered by a screen, register surprise if the screen is removed and there in fact turn out to be two objects rather than one. Shown an obscured *nonmoving* object whose ends have the same color and texture, they display no surprise if the screen is removed and they see two objects. Even if the single object has a different size, color, or texture at either end, so long as parts move together, they infer a single object. It is conceivable that this inference has been learned in the three months since they were born. But since so little time has elapsed, it is much more probable that this concept is hardwired into babies at birth: they display a grasp of the concept of an object (a coherent set of parts moving together) well before they have any words for it.

Here, based on similar experimental methodology, are some other concepts we can conclude that infants already possess at the age of three to five months. They can do crude mental arithmetic, understanding the concept of two or three (Wynn 1990, 1992). They believe that two solid objects cannot simultaneously occupy the same space and express surprise if tricks suggest the contrary. They assume inanimate objects pursue continuous trajectories and are cohesive, and they believe that there can be no action at a distance. Infants are born into the world with a "relatively rich, innately specified understanding of causality, especially in terms of the physical world" (Hauser 1996, 557). All of this is background to the really extraordinary experimental results, which concern what infants bring to the table with respect to the domain of social relations.

Given the demonstration that infants arrive in the world already understanding the previously described primitives, psychologists now constructed video displays in which, for example, a dot moves up an inclined plane, falls back, and moves up again, only to be knocked back by a second dot or pushed gently up by a third dot. From such experiments, researchers have been able to show that an infant can distinguish objects that move only when acted upon by another object from those that are or appear to be self-propelled (Premack and Premack 1994a, 150). Infants interpret as *intentional* an object that starts and stops its own motion. That is, they interpret such objects as animals (including other humans) and try to attract such objects by making faces, as opposed to their techniques for interacting with objects not so identified, for which pushing is the preferred mechanism (Pinker 1997, 322).

The evidence that infants can interpret intentionality is critical in making the argument that humans are hardwired to make what we have come to call moral judgments. That is because moral qualities can only be attributed to intentional objects. The evidence is also highly suggestive that, as in the case of language, some categories for organizing data relevant to social interaction are preformatted at birth and not the consequence of postnatal learning.

In addition to the concept of intentionality, human infants appear to be hardwired to give privileged status to five other key concepts. Together, these six primitives form a "grammar" of social interaction in much the same way that Chomsky's primitives provide a deep structural grammar within which human languages are learned. In addition to intentionality, these are positive/negative valence, reciprocation, possession, power, and group (Premack and Premack 1994a).

Infants assign valence to one object's interaction with another depending on two criteria: whether the action is hard (–) or soft (+) and whether the action has the effect of restricting (–) or maintaining (+) the "liberty" of the object either to remain in motion along a given trajectory or to remain at rest. The first criterion can be observed in very young infants (even invertebrates are attracted by weak stimuli, repelled by strong stimuli). Slightly older infants make use of a second criterion, helping or hurting, in assigning a valence to an action. A precondition for the attribution of helping or hurting is the determination that an object is both intentional and goal oriented. As noted, an intentional object starts and stops its own motion. Attribution of goal orientation requires that object A direct a repeated series of actions all at the same target. A bouncing ball is seen as engaged in play. Put a vertical line next to it, however, and infants perceive the ball as attempting to get over the top of the line. It is the repeated attempt to overcome failure, rather than immediate success, that leads to the attribution of goal.[12] Finally, the actions repeated must vary slightly. Absent variation, one risks losing the attribution of intentionality.

Infants assign to object B a positive or negative valence depending upon whether they perceive it as helping or hindering object A achieve its goal, maintain its liberty, or improve its aesthetic performance. They may also attribute helping to actions by B that permit A to perform an action (bounce higher or faster) in a more aesthetically pleasing fashion.

The concept of reciprocation refers to the expectation that the action of an intentional object on another will be followed by a reversal of roles, in which the acted upon becomes the actor, and that the positive or negative valence of the original action will persist once the actors have changed roles.

Infants are also hardwired to understand the concept of possession, a concept that can apply to both intentional and nonintentional objects. Infants assign valence to acts directed toward possessed nonintentional objects; they do not do so if the object is not possessed. Infants do not expect possessed recipients to reciprocate, even if they are intentional. Thus a possessed recipient is not permitted to retaliate but is excused from the obligation of reciprocating. Children, as possessed intentional objects, are not required to reciprocate the transfers from their parents; neither are they permitted to strike back at them in retaliation for punishment. Thus, children are born with a preformatted distinction between altruistic behavior that requires reciprocation (that between two humans of roughly equal power) and that which may not (behavior between a parent and a child, in which there is a relationship of power and possession, or the grants made by a sovereign to subjects, which may recapitulate that relationship).

Finally, the concept of group is understood as an assembly of inten-

---

12. Consistent successful choice among alternatives can also lead to the attribution of goal. Thus repeated failure is not a necessary condition for the attribution of goal.

tional objects of equal power (not possessed by each other). The infant expects such objects to move together and act together as a group. Physical likeness promotes concept of group but is not necessary for it. Members of a group are expected to act in similar fashions, not to act negatively toward one another, and to engage in reciprocation on behalf of other members.

These six primitives are rapidly acquired because, to use Pinker's characterization of the acquisition of language, "of a harmony between the mind of the child, the mind of the adult, and the texture of reality" (Pinker 1994, 157). As Tooby and Cosmides put it, "Natural Selection shapes decision rules and the cues they monitor" (1990, 405).

Because human babies require so much parental investment when they are born (and adults who provided that care were selected for, because they were more likely to pass on genes predisposing to such behavior), and because parents limit aggression among siblings (again, because parents who kept siblings from killing each other were more likely to pass on more of their genes), it is possible for babies born with a propensity to refrain from first strike both to survive and to have such behavior reinforced by the cultural process of socialization. This is not to say there are no first strikes but rather that there is hardwired receptivity to restraints on them.

It is also likely that we are born with the equivalent of a "mental Rolodex," a database for individuals on which are recorded updated histories of past interactions, along with information on their status relationship: those of power (no reciprocation expected for favors), rough equality (reciprocation expected), and possession (favors to be granted; no reciprocation, or reciprocation of a different kind, expected).

In summary, Chomsky has demonstrated beyond any reasonable doubt that we are born with a preformatted filing system for organizing different kinds of words as well as deep structural rules for linking them together. None of the 5,000+ known human languages violates these rules. Similarly, we are born with a preformatted filing system for organizing social interaction and with a set of deep structural rules governing social interaction. These rules drive universal elements of human culture. The aversion to incest among those with whom one has been raised between the ages of two and eight and the propensity to punish murder (with the possible exception of infanticide) of members of one's group do not represent triumphs of cultural evolution but rather are human universals that have an important biological component.

Evolutionary pressures have selected for hardwired taxonomies, just as much as the innate aversion to having sexual relations among those with whom one was raised. Learning depends on cues received from the external environment. But this learning is structured. Evolution has selected organisms to be particularly sensitive to stimuli that can be reliably detected and could reliably predict the hidden structure of conditions that determined the success of alternative courses of action over millions of years prior to the Neolithic revolution.

In arguing that preformatted taxonomies structure our view not just of biological forms but also of social categories and relations, we are arguing that aspects of our language instinct (the words are Pinker's) also structure our understanding of the world. This argument is fundamentally different from the many anthropological stories—now discredited—about how *particular* language structures determine a *particular* view of the world in different cultures. Eskimos do not have four hundred different words for snow, and the Hopi language does not evidence a culturally distinct view of time. There is simply not much left of the hypothesis advanced by Edward Sapir and Benjamin Whorf that culture or environment determines language, which in turn influences worldview (Sapir 1958; Edgerton 1992, 27; Malotki 1983; Pinker 1994, 63–66; Whorf 1963).

What we are concerned with here is what is *essential* about human cognitive construction of the world—and the degree to which that is reflected in innate taxonomic categories and relations among them. Since a primitive grammar of social relations can be demonstrated in infants as young as five months old, it is difficult to believe that this is due to socialization or learning, any more than the acquisition of grammatical rules in the learning of language. Millions of years of natural selection have provided humans with hardwired modules when they are born, modules that govern expectations about the behavior of other intentional objects, as well as, implicitly, their own. We see in this primitive grammar the evolutionary residue that has selected in favor of organisms prepared to make grants of first move(r) altruism and to reciprocate toward other group members, including those who may not be closely related.

Neurobiology

Our brains are highly complex organs, consisting of overlays of systems with different evolutionary histories. The higher mental facilities that create and process language and visual imagery attempt to impose order on a cognitive and emotional landscape that is in fact highly disordered, as the study of dreams suggests. People who successfully engage in reciprocal relations by initially exhibiting altruistic behavior of either the helping or the failure to harm variety, even when doing so exposes them to danger, and in so doing pass up opportunities for immediate gain, cannot be relying entirely on their faculties for logical and mathematical reasoning to guide and encourage this behavior. Careful ratiocination would counsel defection, a course of action that can be justified on both opportunistic and prudential grounds.

The modern experience of this is not, for reasons already noted, to be commonly found within established social groupings. It can be experienced in negotiations between potentially or actually hostile groups, or between members of different groups, or between representatives of hostile states, or in personal relationships that may be breaking up or becoming established and where the prediction of future interaction is highly uncertain. As suggested in chapter 1, it remains an important puzzle why a world consisting of sovereign states, absent a world government (I exclude here the influence of the United Nations), does not degenerate into continual warfare. While people often observe that actions speak louder than words, the maintenance by states of extensive diplomatic apparatus is testimony to belief in the value of talking, consistent with experimental findings in Prisoner's Dilemma games that the ability to communicate affects outcomes, even though there is no normative reason that it should. The incoherent treatment by Frank of deterrence and disarmament issues is reflective of the limitations of the standard economic model in addressing these issues.

When individuals, faced with such challenges, offer grants of first move(r) altruism, they must be influenced by other, functionally specialized mechanisms that have been evolutionarily adaptive and have neurobiological foundations. Treatment of the role of emotions and their neurobiological foundation is not essential to the arguments developed here: evidence on behavior alone is sufficient. Nevertheless, the results of research in neuroanatomy and neurobiology reinforce arguments already made by providing us a look inside the black box.

The physiological manifestations of an emotion and the feeling or mental image of it are part of a complex of behavioral adaptations linking genetically programmed predispositions to probabilistic influences on behavior within the domain of social interaction. Introspection suggests that what we perceive as emotions, our feeling of emotions, is related in some way to our willingness to make grants of first move(r) altruism. We perceive our emotions as both gifts and at times unwanted baggage bestowed on us as social animals by our evolutionary heritage. Here Trivers is probably on the right track in arguing that the complex demands of initiating and sustaining relations of reciprocity form the evolutionary foundation of a variety of human emotions. The feeling of "liking," he argues, predisposes toward offering a favor (a unilateral transfer) or forgoing first strike—first steps in initiating relationships that may potentially emerge as reciprocal over time.

The propensity to anger, which almost always has a self-righteous component, protects those whose repeated bestowal of favors on non-kin might lead them to excessive vulnerability. Since anger is often the consequent of unreciprocated favors, it provides an emotional impeller for behavioral strategies that involve at least temporary retaliation not clearly in the self-interest of the retaliator. Controlled anger may thus help impel implementation of a Tit-for-Tat strategy.

Gratitude helps calibrate the desire to reciprocate and how large the reciprocation should be. Sympathy, Trivers argues, alerts individuals to favorable opportunities to earn gratitude (where one feels sympathy for another in distress, it is often the case that a favor that costs the grantor little may induce a large degree of gratitude in the grantee). Trivers is not necessarily implying that the feeling of these emotions is the result of such calculations but rather that the consequences of the actions such emotions induce may have a favorable evolutionary calculus.

Guilt is a cost that cheaters bear if they are found out; cheating (defecting) publicly revealed produces shame (Trivers 1971; Pinker 1997, 402–3). The problem of initiating and sustaining relations of reciprocal altruism is so central to human existence that both our emotional and our reasoning capabilities have undoubtedly been influenced by it through evolutionary mechanisms at both individual and group levels. These observations give us insight into mechanisms that may sustain complex social organization, in which context they seem transparently adaptive (functional). But whereas Trivers excels in understanding mechanisms that maintain social interaction once established, he does not address why or how these emotions would have been adaptive in the absence of complex social organization. Recall that Trivers eschews appeal to any selection at the group level, in keeping with the prevailing scientific consensus of the 1970s and 1980s and in contrast to the argument of this book.

Second, I question Trivers's implication that these mechanisms, or all of them, are of relatively recent evolutionary origin. We tend to assume that humans are the only animals who experience consciousness, or have a well-developed emotional repertoire, but increasing evidence suggests we are not unique in this regard. Certainly, a presumption that chimpanzees or bonobos, for example, lack consciousness seems untenable. Much of the neurobiological hardware underlying our emotional repertoire must have preceded the growth of cranial capacity with its vastly expanded neocortex.

Neurobiological isomorphism suggests, for example, that human subsystems controlling fear are virtually indistinguishable from those possessed by birds and reptiles (LeDoux 1996). Emotions are externally manifested, and we can easily attribute them to lower animals, simply based on these manifestations. Indeed, normal humans can reliably attribute them to movements of a chip on a computer screen (jagged fast movements are coded as angry, recoiling movements as fearful). Patients with damage to the amygdala, on the other hand, can accurately characterize the movements of the chip in a technical sense but fail in intuiting the emotional subtext (Damasio 1999, 66–67, 70). Recall that the amygdala is also implicated in ability to forecast trustworthiness based on nonverbal cues and is a structure not part of the evolutionarily recent neocortex, consistent with my argument that predispositions enabling complex social organization are of older evolutionary lineage.

Growing experimental evidence, as well as corroborative data from neurobiology and neuroanatomy, suggests that "reasoning" with respect to social interactions is the consequence of the operation of a functionally specialized set of distinct brain subsystems that operates in parallel with those responsible for mathematical reasoning, statistical inference, and logical analysis. The same, it appears, is likely to be true for what we perceive as emotions (Griffiths 1997). Indeed, there is evidence that both of these systems occupy similar areas of brain anatomy, in particular the amygdala and parts of the prefrontal lobes (Anderson et al. 1999; Damasio 1994, 1999). Imaging studies show both the prefrontal cortex and the amygdala lighting up when subjects wrestle with emotionally salient problems (Hauser 2000, 14).

It appears likely, then, that our pantheon of emotions works collaboratively with "reasoning" specialized to the domain of social relations, providing the backdrop for the emergence of relations of reciprocity. Both the emotional armorarium and the domain specialized reasoning system become increasingly less necessary for their maintenance once established. That is, once relations of reciprocity become relatively established the behavioral guidance of this domain specialized reasoning system and that of the more general system we associate with capabilities in logic and mathematics become more congruent. In market relations, when prices are perceived as parametric, exchange has been drained of virtually all emotional content.

Thus the more complex and highly developed are social and economic organization, the more they can apparently be navigated by the same techniques whereby hunter-gatherers and their animal predecessors foraged for food. The purely competitive model of the economy is the apotheosis of this development: there are no consumer or producer cartels and no unions, and consequently all prices are parametric. No behavior appears anymore to involve strategic interaction. Economic interactions that in actuality have an irreducible social component nevertheless confront the individual as a series of games against nature, in which one's own behavior has no direct effect on the environment. And it is thus that economic models premised on assumptions that humans operate solely on the basis of "higher level" reasoning systems provide tolerably good predictions in analyses of the behavior within a strictly competitive economy.

This leads to the illusion that domain specialized "reasoning" systems, including emotional systems that may help us forecast those likely to be trustworthy, are not relevant in understanding the origin of complex social and economic organization. A central theme of this book has been argument against this illusion. As game theoretic analysis reveals, a willingness to perform altruistic acts is necessary in the initiation of a pattern of nonsimultaneous transfers (reciprocity). As the experiments summarized in chapter 1 reveal, many humans are willing to make these grants, even when considerations of reputation or expectations of repeat encounters have been controlled for.

So the behavior is a real phenomenon. What remains at issue is the explanation for it, and the solution proffered here is that we have hardwired predispositions toward so doing. Natural selection has apparently endowed us with the ability, in making such moves, to ignore or suppress the counsel of reason, narrowly and precisely defined: namely, that there is no strictly rational justification, as Nash would have understood it, for expecting reciprocity and that, indeed, to offer it initially makes one vulnerable.[13] That with a frequency greater than zero we systematically suppress such guidance is impossible to deny, and where such suppression occurs in established social settings in which Tit-for-Tat players predominate, it rarely requires a second thought. Those trying to bring peace to the Balkans, on the other hand, face the issue of origination on a daily basis.

Note that this perspective on the interplay between "reason" (as understood by economists) and other domain specific reasoning/emotional systems differs radically from popular interpretations, even those that embrace some version of modularity. Writing in 1977, Carl Sagan, drawing on the work of Paul Maclean (1973), described the "triune" structure of the brain: three anatomical modules distinguished by different structures and functions, marked by different evolutionary histories and characterized by different concentrations of dopamine and cholinesterase. The core of the brain, Maclean argued, emerged three hundred million years ago in reptiles. Wrapped around this was the limbic system, first observed in primitive mammals two hundred million years ago. The outer

---

13. Environmental influences can overpower genetic predispositions. Those who have been abused as children may find it difficult to love or trust, even though they may be quite intelligent. Their highly developed skills at logical inference help them understand with great precision the nature of the Prisoner's Dilemma, but they may remain incapable of exiting from it, trapped in a recurring psychology of defection.

layer was the neocortex, or new mammalian brain, only sixty-five million years ago. While Maclean's categories are not universally accepted by current researchers (see Ledoux 1996), his basic point that the brain consists of neurobiologically distinct components with different evolutionary histories is.

Sagan speculated that the "R-complex," or reptilian brain, governed "human bureaucratic and political behavior" (Sagan 1977, 60). He then asked whether there was any hope for humanity and answered optimistically by noting the size of the neocortex (the seat of higher brain functions—reason), which enabled us to "resist the urge to surrender to every impulse of the reptilian brain." Sagan went on to discuss the second module, the "limbic system," viewed as the seat of emotion.

Our knowledge of the brain's structure and functioning has advanced since Maclean and Sagan wrote, although their emphasis on modularity remains valid. But Sagan's faith that human "progress" can and will be reflected in the domination by reason (neocortical functions) of other "lower" and older brain systems needs qualification. It is indeed closely related to the Lorenz/Freud thin veneer story, with "reason" substituting in the role previously played by culture/socialization. Sagan's error would appear to lie in identifying "political and bureaucratic behavior" so exclusively with its dark side. One can argue that Nash equilibrium play—reason—leads away from cartels just as much as it leads away from Nuremberg rallies and all they connote. But as we have seen, high level reasoning also leads inexorably to a logic of first strike, if reason is defined narrowly and precisely. The short-circuiting of the behavioral guidance suggested by the logic that leads to this conclusion has been critical to human evolution and remains so for its survival, even if it has the potential to metastasize into the hostility toward the other that reached its apotheosis in Nazi Germany.[14]

Research in neuroanatomy and neurobiology offers increasing promise of helping us understand how this suppression happens. Finance scholars often joke that one needs only two human emotions to fathom the behavior of the stock market: fear and greed. To engage in nondefection behavior in a situation where one is initiating a reciprocally altruistic relationship, individuals must triumph over both: the fear that cooperation will be exploited by one's counterpart and the opportunistic desire to take advantage of possible "chump" (cooperative) behavior by one's counterpart. Both of these emotions, which reinforce the dictates of dispassionate reason, must be suppressed or trumped by other emotions and/or domain

---

14. Moreover, we need to be fair to reptiles: by all accounts they too possess powerful inhibitors on intraspecific violence. See Maynard-Smith and Price 1973 on snakes.

specialized "reasoning" systems, since logic clearly supports the counsel of both greed and fear (see chap. 4), impelling one toward defection. We need to understand not only how some specialized aspects of our cognitive apparatus, closely associated with those that produce emotions, systematically drive a wedge between the predictions of standard economic models and observed behavior but also why they evolved.

Neurobiology and neuroanatomy have received little attention either from rational choice theorists or behavioral economists. The idea that these subjects have relevance to behavioral science is controversial, perhaps no more so than among cognitive scientists in the artificial intelligence field. Patricia Churchland, for example, describes the unreceptive intellectual landscape she encountered when, as a cognitive philosopher, she began to learn neurophysiology in a medical school (Churchland 1995, 22).

One cannot help but be impressed, however, by the clinical histories documented in Anthony Damasio's 1994 book *Descartes' Error,* his more recent book *The Feeling of What Happens* (1999), and a broad range of coauthored scientific publications in which he establishes a strong neuroanatomical claim for the proposition that different functionally specialized parts of the brain, including those responsible for producing emotional responses, are together jointly responsible for our ability as humans to make decisions that permit us to initiate and sustain "normal" social relations. Damasio observes that in patients with damage to the prefrontal lobes and/or the amygdala social impairment often goes along with a reduction in observable emotional affect.

This leads Damasio to argue that emotions are key to our ability to decide "rationally." His understanding of rationality is of course the broad view that argues cooperation in a single play PD to be rational, not the narrow definition insisted upon by Binmore that I endorse. Damasio's evidence that decisions of patients with damage to the prefrontal lobes and/or amygdala are not rational is that these actions are "more often disadvantageous to their self and others than not" (Damasio 1999, 41). Again, this gets to the deep question of what it means to make a rational choice in the context of the sort of problem Alchian and Williams faced.

The model developed in this book maintains that humans possess specialized reasoning systems for dealing with social interactions, systems that have been selected for at the group level and in so doing have benefited the genes predisposing toward them but not *necessarily* the organisms exhibiting the resulting behavior. These systems counsel actions that cannot be defended as rational using Nash's criterion. At the same time, we have evolved capabilities for logical and mathematical reasoning that can be and often are used to identify what actions best serve the material interests of the individual organism and define, normatively, what rational action in game theoretic terms means.

In many cases observed in the field, these systems do not conflict in their guidance, because social interaction is embedded in contexts of repeated interaction where considerations of reputation matter. They will diverge in the absence of such structured interaction or in experimental situations that control for these factors, such as one-shot PD games with anonymity. If we wish to understand the *origin* (not the *maintenance*) of systems of reciprocity, it is critical that we recognize this divergence and the apparent power of "reasoning" systems specialized to the domain of social interactions to override what we consider rational using a precise and narrow definition.

One interpretation of Damasio's clinical results is that he has identified individuals whose capabilities to be rational narrowly defined are intact but whose ability to be rational in the sense Damasio understands it has been destroyed, making them quite capable of performing tasks that enable them to score high on intelligence tests (see also Anderson et al. 1999) but at the same time incapable of negotiating even mild social dilemmas. If we restrict reason to what is commonly measured on intelligence tests, then the traditional opposition of emotion and reason, reflected in Sagan's observations and against which Damasio argues, can be defended. But reason, narrowly defined, can no longer be given quite the star billing Sagan intends.

The issue comes down again to whether we view Williams's initial cooperative move in the first PD games as rational. If the term *rational* is defined narrowly and precisely, it is difficult to so view it, a conclusion that Nash reached and Binmore reinforces. But many will argue that Williams's play was in some sense reasonable if not exactly rational and find this conclusion validated by the empirical finding that Williams (and ultimately Alchian) ended up doing better venturing contingent cooperation than each would have using a strict defect strategy. Thus we can, along with Damasio, wave our hands and reason that cooperation "must" be rational because it appears more often than not to be advantageous. Those of us who reach this conclusion will however, be evidencing a reasoning system specialized to the domain of social interaction, one that has short-circuited or rejected the counsel of our logical faculties, which easily demonstrate that, at least in a single play PD, defect strictly dominates: it is superior for us individually regardless of the play of the counterparty.

In any event, Damasio's clinical histories provide us with the results of neuroanatomical experiments on humans that ethical protocols would never permit us to initiate ourselves. The most dramatic story, around which Damasio builds his 1994 book, is the case of Phineas Gage. In 1848

Gage was the construction foreman on the Rutland and Burlington Railway in Vermont, responsible for blasting operations as a new roadbed was laid. On a warm summer afternoon, Gage, as usual, carefully and systematically supervised preparations. A hole was drilled in the rock and then filled halfway with blasting powder. Normally a fuse was inserted, the remainder of the hole filled with sand, and the charge tamped down with an iron bar that Gage had had made specially for this purpose. On that afternoon, however, Gage was distracted and began to tamp down the charge before his subordinate had added the sand. As the iron hit rock, it generated a spark, igniting an explosion that turned the iron into a projectile, one three inches in diameter, weighing more than twelve pounds, measuring more than a yard in length, and with a seven-inch taper at its top. This missile rose from Gage's hands, entered his left cheek from below, passed through the back of his left orbital cavity, through the front of his brain on the left side, and finally out the top of his skull. Accompanied by a whistling sound much like a Fourth of July rocket, it landed one hundred feet away, covered with blood and parts of his brain.

Gage, however, was not dead. Awake, he was lifted into a wheelbarrow by members of his crew and taken to a local hotel, where with some assistance he got out himself and was able to provide full details of the accident to the arriving physician. Two months later, after Gage survived fever and infection, his doctor pronounced him cured.

But he was not. His personality had been transformed in the sense that he was not capable of distinguishing between appropriate and inappropriate behavior. For the rest of his life he was unable to hold a steady job or form lasting human attachments. Yet his speech was unaffected, as was vision in his remaining eye, and he exhibited no other noticeable cognitive defects.

The significance of this case history is that it provides dramatic evidence that cognitive and affective functions are indeed localized in particular regions of the brain. This view, although broadly accepted today, was strongly contested in the middle of the twentieth century by researchers who argued for a more holistic approach to brain function. Karl Lashley's research, for example, seemed to show that brain damage to individuals was a function of the extent of damage, not its location (Lashley 1929; see also Gardner 1974). Damasio, however, details numerous other cases of individuals who because of tumors or accidents have damage to the prefrontal lobes. These individuals in general have undiminished cognitive capability, as measured by standard tests, but (*a*) their affect is flat, they lack emotion—this can be corroborated to some degree with skin conductance tests and (*b*) they are unable to function effectively as social individuals. In particular they do not seem to be capable of maintaining, interpreting, and acting upon what Cosmides and Tooby call their "social map of the persons, relationships, motives, interactions, emotions and intentions that make up their social world" (Cosmides and Tooby 1992, 163). Damasio's more recent research (1999) places emphasis as well on the study of individuals with damage to the amygdala.

These clinical histories suggest that parts of the brain, independent of those that underlie cognitive processes associated with vision, language, logic, mathematical reasoning, or statistical inference, control emotional responses and that absent access to the common panoply of those responses, individuals are not able to negotiate and/or interpret the fine calibration of behavioral responses necessary to initiate and sustain reciprocally altruistic relations. Damage in certain identifiable regions of the brain will reliably diminish an individual's ability effectively to negotiate social interactions while leaving intellectual powers unimpaired. This is an important finding. Damasio's clinical and experimental investigation of the role and neuroanatomical foundation of emotional subsystems is more profound and nuanced than Frank's often incoherent interpretation of them simply as "precommitment" devices.

A cognitive system specialized to the domain of social interaction is the most plausible explanation for the behaviors identified in the experimental results summarized in chapter 1.[15] Pure calculations of individual self-interest cannot account for the repeated observations that individuals achieve cooperative solutions to Prisoner's Dilemma games, even single play games. A "higher level" reasoning system may fully understand that defecting is the superior individual strategy, irrespective of the choice of the counterparty, yet be overruled—countermanded—by the system specialized to social interaction. Thus Williams plays cooperate, with full knowledge that it is not a rational play (unless Alchian is assumed irrational), and many of us endorse what Williams does as reasonable, irrespective of what Nash tells us.

If a cognitive system specialized to social interaction, perhaps working hand in hand with our emotional armorarium, predisposes us to overcome fear, short-circuit the counsel of logic and reason narrowly defined, and engage in the generosity of first move(r) altruism, evolution has also equipped us with an exaggerated, indeed sometimes obsessive, interest in the behavior of others and willingness to punish those who take advantage of us or violate group expectations, even when doing so imposes costs on ourselves. We have seen this willingness to punish in the collective goods

---

15. The extent to which the behavioral outcome is the result of conscious reasoning, the extent to which the hardwiring may involve propensities to teach or learn these behavioral patterns, or the extent to which these patterns are simply strategies that get selected for is not relevant to the basic argument.

experiments where free riders can be fined and in the ultimatum games described earlier. The Cosmides and Tooby/Gigerenzer and Hug experimental results described in the final section of this chapter give us an additional perspective on these predispositions. It is tougher to see this "punishing" behavior as "generous" in quite the same way as unilateral grants of negative or affirmative altruism to another, although the same type of selection must have favored both. None of this behavior can be accounted for as the result of narrowly rational decision making or selection, at least upon first appearance, at the individual level alone.

The clinical data discussed reveal, as does other evidence, that our ability to make "good" decisions in situations involving social interaction depends on the separate and joint operation of different brain structures—neurobiological subsystems that have different physical locations in the brain and different evolutionary histories. There is no formal reason, for example, why preplay communications should make any difference whatsoever in the outcome of a Prisoner's Dilemma game, but abundant experimental evidence indicates that it does (Frank 1988, chap. 7; Dawes 1988, 197; Rabin 1998, 22). Damasio's work, particularly if combined with the evidence from evolutionary psychology and behavioral economics, helps us understand why.

Our brains are the result of a long evolutionary history, some portions with a longer history than others. We have the intellectual and cognitive powers, thanks to our evolutionarily newer neocortex—to utilize and comprehend natural language, analyze game theoretic problems, and perform complex mathematical calculations. Our closest animal relatives, chimpanzees and great apes, biologically very similar to us, lack comparable capabilities, although they may possess them in more rudimentary form. But they share with us the gift of consciousness that our more distant animal relations lack, as well as the ability to initiate and sustain coalitions and other forms of social relations among non-kin. Their political and social behavior bears many more analogues to that observed in humans than does their mathematical ability. Thus it is unlikely that the higher intellectual capabilities observed in humans, in comparison with chimpanzees, have a great deal to do with understanding the fundamentals of human social and political interaction. The starting point for many social contract theorists, and most modern social scientists, has been to assume the contrary.

We retain brain functions, particularly those that govern such emotions as anger and fear or permit us to "intuit" those likely to be trustworthy, with much longer evolutionary histories than those that make possible language, and as Joseph LeDoux has shown, these systems, in particular those that produce fear as a response to danger, are remarkably similar throughout the mammalian world and possibly also among birds and reptiles. Complementing Damasio's work, LeDoux's research has helped chart the neurological wiring that enables emotional subsystems to countermand the counsel of "higher level" reasoning. Even as our eyes, ears, and other sense organs send information to the appropriate cortical areas for conscious processing, parallel wiring, similar to that shared by far distant animal relatives, connects visual, auditory, and somatosensory input directly to the amygdala, the almond shaped brain organ implicated, as already noted, in the physiology of emotion. This wiring permits emotional responses without input from the cortex. These responses are faster and cruder than those generated by the cortical route. Our different brain subsystems pull us sometimes in different directions, and the prefrontal lobes may play a role in mediating between these channels. With effort and discipline we can sometimes act on the basis of reason, narrowly and precisely defined, not our emotional impulses. But this does not invariably lead to improvement in our material condition. One of the reasons that it is so easy for our emotions to intrude on the operation of reason, and often so difficult for the reverse to occur, is that the wiring connecting cortical areas with the amygdala is much weaker than that traveling in the opposite direction (LeDoux 1996, 265).

Implications

The implications of this reconception of the structure of our mind are only beginning to be digested. The general acceptance of the Chomskian view of language acquisition in lieu of the operant conditioning response approach advanced by B. F. Skinner has had little effect on the presumption by microeconomists and other social scientists that their central task as behavioral scientists is to understand cognition and explain behavior as the consequence of a single general-purpose reasoning capability. Social scientists may accept Chomsky's verdict that general-purpose association learning devices are incapable of explaining a child's inference of rules of grammar: the database to which infants are exposed through heard speech is simply too limited to make this possible. But the process of language acquisition continues to be treated implicitly as exceptional in its reliance on specialized subsystems.[16]

To do otherwise is to begin to conceive of humans as organisms whose behavior is driven not only by rational choices made consciously

---

16. This predisposition persists in spite of the enormous evidence of functional specialization throughout the human body. For a skeptical, and in my view unpersuasive, critique of the Chomsky/Pinker view of language acquisition, see Sampson 1997.

but also by the biological inheritance of a panoply of genetically prepro-
grammed scripts (or a propensity to learn and teach them), scripts whose
survival has been predicated on their ability to favor the propagation of
the genes that control them. It is obvious to anyone who has blinked when
an unexpected object comes flying toward one's eye, or who has sat up and
taken notice when an attractive member of the opposite sex enters a room,
that we embody such scripts and that our behavior can be influenced by
them. In some cases (the blink reflex), we have little control over our reaction; in others (what we do in response to the presence of an attractive
woman or man), we can choose. But neither Pavlov's discovery that involuntary reflexes could be associated with new stimuli nor Skinner's demonstration that voluntary behaviors could be conditioned through rewards
leads most of us to believe that our blink reflex or sexual impulses are pre-
dominantly learned.[17]

To recognize that genetics influences behavior is not inexorably to be
a genetic determinist. We do have control over our voluntary behavior in
particular circumstances—that is why we call it voluntary—and it is meaningful in these areas to talk about our responsibility for it. Rather, that
recognition leads to the argument that these biologically inherited scripts
influence behavior in a probabilistic sense.[18] Moreover, in providing us
tools to address challenges that are likely to be life cycle specific, our hardwiring may only provide epigenetic rules (to use the terminology of Lumsden and Wilson) that facilitate learning by canalizing the acquisition of
information and privileging certain categories. With respect both to their
direct influence on behavior and their influence on the acquisition of culture, our genes give rise to predispositions, not irrevocable instructions
about how to act in particular situations whose specifics could not be predicted in any event by the "as if" programmers of natural selection any
more than the IBM programmers of "Deep Blue" could provide specific
instructions covering how to respond to all conceivable moves by Kas-
parov given all possible configurations of a chess board.

The search for the origins of behavioral influencers using evolutionary models involves considering how well particular behavioral tendencies
are likely to have favored offspring of individuals exhibiting them, in com-

---

17. In a telling observation, David Allyn (2000, 191) has noted that although pornog-
raphy troubles conservatives because it is seen as a threat to social order, it troubles traditional liberals because its persistent appeal is so inconsistent with the tabula rasa view of
learning and cognition.

18. Richard Dawkins makes this point well in his book *The Selfish Gene* (1989). Perhaps because of the potentially inflammatory title of his book, Dawkins has been unfairly
categorized as a genetic determinist, and people have reacted to a social Darwinist agenda
they have, with little evidence, projected onto his work.

parison with the impact on fitness of different tendencies in other organisms of the same species. As discussed earlier, the evolution of complex social organization among hominids requires as a sine qua non a willingness to avoid attacking first: first move(r) altruism forms one part of the Tit-for-Tat strategy.

Propensities toward altruistic behavior toward non-kin—of which this is a kind—cannot have been favored by individual level selection when first appearing in populations. Altruistic behavior definitionally is behavior that increases the relative fitness of other organisms at the expense of the acting organism. Therefore, if the behavioral propensities survived, at some point in our long evolutionary history the strength of group selection must have outweighed the negative effect of individual level selection, allowing situations of structured interaction among non-kin to emerge.

The four necessary conditions for this to have occurred have already been outlined: (1) There must have been a population that periodically divided into relatively small groups. (2) The groups must have varied with respect to the proportion of their members with behavioral predispositions toward altruism. (3) Groups with more individuals willing to make grants of first move(r) altruism must have produced more offspring. (4) Progeny must have mixed periodically or otherwise competed in the formation of new groups. The sufficient condition for first move(r) altruism to be favored by natural selection is for the group level selection effect to have been stronger than the individual level effect (Sober and Wilson 1998, 26) (see chap. 2).

Cheater Detection Modules

I conclude this chapter with discussion of evidence that humans possess not only a module predisposing to the practice of first move(r) altruism but also a domain specific adaptation that gives us a particular concern with detecting cheating on social rules. This propensity can dramatically affect human ability to solve problems in propositional logic and, I will argue, predispose them to act in a manner not necessarily rationalizable as in their own interest. In particular, the obsession with detecting cheating and punishing violators leads individuals to act in ways that could not have been favored, at their initial appearance, by individual level selection but that must necessarily, through group selection, have favored genes predisposing to such behavior.

The foundations of this argument have been established in previous chapters. Retaliation against cheaters only makes sense from an evolutionary standpoint focusing on the individual organism when propensities to do so are already widely shared within the group. But again, showing that a propensity to retaliate against cheaters can sustain itself once broadly established does not provide an account of origin. Retaliation costs the retaliator and produces no individual benefit. Once cheating has occurred the behavior the retaliatory threat was "designed" to deter has already taken place, and whatever benefits accrue as the result of such punishment accrue disproportionately to the group. The optimal strategy for the individual is not to monitor and not to punish but to free ride on the behavior of others who do so. Exactly the same range of arguments involving the practice of first move(r) altruism, and the degree to which it could have been favored by individual level selection, apply in this case.

The proposition that a modular view is relevant in understanding social behavior owes a great deal to research by Leda Cosmides and John Tooby in the United States and Gerd Gigerenzer and his associates in Germany. They have not attempted (as have I) to apply the concept of modularity to Prisoner's Dilemma games or issues involving first move(r) altruism. Nor have they explored at what level evolutionary forces must have operated in favoring a cheater detection module. But they have, in remarkable and compelling experiments, established its existence.[19]

The initiation and emergence of reciprocity in the context of nonsimultaneous transfers require two key components: a first move(r) willing to perform an altruistic act and a mechanism for keeping track of whether or not such grants have been reciprocated. Trivers predicted the latter: "As selection favors subtler forms of cheating, it will favor more acute abilities to detect cheating" (1971, 48). Cosmides and Tooby's and Gigerenzer's research shows that we have evolved functionally specialized systems that help us do this, systems so powerful they will override the counsel of logical analysis in certain cases and, in other cases, apparently vastly improve our ability to conduct it. Our ability to detect violations of conditional rules is much higher when these rules involve a social norm. We are obsessed with detecting and punishing cheaters on social rules: those who receive a benefit but do not abide by a "rule" codifying reciprocity in what can be thought of as an *n*-person Prisoner's Dilemma.

Cosmides and Tooby studied the ability of individuals to detect violations of rules of the form *if p, then q* using an experimental design known as the Wason selection test. Subjects have explained to them a certain rule of this form. They are then shown a set of four different cards, each of

---

19. For a less enthusiastic evaluation, see Davies, Fetzer, and Foster 1995, an article that seems to be one of the few systematic critiques in print. Many of their criticisms involve rather fine points of logic that do not, in their entirety, detract from the force of the Cosmides and Tooby contribution. In particular, the critique does not adequately credit the contributions of Cosmides and Tooby in finding a coherent way of organizing the disparate experimental results utilizing the Wason selection task.

which contains an antecedent (*p* or *not p*) or a consequent (*q* or *not q*). On the reverse side of the cards is the associated consequent or antecedent. Subjects are asked to indicate which cards need to be turned over to verify that there have been no violations of the rule *if p, then q.* The correct solution from the standpoint of propositional logic is that one must turn over all cases of *p* and all cases of *not q* to ensure that no errors have occurred. The consequent *not p* and the antecedent *q* (whatever they are) cannot establish a rule violation and therefore from the standpoint of formal logic need not be examined.

The reasons for this are as follows. Turning over *not p* is not relevant because the rule says nothing about the consequent of *not p.* Looking at the other side of *q* is also not relevant because the condition is *if,* not *iff* (i.e., we have a conditional, not a biconditional, statement). There might well be other antecedents that also implied *q.* Turning over *q* will either show *p,* which will be according to the rule, or *not p,* which will not be a violation of the rule.

For example, suppose you have instructed the university registrar to code all letter grades of C with the number 3. There have been errors in the past, and you have some doubts as to whether the rule is being followed correctly. You have four cards in front of you. They show, respectively, the letter **C,** the letter **D,** the number **3,** and the number **7.** On the other sides of the number cards are the corresponding letter grades. On the other sides of the letter grades are the corresponding coded number grades. Which cards do you need to turn over to make sure that no errors have been made? Since the applicable rules are *if the letter grade is C, then the numerical code is 3,* you need to turn over the card with the letter **C** on it (*p*), to make sure it is coded **3,** and you need to turn over the **7** card (*not q*), to make sure it does not correspond to a letter grade of **C.** Turning over the **D** card (*not p*) cannot detect a rule violation, since there is nothing in the rule that says how the letter grade **D** is to be coded. Turning over the number **3** cannot detect a rule violation, since it may be true that grades other than C (such as C– or D) are also coded 3.

If this is confusing to you, take heart. Where the rule is purely formal, as it is here, undergraduate subjects from U.S. universities (Harvard and Stanford) don't do very well, batting on average about 25 percent. Apparently, whatever tools eons of evolution have given us, facility with the propositional calculus is not one of them. But where the setting is recast as one in which subjects are responsible for detecting *some kind of human cheating on a social rule,* success soars, in some cases *tripling* (to the range of 75 percent correct). This is an astonishing result.

For example, assume the setting is as follows: you are a bouncer in a bar, where the rule is, if you are drinking beer, you must be over twenty. You see four individuals. For two of them you can tell what their age is but cannot see what they are drinking (one is over and one is under twenty). For two others, you can see what they are drinking but cannot tell how old they are (one is drinking beer, the other Coke). Typically more than 75 percent of U.S. subjects and more than 90 percent of German subjects are able to ascertain that you should check the person drinking beer (*p*) and the person under twenty (*not q*).[20] From a logical standpoint, this problem is identical to the grade coding problem.

My initial reaction in reading the results of these first experiments was that perhaps a situation involving cheating triggered an adrenalin rush or some other hormone that concentrated people's minds, making them "better" at solving the logic problem. Checking coding mistakes in the first problem is boring; perhaps catching underage drinkers in a bar is not. It turns out this hypothesis can be decisively rejected. A problem involving detecting cheaters does not necessarily make subjects better at solving an identical problem of logical inference. In some designs the experimenters cleverly switched the antecedent and consequent, so that the correct answer to the inference problem no longer involved detecting cheating (although the problem itself still appeared to involve a social contract). For example, change the rule to *if you are over twenty, then you are drinking beer*. The rule has, because of this switch, become a descriptive rule, like the registrar problem, rather than a deontic rule (one involving a *must* or *should* implication). Subjects still overwhelmingly counsel finding out what the underage patron is drinking and checking how old the beer drinker is, whereas the correct approach to sniffing out rule violation now is to check what the overage patron is drinking and find out how old the Coke drinker is (turn over *p* and *not q*). Subjects persist in examining cases that would permit them to detect cheating on a social contract, *not* those that would permit detection of violations of the logical rule. The concern with detecting cheating is so powerful that it overrides the guidance of our faculties for logical inference. In all of the experimental designs, the rea-

---

20. Gigerenzer and Hug (1992), in replicating Cosmides and Tooby's results using German university students, found the same roughly 50 percentage point difference in performance between social contract and non–social contract problems, although performance on all problems was higher than among U.S. students (Harvard undergraduates in Cosmides's original experiments). Gigerenzer and Hug attribute these differences in part to the more rigorous training that German students receive in Gymnasium and in particular to a group of six subjects who insisted on strictly applying the logic of the propositional calculus to the problems, regardless of how the answers "felt" to them. This highlights the degree to which success with this calculus is a learned competency, not selected for in Pleistocene times, in contrast to a finely honed ability to detect violations of expectations of reciprocity.

soning challenges are formally identical. Nor does the familiarity of the contextual setting appear to affect performance. What differs is the emotive content of the challenge.[21]

In some of the experimental designs explored subsequently by Gigerenzer and Hug, the concern with cheating is shown to be context dependent. Suppose the rule is *if an employee gets a pension, he or she must have worked for at least ten years.* The definition of cheating depends on whether one is employer or employee, although the logical problem is the same. For example, from the standpoint of the employer, the cheater is the employee who has a pension but has worked for less than ten years. For the employee, the employer has cheated if there is an employee who has worked more than ten years but has no pension. Yet performance differs greatly depending upon whether subjects are first told they are the employer or the employee (Gigerenzer and Hug 1992, 153–56; Cosmides and Tooby 1992, 181–89). "Employees" are determined to uncover cheating by employers, even where it represents the incorrect solution to the problem of logical inference, and "employers" are determined to uncover cheating by employees, regardless of whether it represents the correct solution to the problem of logical inference. The hypothesis that different parts of the brain govern logical inference and reasoning about social contracts is supported by evidence from schizophrenics, which frequently shows impaired performance on the former but not the latter.

The striking results of these experiments have been replicated in other studies. Discovering these patterns is akin to holding up a sheet of paper one thinks is blank and suddenly perceiving a watermark—a phenotypic imprint of the legacy of millions of years of evolutionary history. It is precisely because, compared to other animals, we are more altruistic, even to non-kin, and as a consequence end up practicing so much more reciprocity involving affirmative assistance, not just passive failure to harm, that our cheater detection capabilities are so highly developed.

Multiple Adaptations for Social Exchange

This cheater detection module and the related behavioral predisposition to punish violators of social rules complement the propensity to practice first move(r) altruism evident in the experimental results concerning single play or fixed duration Prisoner's Dilemma games, the voluntary provision of public goods, and elsewhere. To the extent that they consider this issue, Cosmides and Tooby have adopted strictly conventional accounts of the

---

21. As the authors put it, "humans have rules of inference that are specialized for cheater detection" (Cosmides and Tooby 1992, 189).

origin of reciprocity (i.e., those associated with the work of Trivers, Axelrod, or Frank). I have argued that, in accounting for the origin of complex social organization, a predisposition to practice first move(r) altruism, supporting by "reasoning" propensities specialized to the domain of social interaction, is as important as a module devoted to cheater detection.

A predisposition to practice first move(r) altruism is, like cheater detection, a domain specific adaptation. It short-circuits and contravenes the prescriptive advice of our deductive logic, which counsels defect (first strike) in a one-shot PD, in a manner as striking as the process whereby the cheater detection module overwhelms whatever limited capabilities we may have for solving problems in the propositional calculus. The persistent and replicable tendency for a substantial fraction of human subjects to play cooperate in single play or fixed duration PD games is the equivalent, for this module, of the watermark represented by Cosmides and Tooby's experimental results.

Cosmides and Tooby's work demonstrates the existence of content specific adaptations of a reasoning process affecting social relations, precisely what is denied by the assumption that our intelligence derives from a general-purpose reasoning ability, one leading to a narrow and very precise definition of rationality. Their arguments regarding our obsession with cheaters are corroborated by findings of Mealey, Daood, and Krage (1996) that experimental subjects are better able to remember faces of individuals who have been characterized to them as cheaters. Cummins (1999) extends the Cosmides and Tooby/Gigerenzer and Hug results in important directions by demonstrating the extent to which triggering of the cheater detection module may be associated with high rank within a dominance hierarchy.

Edward O. Wilson has remarked upon our preoccupation with and our exceptional abilities to sniff out cheaters in discussing how much attention we pay to these matters. "[Cheating] excites emotion and serves as the principal source of hostile gossip and moralistic aggression by which the integrity of the political economy is maintained" (E. O. Wilson 1998, 172). Natural selection has endowed us with a strong drive to detect those who fail to reciprocate when an opportunity subsequently presents itself and with a self-righteous anger that motivates retaliation or subsequent refusal to deal with such parties, even where such behavior is not in our own best interest and even when the failure to reciprocate involves third parties. As I have suggested, this predisposition, so important "in preserving the integrity of a political economy," is also what, under the right political conditions, can be mobilized to sustain group attacks on out-groups.

The propensity, at cost to ourselves, to punish "rule violators" is thus a two edged sword, giving rise to much that is ugly in the human ethogram. But it was an essential precondition for the development of complex social organization. Margins of subsistence were sufficiently thin during the millions of years over which evolution took place that first move(r) altruism could not have been indiscriminate. Indiscriminate altruism could not persist without grave detriment to the practitioner and a likely reduction in genetic fitness. To have any chance of persisting, first move(r) altruism had to be coupled with an ability to keep track of whom one had dealt with and their subsequent behavior and a willingness to punish nonreciprocity.

The research on the Wason selection task shows conclusively that we have a cheater detection module that operates independently of whatever competencies we have for propositional calculus: sometimes improving our performance on it, other times causing it to deteriorate, basically overriding it. The experimental evidence of cooperative behavior in Prisoner's Dilemma games and those involving the voluntary provision of public goods is strong evidence that under certain circumstances, we operate according to a first move(r) altruism predisposition, supported by "reasoning" modules specialized to the domain of social interaction that systematically override the counsel of logic and mathematical reasoning.

The existence of these cognitive modules is consistent with what we know of language structure and acquisition, as well as visual perception, in which there are functionally specialized modules that permit us to see a snowball in our living room as white and a lump of coal outside as black, even though the latter reflects substantially more light; or detect edges in objects; or convert two-dimensional retinal images into representations of three-dimensional objects (Marr 1982). The assertion that modules directly influence reasoning about and behavior affecting our social relations is more difficult to accept, than, for example, when perceptual modules are exploited to create optical illusions. This idea is harder to accept because of the way in which these modules apparently short-circuit the counsel of what we view as our highest evolved competencies—logic and mathematical reasoning—and the way, at least in the former case, they are inconsistent with the fundamental behavioral assumption of the standard economic model (for a similar line of argument, see Stanovich and West 2000).

The two key adaptations addressed, first move(r) altruism and cheater detection with its associated propensity to punish, short-circuit cognitive and behavioral mechanisms that undergird the standard economic model. They have strong evolutionary rationale, if we allow for group selection and in particular modularity. No research effort has done more to sensitize economists and other social scientists to the likelihood of modularity than the heuristics and biases program pioneered by Daniel Kahneman and Amos Tversky. It is one of the great ironies, therefore, that it has so little to tell us about these cognitive and behavioral adaptations. Chapter 6 explains why.

Modularity and the "Heuristics and Biases" Research Program

Much of economic theory has been guided by a methodology that, in its more enthusiastic moments, seems to glorify the irrelevance of empirical research on how people actually behave (see, e.g., Selten 1998). In this light it is not surprising that with one or two important exceptions, economists' knowledge of or interest in experimental methods historically has been limited. In recent years, multidisciplinary participation in experiments using human subjects has begun to change this and has been associated with an increased willingness to use these methods and consider the implications of what they show. As Selten's comments indicate, these results are now, in the area of strategic interaction, so broad and so consistent in their identification of deficiencies in the predictions of standard models that a number of theorists have found it desirable to rethink what explanatory or predictive claims are actually made for normative theory.[1]

A second program has been pioneered by Amos Tversky and Daniel Kahneman and popularized among economists by Richard Thaler and others. From the standpoint of intellectual history, perhaps even more significant than its particular findings is the fact that, whether they dismiss or embrace the heuristics and biases research program, most economists are aware of it. The program has had a distinctly higher profile and a larger impact to date on economics than the experimental research identifying anomalous behavior in situations of strategic interaction (see the prologue and chap. 1).

There are some overlaps between these two bodies of work, but for reasons outlined subsequently, their areas of inquiry are largely disjoint. Most of the research in the heuristics and biases program has involved (a) defects in the way we use data to form and update beliefs and (b) the study

1. In games against nature, we make choices, but payoffs depend on outcomes "dealt" to us by natural processes, not on the decisions of other humans. These outcomes are not known to us in advance, although the various possibilities and their likelihoods can often be described probabilistically. Both playing roulette and deciding where to go fishing are games against nature. Techniques of statistical inference are relevant, however, for the latter but not the former problem.

of choice in games against nature (decision theory). Decision theory places great emphasis on human capabilities for statistical inference. It emphasizes as well the actual process of making choices within risky or uncertain environments. Such capabilities are simply not relevant for decision making in a one-shot PD, because the counsel of normative game theory (defect) is independent of consideration of how the other party may play.

Decisions in situations of strategic interaction are not the only types of decisions humans make. Many of the others do involve games against nature—foraging, for instance—circumstances where intuitive abilities to perform statistical inference can be quite valuable. Choice, for instance, about where and how intensely to search for food had critical implications for our hunter-gatherer ancestors—and their ancestors. The heuristics and bias research program, taken in its entirety, suggests that we are objectively poor at such inference. In the language of modularity, Kahneman and Tversky can be viewed as stating that domain specific modules, heuristics and biases, cause us to analyze formally identical problems in different ways. They call this process framing, and it represents an obvious violation of the assumptions of rational choice theory—different from those documented earlier but a violation none the less.

There are real questions, however, why, from an evolutionary perspective, some of the short-circuiting Kahneman and Tversky identify should have been favored by natural selection, particularly with regard to human capabilities to calculate updated probabilities conditional on new data in accordance with Bayes' law.[2] Ironically, the heuristics and biases program appears to provide the strongest evidence for modularity in areas where we would least expect it from an evolutionary standpoint, and it has little to say about areas where it is essential to account for the origin of complex social organization.

Although Kahneman and Tversky were trained as psychologists and began their research very much within established disciplinary traditions, their seminal work now underlies an empirically based challenge to the dominant methodology in economics. Within their work one finds empha-

---

2. Bayes' law, formalized by Thomas Bayes in the eighteenth century, is a systematic means of calculating posterior probabilities based on prior probabilities and new information. Suppose two different individuals are responsible for securing my departmental suite, Tom 80 percent of the time and Dick 20 percent. I know from prior experience that Tom is responsible, and leaves the main door unlocked only 10 percent of the time, whereas Dick is less so, and forgets to close up 9 times of 10. My prior probability is that there is an 80 percent chance that Tom will secure my office. But if I find the door unlocked tomorrow morning, what is the posterior probability Tom was on duty? Bayes' law tells me it's still about a third. In 100 nights, on average, Tom would leave the door open 8 times ($80 \times .1$), and Dick 18 times ($20 \times .9$), so the probability Tom was on duty, given that the door was unlocked, is $8 / (8 + 18) = 4 / 13$.

sis on anomalies—behavior inconsistent with the predictions of the standard model—and on a series of "biases" in human reasoning that account for them.

These biases, the program claims, arise under empirically replicable conditions in which learning and calculation will violate the prescriptions of logic, probability theory, and/or Bayesian statistical inference. Continuing in a tradition established by Herbert Simon, Kahneman and Tversky have advanced, as explanation of these biases, a variety of heuristics— rules of thumb—whereby humans do well enough, most of the time, in making their judgments. They add to the Simon tradition, however, an emphasis on how these heuristics sometimes produce not random errors but *systematic* deviations from the "normatively correct" judgment.

The Kahneman and Tversky program is partly concerned with how people think and reason and how they draw inferences from data. Here it focuses on whether human *beliefs* or *expectations* are formed rationally: according to the best available logical or statistical algorithms. Their research and that inspired by it search for regularities in the ways humans process information, regularities that are at variance with what should happen if reasoning were strictly logical, based on known rules of probability, or followed "normative" rules of statistical inference. These include, for example, the representativeness heuristic, which causes people to assume incorrectly that parts of a phenomenon will necessarily exhibit characteristics of wholes; the availability heuristic, in which the subjective probability of an event increases depending upon the ease and vividness with which it can be visualized; and the anchoring heuristic, whereby the subjective estimate of an outcome is influenced by the starting point, or status quo.

The latter heuristic is typical of the overarching Kahneman and Tversky emphasis on frame dependence: inferences about and choices regarding a formally identical problem will be influenced by the context or frame in which it is presented. Frame dependence is inconsistent with assumptions implicit in the Skinnerian model of operant conditioning. In challenging that model, Kahneman and Tversky also challenge the model of learning and decision making underlying the standard economic model, in particular the expected utility framework, the approach to decision making under risk or uncertainty first advanced by von Neumann and Morgenstern in an appendix to their 1944 book on games and economic behavior.

Kahneman and Tversky have argued repeatedly, based on their experimental results, that individuals will treat formally identical problems differently depending upon how they are presented. For example, a military commander is in a pinch. If he does nothing six hundred of his soldiers will die. He has a choice of two escape routes. Under option A, two hundred soldiers will escape. Under option B, there is a 1/3 chance that all six hundred soldiers will be saved and a 2/3 chance that none will be saved. What is the appropriate counsel to the commander?

Now consider a commander in a situation where six hundred of his soldiers are again at risk and with two possible escape routes. His advisers tell him that under option A, four hundred soldiers will die and under option B there is a 1/3 chance that none will die and a 2/3 chance that six hundred will perish (Kahneman and Tversky 1979). In the first "framing" of the problem, a preponderance of experimental subjects recommend option A—they are apparently attracted by the certainty of saving two hundred lives. In the second case a preponderance of subjects choose option B, the riskier option, apparently attracted by the possibility of saving all six hundred. But the two problems, Kahneman and Tversky argued, are formally identical, and expected utility theory predicts that options A and B should be equally preferred under the two presentations: in particular, these findings contradict the assumptions that preferences should be stable or invariant to how a problem is presented.

Under option A the fate of the remaining four hundred soldiers is left unspecified. Kahneman and Tversky presume that subjects, if they are logical, should reason that they die. Perhaps, since their fate is not explicitly stated, subjects conclude that there is still some positive probability they might be alive. Under the second scenario, the four hundred under option A are unambiguously dead, but the fate of the remaining two hundred is not explicitly stated. Perhaps we reason that there is some likelihood that a number of them are dead as well. If such reasoning were operative we could conclude that the expected number alive is actually greater with option A under the first scenario than under the second, explaining the preference for it.

These possibilities are raised not to suggest that this interpretation disposes of the anomaly—I doubt that it does—but to indicate how carefully results must be scrutinized before concluding that we are faced with a regularity with real, out-of-sample predictive power. Kahneman and Tversky rarely consider *why* we reason as we do. In this instance the evolutionary logic for a preference for saving more members of "our" group is perhaps so obvious it needs no further consideration. But in other instances, bringing to bear considerations of the challenges posed by ancestral environments and the adaptations that likely resulted can be of considerable usefulness in this task of critical scrutiny.

As an example of the representativeness heuristic, humans expect "parts" of a phenomenon to exhibit characteristics of the whole, and in particular they expect this to be true with respect to the degree of randomness exhibited by a series of statistically independent realizations. Whereas this heuristic works well in reasoning from information on parts of an apple or a piece of wood to characteristics of its entirety (and vice versa), it works poorly for phenomena involving probabilistic outcomes. Thus people tend to assume that because 100,000 flips of a (fair) coin are very likely to produce a proportion of heads (or tails) very close to .5, it is also true that 10 flips of a coin are very likely to produce 5 heads and 5 tails (a 50 percent split). The binomial distribution tells us otherwise (the correct probability of exactly 5 heads in 10 tosses is less than a fourth—.246). Most subjects have very poor intuition about these matters. Because truly random processes were rare in ancestral environments, there is an evolutionary explanation, discussed in greater detail in what follows, for why this is so.

Closely related to this bias is a tendency, in thinking about the outcomes of random processes such as coin flips, to underestimate the likelihood of runs of heads or tails, say, three or four in a row. In general, humans are too willing to attribute structure, in particular, positive autocorrelation, to the results of a random process, identifying a "hot hand" in the performance of basketball shooters, the equivalent of a string of heads, when the performance records are statistically indistinguishable from what would be produced by the rough equivalent of a string of coin tosses (Gilovich 1991, 11–17). When asked to characterize what they think a string of random coin flips will look like, subjects include far too few runs, because they tend to assume that the proportion of heads will be roughly 50 percent even in very small series of realizations (such as two or four). A related phenomenon, Kahneman and Tversky claim, is that humans lack an intuitive understanding of the fact that the variance of an estimate of a population parameter, say, the mean of a population, shrinks as the size of the sample upon which the estimate is based increases. This last claim has, however, been disputed (see Cosmides and Tooby 1996; and subsequent discussion).

As an example of the availability heuristic, one can point to the common tendency for subjects to increase disaster preparations after a memorable event, such as an earthquake, even though there may be no objective evidence that the probability of a second disaster has increased as the consequence of the one that just occurred (Kunreuther et al. 1978) and the reverse may be true, inasmuch as pressure on a fault has now been relieved.[3]

As an example of an anchoring heuristic, Kahneman and Tversky

---

3. Of course, sometimes major aftershocks do occur, in which case it would have been rational to stay out of one's house. Similarly, canceling plans to fly to Europe after the TWA 800 crash *would* have been rational if the crash had been due to a terrorist bomb, presaging a series of attacks on U.S. flag carriers. So the availability heuristic does not necessarily serve us poorly.

asked subjects to estimate the number of African nations in the United Nations. The experimenters first spun a wheel with numbers from 0 to 100 on it and then asked subjects whether their estimate was higher or lower than this apparently randomly chosen number (the wheel was actually rigged to stop at either 10 or 65). The median estimate of the number of African countries in the United Nations was 25 for those who received 10 as an anchoring point and 45 for those who received 65 as an anchoring point.

The Kahneman and Tversky research program has produced a variety of striking findings and, due in part to the efforts of behavioral economists, has been one of the more "successful" interdisciplinary conversations in which economists have engaged over the last quarter century. In spite of this success, the program in its current incarnation does not offer a substitute for or a fully adequate complement to traditional economic theory as the foundation for an empirically based science of human behavior.

I adduce several reasons for this. First, the burgeoning menu of heuristics and biases has proved capable in a number of instances of accounting, ex post, both for a phenomenon and its opposite. Second, new research indicates that some of the findings of Kahneman and Tversky that do not suffer from this defect are less far reaching in their implications for cognition or behavior than was first apparent. Finally, the program has essentially nothing to say about the cognitive underpinnings of behavioral predispositions central to the origin of complex social organization. It focuses on the rationality of judgments—how beliefs and expectations are formed in games against nature—not on the rationality of optimization in games with other humans.

My intent in pointing out limitations in the heuristics and biases program is not to suggest—as have some of its critics—that the decision-making assumptions embedded in the standard economic model form a complete and satisfactory foundation for a comprehensive empirically based behavioral science. Enough has been said in earlier chapters to indicate that this is not my position. In critically examining some of the applications of behavioral economics to finance, for example, I do not intend to endorse the traditional view that financial markets are, after all, efficient, *even though some of my concerns are echoed by those who do hold that view.* My critique of the contributions of this program revolves in part around how adequately, if in some cases at all, it has accounted for phenomena that are indubitably anomalous from the standpoint of the standard economic model and in part around whether in some instances the Kahneman and Tversky approach has overstated the behavioral implications of biases it has identified.

It is perhaps ironic that the Kahneman and Tversky program, which has done so much to sensitize economists to the possibility of modularity, should end up being criticized for having gone too far, through its emphasis on framing, in its questioning of the relevance of the Skinnerian operant conditioning model, the prototypical domain general learning mechanism.

The Orthodox Alternative

Because of a series of startling experimental results accumulated over more than a quarter century, the heuristics and bias approach is now on the verge, among those who recognize the lack of correspondence between the predictions of normative economic theory and a large body of observational and experimental evidence, of becoming, if not orthodox, at least the orthodox alternative. Attainment of this status means that its claims warrant greater scrutiny. Much of what Kahneman and Tversky and those working in this tradition have discovered and documented will withstand such reexamination: they have generally been very careful in their exposition. But the interpretation of results will alter, and the scope of their relevance may narrow, in some cases quite significantly. And given the larger explanatory responsibility of an approach that aspires to comprehensiveness, we must also focus more precisely on what types of behavior the program has not elucidated.

Participants in this research program can take pride in their careful demonstration that in many instances human behavior does not correspond well to the predictions of the standard economic model. But ultimately we need more than just the identification of anomalies. It has been relatively easy ex post to adduce various heuristics with psychological resonance to account for a result, but it has proved more difficult to develop a framework with strong predictive power, inasmuch as different proposed heuristics may suggest that behavior will go in two entirely opposed directions. As Kahneman, Knetsch, and Thaler noted in 1986, "Parsimony requires that a new behavioral assumption should be introduced only if it specifies conditions under which observations deviate significantly from the basic model and only if it predicts the direction of these deviations" (1986, 233).

This is a sound methodological precept and one equally relevant to the exploration of the domain specific adaptations in cognition and behavior that have figured prominently in earlier chapters. I believe that these "new behavioral assumptions" or modules can withstand this test. For example, "first move(r) altruism" predicts that when subjects find themselves in a single play PD, their behavior will deviate from the predictions of the standard model in the direction of more nondefection. Estimates of the magnitude of the deviation require a statistical, empirical methodology whose normative relevance is not admitted in canonical theory. Its size may vary in a predictable fashion as a function of whether preplay communication is allowed or how large are the temptations to defection, but the existence of the deviation as an empirically important phenomenon is hard to question at this point.

Similarly, the "cheater detection" module predicts that when faced with problems of propositional logic in a context where a social rule is at stake, subjects will focus disproportionately on uncovering evidence of cheating, irrespective of the "normatively correct" solution to the problem, as a prelude to punishing such behavior or making certain it is punished by others. More generally, this module is reflective of a propensity to punish violations of norms, even when deterrence has failed and the act of punishment does not serve the individual interests of the actor narrowly defined.

If one does an overall assessment of the heuristics and biases program, however, the multiplication of heuristics and their often very general definition have created a situation where this precept is not always being observed. One way in which the focus of the program may be sharpened is to insist that when the menu of heuristics and biases can account both for a phenomenon and its opposite, we have an underspecified model. Another way is to subject it to the discipline of an evolutionary perspective.

First, though, it is important to understand why the Kahneman and Tversky research program has proved of such limited relevance in understanding the origin of complex social organization. Those dissatisfied with the gaps between the predictions of economic theory and observational and experimental data should understand that their dissatisfaction can be at best only partly resolved within this body of work.

As advertised in the title of their 1974 article (Tversky and Kahneman 1974) and their 1982 book (Kahneman, Slovic, and Tversky 1982), the program is principally concerned with judgment, and, implicitly, decision making, under uncertainty. It is about the ways in which humans do and do not make good use of available information in situations where there are many unknowns and where relations among variables are neither necessary nor sufficient but are probabilistic. The choice situations investigated in this program concern circumstances where outcomes for the individual do not depend directly on the choices of other individuals. Thus, if there is concern with games in the Kahneman and Tversky research program, it is principally with games against nature, not against other humans.[4]

---

4. An exception to this is the large experimental literature on fairness, some of which is discussed in chapter 4.

In contrast, at the core of the challenge of establishing and maintaining social relations is a problem, captured in the single play Prisoner's Dilemma, where the outcome for each depends on the choice made by the other but where, at least from the standpoint of normative game theory, neither the acquisition of more information nor the refining of skills in statistical inference makes *any difference whatsoever* in the conclusion about how one should play. The Kahneman and Tversky program can be at best only a partial challenge to the standard economic model because it addresses only a subset of deviations of human behavior from the "basic model" and perhaps not the most fundamental ones.

To be fair, neither Kahneman nor Tversky has claimed that their research is relevant to the problem of explaining, for example, first move(r) altruism.[5] They have tried to stick with problems where the "normatively correct" solution is apparently uncontroversial, although, as we will see, this effort has not been entirely successful. To appreciate the issues at stake, consider how the heuristics and biases program would approach the issue of decision making in a Prisoner's Dilemma. The standard methodology is to look at a particular decision-making problem; define the "normatively correct" solution to it; measure behavioral deviation from the counsel of the normative rule; describe that deviation as a "bias"; and then identify the "heuristic," or quick and dirty decision-making rule, that is responsible for the bias. One reason Kahneman and Tversky do not address the PD problem may be because, as Rapaport and Chammah note in discussing the game back in 1965, "whatever choice is recommended by 'rational considerations' has something wrong with it in spite of the fact that nothing remains unknown about the situation. In other words, the chooser cannot do better by finding out more." The "normatively correct" decision can be identified as defect, but intuition may rebel against this identification.

The challenge of dealing with a Prisoner's Dilemma does not have to do with the human brain's difficulty in grasping the choices and their consequences, nor is it that individuals are overwhelmed with information, some of which may be ambiguous. The dilemma does not involve difficulty in applying the propositional calculus or Bayes' theorem or calculating the binomial distribution. The payoffs are clearly specified, and information about the prior behavior of the other player(s) is irrelevant to the decision problem because it does not affect the dominance of the defect strategy. Thus neither the Kahneman and Tversky results about biases in the way information is processed nor the emphasis by Herbert Simon (1987) on limitations in the information processing capabilities of humans, a tradi-

---

5. Amos Tversky died in 1997.

tion out of which the Kahneman and Tversky research emerged, is germane to understanding the first of the key behavioral propensities upon which human altruism to non-kin and, ultimately, complex social organization depend.

Moreover, to assert that the normatively correct rule for the PD problem is defect, and to claim it as the gold standard against which actual human behavior should be measured, with deviations identified as "biases," will likely lead to philosophical objection. How many social scientists are prepared to characterize the play of cooperate in a one-shot PD game as a deviation from the "normatively correct" decision, a bias we should try to correct? Some hard core adherents to the standard economic model perhaps will, but the issue would, no doubt, be contested. As suggested, one can reasonably interpret a propensity to make grants of first move(r) altruism as a "heuristic," or rule of thumb, that has been favored by natural selection, albeit at a level above that of the individual organism. I am personally not prepared, however, either to claim that playing a strictly dominated strategy is rational or to advocate or initiate a systematic program to "debias" humans by eliminating this heuristic, even were that possible, and even though in some cases, such as reducing cartel stability, facilitating the breaking up of terrorist cells, or weakening intergroup conflict based on within group solidarity, it might be socially beneficial. Such benefits would vanish in a more complete accounting, for we would discard along with the bathwater the behavioral foundation for complex social organization above the level of the family.

The two player one-shot PD problem is an unusual case because the intuitive unattractiveness of the normative rule is widely acknowledged. But it is increasingly apparent that in a number of the decision challenges studied by Kahneman and Tversky the "normatively correct" decision rule they identify is less obvious or straightforward than the investigators have suggested. This is particularly so with respect to their conclusions about how poor we are as intuitive statisticians.

Base Rate Neglect?

One of the most frequently repeated conclusions of the program is that humans exhibit a systematic tendency to ignore base rate data in calculating posterior probabilities in the light of new information. The issue can be illustrated with a problem often used in these experiments. In the standard medical diagnosis problem, subjects are told that a test to reveal a disease with a one in one thousand incidence has a 5 percent false positive rate and are asked to calculate the probability that an individual testing positive has the disease. Sophisticated medical practitioners, for example, Harvard

Medical School residents, appear appallingly unable to give the normatively "correct" answer: approximately 2 percent.[6] Since subjects commonly answer that the probability is 95 percent, they have apparently failed to incorporate in their judgment the information on the very low incidence, or base rate, of the disease.

The application of Bayes' theorem is not in principle a complex task. A computer can process the information with a few lines of programming. The idea that natural selection was unable to "design" such a computer seems puzzling when placed alongside the remarkable success of human vision, which no human engineers have been able fully to reverse engineer, in light of the utility of inference capabilities in facilitating foraging and enabling complex social organization and in light of the ability of animals, including single celled animals, to "learn" using inductive algorithms.

Kahneman and Tversky do not generally ask why the brain operates as it does: their task, as they see it, is to understand how it operates. The Simon tradition attributes biases to computational complexity, but such an appeal seems of limited relevance here, since the calculations involved are in principle simple. Could one attribute these results to some heretofore unidentified "module" that can short-circuit "normal" processes of logical or statistical inference? But if some kind of module conflict is the explanation for the poor performance on the medical diagnosis problem, we advance to the next question: why would evolution select for a module that made us perform so poorly as intuitive statisticians?

Such questions have not generally been asked within the heuristics and biases research program.[7] Partly as a consequence, the biases documented have begun to take on the status of museum pieces: artifacts

---

6. This conclusion assumes that the person tested was drawn randomly from the population and that the rate of false negatives is 0: everyone who has the disease tests positive for it. Under these circumstances, if one randomly tests 1,000 people, one will likely pick up 50 false positives and 1 true positive, giving a posterior probability that an individual testing positive for the disease actually has it of 1/51, or about 2 percent. Another famous experimental test is the taxicab problem: 85 of the cabs in a city are green, 15 blue. A witness to a nighttime accident identifies a blue cab as involved, but color identifications after dark are known to be only 80 percent accurate. What is the probability the cab actually was blue? The correct answer is about .41. In 100 identifications, one would expect to "see" 29 blue cabs, 12 that actually were blue (15 × .8) and 17 that weren't (85 × .2). Twelve out of 29 is about 41 percent, so even though one can correctly identify cab color 80 percent of the time, the probability it is blue given that one saw it as blue is just over half that, because there are so few blue cabs (we assume the blue cabs are just as likely to be on the road at night as the green cabs). The issue is whether we are biologically predisposed to process these problems more easily when they are stated, as they are here, in frequentist terms.

7. An exception is Einhorn, who argues that the persistence of suboptimal rules in the face of Darwinian selection is not a contradiction, because it is only relative advantage vis-à-vis one's environment that matters (Einhorn 1982, 283).

enclosed in glass cases, maintained at constant temperature and humidity. They are cherished and nurtured, admired for their beauty and apparent ability to account for anomalous behavior. In some cases, however, in a matter that suggests problems from a scientific standpoint, biases have been used to "explain" both a phenomenon and its exact opposite.

Even those cases that do not suffer from this problem need to be brought out of the museum and studied in the light of evolutionary considerations. We need to know which ones surviving this screen would have been truly important from the standpoint of relative fitness. As it now stands, the anomalies elicit the same kind of fascination we associate with optical illusions or mathematical puzzles, like the St. Petersburg problem.[8] We study them, it is argued, for the same reasons we study optical illusions: because they can provide a key to how the mind works and, it is claimed, because by educating people to recognize these illusions, we can help them make better decisions (Nisbett and Ross 1980, xii). But to what degree are these cognitive illusions, like optical illusions, generated in part by the framing of problems in ways that defeat, or show in an unfavorable light, capabilities that are in fact more robust and have a stronger evolutionary rationale? How much of their effect is due to the fact that the experimental problems are presented in ways that come in "under the radar screen" of our cognitive processors?

By drawing two lines of equal length, with arrowheads flared in on one and out on the other, we can trick the brain into thinking one line is longer than the other. But most of the time we do very well indeed in judging the relative length of two parallel lines. Is there a danger that in focusing on the ubiquity of processing errors we have developed an unbalanced view of human inductive capabilities? One of the difficulties is that the heuristics and biases research program takes as given the one true normatively correct answer to the kinds of problems it poses. The history of statistical theory is one of heated controversy about how best to make inferences, not a uniform march to consensus.

Economists are generally taught differences between a classical hypothesis testing approach on the one hand and a Bayesian perspective on the other, but this underestimates the degree of diversity in statistical approaches. In fact, the Fisherian emphasis on significance levels is not identical to the Neyman/Pearson/Wald approach to discriminating

---

8. One is offered the opportunity to flip a coin. If heads on the first toss, one gets $1. If heads does not appear until the second toss, $2; the third toss $4; the fourth toss $8, and so on. The mathematical expectation of the game is infinite, but few reasonable people—in particular those who have some risk aversion—will wager their fortunes to play it. The St. Petersburg paradox stimulated von Neumann and Morgenstern to develop a theory of expected *utility*, rather than expected *value*, to explain choice under uncertainty.

between two hypotheses based on the relative costs of Type 1 and Type 2 errors. Disagreements between Fisher and Neyman and Pearson were public and severe. Gigerenzer and Murray have made a strong case that the hybridization of these two approaches in "classical statistics" is a creation of textbook writers (Gigerenzer and Murray 1987).

Both approaches are, in turn, different from the explicit subjectivity inherent in a Bayesian approach, in which, aside from textbook problems involving colored balls in urns, base rates are not known objectively or, where prior frequency data are available, there are legitimate differences in subjective views about exactly how narrow a category one should use in calculating such base rates. In the medical diagnosis problem, doctors apparently rebel against using base rate data because they see each patient as unique, rather than as part of a class for which past frequency data may be relevant. As Gigerenzer and his colleagues noted in 1989, before his adoption of a more explicitly evolutionary perspective in trying to discriminate among these:

> If we put some of the various cognitive functions that have been seen as intuitive statistics together, we get a picture of an eclectic brain whose different homunculi statisticians control different functions. Elementary functions such as sensory detection, discrimination, and recognition in memory are controlled by a statistician of the Neyman-Pearson-Wald school, causal reasoning by a Fisherian statistician, perceptual estimation and judgment by a statistician of the Karl Pearson school, and induction and opinion revision by a Bayesian statistician. To read the current psychological literature on cognitive functioning, it would seem as if each of the homunculi operated in ignorance of the other, and by dogmatic adherence to a single statistical school. (Gigerenzer et al. 1989, 233)

Some of the interpretations of the relevance of findings in the Kahneman and Tversky program are misleading because of suggestions of greater consensus than exists regarding what should be the normative "gold standard" of the basic model. As a consequence the research has tended to portray the intuitive statistical capabilities of the average human in a less favorable light than is warranted. None of us is perfect, and identification of cognitive illusions can obviously be enormously valuable. Indeed, my sense is that the greatest contribution of the program and the methodological and philosophical issues it raises so far has been to illuminate our practice as social scientists and to point toward ways in which that practice might be improved.

The development of double blind experimental methodology in medical research, for example, is a triumph of human ingenuity and reasoning. Much of our belief in the effectiveness of certain treatment rules is not based on such studies, however, and is often biased by the general absence of data on outcomes for those who did not receive the treatment. This is a bias that Kahneman and Tversky's work has identified and encouraged us to overcome. We admit to college or hire for our departments based on a personal interview, and we have a strong incentive to believe that this expenditure of time is worthwhile and that the contribution of professional judgment adds value. But this is largely faith, since we have no knowledge of how those we rejected would have performed had they been admitted or hired and we are generally not prepared to, or in a position to, conduct the experiments necessary to ascertain the true efficacy of the treatment.

But although we are often much poorer scientists than we could be, we are not necessarily as poor intuitive statisticians in our day-to-day life as the research results have suggested. And this is important, because evolutionary considerations suggest we should be relatively good intuitive statisticians, better than Kahneman and Tversky suggest, in solving complex problems of statistical inference, particularly those associated with foraging.

The observation that many of the Kahneman and Tversky results are puzzling from an evolutionary perspective has canalized research effort among evolutionary psychologists in an effort to discover what really is responsible for them. Recent research has now shown, in designs such as the medical diagnosis problem, that humans are actually quite good at applying Bayes' theorem, *provided both inputs given and output requested are stated in frequentist terms, rather than as single event probabilities.*

This discovery was foreshadowed in research by Fiedler (1988) on the "Linda" problem. Told that Linda is a bright, single, outspoken 31-year-old philosophy major who in college had been deeply concerned with discrimination and social justice and had participated in antinuclear demonstrations, subjects are asked to rank order the respective probabilities that (a) Linda is a bank teller and (b) Linda is a bank teller and active in the feminist movement. Most subjects in the original experiment and in subsequent replications commit what Kahneman and Tversky call the conjunction fallacy. They rank the latter probability higher than the former, even though, because the set of bank tellers must be greater than or equal to the set of feminist bank tellers, this is a logical impossibility.

Fiedler (1988) showed that if the question were rephrased, results were quite different. Instead of asking subjects to rank single event probabilities, they were asked instead, "To how many out of one hundred people who are like Linda do the following statements apply?" Seventy to

80 percent of subjects then correctly state that the frequency of bank tellers will be greater than the frequency of bank tellers active in the feminist movement. In other words, once the problem is restated in frequentist terms, the apparent conjunction bias disappears.

Subsequent experimental results indicate that when problems are posed in frequentist terms, subjects are quite capable of intuitively applying Bayes' theorem to inputs defined as frequencies rather than subjective probabilities, producing outputs in which base rate neglect disappears. Elaborating on broader work by Gigerenzer and Hoffrage (1995), Cosmides and Tooby (1996) have demonstrated exhaustively that the same type of rephrasing eliminates base rate neglect in the medical diagnosis problem. A mounting body of evidence suggests that in fact a number of the biases identified by Kahneman and Tversky disappear when problems are rephrased in this manner. Their conclusions that humans are not capable of processing these problems correctly and that the explanation for this is inadequate weight given to base rates must at least be reconsidered. It appears that although humans are not very good Bayesians where problems are phrased in the language of single event probabilities, they are quite good intuitive Bayesians where they operate on frequencies. Similar clarifications have been obtained with respect to the "overconfidence" bias (Gigerenzer, Hoffrage, and Kleinbölting 1991).

One might respond that these restatements in frequency terms just make the problems easier or "too easy." But that response points critically to what we need to explore. We need to understand, from an evolutionary perspective, why certain ways of posing the problem are more easily processed by the human mind than others. One might also argue that these results simply confirm the Kahneman and Tversky emphasis on the importance of framing. The difference in approach, however, is that the search for frames that are likely to trigger different or better performance by humans is guided by evolutionary considerations. This can make a big difference in directing research in certain directions and in increasing the productivity of our research effort.

The concept of the meaningfulness of a single event probability remains controversial among statisticians, and the choice as to whether one sees him- or herself as a Bayesian as opposed to a "frequentist" is as much philosophical as scientific. The Gigerenzer and Hoffrage/Cosmides and Tooby position is that since the "modern" understanding of probability and percentages is less than two centuries old, it is extremely unlikely that evolution selected our cognitive facilities to be proficient working within this framework. On the other hand, it is likely that we have been selected to update and maintain frequencies and draw inferences from such data. "From animals to neural networks, systems seem to learn about contingencies through sequential encoding and updating of event frequencies" (Gigerenzer and Hoffrage 1995, 686). Indeed, studies of animal foraging behavior, particularly among bumblebees and birds, have indicated they are able to effectuate the well-calibrated feats of statistical inference that humans, according to the biases and heuristics program, cannot (Brase, Cosmides, and Tooby 1998, 4).[9]

Kahneman and Tversky's position, in a published debate with Gigerenzer, is that "the refusal to apply the concept of probability to unique events is a philosophical position that has some following among statisticians, but is not generally shared by the public" (Kahneman and Tversky 1996, 585). They go on to claim that "whether or not it is meaningful to assign a definite numerical value to the probability of survival of a specific individual, we submit a) that the individual is less likely to die within a week than to die within a year and b) that most people regard the preceding statement as true—not as meaningless, and treat its negation as an error or a fallacy" (586). In his rebuttal Gigerenzer argued first that faced with an individual near death, many people will, quite reasonably, attribute a higher probability to that individual's dying within the next week as opposed to the period of time represented by *the remainder of the year excluding the immediately upcoming week,* an interpretation of the problem he sees as perfectly reasonable.[10] Moreover, he asks pointedly, "How can people's intuitions be called upon to substitute for the standards of statisticians, in order to prove that people's intuitions systematically violate the normative theory of probability?" (Gigerenzer 1996, 593).

The lesson to be taken from this debate is that the choice of a normative baseline against which "deviations" are measured is more arbitrary in many cases than has been suggested. Kahneman and Tversky argue that humans do not give sufficient weight in making their judgments to the information that can be extracted from base rates. But there will always be legitimate issues regarding whether a base rate is relevant for the particular problem at hand. Induction "works" well when the underlying process is stable and the chosen reference category appropriate. Neither of these determinations can be made unambiguously. Induction might fail to yield

---

9. Recent research by Knowlton, Mangell, and Squires (1996) adds support to the proposition that we are armed with tools that make us good intuitive statisticians. Knowlton and colleagues presented subjects with one, two, or three of four possible clues as to whether it would rain or shine the following day. The clues had predictive power, but the links were complex and probabilistic. After as few as fifty trials, subjects were able to predict the "weather" with 70 percent accuracy, even though they were completely unable to articulate the structure of the underlying model.

10. Kahneman and Tversky's rhetorical point is that the period "within a year" subsumes the period within a week; therefore the probability of the latter cannot be greater than the probability of the former.

good predictions because the underlying structure has in fact changed, or because the reference category is not appropriate to the problem, or because there never was in fact any structure, as in the case of a roulette wheel.

Finally, in terms of the posited behavioral predisposition systematically to underweight base rate information, we should recall that this tendency is in direct conflict with the conclusions of some of the original experiments in this paradigm, those conducted by Ward Edwards (1968). Edwards found that subjects were too *conservative* in updating probabilities based on new information. In other words, they gave too much weight to base rates (Gigerenzer et al. 1989, 219). Other experimenters have also documented conservatism (Camerer 1995, 601–2), and Edwards's work and his conclusions coexist uneasily with the Kahneman and Tversky heuristic.

Griffin and Tversky (1992) try to reconcile these apparently contradictory findings, arguing that people put too much emphasis on the strength of evidence (they neglect base rates) and not enough on its weight (they undervalue evidence that is weak but based on a large sample). On the other hand, Deirdre McCloskey has repeatedly admonished economists to pay more attention to the size of coefficients and less to their statistical significance, suggesting that economists suffer from just the opposite bias: they overvalue evidence that is weak but based on a large sample, such as economically unimportant but statistically significant coefficients (1983, 496–98; 1985; 2000, 187–207). The existence of analyses suggesting biases in opposing directions is symptomatic of a more general problem besetting the heuristics and biases program. A tendency systematically to overweight base rate data and a tendency systematically to underweight base rate data cannot both be essential human predispositions. If these heuristics are to be developed into a model with real predictive capability, more specification, ex ante, of conditions under which one or the other is likely to obtain is needed.

One can of course construct and logically justify another normative standard—ignore all base rate data—that summarily disposes of the preceding debate. This may strike some as silly, but its logic follows naturally from Hume's concerns with what W. O. Quine would later call the "scandal of induction." The beauty of an evolutionary approach is that we do not have to go down this route. It *does not matter* for our purposes whether the use of induction can be logically justified and thus whether decisions based on such a methodology are rational. What matters is whether selection pressures would have permitted posited predispositions to persist. All that we need in order to explain why humans use inductive reasoning is the presumption that those organisms that had a propensity to do so enjoyed a reproductive advantage over those that did not, buttressed with statistical evidence that behavior of individuals is to some degree reliably predictable by past overt behavior.

From this perspective, it is no longer a puzzle why animals, including single celled organisms, can "learn," using inductive algorithms. Induction worked, and it works, when it does, because much of the world consisted and consists of relationships and processes that have sufficient structural stability that it is meaningful to talk about reference categories, keep tabulations of base rates, and take action in accordance with estimates of contingent probabilities based on past experience. Insurance companies try to identify and operate over structurally stable processes and exhibit more caution around those that are not. So, too, do individual humans. This, then, is an evolutionary explanation for why we do—not a philosophical justification for why we should—use induction. If we are interested in understanding essential features of human nature, that is all we need.

Accepting the practical usefulness of induction, a prerequisite for any serious study of statistical analysis or decision theory, how people do and should handle base rates in actual decision problems is often as much a question of art as science. Kahneman and Tversky interpret the results of the medical diagnosis problem as showing that people may err in attributing uniqueness to events that are reasonably considered part of common categories for which past frequency data (base rates) are relevant. Their interpretation turns on how reasonable we find it to equate testing people for a disease with trying to determine the color of balls one draws from an urn.

Doctors, and, to an even greater extent, clinical psychologists, cherish the belief that their experience and trained intuition give them an ability to make individual level (clinical) predictions that will be, on average, superior to those obtainable using actuarial methods. Recent research on the value added by the subjective judgment of experts to diagnoses relative to what can be predicted from a random linear combination of objective data shows that this belief is largely a matter of hubris (Dawes 1988, chap. 10). We would no doubt benefit if doctors had better training in probability and statistics. At the same time, there will always be legitimate questions about the relevance of the reference class for which base rate data are presented. What does seem clear is that people can understand problems in statistical inference much better when they are posed in frequency terms, a finding that has implications for instructional strategies in medical schools and elsewhere.

Intuitive Estimates of Hazard Functions

Some, perhaps many, of the Kahneman and Tversky results will prove more robust. We may understand these better, however, if we examine them from an evolutionary point of view. It does seem evident, as noted, that in confronting random processes people expect that the proportion of outcomes in a series of trials will tend to be equal to the probability of a particular event in a single trial. Thus in trying to infer whether a process is truly random, subjects are prone to misclassify outcomes with long strings of "hits" (e.g., strings of heads or tails in a sequence of coin tosses) as possessing structure, or duration dependence, when they are in fact the result of a random process.

This phenomenon is evident in the belief among basketball players and fans that when you're hot you're hot and when you're not you're not. If streak shooting is a myth, then the probability of making a basket on the next shot is independent of the previous record of successes and failures. Whether there has been a streak of zero baskets, one basket, two baskets, three baskets, or more, the likelihood of making the next shot should be unaffected. Belief in streak shooting implies belief in duration dependence: that the likelihood of making the next shot depends in part, at least for a while, on the string of immediate past successes.

The problem is similar although not identical to the gambler's fallacy. The belief that because the roulette wheel has come up red four times in a row there is now a greater probability it will come up black also implies a hazard function that changes depending on the duration of the previous streak. In both instances predictions are biased because humans underestimate the likelihood that random processes can produce long strings of identical outcomes. In the case of the roulette wheel, however, there is simply no way to rationalize belief in duration dependence, since, if the wheel is true, the gambler has available mechanical information about its construction that should lead to the conclusion that its realizations are independent of each other. In the case of streak shooting, it is at least conceptually possible that shooting success is duration dependent: a string of successes *could* increase a player's confidence and improve the odds of making the next few shots.

In both cases, though, we have belief in a changing hazard function, whereas for a random process the hazard function is flat over time (Kiefer 1988). Many natural processes, such as storm fronts or animal stampedes, do have an underlying structure and a changing probability of continuation based on duration (a changing hazard function). Evolutionary forces may have hardwired in us a tendency to place a high subjective prior probability that a time series process has such a structure. Given the paucity of devices for producing series of truly random outcomes in hunter-gatherer environments, this bias may have been adaptive in our prehistory, though it outfits us poorly for forays into casinos or stock markets.

Gambling casinos and stock markets were not features of hunter-gatherer existence. From a logical standpoint it may seem perfectly obvious to students of statistics and probability theory that applying econometric time series (ARIMA [autoregressive integrated moving average]) techniques to the prediction of roulette wheel outcomes is silly. But naive subjects do not have this intuition, which is gained only with study and sometimes with difficulty. Influential finance theorists are persuaded that the stock market is, like roulette wheel outcomes, a random walk. Yet technical analysts continue to try to squeeze information about the future from the past, applying time series techniques to data in the hope of making money. We cannot state as unambiguously that this effort is a waste of time, because the securities markets are more complicated machines for producing outcomes than is a roulette wheel, whose basic design, assuming it is fair, is transparent.

Nevertheless, continuing investment in technical analysis should probably be interpreted as further evidence that humans are predisposed to believe that statistical processes have structure: that useful data for predictive purposes can be garnered from past realizations of the process. The bias may not serve our interests in casinos and stock markets, but it probably does in most of our interactions with the natural world. Moreover, once one is beyond a single play environment, it can be valuable in situations of strategic interaction, where it may trump the counsel of canonical game theory that leads to the conclusion, as Telser put it, that reputation or reliability is not an inherent personality trait and therefore that data on past overt behavior are not germane for predictions of counterparty action.

The Kahneman and Tversky program has its origins in well-established traditions in cognitive science and has consequently not been concerned with how our reasoning processes may have been affected by adaptation to encountered environments. In spite of the program's iconoclasm with respect to the standard economic model, Kahneman and Tversky approach the mind in the spirit of treating it as a black box and trying to find out how it works by asking what it does. An alternate approach has been championed by evolutionary psychologists. It insists first on taking advantage of our knowledge that this black box was "designed" by natural selection over millions of years of hunter-gatherer existence. That information permits us to channel research effort in directions that are likely to be particularly fruitful and to probe more deeply when confronted with experimental results that seem inconsistent with this indisputable fact.

Cosmides and Tooby illustrate the differences in results that these two approaches may produce through the following analogy. Suppose one is handed a black box and asked to investigate how it works. Applying the standard approach of cognitive science, one might discover that if placed upon loose papers it will prevent them from being blown away in the wind.

One might also discover that one can warm one's hands on it during a cold winter morning. And, through trial and error, one might stumble upon the fact that one can kill someone by throwing the device into his or her bath. Thus, three years of National Science Foundation funding would lead to the conclusion (in Cosmides and Tooby's language) that what one has here is an electric powered heat-generating paperweight (Cosmides and Tooby 1994a, 95).

If, on the other hand, one stopped before plunging ahead and first explored what the item had been designed for, one might pause to examine the box in which it was packaged and discover that the device had been designed to toast bread. This information could permit the construction and execution of a more focused and ultimately more productive inquiry into how it worked. With respect to the human mind, the equivalent of the information on the appliance box is knowledge that the system modules were "designed" by natural selection to solve recurrent problems in hunter-gatherer life.[11]

An explicitly evolutionary perspective has been less necessary in the relatively successful research programs in language acquisition and visual perception, where the functions of the subsystems investigated are more or less obvious. With respect to human social relations, the evolutionary perspective and assumptions about how evolution operated are more critical. From this perspective, many of the Kahneman and Tversky results seem puzzling. In their 1974 article, Tversky and Kahneman argued, "in general, these heuristics are quite useful, but sometimes they lead to severe and systematic errors" (Tversky and Kahneman 1974, 1124). On balance, however, the heuristics and biases research program has focused on the errors, not on the putative usefulness of the heuristics (Gigerenzer 1991, 101).

Kahneman and Tversky have shown that we are not very good at employing a number of advanced statistical, logical, and mathematical skills. But this is not in itself terribly surprising to students who have struggled through such subjects; most of us need structured education to understand them. Modern statistics is only a few centuries old, mathematics perhaps a couple of millennia. We have formal educational institutions for transmitting and developing accumulated human knowledge in these

---

11. My own view, defended at length in chapter 5, is that the repeated emphasis by Cosmides and Tooby on the Pleistocene is too limited and can lead to an underemphasis on modules that may have an older evolutionary lineage. In particular, I argue that the propensities necessary to enable complex social organization were likely evident six million years ago in the common ancestor of the three surviving chimpanzee species and thus predate the developments and refinements stressed by Cosmides and Tooby in their emphasis on the Pleistocene.

areas: unlike the case of language, people do not pick up these principles automatically. Although children learn how to speak without instruction and without encouragement, they do not necessarily learn how to read, how to write, or how to do more than rudimentary arithmetic. Do away with formal education and you will not do away with language: the overwhelming majority of children will still learn to speak and understand spoken language. However, most of them will be illiterate and innumerate. Literacy and advanced numeracy are accidental by-products of our evolutionary history. The ability to speak, as well as the ability to learn inductively by keeping track of frequencies, on the other hand, is probably essentially human, whereas the ability to grasp number concepts larger than four is not (Ifrah 2000, 6–10).

Cosmides and Tooby argue that we are endowed with relatively good domain general capabilities for keeping track of statistical frequencies and updating them based on new information.[12] In particular, they maintain that tabulating frequencies, as opposed to percentages, enables one also to keep track of the sample size and thus the reliability of frequency based prediction. Thus 7 out of 50 and 70 out of 500 both yield an "event probability" of 14 percent, but one can place more reliability in the latter estimate because of the larger number of trials. Thus they imply that if data are tabulated in the evolutionarily favored input format, we actually have a good intuitive understanding that the variance of the estimate of a population parameter decreases with the size of the sample upon which the estimate is based.

Maintaining data in a frequency format also makes it easier to update statistics upon the arrival of new information, and it is easy after the fact to construct from these databases new reference categories. For all these reasons they argue that the ability to collect, manage, and update frequentist probabilities (but not single event probabilities) has been selected for. This capability is "designed" to deal with life span specific challenges that individuals face: in other words, challenges whose content does not necessarily recur over thousands of generations and for which it would be evolutionarily useless to produce hardwired behavioral predispositions.

In contrast, selection for a hardwired module predisposing against sexual relations among those with whom one has been raised, whose deleterious genetic consequences are a recurring feature of the evolutionary environment; or selection for a module dedicated to detecting cheaters; or,

---

12. Some readers may initially find this confusing (I did) since Cosmides and Tooby's emphasis on domain generality here stands in striking contrast to their emphasis on a specialized module that can be evoked in the cheater detection studies of the Wason selection experiments.

I would argue, selection for a module predisposing to first move(r) altruism is readily explicable. Humans need not learn these lessons over and over through trial and error. The hardwired module is specialized to a recurring problem; the domain general capability as good intuitive statisticians is specialized to deal with life span specific problems.

The underlying methodological principle, again, is to organize research by first asking questions about "design," with the assumption that natural selection operated to solve recurring problems of ancestral existence. Thus adaptation to ancestral environments provides us with color correction modules that enable us to see grass as green both at high noon and at dusk, even though the objective properties of light reflected off vegetation are quite different at these two periods. In contrast, our color correction modules are worthless as one tries to find one's green car under the sodium lights of an airport parking lot, hardly a challenge that was a recurring feature of Pleistocene existence.

Too Many Heuristics?

It is now time to ask whether behavioral economics without an evolutionary perspective—essentially the Kahneman and Tversky research program—can provide the foundations for an empirically based behavioral science. Gigerenzer expresses his concerns with the results of this research approach.

It is understandable that when heuristics were first proposed as the underlying cognitive processes in the early 1970s, they were only loosely characterized. Yet, 25 years and many experiments later, explanatory notions such as *representativeness* remain vague, undefined, and unspecified with respect both to the antecedent conditions that elicit them and also to the cognitive processes that underlie them. My fear is that in another 25 years researchers will be stuck with plausible yet nebulous proposals of the same type: that judgments of probability or frequency are sometimes influenced by what is similar (representativeness), comes easily to mind (availability) and comes first (anchoring). The problem with these heuristics is that they at once explain too little and too much. Too little because we do not know when these heuristics work and how; too much because, post hoc, one of them can be fitted to almost any experimental result. (Gigerenzer 1996, 592)

He grants that Kahneman and Tversky have had an enormous stimulating effect on research.

But the sheer proliferation of studies is not always identical to progress. An ever-larger collection of empirical results, especially results that seem to vary from study to study in apparently mysterious ways, can be more confusing than clarifying. If the psychology of judgment ultimately aims at an understanding of how people reason under a bewildering variety of circumstances, then descriptions, however meticulous and thorough, will not suffice.

He concludes his exchange with Kahneman and Tversky in this fashion: "As I see it, there are two ways in which a theory can fail: by being wrong or by being indeterminate. The latter may be worse for scientific progress, because indeterminate theories resist attempts to prove, disprove, or even improve them" (Gigerenzer 1996, 596). Somewhat ironically, the Kahneman and Tversky program is now having levied against it some of the same criticisms long applied to the standard economic model where rational choice is understood to mean that people act in satisfaction of their desires.

Gigerenzer's judgment may be overly harsh, but what frustrates him can be illustrated by considering a recent work applying the Kahneman and Tversky framework to behavior in financial markets: Gary Belsky and Thomas Gilovich's *Why Smart People Make Big Money Mistakes* (1999). Gilovich has been a pioneer in behavioral psychology, and although this book is directed at a popular audience, it references and attempts to distill many of the important conclusions of the Kahneman and Tversky program. The work does contain a great deal of sound financial advice, whatever its underlying rationale, advice almost completely consistent with my own financial strategies, one of the reasons I probably find it sound.[13] Still, the book might better be titled "Smart People Make Big Money Mistakes." That statement is undoubtedly true, is illustrated profusely in the work, and would still resonate with an upscale readership that knows its truth.

It is in claiming to *explain* (not simply point out) these errors ("Why . . .") that behavioral economists sometimes seem to border on proffering snake oil, because they suggest that these errors were ex ante predictable. For example, drawing on the work of Thaler, Belsky and Gilovich suggest that bonuses are normally spent quickly, rarely making it to the bank, because there is different mental accounting for them. Thaler has made a real contribution in developing and documenting the framework of mental accounting (1990). The questions at issue are its implementation and

---

13. These include advice to buy and hold index funds, a key conclusion of the efficient market perspective.

the explanation of why particular accounting schemes rather than others are used. The Thaler story about the treatment of bonuses is inconsistent with Milton Friedman's permanent income hypothesis, which provided an explanation for the divergence between time series and cross section studies of the consumption function and for which there is a considerable body of supporting empirical confirmation at the aggregate level (1957). Friedman's theory was, of course, at variance with the standard Keynesian treatment of the consumption function, which viewed consumption behavior as determined by current receipts of money. The Keynesian view would suggest no differential treatment of a bonus as compared with regular income: both would be run through the standard consumption function and induce additional spending in accordance with the marginal propensity to consume. Thaler's and Belsky and Gilovich's views seem to go to the opposite extreme from Friedman's; these researchers argue that the propensity to spend out of a bonus is *higher* than out of current income. Perhaps the behavior that Thaler tries to capture applies only to households that are liquidity constrained, unable to borrow to smooth their lifetime consumption streams and thus faced with a propensity to consume out of transitory income = 1.

The idea that people segregate their money into mental accounts that they treat differently, ignoring the essential fungibility of cash, has psychological resonance. In order to advance the theory so it has real predictive power, however, we need to know under what conditions people use certain accounting schemes rather than others. There are several possibilities. The first, which can possibly be dismissed, is that these categories are completely idiosyncratic, in which case knowledge that they exist would give little predictive power in the aggregate. The second possibility is that there are systematic patterns in these accounting schemes that are learned and therefore culturally determined, just as there are different languages and different national accounting conventions. A third possibility is that there are some universal or essential ways in which individuals set up these categories, frameworks, and taxonomies that have been evolutionarily selected and are hardwired at birth. None of these types of questions has been asked within the heuristics and biases program. Consequently, merely demonstrating the operation of segregated mental accounts does not take us very far down the road to an empirically validated theory with real predictive power (for an empirical investigation of these issues, see Levin 1998). In the particular application at issue, what we need more of is evidence that leads to a systematic and predictable account of how people set up and spend from different types of accounts. The prediction that people will put nearly all bonus money into savings, the conclusion of the Friedman analysis, could, although it was certainly not interpreted in this way by Friedman, be explained as reflecting the operation of mental accounting. But it is exactly the opposite behavior from that "explained" by Thaler.

At the start of their book, Belsky and Gilovich are candid about the apparent indeterminacy of the heuristics and biases program, resulting from the ease with which one can access a heuristic from the current menu, regardless of in which direction the "bias" goes.

> We don't want readers of one chapter to throw up their hands in dismay when the next chapter seems to be saying something quite opposite. In chapter 7, we'll talk about herding, which is the tendency many people have to rely too much on the opinions or actions of others. . . . On the flip side, however, chapter 6 focuses on people's tendency toward overconfidence, which causes them to have more confidence than they should in the reliability of their own judgment or experience. How can we reconcile these two concepts? We can't, really. The fact of the matter is that sometimes people make mistakes because they behave like sheep, and sometimes they err because they behave like mules. The critical task is to try and identify which tendency is harming us in which circumstance and then try to break the habit. (Belsky and Gilovich 1999, 26)

Here is an admirable and disarming frankness about the limitations of the approach. But the limitations remain. Let us consider another example. An inherent human aversion to realizing losses has been used to explain both why people sell out too quickly when the stock market falls and why they hold onto their losers too long in hopes of recovering losses. We have a problem, however, if a heuristic or psychological principle is used to account both for a phenomenon and its opposite. Some scholars, for example Shefrin and Statman (1985), have argued that there is a predisposition, based on an essential human tendency, loss aversion, for people to sell their winners too early and hold on to their losers too long. deBondt and Thaler (1985, 1987), on the other hand, argue that stocks that have done extremely poorly over the past three years do much better subsequently than those that have done extremely well. If deBondt and Thaler are correct, and mean reversion is common because of systematic investor overreaction, and Thaler is coprincipal in a mutual fund that has done well managing money according to these principles, then investors who sell their winners and hold their losers are doing exactly the right thing. But if some stocks are losers (i.e., have fallen greatly in value) it cannot be the case that, in the aggregate, some people are fools for holding on to them at the now lower value and, at the same time, other people are fools for not acquiring them.

Ex post, depending on whether the stock subsequently recovers, many people will view themselves as foolish for having done one or the other. But ex post regret is not the same thing as ex ante foolishness. There will be others in each instance who feel exactly the opposite of foolish. Advocates of behavioral economics invite readers or listeners to *recognize* a psychological mechanism they identify as "explaining" ex post a behavior now regretted. This is an extremely effective rhetorical device, but it is not a scientific validation of the predictive capabilities of the framework.

Given the broad menu of heuristics and biases, we are getting to the point where there is one sure thing in this uncertain world: *whatever* one does as the market or an individual security crashes or soars, (1) there will be occasions when you will experience regret, (2) there will be an article in behavioral economics that will helpfully inform you that what you did was wrong, and (3) this article will offer (ex post) an "explanation" of why you did it! (Belsky and Gilovich 1999, 61). This is hyperbole, but the scientific issue is an important and troubling one.

The authors cite research by Terence Odean (1998), who finds that people are more likely to sell stocks that have risen in price than those that have fallen. But this is not irrational if, as deBondt and Thaler have argued, stock prices exhibit mean reversion as the result of systematic investor overreaction to good or bad news.[14] Of what use is reference to a "sunk cost fallacy" if it explains both why people dump their winners too quickly and dump their losers too quickly? People are urged to forget the past (Belsky and Gilovich 1999, 75) but to avoid the fallacy of having too short a memory (148). Failure to act, the result of decision paralysis, will cost you money, but of course so too will precipitous action. The same ambiguity about the value of historical evidence is reflected in Robyn Dawes's 1988 book, where he concludes that "I have no simple solution to the problems raised here" (Dawes 1988, 120). He cautions against mindless extrapolation from the past but, quoting George Santayana, also warns that it may well be true that "those who do not remember the past are condemned to relive it."

With respect to regret-inducing decisions based on historical data, which are, after all, what most of us must base our decisions on, behavioral economics has available too many ex post explanations for why one's decision making was flawed. On page 176, Belsky and Gilovich (1999) sug-

---

14. Ignorance of regression toward the mean is another bias behavioral economists rightly warn against.

gest that several hundred years of stock market history have shown that all too often stock market investors buy stock in companies or shares in mutual funds, presumably for sound reasons, but then sell their shares the minute "the market" turns against them. But of course not dumping shares the moment the market heads south is precisely what opens an investor to the criticism that he or she is holding on to losers too long!

According to historical accounts, the heuristics and biases research program got its start in an observation by its progenitors that Israeli flight instructors undervalued the effectiveness of reward and overvalued punishment, simply because, due to regression toward the mean, poor performances statistically tended to be followed by better ones and exceptionally good flights by more average performances. Thus rewards seemed to produce deterioration in performance and rebukes the reverse, even though no such inference should have been drawn. Human subjects fail to understand the spurious correlation due to regression to the mean.

The current weakness in behavioral economics involves the claim to having explained, rather than simply described, outcomes that are anomalous from the standpoint of the standard economic model, which in finance gives rise to the efficient markets paradigm. Because of heuristics that can "explain" biases in either of two opposing directions, the apparently successful retrodiction is spurious, although, as in the case of the Israeli flight instructors (whose spurious correlation had a different origin), this apparent success has strengthened belief in the efficacy of the approach. There is something for everyone: people who hold a stock too long *and* people who sell it too quickly both experience regret about the choices they have made. Behavioral economics appears to provide an explanation for both mistakes. *But not both of these mistakes can be the consequence of human behavioral propensities that are essential.*

It is possible to find evidence that under some circumstances at some ages, some people suffer from overconfidence. Adam Smith believed that young males suffered systematically from an exaggerated estimate of their own invulnerability, explaining their willingness to enter military careers. The majority of automobile drivers believe that they are better than the average driver. But the entire full service brokerage industry can be interpreted as evidence that some people at some ages under some circumstances also suffer from underconfidence.[15] Where behavioral economics in the aggregate has sometimes overreached is in claiming to have identified essential human predispositions that can account for an anom-

---

15. Even though virtually all of the information full service brokers can offer is available free of charge elsewhere, customers apparently lack confidence in their ability to make their own judgments or enjoy having another to blame if things go badly.

aly even though the body of experimental and observational evidence underlying that predisposition is ambiguous and sometimes points in the opposite direction.

The problem of indeterminacy of prediction is illuminated in a 1988 work on gambling by Wagenaar, addressing what people do after they have experienced a streak of wins or losses: "The representativeness heuristic predicts that people will increase their bet after a run of losses, and decrease it after a run of gains." (If the probability of winning is, let us say, .5, then people mistakenly assume that what will be true of the proportion of wins for a very large number of trials—it will approach .5—will also be true, or be representative, for a small number of trials.)

> This is indeed what about half the players of blackjack do. . . . But the other half show the reverse behaviour: they increase their bets after winning, and decrease them after losing, which is predicted by the availability heuristic. After a run of losses, losing becomes the better available outcome, which may cause an overestimation of the probability of losing. [The] repertoire of heuristics predicts both an increase and decrease of bet size after losing, and without further indications about conditions that determine preference for heuristics, the whole theoretical context will be destined to provide explanations on the basis of hindsight only. (Wagenaar 1988, 13)

The ambiguity of the heuristics and bias approach is actually reflected in Kahneman and Tversky's seminal 1979 article on prospect theory, where they predict *"that a person who has not made peace with his losses* is likely to accept gambles that would be unacceptable to him otherwise" (Kahneman and Tversky 1979, 287; my italics). How can we predict in advance under what conditions an individual will have made peace with his losses?

Wagenaar's work is cited in Jon Elster's 1999 work *Alchemies of the Mind* (Elster 1999, 7). Elster is acutely aware that a framework that predicts, given certain conditions, a particular behavior about half the time and its exact opposite the other half lacks any real predictive power. And yet there is clearly a very strong intuitive appeal, and consequently a market, for such models. Elster's provocative discussion of proverbs (11–13) provides insight into the appeal of the heuristics and biases approach. He identifies a number of compelling instances in which popular proverbs providing absolutely contradictory advice simultaneously coexist. *Haste makes waste,* but *he who hesitates is lost. Absence makes the heart grow fonder* but *out of sight, out of mind.* A study of proverbs reveals that again, regardless of what you do, the master of proverbial wisdom will be able to adduce a wise saying explaining why what you did was wrong (or right).[16] No matter what behavior is observed, there will be a proverb apparently providing an (ex post) explanation of why it happened. Such discourse may be entertaining, and in each case the mechanism identified may appear to have psychological resonance. But this exercise in providing appealing after the fact "explanation" is not scientific, in the sense that absent an ability to specify under what conditions one or another mechanism will kick in, the analysis does not give rise to testable hypotheses.

One cannot help but observe that to some degree, the success of the heuristics and biases program, with its large menu of heuristics from which to choose, is remarkably similar to the success over many centuries of persisting proverbs. Elster makes a plea for the relevance of ex post explanation via reference to mechanisms. It is in some sense an appeal to Coase's position in opposition to Friedman's (see the prologue). Thus Elster should be understood as defending the type of "explanations" offered by the heuristics and biases literature. But his argument is unconvincing. What he advocates cannot be termed behavioral *science*. For centuries people have ex post attributed bad luck to walking under a ladder or having one's path crossed by a black cat, even though, as in the gambling example earlier, there is no systematic relationship between these events and the type of luck subsequently experienced. As Dawes notes, good stories may be psychologically compelling, but they often lack validity (1994, 76). The progress of science has been based on rejection, not acceptance, of mechanisms that lack validity.

In important cases we may be better able to validate the operation of mechanisms, and this type of explanation is certainly what Elster is arguing for. But in these instances, and where the accounts we offer do not claim or do not have out-of-sample predictive power, I think it is more straightforward to indicate that what we are offering is historical, not scientific, explanation. I expand on this point in chapter 7.

Elster is pessimistic about the possibility of a true behavioral science, a pessimism reflected in his remark that "any economist worth his or her salt is able to tell a story demonstrating that a given piece of behavior is rational, and any sociobiologist showing that it is fitness enhancing" (Elster 1999, 15). Elster's characterizations, of course, have an element of truth to them. Critics of evolutionary explanations of adaptations often call them "just so stories," and the same appellation can legitimately be applied to many forays into the explanation of behavior, some more seri-

---

16. It is interesting that stock market forecasters also appeal to proverbs to explain or rationalize their actions. For example, *the trend is your friend* or *don't fight the tape.* See Shefrin 1999 (67).

ous than others, by economic theorists. But identifying instances of such sophistry is a prelude to criticism insisting that disciplines that claim to be scientific develop models with true out-of-sample predictive power. *Elster asks us to accept this feature of the economic and/or sociobiological enterprise as inherent in the enterprise.* Such acceptance surrenders any aspirations to true behavioral science and requires, in my view, that both economics and sociobiology/evolutionary psychology be reclassified as humanistic studies: areas of inquiry that do not aspire to the development of testable, refutable hypotheses.

If, as Elster shows, popular essayists such as Montaigne (Elster 1999, 16) provide numerous instances of advice and the exact opposite of that advice, we can conclude that what we have in Montaigne's essays is entertaining literature, not a practical guide to action. If, as the heuristics and biases literature reveals, we have an explanatory framework that is ready and able to explain the existence under specified circumstances of both a phenomenon and its opposite, we must conclude that what we have is not behavioral science, at least insofar as such an enterprise aspires to prediction.

The problem with Elster's intelligent and insightful analysis is that it seems to end up as a defense of pop sociology or pop economics. There is ample evidence that humans enjoy the search for ex post explanations that make their behavior apparently comprehensible. At some intuitive level, these "explanations" provide value. But when different mechanisms are equally capable of explaining both a phenomenon and its opposite, we have lost out-of-sample prediction. In my 1981 work on North and Thomas I characterized (and implicitly criticized) their "model" as predicting that high land-labor ratios would be associated with the absence of coercive labor regimes *except where they weren't,* as in the instances of U.S. slavery and eastern Europe after the plague. Whenever we have a model within which specified conditions "explain" both a condition or course of action and its exact opposite, we have the illusion of explanation without its reality. We are offering narrative history, which is to be commended, provided it is so identified, but suggesting that we are providing scientific explanation, which is not, because the claim in this case is unwarranted.

Elster points out correctly that most attempts to specify social scientific "laws" are not deterministic but are statistical or probabilistic: thus they are incapable of explaining individual cases, although they may be able to provide a useful prediction of the behavior of a larger group. He defends the study of mechanisms on the grounds that although they also cannot predict individual cases, they "can at least explain individual events after the fact" (1999, 44). But these ex post "explanations" are not the same as explanations based on models or algorithms with out-of-sample predictive power. They are historical, not scientific, and it is important not to confuse one with the other. Elster's plea for disaggregation (44) is not really an argument against the search for relations with predictive power, even if that predictive power is only probabilistic or statistical, but rather a suggestion that disaggregation may improve our search for them.

Both the heuristics and biases approach and a great deal of standard economic analysis come dangerously close to providing, after the fact, "just so" stories. Behavioral science cannot call itself that if it remains limited to such accounts. Thus, if we are overwhelmed with evidence that people are both overconfident and underconfident, we need to start carefully disaggregating the data by age, sex, and domain to see if there are truly robust tendencies that we can identify as essential. If so, such predispositions should have out-of-sample predictive power. Considerations of selection pressures in the environment of evolutionary adaptation may help canalize the search for such mechanisms or help us understand those we stumble upon.

The argument that research in behavioral economics and finance needs to be more disciplined by an evolutionary perspective must be understood carefully. Appeal to Darwin has often been a knee-jerk reaction by proponents of the standard economic model whenever its behavioral presuppositions are questioned. The understanding of the levels at which natural selection may operate is more catholic here, and the aim of an emphasis on the importance of adaptation in ancestral environments is to canalize experimental research and its interpretation in directions that may be more productive in the long run.

In his Nobel lecture, Maurice Allais wrote that "a theory which cannot be confronted with the facts or which has not been verified quantitatively is, in fact, devoid of any scientific value" (1997, 6). It is remarkable how many of the criticisms of behavioral economics, particularly that of indeterminacy, have begun to echo complaints levied against the standard model and the applications of the rational choice approach in other domains.

CHAPTER 7

The Invisible Hand and the Blind Watchmaker

The heuristics and bias program has generated a body of striking experimental results that all serious students of human behavior need to address. It has increased our receptivity to what can be learned from experimental methods. And it has introduced into our vocabulary the important concept of framing: the idea that people may reason about and respond differently to the same formal problem presented in different contexts. The research generated and language employed by this program are very much consonant with the postulate of cognitive modularity developed in chapter 5.

But the conversation between heuristics and biases researchers, on the one hand, and rational choice theorists, on the other, has not led and does not appear to be leading in the direction of a *comprehensive* empirically based behavioral science. Setting aside the challenge posed by an expanding menu of heuristics, such a science must ultimately address not only issues historically of interest to decision theorists but also those in the purview of game theory. Simply put, the Kahneman and Tversky program has little to say about the most troublesome behavioral deviations from those predicted by the standard normative model, deviations troublesome because they are foundational to an understanding and explanation of the origin of complex social organization.[1]

---

1. For exceptions, see Dawes and Thaler 1988 and Shafir and Tversky 1992. In the latter paper, the authors question the relevance of altruism (they refer to it as ethical thinking) in explaining mutual cooperation in the single play PD game by showing that cooperation levels go down if the second player is informed in advance of what the first has done (irrespective of whether the first player chooses cooperate or defect). For example, knowledge that the first player has cooperated moves some second players from the cooperate to the defect column, presumably because knowledge that the first player has cooperated increases the temptation for defection (the highest possible payoff is now available with certainty). But it also moves some players—a smaller number but a larger percentage increase—away from defect to cooperate. According to canonical game theory, of course, none of the players should have been in the cooperate column in the first place: any level of cooperation above zero is a deconfirmation of the predictions of Nash's analysis. Shafir and Tversky attribute the willingness to cooperate when the outcome is not known to "quasi magical thinking"— pointing out that millions are prepared to vote when the outcome is uncertain, apparently

295

These deviations appear most strikingly in situations involving strategic interaction. They include predispositions to play cooperate even in single play PD games and, where repeated interactions have been established, to monitor others obsessively for signs of violations of social rules and to punish those who do not reciprocate. It is discomfiting to label these deviations as biases, for the term brings with it the implicit suggestion that human progress lies in eliminating them. The problem here is not that subjects fail to make correct logical or statistical inferences; the issue is not deficiency in the rationality of beliefs or expectations. When an individual rejects a proposed division in a one-shot ultimatum or dictator game, for example, it cannot involve a problem in the way beliefs have been formed, nor is there even any element of uncertainty about what the outcome will be.

Reading the contributions in the Hogarth and Reder collection (1987), particularly those by Simon and Thaler, one has a sense not of the integration of new experimental results into the ongoing development of a progressive discipline, as would typically be the case in a natural science, but rather of an intellectual logjam. Matters are scarcely different a dozen years later.

The logjam can be broken, I believe, if two things happen. First, those committed to a rational choice approach need fully to understand that evolutionary theory does not preclude selection for behavioral predispositions at levels above that of the individual organism. Abandoning the facile view that evolutionary theory provides ironclad justification for the assumption of strict behavioral egoism is an essential step. Too often has an improper understanding of the constraints that natural selection places on the evolution of human predispositions constricted thinking, leading to head in the sand denials of evidence of other-regarding behavior; to almost schizophrenic approaches (witness Frank; see chap. 4 in this volume) among those committed to acknowledging such data; and to prolonged, contorted, and unsuccessful attempts to explain phenomena that, within the framework developed in this book, are not anomalous.

Those skeptical will wish to examine, consider, and/or dispute the evidence that group or multilevel selection has operated in human and other populations, but were that to happen, and as that happens, the terrain of discourse will alter from one involving mostly logic to one involving a more productive balance of logic and evidence. For others, recognizing the possibility of multilevel selection should undo an intellectual straitjacket and open the way for more systematic explorations of essential human

---

believing that their participation can somehow influence the outcome, but few will participate after the outcome has been determined. Thus conflicts about announcing predicted winners of national elections before polls on the West Coast or Hawaii have closed.

predispositions and the conditions under which they will and will not manifest themselves.

Bruce Bueno de Mesquita has observed, "We must not be lulled by apparent empirical successes into believing that scientific knowledge can be attained without the abstract, rigorous exercise of logical proof" (1985, 128). The behavioral assumptions underlying the application of the axiom based choice theory he favors presuppose a process of natural selection that operates only at the level of the individual organism. Game theory premised on self-regarding preferences can be helpful in illuminating mechanisms that sustain cooperative solutions once established. What it has not provided is an intellectually coherent account of origin, any more than, within an evolutionary framework, have models based on individual level selection alone.

If we are serious about predicting human behavior, we can do better. How? By using systematically developed empirical regularities to characterize behavioral predispositions that, in environments in which they exist only at low frequency, do not advance the material welfare of the actor—and the domains in which these are likely to manifest themselves. Such action tendencies, in low frequency environments, are not rational in the sense defined at the start of the book. This category includes the type of behavior counseled by nonconsequentialist ethical systems that, in contrast to utilitarianism,[2] for example, do not condition the search for what is right on consideration of the consequences of actions. Some of what we do, voting for example, or playing cooperate in a one-shot PD, or rejecting positive offers in a single play ultimatum game with anonymity, cannot plausibly be explained as the consequence of strategic thinking, even though, because of the high value placed on such thinking in our societies, we will often bend over backward trying to persuade ourselves that the contrary is true.

And preserving a role for choice defensible as rational in explaining the *maintenance* of cooperative or reciprocal relations requires rethinking the logic and implications of the hard and fast distinction commonly made between games against humans and against nature. The former are assumed to involve strategic interactions for which the logical and mathematical tools of game theory are sufficient. Nonstrategic interactions, on the other hand, are assumed to benefit from the use of algorithms for making statistical inferences, with the notable exception of games of chance and mechanisms like stock markets that may mimic them.

---

2. The assumption of utility maximization, which underlies rational choice theory, does not require acceptance of utilitarianism, which embraces interpersonal comparisons of utility. But both entail the belief that behavior is or should be goal oriented and thus evaluated in terms of its consequences.

Are techniques of statistical inference applied to past data relevant for predicting the behavior of an individual human or a group of them? Is it rational to form expectations of the behavior of others using these algorithms? Is it rational to predict our own behavior from such data? The approach of game theory generally assumes not: it assumes that our behavior and that of others are a function only of the situations we find ourselves in, not our dispositions.[3] But a great deal of evidence, including the obvious point that we are animals with an evolutionary history and thus not separate from nature, suggests that the position is a poor one to adopt from a practical standpoint. Humans do and probably should use such expectations, not only in influencing behavior when not choosing rationally, but also in coordinating on certain equilibria when they do. Expectations based in part on data on past behavior of similarly situated humans, or the particular individual(s) in question, may be more rational in the sense that the word is applied to expectations than those that are not.[4]

Experimental research on human subjects will continue to play a critical role in identifying these regularities. But like other once revolutionary endeavor such enterprise can, over time, become routinized and the rate of scientific advance slow. What can be beneficial in maintaining focus and breaking logjams is adoption of an explicitly evolutionary framework conditioning the interpretation of results and the direction of research effort. Recent work by Gigerenzer and Hoffrage (1995) and Cosmides and Tooby (1996) (see chap. 6) indicates that this is a promising approach in helping us understand, for example, which items of the menu of heuristics and biases are truly robust, rather than artifacts of the way experimental questions have been posed, and, where different heuristics may imply contradictory behavior, under what conditions we are likely to observe one rather than another.

The value added that these scholars have contributed by focusing an evolutionary spotlight on research in the heuristics and biases tradition, however, does not require them to address or accept the possibility of group selection, nor do they. While enthusiastically endorsing their call to

3. Aside, one might argue, from the assumed disposition efficiently to pursue our material welfare.

4. We can focus the issue by considering the problem of whether or not to allow a prisoner to be paroled. Is a consideration of the opportunities and potential penalties the individual will face upon release the only grounds for attempting to predict behavior? Or is the record of behavior while in prison relevant in deciding whether or not to parole? Presumably Telser would argue the former. Debate about the appropriate criteria is mirrored in psychology, with the distinction between an emphasis on situational factors, arising from a behaviorist social learning perspective, and an emphasis on dispositional factors: the proposition that humans may have personality traits and indeed that these may, to some degree, be heritable.

examine the results of experimental research under an evolutionary lens, I distinguish broadly between the research on decision theory (most of the heuristics and biases literature) and that on game theory, the body of work summarized in chapter 1. Wherever we study strategic interaction, it matters a great deal that the evolutionary perspective include awareness of controversies surrounding the different levels at which natural selection may operate.

Adopting an evolutionary perspective does not mean assuming the brain was designed to solve the challenges of life unique to the 11,000 years after the beginnings of the Neolithic revolution, nor does it imply that there has been much time to evolve genetically in response to the industrial revolution and the onset of modern economic growth in the past 250 years. To the degree that design appears to be adaptive, it is because of environmental challenges common to the hunter-gatherer existence and the epochs preceding it and the era after the agricultural revolution. This point is an important feature distinguishing current approaches from those characterizing 1970s sociobiology, which tended to presume adaptation to currently encountered environments.

A corollary of a position emphasizing the long time frames over which adaptation occurs is that although the cognitive tools refined in relatively recent evolutionary history have *as an unintended side effect* proved useful at solving problems in higher mathematics and advanced probability theory, *they were not designed to do so.* We will therefore gain little insight into the design of cognitive structures or behavioral adaptations by presuming they were "intended" to address problems that are common now but were absent during the Pleistocene era or earlier. There are reasons why it is more common and far easier for people to acquire phobias about spiders, snakes, enclosed spaces, heights, and thunder than about cars, trucks, or knives, even though the latter set of threats is far more dangerous in modern life. The explanation for these tendencies is evolutionary and historical, and the biological substrates responsible are, under current conditions, not adaptive, functional, or efficient, to use the lexicons of biology, sociology/anthropology, and economics, respectively.

What was Pleistocene life like? I enjoy wilderness travel in Yosemite and the high Sierras: there is something elemental I have always felt about such adventure. Pleistocene life on the savannas of Africa might be described as the equivalent of an extended backcountry trip without the benefit of Gore-Tex, freeze dried food, or bottled fuel. Moreover, it was a trip whose routines did not alter for thousands of generations, up until the beginnings of agriculture and the domestication of animals, roughly ten or eleven millennia ago. It was in that extended human adolescence, the Cosmides and Tooby program argues, that the modular structure of human cognition was refined through the trial and error process that Darwin first identified.

But—and here my emphasis differs from Cosmides and Tooby—these adaptations built on earlier capabilities. One set, for which there had been and continued to be strong and continuing selection pressure at the individual level, included cognitive and behavioral algorithms facilitating foraging. These algorithms lead to our facility with the techniques studied in courses in decision theory. They are central to the learning mechanism implicit in behaviorist psychology, a mechanism that has been explored fruitfully with respect to both human and animal behavior. And in modern settings they serve the set of behavioral propensities upon which microeconomics is generally premised.

But success at obtaining food from the natural environment is only one outcome that has been favored in evolutionary history. So too has been the avoidance of death at the hands of other members of the same species, a precondition for establishing complex social organization. Other cognitive and behavioral modules, specialized to the domain of social relations among non-kin, were also under selection pressures. They also built on evolutionarily older modules, these modules inhibiting intraspecific violence, which would not have been favored initially by individual level selection.

Modularity—domain specific adaptations that prespecify taxonomic categories and relations among them and in so doing can govern action—applies to the realm of social relations as much as to language. We know that aversion to incest among siblings raised together is universal among human cultures. We also know that incest avoidance is evolutionarily adaptive because it avoids the negative genetic consequences of inbreeding. Humans do not need to conduct controlled experiments each generation to discover empirically that inbreeding increases the probability that various recessive genes will manifest themselves.

Studies of Israeli kibbutzim and the sim-pua system in Taiwan support the conclusion that humans are predisposed to avoid sexual relations with those they were raised with between the ages of roughly two and eight.[5] These studies are consistent with the view that we do not in fact

---

5. Degler (1991, chap. 10) provides a comprehensive history of social scientific treatments of the incest taboo. What is remarkable is how recent is the consensus that the Westermarck thesis is correct and that Freud, Malinowski, Lévi-Strauss, and a host of other anthropologists were wrong. The consensus has been driven by a growing understanding of the weakness of functionalist arguments explaining the incest taboo as "necessary" to drive exogamy (functionally beneficial in linking kin groups together), empirical studies demonstrating that incest among animals in the wild is rare (the contrary was assumed as late as the 1960s), and evidence that unrelated humans reared together have an aversion to sexual rela-

need to teach children an aversion to incest, although children do have to be taught not to touch a hot stove or learn this through trial and error. We are born with dedicated modules that embody the evolutionary wisdom of millions of years.

In a similar fashion, the genome stores templates providing the building blocks for language and its structure, although particular environments into which a child is born store vocabularies, which are learned through standard Skinnerian mechanisms. Nor do we learn to interpret the world visually via a domain general Skinnerian mechanism alone. Our ability to see is the consequence of an interacting complex of modules dedicated to specific domains, such as edge detection, or the maintenance of perceived color constancy for objects, even as lighting conditions change (Marr 1982). Thousands of generations of natural selection have encoded recurring features of the natural environment in specialized modules for interpreting the sensory impulses generated by the rods and cones in our retinas.

Implications for the Core Social Scientific Traditions

For the sociological and anthropological traditions, culture and social structure have long been considered emergent properties, neither influenced by the genome nor reducible to the characteristics of individuals whose behavior they organize. I have argued, in contrast, that acquisition of certain universal norms is favored by biological, genetically influenced predispositions, just as is the acquisition of language adhering to the rules of universal grammar. We are differentially prepared to learn in certain directions.

Having said this, an important range of cultural variation remains, sustained by patterns of belief about the material world and about what others believe. That variation has real consequences for social and economic outcomes. The argument is not, therefore, that we should abandon the concept of culture but rather that we recognize factors limiting its variation. If these limits have a biological underpinning, blanket rejections of reductionist models are not sustainable. The understanding of culture, both its universal and variable components, can, in fact, be undertaken with reference to attributes of individuals.

Methodological individualism has long been a key tenet of the rational choice tradition but has typically been paired with restrictive assump-

---

tions. The latter research is based in particular on studies of the offspring of Israeli kibbutzim and the marital success (poor) of children reared together in Taiwan under the sim-pua system. See also Brown 1991 (chap. 5).

tions about essential human predispositions. The argument here poses challenges for this tradition as well. Most important, it questions the legitimacy of invoking an evolutionary rationale for the assumption of egoism narrowly understood.

Although humans may perceive their behavior toward children, siblings, or even their genetically unrelated spouse as genuinely altruistic, they more rarely perceive their other social relations as having this character. There are several reasons for this. The first is the popular identification of altruism with affirmative altruism—positive acts of assistance—an identification that hides from view its more empirically important form: failure to harm. Second, altruism directed toward non-kin leads to behavioral interactions that are more explicitly organized on a quid pro quo basis, that is, on the basis of reciprocity. In its developed state it is, objectively, mutualistic rather than altruistic. This often reciprocal character makes it difficult to recognize and acknowledge the altruistic predispositions necessary for such behaviors to originate.

Because organized social existence is regulated by a widespread willingness to punish those who violate its regularities, a marginal invader of such a group can find it rational to behave according to these norms. If such behavior is rational, as defined at the start of this book, it cannot be altruistic. Once the basic structure of a cooperative group has been established, once Tit-for-Tat players dominate the group, for example, cooperative behavior by the marginal invader becomes increasingly self-serving. Conditionally cooperative behavior has been drained of altruistic consequence and is no longer altruistic, although its form remains unchanged. Propensities to behave in unambiguously altruistic ways, necessary for cooperation based on mutuality to originate, fade into the background, a reservoir that is called upon in exceptional circumstances, where the structure of civil society, or social relations, or the particular intermediate level coalition or relationship is called into question; or where individuals are trying to initiate a new regime of cooperation and reciprocity where only hostile relations existed before.

It is only in these circumstances, or under controlled experimental conditions, that fundamental behavioral propensities that made and make possible humans' extraordinary reciprocal social life again show themselves clearly. In such instances playing cooperate in what could be a one-shot PD again has a truly altruistic character, because it may risk the organism's survival in a fashion that might, but might not, establish or reestablish relations of reciprocity. Episodes of this type form the foundation of much dramatic literature and art, are often featured in news reports, and bring into sharp relief issues of individual character and human nature that are disguised or suppressed during more ordinary times.

Thus it is that the assumptions reflected in the standard economic model, and the explanation of order as reflecting the operation of an invisible hand, seem to be confirmed by introspection: it seems to be the case that our social relations among non-kin have no altruistic character. In established social interaction this is largely true: it is not to the benevolence of the butcher that we appeal in order to get our meat, it is to his self-love. It is only in the rare moments when civil society breaks down, or in the initial stages of love or the final stages of divorce, that we get a glimpse of the human propensities that made it possible in the first place, as well as those they had to overcome.

Mandeville's *Fable of the Bees* has been a touchstone for economists' discussion of human cooperation for over two centuries, providing underpinnings for Smith's invisible hand metaphor, and the life of the social insects formed a backdrop for discussions of human society by the original social contract theorists. We know now that the explanation for the high degree of social organization among bees, ants, and wasps must be somewhat different from the isomorphic forms among humans. The bees in a hive are all closely related and reproduce using a haplo-diploid system. Males develop from unfertilized, females from fertilized eggs. Consequently, males have half the complement of chromosomes possessed by their sisters. Sisters share on average three-quarters of their genetic inheritance with each other but only a quarter with their brothers.

From the standpoint of inclusive fitness theory, it is not entirely surprising that sisters are highly altruistic toward each other (75 percent genetic overlap), somewhat altruistic toward their queen mother (50 percent overlap), and not very altruistic at all toward their brothers (25 percent overlap). The implications of the peculiar inheritance system of Hymenoptera and the extent to which the predictions of Hamilton's model are borne out by evidence are developed in E. O. Wilson's *The Insect Societies* (1971, especially chap. 17; see also Hamilton 1964).[6]

Humans groups are comprised of individuals with much greater average genetic distance between them, and we reproduce using a diploid mechanism. A different balance of selection pressures is therefore necessary to explain altruism, especially that exhibited toward non-kin. Because of the difference in reproductive systems, the burden that between group

---

6. On the other hand, haplo-diploid inheritance does not explain complex social organization among termites. And whereas most of Wilson's analysis is within the context of individual level selection models, the consensus is now moving to allow some role for group, that is, between colony, selection as well (Wilson and Sober 1994).

selection must bear is higher in explaining the origin of complex social organization in humans.

In thinking about the appropriate relationship between evolutionary biology, economics, and social science in general, one cannot help but be struck by the apparent analogy between the blind watchmaker and the invisible hand. The blind watchmaker is a metaphor for mechanisms leading to the appearance of design in living organisms: the intricate and marvelous results of the operation over generations of natural selection. The invisible hand was addressed as an apparently similar marvel: the coordination of specialized economic activity in the absence of a central planner. The two ideas seem on the face of it analogous: in the former the appearance of design results from the "efforts" or "strategies" of genes to replicate; in the latter social and economic organizations seem to arise organically from the efforts of individual organisms efficiently to advance their material self-interest. But the two metaphors have different underpinnings. Genes may be "selfish," since they persist only if they foster behavioral predispositions in the organisms containing them that foster their persistence. This does not preclude individuals constructed according to genetic scaffolding from being predisposed to act in an altruistic fashion.

To claim that the invisible hand metaphor explains the hidden order of society is at best a partial truth. It tells us virtually nothing about the *origin* of complex social organization but rather gives us insight into how it is *maintained* in a market society. What we may interpret as the result of the invisible hand is in fact an indirect manifestation of the workings of the blind watchmaker, played out within a technological environment unanticipated by the selection pressures of earlier epochs.

What Smith interpreted as man's natural tendency to truck and barter, from which so much follows, reflects the evolution of the generalized reciprocity (nonsimultaneous exchange) of hunter-gatherer times to the more simultaneous exchange made possible by the invention of agriculture, the development of stored food, the social contrivance of money, and the greater division and specialization of labor. But the human propensity to practice generalized reciprocity in turn reflects the heritage of behavioral propensities with more ancient lineages, in particular, a fundamental willingness to play cooperate in what could be one-shot PDs. Smith explored these propensities extensively in *The Theory of Moral Sentiments* ([1759] 1976).[7]

The standard economic model captures in a parsimonious fashion important and essential human behavioral propensities. Within circum-

---

7. Smith spoke of such inclinations as benevolence, sympathy, and empathy, not specifically of altruism, a term introduced, and distinguished from egoism, in 1851 by the French sociologist Auguste Comte (Batson 1991, 5).

scribed spheres of activity it provides good predictions of the direction of changes in behavior in response to changes in environmental (situational) conditions. But it is incomplete as a general model of human behavior. At some level most economists and rational choice theorists recognize the weakness of the model—the wide gap between normative predictions and actual behavior, particularly where bargaining or strategic interactions are concerned—but efforts to develop a comprehensive empirically based behavioral science from within the tradition have been stymied. Why?

Melvin Reder's thoughtful and carefully argued book *Economics: The Culture of a Controversial Science* depicts a discipline uninterested in the reasonableness of its assumptions; unconcerned with its poor ability to predict, explain, or control; and consequently incapable of developing general laws with widespread applicability (Reder 1999, chap. 2). This diagnosis is perhaps too harsh in terms of the discipline as a whole. I share with William Baumol a minority view that macroeconomics has achieved significant scientific advance in the twentieth century, in part because of a persistent concern with addressing practical problems such as inflation and unemployment, and a development of theoretical models that, in general, have been better disciplined by repeated confrontation with data (Baumol 2000, 11).[8]

Reder's book nevertheless paints a picture of a field of study that, in spite of aspirations to universality, is remarkably insular. Operating within a highly elaborated paradigm, particularly in microeconomic theory, the discipline frequently exhibits signs of an almost hermeneutical imperviousness to deconfirming evidence. Whereas similar behavior characterizes the history of many natural sciences, and whereas philosophical

---

8. For example, Milton Friedman's claim that inflation is always and everywhere a monetary phenomenon is accepted as broadly true by most economists and as consistent with a wide range of historical evidence. Supply shocks or technological innovations affecting velocity may lead to one-time upward or downward movements in the aggregate price level. But few today argue that a sustained upward movement in price levels over the medium to long run is likely to be observed in the absence of a persistent increase in the supply of the transactions medium relative to the growth of transactions demand for real balances (roughly proportional to real GDP). Similarly, econometric evidence on the interest elasticity of the demand for money has led most economists, including Friedman, regardless of their views about the conduct of monetary policy, to abandon the view that the demand to hold cash is interest insensitive. A final example: supply side economists predicted confidently that cutting tax rates would raise total tax revenues. When that did not happen following the Reagan tax cuts in the first half of the 1980s, the implicit labor supply elasticities in the model were called into question, and the intellectual stock of the theory fell. In part, the judgment of the relatively greater value added in macroeconomics is based on the fact that the subdiscipline, aside from monetary theory, hardly existed in 1900, whereas most of the implications of the use of foraging algorithms by humans in advanced societies had already been worked out by that date. With respect to microeconomics, it is not all in Marshall, but a lot of it is.

issues regarding what should be the appropriate tolerance for deconfirming evidence apply equally in the social and natural sciences, the latter nevertheless have a record of progressivity superior to that of much of the social sciences.

Anticipating a More Integrated Curriculum

In progressive disciplines, logic and evidence ultimately change people's views. Suppose, fifteen years from now, the relevance and implications of multilevel selection and modularity have been more widely accepted and an integrated curriculum in behavioral science has been adopted across institutions of higher education. What would be the place of economic inquiry within such a curriculum? Such a curriculum, I suggest, would begin with a broad overview of evolutionary theory and what we now know of the history of hominid evolution. The emphasis would, to the degree appropriate, be on species typical characteristics and would defer to specialized courses the intellectual history, evidence, and debates about the heritability of individual differences among humans and the existence of statistically and behaviorally significant genotypic differences among human groups ("races") and between the sexes.[9] Evidence from paleontology; molecular biology; anthropological studies of hunter-gatherer societies; and, to the degree relevant, animal studies would be adduced. Evidence from experimental research in economics and cognitive and social psychology would be summarized.

The purpose of this overview would be to lay an evidential foundation for statements about the types of domains within which one can productively assume the operation of domain general learning mechanisms and the efficient pursuit of an actor's material self-interest. Specialized courses in anthropology and sociology, focusing on cultural variability within evolutionarily bounded constraints; in political science with an emphasis on the consequences of variation in political structure and public policies; and in economic history, stressing the implications of develop-

---

9. Experimental evidence documenting some systematic differences in the operation of cognitive mechanisms between males and females is now widely accepted. Arguments with respect to race remain much more controversial, in part because racial categories are much more poorly defined. There are obvious systematic and functionally important differences between the physiological structures of men and women. It would not be surprising if there were also some systematic differences in the operation of cognitive mechanisms. This presumption holds in only the most minor ways in the case of racial differences. Even in the case of gender differences, however, we should keep in mind that we are talking about differences between the means of two distributions; these differences may not and often will not apply to differences between the reasoning mechanisms of a specific man and a specific woman.

ments in technology and of law would follow. So too would courses in microeconomic theory per se, with a focus on specialized subject matter topics and an emphasis on the study of foraging behavior in modern environments.

Optimal foraging models were originally developed to study nonhuman animals but have also been applied with considerable success to hunter-gatherer societies. The close relationship to economic modeling can be seen both in the categories employed and in the techniques used, which include constrained maximization and linear programming. Optimal foraging models normally specify a goal (food acquired per unit time), a currency (typically calories), constraints (generally time), and choice options (where to search, what to search for, what algorithms to use) (Kelly 1995, 73–108).

Studies showing the success of optimizing models in explaining animal foraging behavior have been interpreted by some as suggesting that animals are good economists. We might, in contrast, put the reverse spin on this. These studies drive home the point that humans are good foragers, just as their ancestors have been for hundreds of millions of years— not just two million years. The realization that relatively unfettered markets conduced to economic growth represented a discovery of an institutional structure within which human foraging propensities could be harnessed for mutual advantage within a complex social environment not anticipated when these propensities first emerged. A great deal of microeconomics can therefore be thought of as the study of optimal foraging behavior in an environment never anticipated by the forces of natural selection.[10]

By and large, foraging behavior represents a game against nature. But human-human interactions are qualitatively different, as are the associated challenges of establishing and maintaining relations based on expectations of reciprocity. Even in extremely hierarchical social structures, such relations characterize interactions at any of a society's different levels, and even in politically unbalanced relationships, there is invariably a role for such expectations. To make mutually beneficial reciprocal relations possible, evolution favored modules other than those facilitating foraging, which were not designed, or well suited, to achieve such ends. Unlike the foraging modules, these must have required group level selection to spread, because at low frequencies they do not involve the efficient

---

10. Similarly, experiments designed to show that pigeons are good economists study foraging behavior in controlled, as opposed to uncontrolled, environments. Optimal foraging depends on the operation of the domain general learning mechanisms upon which behaviorist psychology has focused.

pursuit of material self-interest and consequently could not have been favored by individual level selection.

An evolutionary perspective allowing for both individual and group level selection can help us sort through where and why the standard economic model works relatively well and where it does not. Consider three domains for its application: navigation and decision within the competitive model, behavior within situations of strategic interaction, and behavior with respect to the holding of financial assets. Arguably the best results occur in the first domain, in which prices confront individuals parametrically and what individuals must do is search over the price space of outputs and inputs in order to sustain themselves. The model does relatively well in predicting the direction of changes in behavior in response to changes in incentives (prices) because it is applied to behavior closely analogous to the foraging activities that hunter-gatherers and their ancestors pursued for millennia. Evolution has endowed us with relatively sophisticated search algorithms and intuitive techniques for statistical inference; the closer these are to foraging problems, in general, the better the model does.

Markets succeed in converting games against humans into games against nature or, in more technical terms, optimization against a fixed environment. Economic theory has much greater difficulty in dealing with bargaining: situations where parties must decide how they will divide a surplus that will vanish if they do not agree (see in particular the contrast in the results of market vs. bargaining experiments in Roth et al. 1991). This could involve labor-management conflict, disputes about the price at which a car is to be bought, or the salary at which an individual agrees to leave her old job for a new one. Game theory has had very limited success in elucidating the outcomes of such interactions (Roth 1995b). Evolutionary analysis, on the other hand, has shed light on the surprising experimental frequency of "fair" divisions in such situations (Skyrms 1996, chap. 2).

Finally, consider the mixed results in the area of finance, discussed in chapter 6. Although the predictions of rational choice theory are not shockingly contravened, as in single play PD games, these markets are riddled with apparent deviations from what the standard normative model would predict. Indeed, outside of experimental data on choice among gambles, the study of financial data provides perhaps the most fertile arena for identifying the type of anomalies collected by the heuristics and biases program. Why are these anomalies so prevalent in this area?

An evolutionary explanation is that we are dealing with phenomena (casinos and stock markets) that lacked even approximate counterparts in Pleistocene existence or earlier. In such times there were no established asset exchanges, there was not much stored wealth, and there were few truly random processes. Financial markets differ from goods markets. In financial markets, the underlying assets traded are homogeneous, at any moment of time price dispersion around the world is low, and it is generally possible for an individual to buy and sell as much of a particular asset as he or she wants. Goods markets, in contrast, are usually characterized by a dispersion of availability, price, and sometimes quality. Their navigation, one can argue, is more strongly facilitated by foraging algorithms.

Humans attempt to apply to truly random processes tools that work well in foraging: tabulating histories of past occurrences, maintaining updated tables of contingent frequencies, and attempting to predict the future based on past history. Casinos exploit this predisposition by providing players at roulette wheels with pads of paper on which they can keep track of recent outcomes. The financial services industry caters to this predisposition by providing reams and megabytes of data on past performance of individual securities. If financial asset prices are, like realizations of roulette wheels, truly random processes, however, "foraging" among individual assets is a waste of time, unless one has access to information not widely available in the market. Buying and holding an index fund is the best strategy, just as not playing roulette in a casino is the best (wealth maximizing) strategy.

Nevertheless, a great many individual investors believe they can systematically beat the odds at the roulette wheel, and systematically beat the index in the stock market. They believe they are operating in environments in which foraging theory is applicable, as are statistical inference techniques for predicting future price from past behavior. In doing so, many market participants persist in trading off expected return for greater risk, as do roulette players, clearly violations of the predictions of the normative model.[11] With the exception of blackjack using a card counting strategy, the expected value of any casino game is negative. In stock markets, feverish and expensive attempts to beat the market generally lead to lower returns and higher tax liabilities than a buy and hold strategy.

But the reasons for anomalies in investors' behavior are different from those that explain behavior in Prisoner's Dilemmas. In the case of financial assets, evolutionary pressures have prepared us poorly to deal with truly random processes, for they are a recent development. As a result, individual behavior introduces noise into financial asset prices, ren-

---

11. On the other hand, the random walk hypothesis is not universally accepted, and hundreds of thousands of dollars continue to be invested in the development of computer models aspiring to discern structure in the apparently chaotic data produced in the financial markets.

dering questionable the standard economic model's assumption that the market is efficient and prices securities at fundamental value based on all available information. Consequently individual securities and the market as a whole may be undervalued or overvalued for sustained periods of time.[12]

In the PD case, in contrast, evolutionary pressures prepared us relatively well but not in ways captured by the standard economic model.

Microeconomics as Topics in Advanced Foraging

Within the imagined social and behavioral science curriculum, economics would survive as a subject of specialized study, particularly in the areas of national income accounting and monetary policy and macroeconomics, and as one with a distinct intellectual culture in microeconomics resulting from its comparative advantage in the analysis of foraging. But because the study of foraging behavior cannot be the exclusive foundation for a comprehensive behavioral science, the subject matter definition of economics would reemerge as its unifying characteristic. The discipline would be reestablished within the more limited Marshallian parameters as the "study of mankind in the ordinary business of life." As a means of emphasizing rhetorically the important but restricted domain of microeconomic inquiry, one might even consider retitling the first course in microeconomics "Principles of Foraging in Advanced Technological Societies" and follow it with more specialized courses such as Intermediate Foraging, Mathematical Foraging, International Foraging, and Foraging in Labor Markets.

An understanding of the taxonomic categories whereby we organize thinking about economic interaction, the statistical apparatus (national income and product accounts) underlying the measurement of economic categories, and the framework relating these categories to each other represents and would continue to represent a specialized range of knowledge historically particular to the discipline. In this imagined integrated curriculum, what would not survive would be the widely proclaimed view that the essence of economics is an *approach* to studying human interaction equally applicable across the entire range of human behavior. In spite of its failures in the areas of prediction, explanation, and control, and in spite of the often ambivalent attitude toward the role of new empirical findings

---

12. I am skeptical of the view, however, suggested by the heuristics and biases literature, that the direction of these pricing errors can be shown to be predictable. Financial market prices are not as close to a random walk as efficient market theorists believe, but they are closer to it than is the belief of the typical investor.

in advancing the subject, economics remains a discipline acutely concerned with its status as science and indeed, as E. O. Wilson notes, proclaiming itself the Queen of the Social Sciences.[13]

The claim to royal status has rested implicitly on the discipline's incorrect view that it possesses a privileged understanding of the implications of evolutionary theory for human motivation. That view is facile and incomplete. Cognitive capabilities and behavioral predispositions other than those typically assumed in economic models have been favored by natural selection. Our tasks in part are to try to understand what they are using scientific and empirically based methodologies and to use the results of such studies to build behavioral models or algorithms with more predictive success than those that can be deduced from models based on strict egoism and the assumption of optimization alone. In the past, none of the social sciences has been in the forefront of championing such efforts.

Responding to challenges that the behavioral assumptions underlying the discipline are unrealistic, economists have defended their methodology on the grounds that the proof of the pudding is in the eating, that the assumptions are simplifying, and that what matters is the relative ability of such models to predict and explain observed phenomena. I use *explain* in this context to mean the retrospective prediction of data that played no role in the construction of the model or forecasting algorithm. Such a position is defensible when adhered to consistently. In practice, however, much theorizing has consisted of ex post rationalizations of stylized facts. Not only have the models often lacked out-of-sample predictive power but the within sample stylized facts explained have sometimes borne a questionable relationship to the phenomena whose essential features they were supposed to capture.

If we aspire to the status of scientists, and are to dismiss concerns about the reasonableness of model assumptions, we must hold ourselves accountable according to the standards of prediction and explanation. In other words, one can defend "unrealistic" assumptions if the models employing them produce tolerably good predictions or explanations, but absent that, it's time for business as usual to stop. For example, if the assumption that individuals efficiently pursue their material self-interest leads to the prediction that players will defect in single play Prisoner's Dilemmas, and experimental and observational data repeatedly contradict this prediction, it is time to explore alternate approaches.

These approaches should include the incorporation of empirically

---

13. Wilson's treatment of economics is one of the weaker sections of his book. But his lack of appreciation for some of its nuances does not minimize the resonance of his judgment: that the claims of economics to scientific status have been purchased at a high intellectual price.

validated cognitive modules that systematically short-circuit the behavioral counsel of foraging algorithms. Instead, when confronted with admittedly unrealistic assumptions that predict poorly, rational choice theorists often seek to preserve its fundamental assumptions, to provide some twist to the model that accounts better for the observed behavior. Thus the extraordinary efforts to explain how nondefection in the single play or fixed and known duration Prisoner's Dilemma somehow results from the efficient pursuit of material self-interest. The quixotic character of these efforts is obvious in the literature on the single play version but hardly less so in the treatments of the fixed and known duration game. Yet many economists and rational choice theorists remain, deep down, wedded to the behavioral assumption underlying the standard economic model: that humans calculate how they can best advance their material self-interest and act in accordance with these calculations *in all domains.*

Humans do calculate, they do optimize, and they are generally interested in their material welfare. There is sound evolutionary justification, as noted, for assuming that we have these capabilities and inclinations, and foraging behavior by birds and bees suggests that we are not the only animals that act in an analogous fashion. But there is nothing magical about these assumptions: they do not exhaustively capture human behavioral propensities and to treat them as a shibboleth is not justifiable from a scientific standpoint.

One can of course argue that the behavior of rational choice theorists with respect to the treatment of deconfirming or anomalous evidence is no better and no worse than that of most natural scientists—or many other social scientists. But perform the following thought experiment. Consider microeconomics today as it was twenty-five years ago, or even a hundred years ago, as does Baumol. Do the same for any of the natural sciences. Which shows evidence of greater progressivity? Whereas economists happily apply this test to *other* social sciences, they are generally loath to do so reflexively. And yet, its aspirations notwithstanding, microeconomics has made relatively slow progress in building foundations for a progressive empirically based science of human behavior.

Many economists, particularly those adhering to the intermediate position described earlier, do grant an exception to the assumption that humans pursue their own individual self-interest, and they are willing to assume that children's welfare enters parents' utility functions and that parents are therefore prone to sacrifice their own material welfare for that of their children. But why? What is the basis for this acceptance? And what are the reasons for the hard perimeter limiting the consideration of such tendencies to behavior among kin?

As this book has indicated, there are indeed subtle differences in understanding the origin and maintenance of social relations among kin and non-kin. But, with limited exceptions, these differences have not been systematically explored by economists. In general, rational choice theorists have given little thought to the criteria that should underlie assumptions made about human behavior that extend beyond strict egoism. I suggest that two related criteria should *converge* in support of admitting a behavioral propensity. First, it should be evolutionarily plausible. That is, one should be able to provide a plausible account of why genes predisposing to such behavior would likely have persisted and increased in frequency upon first appearance. Second, the propensity should be validated by observational and/or experimental evidence. Whether or not a propensity is "rational" in the sense in which that term is used in the standard economic model should ultimately be irrelevant or at least subsumed within the scope of this enterprise. If a propensity to act "rationally" within certain domains is a central feature of the human psyche, it is because genes predisposing to such calculations and the willingness to act on them have been relatively favored. The rationality assumption can have no favored or privileged status beyond this.

Egoistic considerations push individuals in directions that conduce to cartel breakup, to the elimination of racial discrimination, away from voting, away from voluntary contributions toward public goods, and toward first strike. We may believe, depending on our political views, that some of these effects are socially desirable and some are not. But such normative views are irrelevant to a positive social science. To build a discipline on the proposition that such motivations exhaust the range of essential human predispositions is to lead to the unsustainable conclusion that there are no cartels, no racial discrimination, no voting, no voluntary contributions to public goods, and no restraint on first strike (defect) in single play PDs. The issue for a positive behavioral science is not to tote up a scorecard in terms of what is good or bad but to understand essential human predispositions and to embody them in models or forecasting algorithms with good predictive power, at least in an aleatory sense.

The development of experimental economics, surveyed in the *Handbook of Experimental Economics* (Kagel and Roth 1995), has been valuable in moving the social sciences in a more progressive direction. What is encouraging about much of the work summarized, for example that on public goods provision, is involvement, within the framework of a shared methodology, of participants from sociology, social psychology, political science, and economics, as well as evidence that minds do appear to have been changed (not immediately—that is to be expected—but eventually) as the result of experimental results. Research treated in the *Handbook* extends beyond the types of issues explored within the heuristics and biases program (Camerer 1995). It also includes results referenced repeatedly in this book, especially those involving Prisoner's Dilemmas; the closely related work on the voluntary provision of public goods; and work on human bargaining behavior involving ultimatum, dictator, and impunity games (see, in particular, Roth 1995a, 1995b; Ledyard 1995). Experimental research has the potential to help remake the study of human behavior into a discipline more like a natural science, because it provides a methodology for testing and validating assertions about essential predispositions.

Sociobiology and Gene-Culture Coevolution

In his 1998 book *Consilience,* Edward O. Wilson argues that we are and should be moving toward a unification of the natural and social sciences, a theme he has advocated in one form or another for over a quarter century. It is a proposition that many social scientists react to with suspicion. On first encounter, the idea seems at best utopian, at worst outlandish. But a review of literatures in cognitive psychology, evolutionary biology, paleoanthropology, and other sciences leads to two unavoidable conclusions. First, relative to the social sciences, these disciplines have, overall, been more progressive. In the last twenty-five years, scholarly effort has produced significant new observational and/or experimental data, data that have changed the theoretical consensus within these disciplines. In a number of cases these advances have been facilitated, indeed revolutionized, by technical advances in instrumentation, far more so than has been the impact of the availability of computers on the social sciences. In spite of the often-acrimonious disputes that have characterized and continue to characterize these fields, consensus on theory and methodology is more broadly shared than is true among and within the social sciences.

A second conclusion is that much of this scientific advance is relevant to the study of human behavior. Both of these observations engender qualified sympathy for the program I understand Wilson to be advancing. The initial incarnation of that program was reflected in his 1975 work *Sociobiology,* which, as its name suggested, proposed providing biological foundations for the social sciences. A legitimate question is whether what is advanced in the book you are reading is simply sociobiology redux. The answer is no, or at least, not exactly. Early sociobiological treatises often reached for the stars and, in so doing, overreached. The overreaching resulted in two main features, neither of which is shared by the framework informing the previous chapters.

First, sociobiologists were eager to examine contemporary human behavior, identify in what ways it might be adaptive, and thereby explain it. A typical problem was that if natural selection favored behaviors likely to lead to the spread of genes predisposing to them, it was hard to account, for example, for why families used contraception and for why economically successful families often tended to have fewer children. In contrast, the perspective adopted here is that evolution has favored designs that were adaptive to environmental features recurring over millions of years of human prehistory. In many instances, because of commonalities between that early environment and the one we inhabit today, our designs do seem wonderfully adaptive. But in other areas, technological progress since the agricultural revolution has so changed the world we live in that we should not expect this to be necessarily true, nor is it.

Second, in some versions sociobiology came to be synonymous with biological determinism, which eliminates any role for human freedom, choice, or responsibility. Parents and teachers, confronted with a student who has played hooky and claims, not that the dog ate his homework, but that his genes made him do it, are likely to give such explanations short shrift. So should we. Genes may influence predispositions, but except in the case of reflex actions, they do not automatically program a response to a particular stimulus or situation. The reason for this is obvious. Much of the life experience of an individual is so idiosyncratic that it would be impossible for evolutionary forces to "anticipate" and hardwire a response to categories of circumstance characterized at that fine a level of detail. That is why we are endowed with, in addition to specialized domain specific cognitive modules, domain general capabilities that permit us to learn and reason: logic, mathematical reasoning, and an intuitive understanding of statistical inference. There is no particular reason why evolution might not have favored organisms that, when all was said and done, are free to choose.[14]

Because, given perceptual input, humans choose based on discretion, not on hardwired rules for specific circumstances, the prediction of any individual's behavior in a particular circumstance can be at best probabilistic. Knowledge of evolutionarily favored behavioral predispositions holds out the reasonable possibility, however, of giving superior predictive capability over larger numbers of individuals or instances. Cultural variation will, of course, influence behavior, but it will do so within a bounded range.[15]

---

14. As Lumsden and Wilson put it, "genes and free will are partners of necessity and not partners of convenience" (1983, 55).

15. Again, quoting from Lumsden and Wilson, "genes and culture are held together by an elastic but unbreakable leash" (1983, 60). Many have interpreted this as arguing for the unsustainability of social reform. This is too harsh a reading. Culture cannot go in any direction it wants, because if it is too "dysfunctional" it will destroy or dramatically reduce the

There is a final and important way in which the approach adopted here differs from positions advocated by sociobiologists such as Lumsden and Wilson (1981, 1983). Criticized for minimizing the role of culture in his earlier work, E. O. Wilson made great efforts in his collaboration with Lumsden to incorporate a role for it by developing a model of gene-culture coevolution, emphasizing environmentally determined "epigenetic rules" that canalize learning in certain directions and therefore favor certain "norms" over others. In doing so they appealed to the same growing body of evidence supporting modularity in cognition that has been a recurring theme in previous chapters. Lumsden and Wilson also explored the role of feedback through natural selection in leading to the hardwiring of these rules, thus, for example, explaining the almost universal avoidance of brother-sister incest.

Where they differ is in positing a much faster rate of coevolution than is assumed in this book: "In as few as fifty generations—about a thousand years—substantial genetic evolution can occur in the epigenetic rules guiding thought and behavior" (Lumsden and Wilson 1983, 152). Evidence of relatively recent environmental influences on genetic variation does exist in the areas of the immune and digestive systems. It has long been plausible to argue, for example, that African Americans' susceptibility to sickle cell anemia is due to the increased resistance from malaria, endemic in Africa, afforded by the heterozygous form. The absence of lactase deficiency among groups with a pastoral heritage is also often cited (Ridley 1999, 192–94; see also Durham 1991). Lumsden and Wilson's suggestion that such mechanisms have produced differences in cognition and behavioral predispositions is, however, much less firmly established.

An implication, which they do not explicitly explore, is that Europeans or perhaps Eurasians might, because of their history, today have higher frequencies of hardwired taxonomies favorable for learning about and understanding recurrent features of advanced technology than would members of Stone Age tribes. If this hypothesis were true, we might expect to see significant differences in the blood chemistry of surviving Stone Age tribes as compared, with, let us say, Europeans who have been dealing

---

number of individuals whose lives it influences. To take an extreme example, a culture that extolled the virtues of matricide and patricide as soon as children were physically capable of so doing would not long survive. Within the boundaries defined by a broad "functionality" constraint, there is space for cultural variation, including "progressive" variants that we may not yet have witnessed. The problem with traditional structural-functional analysis is that there are many conceivable structures consistent with the constraint. Demonstrating "functionality" does not therefore account for why one structure or another prevails. For that one may need historical or case specific methods. The problem is formally identical with that associated with rational choice models that generate multiple equilibria.

with advanced technology for at least a thousand years (see also Boyd and Richerson 1985). Such differences are, however, as in the cases described earlier, relatively minor, sufficient to give us insights into historical patterns of migration but unlikely to represent cognitively or behaviorally significant effects of gene-culture coevolution (Cavalli-Sforza, Menozzi, and Piazza 1994; Lewontin 1972). Jared Diamond argues anecdotally that denizens of hunter-gatherer societies have little difficulty mastering advanced technology once exposed to it and that there is little to suggest that they are in any way less intelligent than we are (he provocatively argues the contrary) (Diamond 1997, 19). New Guinean tribespeople, first contacted by advanced society in the 1930s, have had little difficulty, within a generation, coming to terms with it. And the grammars of languages used by surviving hunter-gatherer societies are no less complex than those used by members of industrial societies (Pinker and Bloom 1990, 707).

It is ironic that a move to integrate culture into the study of biological influences on cognition and behavior should have a potential to resurrect old beliefs about significant differences in inherent capabilities of peoples at different levels of technological and scientific development. Tooby and Cosmides provide little historical perspective on the origin of the standard social science model. But it emerged in the United States in the work of Franz Boas at Columbia and his student Alfred Kroeber at Berkeley and was specifically directed at an earlier attempt, associated (justifiably, to some degree) with Darwinian ideas, to provide a biological foundation for the social sciences. That effort was driven by the idea that just as species had evolved from "less advanced" forms, so too had human groups, which could be ranked on an evolutionary scale. Such differences, it was argued, for example between hunter-gatherers and technologically advanced societies, had a biological foundation, reflecting innate differences among the capabilities of the "races of man." It was against this view, and in favor of an essentially universal human nature, that Boas and Kroeber campaigned. Their insistence on a complete severance of culture from biology, congruent with positions taken by European sociologists such as Durkheim, was intended to prevent such ideas from resurfacing (Degler 1991, chap. 4).

It is important to understand that the attack on the SSSM orchestrated by Tooby and Cosmides, and endorsed with some qualification in this book, is not intended to and does not have the effect of resurrecting the discredited views against which the SSSM was counterposed. Models of gene-culture coevolution, however, do suggest, in an unintended fashion, that there may be something to these earlier views. The issue is not whether the process of gene-culture evolution is theoretically possible. The issues are the timescale involved and the extent to which it is empirically relevant for the period after the Neolithic revolution.

By assigning cognitively and behaviorally significant gene-cultural coevolution in response to recurring environmental challenges only to the much longer epoch spanning the transitions from *Homo habilis* to *Homo erectus* to *Homo sapiens,* we allow the cultural variation of the last ten thousand or even thirty thousand years a space of its own, bounded by biological constraints but within that space free to vary according to historical or case specific factors and with an independent influence on economic and social outcomes.

Rational Choice Theory within an Evolutionarily Informed Behavioral Science

Economics has its roots in eighteenth century moral philosophy. Like the Chicago school economists of the twentieth century, and unlike nineteenth century social scientists such as Henri St. Simon, Auguste Comte, and Emile Durkheim, such moral philosophers took the individual rather than society as the unit of analysis. But they also assumed such individuals were reasonable men, *hommes éclairés,* whose implicit range of cognitive mechanisms and behavioral inclinations was broader and less restricted than that of twentieth century economic man.

The eighteenth century "reasonable" individualist retreated under the attack of nineteenth century sociology, presaged by Condorcet or one of his correspondents who in 1792 first used the term *social science.* According to nineteenth century sociology, society was a more fundamental entity than the nation-state, was more than the sum of its individual members, had its own dynamics, and required its own "social science" to understand and explain it (Gigerenzer et al. 1989, 39). The development of state statistical offices and comprehensive demographic, economic, and social data in the nineteenth century also posed a challenge to the "reasonable man" individualist view.

Although statistics clearly implied that "society" was the sum of its individual members, such data were also used to conclude that societies or cultures had features—emergent properties—that were more than the sum of their individual components. Thus Durkheim used data showing that countries and sociocultural groups had relatively stable and unique patterns of crime, suicide, and marriage rates as evidence that such concepts as society, culture, and national character were meaningful (Rosenberg 1980, chap. 2).

Much of the battle among the social sciences in the last half of the twentieth century has recapitulated these earlier disputes about whether the individual or society/culture is the appropriate unit of inquiry, with economists and psychologists generally adopting the former position and classical sociology/anthropology the latter. Of course twentieth century economic man is not exactly the eighteenth century *homme éclairé.* One might say that he has retained the individualism but dispensed with the "reasonableness."

The standard economic model embodies behavioral motivations and an optimizing technology that served well our ancestors' foraging activities and were selected for over hundreds of millions of years at the level of the individual organism. The model is useful for analyzing and to some degree predicting the modern analogue of foraging: search and decision in competitive goods, services, and assets markets in which prices confront all actors as parametric. But with respect to the origin of complex social organization at the macrolevel, or with respect to the formation of coalitions, friendships, economic cartels, or political alliances, in other words, social organization at initial and more intermediate levels, the model performs poorly. The reason is that operation within all of these situations of strategic interaction brings into play domain specific modules such as propensities to play cooperate in what could be one-shot PDs, or to monitor and punish those who do not reciprocate, which could not have arisen as the result of selection at the individual level. One needs an evolutionary framework incorporating multilevel selection to account for them.

If we are to construct a coherent empirically based behavioral science, those specializing in the study of optimal foraging will need more seriously to recognize the domain specific applicability of its techniques and, in other areas, allow the perspective to be complemented by scientific research relevant to the study of strategic behavior. The apparent claim by some economists that not only does it not matter if the assumptions of the model are unrealistic, but it also does not matter if the resulting model predicts poorly, is not sustainable. The view of economics as the search for ways to make what works in practice work in theory (Reder 1999, 12) is an almost perfect recipe for ex post rationalizations that seem to explain but in fact lack both explanatory coherence and retrodictive/predictive power, precisely because they are ex post rationalizations.

Yet we would be foolish to deny the powerful influence of internally coherent theoretical frameworks to which adherents attach strong subjective probabilities of validity. The physicist Arthur Eddington wrote half seriously that no fact should be accepted as true until it had been confirmed by theory. Lumsden and Wilson observe (and they are by no means the first) that "unless an attractive theory exists that decrees certain kinds of information to be important, few scientists will set out to acquire the information" (1983, 63).

One of the goals of this book has been to advance the development of such a framework, an attractive theory that links an evolutionarily informed search for behavioral predispositions and cognitive mechanisms widespread in human populations as a means of strengthening the foundations of a comprehensive, empirically based behavioral science. An unusual and unlikely combination of ideas underlies this approach: admitting group as well as individual level selection, allowing for the modularity that permits altruistic as well as egoistic inclinations, and accepting the principle of methodological individualism. Each poses challenges of intellectual digestion, inasmuch as each is a hot button issue for, respectively, evolutionary theory, the economics/rational choice tradition, and sociology/anthropology. Each, however, has much to recommend it, and collectively they open up new avenues for productive inquiry.

To the manifest discomfort of sociologists and anthropologists, economists have aspired to a social science with widespread applicability across time and space. The standard economic model has been based on exploring the implications of a set of predispositions that are essentially human. The inability of the approach to meet its universalistic aspirations is explained not necessarily because the quest itself is quixotic but rather because this set of predispositions is incomplete and because economics has shared with other social sciences a view of cognition with little space for the type of hardwired taxonomic categories and relations among them stressed by researchers in linguistics and visual perception. Nevertheless, the economist's quest for a comprehensive social science, unique among the disciplines, remains a worthwhile aspiration.

Traditional sociology and anthropology have been hostile to rational choice approaches but not for this reason. Rather, hostility has been driven by doubts, fueled by belief in the overwhelming centrality of culture, that the concept of essential human behavioral predispositions is meaningful. Movement toward a more unified and scientific framework for the study of human behavior requires us to take seriously such inclinations and the evolutionarily conditioned influence of specialized brain subsystems on them.[16] I have emphasized earlier what this would mean for economics, but the acceptance of this view poses at least as much of a challenge, in different ways, for other social scientists. The issues here do not

---

16. Among economists, Gary Becker has perhaps pushed hardest in this direction. His suggestion that human preferences over generalized commodities do not vary much between the rich and poor, or even between members of different cultures or societies, is a reflection of this aspiration (Becker 1976, 8). Some experimental evidence consistent with this position: newborn infants (regardless of acculturation) prefer sweet to bitter, and they prefer sweet in the following order of preference: sucrose, fructose, lactose, and glucose (Lumsden and Wilson 1983, 69).

represent the same turf battles that have been waged for decades. This is *not* simply a question of sociologists and anthropologists reclaiming ground "lost" to economics or vice versa.

Why is the prospect of admitting group level selection, and what it may imply for human behavioral propensities, troubling to many theorists? I believe it is because within the rational choice tradition so much theory operates in an empirically undisciplined atmosphere. Thus to admit anything other than egoistic preferences is apparently to open the floodgates to assumptions about human behavior—often derisively attributed to sociologists and anthropologists—that rational choice theorists *know intuitively* to be wrong. But we cannot advance theory within a largely data free zone and claim that what we are doing is science.

Implications for Models of Human Behavior

Heterodox scholars who have experimented with the implications of unconventional utility functions can argue that much has changed in economics within the past quarter century, and can cite their own efforts as evidence in favor of this view. But it is also true that much has not changed. A recent article by Edward Lazear (2000) contains a useful survey of contributions made by economists to problems not traditionally viewed as within the purview of the field. But its title, "Economic Imperialism," testifies that ambitions for territorial expansion are alive and well. This emphasis on turf battles is enormously debilitating. Lazear identifies the distinguishing features of the economic approach with the assumption of rationality, the use of constrained maximization techniques, the concept of equilibrium, and an emphasis on efficiency. A flavor of his rhetorical posture can be garnered from this excerpt.

> Economics is not only a social science, it is a genuine science. Like the physical sciences, economics uses a methodology that produces refutable implications and tests these implications using solid statistical techniques. . . . Other social sciences that are unwilling to assume maximization are in the position of being unable to predict in new situations. (Lazear 2000, 99–100)

Most troubling about Lazear's stance are the criteria he uses for evaluating the success of a social scientific discipline. In spite of the mantle of science, which he wraps around economics (but not other social sciences), and the incantations about the importance of testing hypotheses using solid statistical techniques, the most frequent appeal in the article is to validation of success via a "market test." Economics is viewed as successful because it has attracted the most students and has had the most outbound influence on other subdisciplines (Lazear 2000, 99). This is an ultimately indefensible criterion for validation, regardless of who advances it.

Such evidence can be suggestive, but a good rank and tenure committee does more than count citations. It may be that a discipline has attracted adherents because of its predictive and explanatory successes. But it can also simply be because the tenets of the approach or the elegance of the models happen to satisfy practitioners' aesthetic or expressive needs. Economists—and rational choice theorists in general—have been quick to apply this critique to others but reluctant to apply it reflexively. Such appeal may or may not be correlated with whether models provide good explanatory or predictive power.

The success of a contribution in satisfying aesthetic or expressive needs is an appropriate criterion for judging work in the arts and humanities but not in the sciences. Science is not a popularity contest. Organized religions count hundreds of millions of believers. Surely the number of adherents to a particular religion is not a measure of the scientific validity of its basic tenets. Psychoanalysis was wildly popular in the United States in the 1950s and early 1960s in the absence of any evidence that recovery rates of patients receiving the therapy (about a third) were systematically different from those who received no treatment.

At its inception, the bases of scientific belief were radically distinguished from those underlying religion. It is this radical worldview, with its emphasis on observation and prediction, that underlies scientific achievement over the past several centuries. If, as social scientists, we are to do more than pay lip service to that tradition, we must hold ourselves accountable to tests of explanation and prediction. When these tests are failed, repeatedly, it is not acceptable to fall back on the Coasian view that we can continue to embrace a model simply because of its "intuitive" appeal—which may simply be another way of saying that it satisfies our expressive or aesthetic tastes or needs.

The justification for constructing models in the social sciences cannot ultimately be the satisfaction of these needs. Ronald Reagan used to tell stories that from his vantage point certainly "should have been true" (Fitzgerald 2000). The stories clearly satisfied his expressive needs, but a historian concerned with evidence could legitimately point out that many were inventions, in some cases recollected dialogue from some of his films. We must also sometimes reject beautiful models, as did Francis Crick. There can be no warrant in the social—or natural—sciences for retaining a model that consistently predicts poorly simply because it feels intuitively correct. No discipline in the social sciences, including economics, can avoid attention to or be unaware of the role that aesthetic and expressive needs sometimes play in producing attachments to a particular model or approach.

The techniques of constrained maximization provide the basis for mathematical models of the operation of a powerful foraging module that all humans possess, honed over hundreds of millions of years of evolutionary history. But it is not the only cognitive module governing human behavior. Lazear implicitly believes that it is and that therefore constrained maximization techniques are the only appropriate tools to be used in developing behavioral predictions.

The assumption of the universal applicability of a foraging module cannot be justified on axiomatic grounds or by a casual appeal to pop Darwinism. When models based on it repeatedly fail predictive tests, one has a strong signal that it is being inappropriately adduced or at least that there is something else going on as well. There are then complementary directions in which one can proceed. The first is to retain the constrained maximization metaphor but introduce "unorthodox" (as Lazear calls them) utility functions, in such a manner that their maximization yields the observed behavior. For examples and review of recent work along these lines see Rabin 1993, Camerer 1997, or Bolton and Ockenfels 2000.

What is encouraging about this work is the extent to which the behavioral assumptions underlying the models are more carefully justified with respect to evidence on human behavior than is typical in models informed by the stronger version of rationality and the extent to which scholars committed to this enterprise are often equally committed to active participation in advancing experimental research as a means of testing, modifying, and refining the theory. At the same time, given the acknowledged incentives of the profession, which have historically placed a very high premium on formalization, it may be desirable to go a bit slow.

Heterodox models have many of the strengths and weaknesses of sociologists' appeal to norms and in a sense they represent an attempt to translate Parsons's "autonomous social structure" into the language of utility functions. When one gets down to the micro level of individual human behavior, however, there are many possible ways in which this might be done, and that is the current difficulty. Some formulations stress unconditional propensities to cooperate, some of which are obviously necessary to understand cooperation in one shot PD games. Rabin's model stresses that people act in anticipation of how others will act toward them; their willingness to act reciprocally is contingent upon the expectation of behavior of others. The dynamic Rabin characterizes is likely to be helpful in understanding some of the cross-cultural and cross-individual variation observed in behavior in these games (Roth et al. 1991; Henrich et al. 2001). But it is of less use in understanding baseline deviations from Nash or subgame-perfect equilibrium levels. Still other formulations, such as Fehr and Schmidt 1999 or Bolton and Ockenfels 2000, stress a posited taste for fairness by assuming that individuals obtain disutility from unequal outcomes. They too have undoubtedly captured part, but only part, of the elephant. Work is now underway in many quarters trying to identify domains in which the predictions of such models differ and then to conduct empirical tests as a means of trying to differentiate among them.

Formal modeling must ultimately prove its mettle by elucidating or calling to our attention empirical phenomena otherwise overlooked, and in general providing out-of-sample predictive power superior to alternative approaches, such as the more purely statistical. The record to date of such efforts, even heterodox efforts, has been mixed (Charness and Rabin 2000). Like the normative approach in sociology and anthropology, most of this work so far has contained little explicit consideration of where these "unusual" tastes come from. Are commonalities, in terms of a "taste" for fairness, a willingness to cooperate if one expects others to, or a baseline inclination to cooperate, simply accidental? What can be characterized as essential and what learned, and thus, in principle, manipulable?

An effort to provide a systematic and compelling evolutionary rationale for essential human cognitive and behavioral predispositions can assist in advancing this enterprise. It can do so at a most basic level by, in a Bayesian sense, modifying our priors, making us more likely to find certain results plausible. In the process, it can help canalize experimental research, as the work of Gigerenzer and Hoffrage/Cosmides and Tooby has demonstrated with respect to our capabilities as intuitive statisticians (see chap. 6).

The most obvious benefit of adopting the more nuanced Darwinian perspective advocated in this book is a weakening of priors in favor of the strong version of rationality insofar as it applies to preferences or goals (people act in all domains in order to advance their material interests efficiently). It should make us more interested in and more receptive to experimental and observational evidence demonstrating the particular nature of behavioral predispositions or action inclinations at variance with those inherent in strong rationality and less likely to reject ab initio heterodox models that try to model these on the grounds that essential human behavioral predispositions are axiomatic or so obvious that they can be identified in an armchair. It should provide us an additional comfort level in finding plausible certain empirical results and modifying models accordingly as, for example, did Hamilton's analysis of kin selection in encouraging theorists to abandon strong rationality by including family members' utility in objective functions (see Becker 1976).

The research frontier now involves relations among non-kin. One of my objectives in this book has been to emphasize that allowing for group selection undoes the intellectual straitjacket that otherwise requires dismissal of the possibility that relations among non-kin are driven ultimately by anything other than the efficient pursuit of material self-interest. The efforts to develop an improved behavioral science based on a close interplay between modeling and empirical testing are at an early stage and will progress more slowly if large numbers of social scientists dismiss such research as irrelevant for predicting how people behave.

Note, however, that my position is based more on challenging the narrow range of goals and preferences consistent with strong rationality than on questioning human abilities to form rational expectations in the Muth sense. Of course we have deficiencies in this regard. But we don't do badly in this area because our capabilities depend on and benefit from foraging algorithms that have been selected for, honed, and refined by natural selection over millions of years. We use rational expectations both when we act, and assume others act, in ways that can be justified as consistent with the strong version of rationality, and when we don't, or assume that others do not. Thus, in an ultimatum game, rejection of positive offers can never be justified as consistent with strong rationality. Nevertheless, evidence (differences in offers in dictator and ultimatum games) suggests that the amount one proposes may be influenced not only by interest in the counterparty's welfare, or a taste for more equitable division, but also by a rational expectation of the likelihood of rejection based on past observed frequencies. Again, a rational expectation of human behavior in the Muth sense can differ from an expectation of behavior based on the assumption that people will act rationally.

While the effort to construct alternative utility functions has in many ways been constructive, and stimulated additional rounds of empirical testing, there are also arguments for deferring it until more solid empirical regularities have been established and rough consensus achieved on them. This is particularly so where the value of perhaps hastily constructed blackboard models is not obvious in comparison with other predictive techniques not dependent on a choice theoretic technology.[17]

Constrained maximization models need not require strictly egoistic preferences, but metaphorically they do imply a single general purpose reasoning module. As indicated in chapter 5, there is a substantial body of

---

17. Excessive concern with the elaboration of "the model" to the neglect of what it can actually inform is a phenomenon evident in other social sciences as well. See Rule's discussion of Parsonian sociology as developed by its most recent exponent, Jeffrey Alexander (Rule 1997, chap. 4).

evidence, both direct and indirect, including information on actual brain wiring, that suggests that this assumption is unrealistic in ways that matter. Consequently, there is reason to doubt that the metaphor is entirely or universally appropriate in modeling human cognition and behavior, either in the sense that it captures essential features of underlying mechanisms or in the sense that it will actually add predictive value in comparison with alternate approaches. It is a method in which rational choice theorists of the orthodox or unconventional variety have a lot invested, but that should not in and of itself commend it to us as essential to our inquiry.

There remains the problem that heterodox work of any stripe elicits among many orthodox economists much the same reaction as does the appeal by sociologists to "norms." It is sometimes said these models don't "feel" right, that they "seem" intuitively wrong. As just mentioned, there are important issues regarding the appropriate timing and content of a heterodox research agenda. But the reactions here go beyond differences within the heterodox program and reflect skepticism about whether it has value at all. If the profession is to progress in a scientific fashion, it cannot collectively allow so much of its development to be driven by aesthetic preference.

Here is where, as I have argued, a broader evolutionary perspective can be particularly salutary. Behind the intuition expressed by skeptical theorists lies the specter of pop Darwinism, a view of Darwin as expositing a model of natural selection that can operate only at the individual level. If group selection is a possibility, then a considerably wider range of essential human predispositions becomes consistent with evolutionary theory. Important examples developed in this book include what I have termed a PD solution module. On the other hand, if the possibility of group selection is not admitted, we are more likely to continue to tolerate and inhabit a quasi-scientific world of coherent, internally consistent, perhaps even beautiful models *that don't fit the data.*

There is little doubt that the incentives to formalize will continue because it is an activity to which the rational choice tradition has historically awarded some of its highest accolades. The way of thinking that justifies this tradition, however, has in many instances been based on a deep-seated belief that the most important behavioral and cognitive assumptions underlying the work are, in the end, so obviously true as to be axiomatic. Pop Darwinism has hovered in the background for those within the tradition who may waver. A central thrust of this work has been to question both the underpinnings of pop Darwinism and consequently the axiomatic quality of the strong version of rationality.

Every scientific discipline has dealt with the fact that practitioners bring to their work prior beliefs and aesthetic preferences governing how they think research should proceed and what empirical observations are likely to be viewed as plausible. But in those sciences that have managed to be progressive, evidence and logic ultimately change minds. Pop Darwinism has powerfully affected prior beliefs in research in the social and behavioral sciences. It needs to be abandoned. We are ultimately faced with a choice: aesthetically pleasing, mathematically tractable, badly predicting models inconsistent with a broader evolutionary theory or a scientifically progressive research effort building on some of the results surveyed in these pages.

Lazear argues that social sciences unwilling to assume maximization are simply "unable to predict in new situations." I disagree. Faced, for example, with the problem of predicting behavior in single play PDs, one can go with the standard choice theoretic methodology, which gives a nice, clean, unambiguous, and wrong prediction. One can try to tinker with utility functions to square their maximization with results, but to what end? If players were pure altruists, with the welfare only of the counterparty at issue, cooperate would be a strictly dominant strategy, but this does not track the data well either. We may ultimately be able to construct formal models with superior predictive power. But I doubt this will be possible unless their components have strong evidentiary foundations in experimental and observational data.

There are alternative non-model-based predictive approaches, for example, a probabilistic or statistical methodology sometimes denigrated by theorists. Such an approach deviates from the view that the maximization metaphor is appropriate or useful in all domains, but why should such a claim be privileged? The forecasting methodology used can be simple—a prediction based on past frequencies of nondefection in experiments; or more sophisticated—using regressions with dummy variables for whether preplay communication was allowed and including variables for the size of the temptation for defection. In either case, the resulting prediction is likely, I maintain, to be superior to one based on choice theoretic methodology *given our current state of knowledge*.

We need to be careful in distinguishing exactly how this statistical approach differs from the possible use of data by actors in standard models. A rational choice approach can, for example, allow a role for use by players of a statistical methodology in explaining how humans coordinate on a cooperative equilibrium in a PD game of indefinite duration. And such methods could arguably be normatively relevant in a fixed and known duration game to the degree that they were used to forecast a propensity of one's counterparty or counterparties to play irrationally. But, at least in the latter case, there is an asymmetry here, reflecting the fundamental attribution bias. To the degree that the relevance of statistical techniques is admitted, it is to predict the behavior of others, who may, presumably, have inclinations and dispositions, in contrast to the actor employing the technique, who is assumed to be clear eyed and influenced only by situational factors. Obviously, this asymmetry cannot be universally applicable, since each individual in the group of others is herself an actor. Finally, of course, neither a descriptive nor a normative rational choice approach can allow any role for a forecasting algorithm in the single play game because forecasts are irrelevant: defection is strictly dominant.

But we can allow such a role. As social and behavioral scientists, we have an interest in prediction different from that of either player in the one-shot game. Our payoffs are measured not by the rewards each player receives but by how well we predict what each of them does. If we are actually one of the players, it comes down, in part, to *how well we predict our own behavior.* My claim is that for social and behavioral scientists, a statistical methodology is relevant for us in each of these games, in none more so than in the single play game. The search for essential human predispositions, for which the study of single play games is so important, is the search for appropriate base rates in a comprehensive empirically grounded behavioral science.

There ought to be a place in our forecasting methods for well-established empirical regularities, such as positive nondefection rates in one-shot PDs, the fact that one cannot offer much less than 30 percent of the stake in an ultimatum game and expect it to be accepted, or the evidence that most human subjects are not prepared to reason more than two or three stages via backward induction (Camerer 1997). None of these regularities has an obvious choice theoretic foundation. But there is no stone tablet that says all human behavior can or should be modeled using the mathematical metaphor of constrained maximization. That metaphor is probably a very good characterization of the cognitive operation of foraging modules. When people play cooperate in a single play PD or reject a positive offer in an ultimatum game, I believe that the behavior is not driven by a single general-purpose foraging module, but by conflicting guidance from different ones.

Experimental and observational data have the potential to establish robust empirical regularities about the conditions under which specialized modules kick in and what, for example, is required to trigger the likelihood that humans will frame a choice as a PD solution problem. It makes no more sense for a social scientist to throw away these data than it does for a psychiatrist to ignore data on past behavior in trying to predict whether a mental patient or a presently incarcerated prisoner is a threat to society.

If we have well-established empirical regularities describing how people play in particular types of situations, why not use them for predictive purposes? From such regularities, in conjunction with the use of constrained maximization techniques where applicable, a more powerful social science can ultimately be constructed (for similar argument, see Crawford 1997, 236). For illustration of how such regularities can be used practically in addressing real world policy issues, see Korobkin and Ulen 2000.

The distinction between the two roads followed when the standard economic model fails predictive tests corresponds roughly to that made between "conventional" and "unconventional" attempts to deal with the experimental evidence indicating violations of expected utility theory (Starmer 2000). The difference between Starmer's subject and the one addressed here, however, is that whereas skeptics question the practical relevance of evidence that people systematically violate the theory of expected utility (Starmer 2000, 368), it is very difficult to question the practical relevance of evidence that the rate (the base rate) at which subjects play cooperate in single play Prisoner's Dilemmas deviates systematically from zero.

The concern that rational choice proponents such as Lazear exhibit with respect to exporting its methods to new domains may be reflective of their limited scientific advance since the time of Marshall. If we are able only to make small improvements in the power of our tools, it would be nice if progress could be measured in the expansion of their applicability. To the degree that such efforts produce models with good predictive or explanatory power, efforts should be encouraged. But the argument for devoting substantial resources to the elaboration of models that are elegant, internally consistent, and "intuitively appealing" but are consistently contradicted by data can be advanced only with the most careful justification.

When Prediction Fails: The Role of Historical Explanation

When using the term *explanation* along with *prediction,* I have indicated that I mean out-of-sample explanation. What of models that track the data from which they are constructed but lack predictive power, for example, those that generate or can rationalize multiple equilibria? Such models ultimately depend for their closure on historical explanation. In adducing historical explanation we have reached the limits of behavioral science. *We acknowledge that a particular branching could not have been predicted ex ante.*

What does historical explanation involve? It involves telling stories. As an economic historian, I value highly this enterprise, which will be part of any complete account of a phenomenon we investigate. But there is a reason history departments are not included within social science divisions within universities. A good historian will use objective—scientific—methods to evaluate documents or data and draw inferences from them. But the explanations advanced are retrospective and case specific. They are scientific in the sense that the mechanisms described are founded on evidence and logic. But they are not scientific in the sense that they do not give rise to refutable propositions. The reason for this is not that the basic structure of the causal argument is different, but rather that historical explanations are so narrowly specific that they are by definition applicable only to the instances examined. There can be no out-of-sample prediction because such explanations are intended to apply only to the particular circumstances in question. The situation is so unique that there is available no appropriate reference category and there are no previously collected data relevant for prediction. Such explanations can be "tested" not with new data but only with thought experiments—counterfactual history—in which antecedent conditions are hypothetically removed and hypothetical consequences examined.

To call historical explanations unscientific would be unfair. Myths are beliefs based neither on evidence nor on logic and thus clearly lacking scientific foundation. Myths are one item good historians assiduously avoid trafficking in. So perhaps *ascientific* is the better word to describe such explanation.

The work of historians may be dismissed as "just telling stories." It should not be. A historian may trace, for example, the consequence of a particular Supreme Court decision. She will not claim, and rightly so, that its outcome was knowable in advance. Had it been an easy case, it never would have advanced to the highest court. Tracing its consequences and the mechanisms whereby they are experienced is a valuable contribution to our understanding. And a good historian will go back and discuss the reasoning and political maneuvering whereby the Court was able to fashion its decision. This is explanation, but it is historical, in the sense that there is no claim to positing a model with out-of-sample predictive power, no claim (or there should be no claim) that the decision was ex ante predictable. In fact, unsupported after the fact claims that outcomes were predictable ex ante are common in historical and journalistic accounts. But these should be treated with skepticism, because they imply an underlying social scientific model that has not been validated by ex post out-of-sample retrodiction. There is no reason to apologize for historical explanation, but it serves us poorly to claim social scientific explanation when we have not provided it.

Similarly, delineating the consequences of particular technological trajectories is valuable, even when a particular trajectory could not have been predicted in advance. It was not inevitable that the United States would adopt a television standard (NTSC) inferior in a number of ways to the PAL and SECAM standards emerging subsequently in Europe and elsewhere.[18] But once the U.S. standard was adopted network externalities produced lock-in, as path dependency theorists such as Arthur (1989) and David (1985, 1994) have argued. Lock-in is not necessarily forever, and the gradual replacement of this standard by high-definition television (HDTV) will end it, but in this case it will have endured half a century.

Historical argument begins when we have exhausted our ability to provide scientific explanation. The process of evolution is necessarily a historical one, and thus the chain of events that gave rise to conditions under which life evolved on earth and eventually yielded *Homo sapiens* is unavoidably path dependent. But evolutionary explanations involve path dependency on a much grander timescale than the preceding examples. Suppose we accept the claim that there are common features of human societies we can call universal culture. This book argues that these commonalities are not explainable as the inevitable consequences of the interaction of rational self-interested agents, as the canonical economic model would have it. Nor are they the result of a statistically unlikely concatenation of accidents producing similar outcomes in region after region of the world, as a variant of the sociological/anthropological tradition, or a theorist emphasizing the path dependent character of norms and institutions, might argue. Nor are they the consequence of localized invention followed by universal diffusion.

Instead, at the bedrock of universal culture, as at the bedrock of universal grammar, we find evolutionarily designed *hardwiring*. In both cases, cognitive modularity is central to understanding the functioning of these legacies, and in the former case, and perhaps the latter, group selection is a necessary mechanism in this design process. In both cases, historical explanation begins *earlier,* in delineating the evolutionary processes that produced the human genome.

Models that, by demonstrating a multiplicity of equilibria and therefore predicting an inability to predict, add to our understanding when in fact the phenomenon is difficult to predict. Unquestionably, appeal to historical or path dependent explanation will be part of any evolutionary account. But it is important not to throw in the towel too soon. It is too easy to excuse our predictive failures on the grounds that human behavior is notoriously difficult to predict. In fact, within certain domains human

---

18. NTSC (National Television System Committee) began broadcasting in 1954. PAC (Phase Alternation Line), developed in Germany, is based on NTSC. SECAM (Sequential Couleur avec Mémoire) was developed in France.

behavior in the aggregate is easier to predict than some natural processes, such as the weather. We should push scientific methods as far as they will take us in this direction before we switch into historical mode. And we should be prepared to use statistical methods where mathematics and deductive logic alone perform poorly.

Behavioral science is good enough, or should be good enough, for example, to enable us to make good predictions of how one hundred randomly chosen pairs of human subjects will play a one-shot PD. My back of the envelope prediction is that, irrespective of from where the sample of subjects is drawn, about half will achieve mutual cooperation, upward of two-thirds if preplay communication is allowed. Historical argument is not front and center in this exercise, although the species typical hardwiring underlying the result does have an explanation that is ultimately historical. It is not necessary in developing this prediction that I posit a utility function maximized under constraint. If you probe and ask what metaphor or model I have of mechanism, I will reply that it is one in which the foraging apparatus that pushes us toward the Nash prediction is short-circuited by another module specialized to the domain of PD type interactions. But as we await the neurobiological and neuroanatomical research that may further validate this view, I am perfectly content to rely on a simple statistical algorithm, based on prior experimental data, because I am confident it will outperform the more elegantly derived conclusions of the standard economic model based on the strong version of rationality.

Conclusion

This voyage began with issues of data and method. Where has our journey left us with respect to these issues?

1. The purpose of the social and behavioral sciences is to forecast and retrospectively predict human behavior, and the purpose of building models of behavior is to facilitate this enterprise. What we are after is a methodology for producing rational forecasts. Forecasts (expectations) are rational if they take advantage of all available data and are produced using the best available statistical and/or logical algorithms.

2. The model building exercise is only as good as its predictive and explanatory successes. The enterprise cannot be defended, at least as part of a social science, simply because, in the opinion of the model builder, the models intuitively provide insights into the process under study. To a man with a hammer the whole world

looks like a nail. To a social scientist invested in a rational choice methodology and the techniques of constrained maximization associated with it, every aspect of human behavior looks like a constrained maximization problem.

3. This book began with the problem of predicting behavior within a Prisoner's Dilemma, in the limit, a single play PD. The methodology of constrained maximization, applied to this situation of strategic interaction, yields an unambiguous prediction: there is a unique Nash equilibrium, one involving mutual defection, and it is the one players should arrive at. Similarly, the analysis of an ultimatum game yields a unique (subgame perfect) equilibrium, also the outcome at which rational players should presumably arrive. From the standpoint of a set of aesthetic values typically held by rational choice theorists, these predictions have much to recommend them. They are "choice theoretic," and they do not make use of "ad hoc" behavioral assumptions. Historically, these have been powerful evaluative criteria in economic discourse: the first betokening a "good" model, the second one that is "bad." And the predictions make very efficient use of data, in fact extremely efficient use, since they make no use of data at all. Talk about parsimony! Data on the past behavior of the players, or of others like them, is of no relevance in forming the prediction, and even if it were relevant descriptively, it wouldn't matter normatively, because defection is strictly dominant. Given all of these "aesthetic" criteria in their favor, one feels almost embarrassed continuing to point out that as predictions, they are *repeatedly, overwhelmingly, unambiguously* contravened by experimental data.

4. When this critique is raised, skeptics often ask what is the alternative. First, we must again remind ourselves why we are in this business. Predictive success is what matters. The elegance or beauty of the model is ultimately irrelevant. Francis Crick constructed a beautiful, elegant hypothesis about how triads of base pairs coded for assemblage of proteins from among amino acids. The analysis was so beautiful, said some scientists, it should have been true. But it was not, and when experimental evidence inconsistent with it appeared, Crick abandoned his hypothesis (for details, see Ridley 1999, 50–52). Beauty is not always a guide to truth. And sometimes beauty is in the eye of the beholder. In the case of the single play PD, a simple statistical forecast based on the past behavior of the players, or of similar players, will almost invariably provide a superior forecast of behavior than does the Nash equilibrium pre-

diction. One can throw whatever pejorative terms one wants at the forecast: ad hoc, not choice theoretic, mindless, inelegant. *But its predictive success is superior.*

5. This book has gone considerably beyond this simple point. It has tried to get under the hood of human decision making, studying the evidence for cognitive modularity that makes intelligible this behavior in the context of straightforward self-serving behavior in other domains. And it has explored the history of design of the human behavioral machinery, its evolutionary history, arguing that the operation of natural selection provides fewer restrictions on the range of essential human predispositions than rational choice theorists have generally supposed.

6. Faced with two predictive technologies, one viewed as elegant that predicts poorly and one viewed as inelegant that predicts well, which is it? *If we are to do science, it must be the second.*

The methodology of constructing models of constrained maximization works well in explaining and predicting foraging behavior and its modern analogues. On the explanatory side, the idiom does a good job in capturing metaphorically the cognitive modules that facilitate foraging—in humans, sheep, birds, and bumblebees. The neat thing about the method is that in the right domains, it permits tolerably good predictions of behavior in the absence of data on the past actions of the individual or individuals in question. But we need to recognize the limitations of the method and also that, as a practical matter, most of us would not throw away data on past performance of individuals in question if we were trying to make such predictions.

The psychology of William James, which placed heavy emphasis on instincts, was eclipsed in the twentieth century by the behaviorism of John Watson and B. F. Skinner. But the concept is coming back in vogue, with Stephen Pinker, for example, emphasizing a language instinct. I doubt it is helpful to suggest that humans are maximizing anything when they learn a language. They just do it, because genes predisposing to such behavior or cognition have been favored in the past.

The title of this book asked whether we are altruistically inclined. The question posed can now be answered in the affirmative, although in slightly different ways than has been traditional. We are altruistically inclined toward our children, parents, and other relatives, as the theory of kin selection has recognized since the 1960s and as most of us have been willing to allow. But our relations with non-kin also have an altruistic foundation, reflected experimentally, among other ways, in our willingness to play cooperate in single play PDs. In these relations with non-kin, what altruism initiates, interest can help sustain. Our ongoing interactions with others can, under the right conditions, be sustained by calculations of interest alone and be favored by individual level selection. But they cannot originate as the result of such calculations, nor can they arise evolutionarily through selection operating only at the individual level.

The sobering news for the rational choice tradition is that its preferred modeling techniques are limited in their applicability. But the canonical version of the sociological/anthropological tradition also faces a challenge. The reification of social structure is not, as Parsons suggested, a solution to the problem of order. Explanation of the universal component of that structure can be pushed back further. Opposition to any possible biological or genetic influences on "culture" is not sustainable, and methodological individualism can be defended, although not with the same implications as those commonly imagined by economists.

At the same time, while biology may determine underlying parameters of universal culture, just as it does for universal language, there is much room for cultural and institutional variation. And, in contrast to variation in specific languages, such variation is likely to be consequential in terms of social and economic outcomes. Thus, just as there will continue to be a role for constrained maximization techniques in, for example, the study of market behavior, there remains an important role for the descriptive, case specific methodologies of the traditional sociologist and anthropologist, as well as the narrative and closely related techniques of the historian. In fact, if they are to be used productively, these approaches need to be employed in a complementary fashion.

Responding to the continuing challenge involved in bridging the divide between the rational choice and the sociological/anthropological traditions will require the development of a social science that, in a more progressive fashion, systematically incorporates new experimental and observational data—including the results of research within the natural sciences—within an evolutionarily conditioned theoretical framework. That process, and continuing debates about exactly where we set the boundary between historical and social scientific explanation, will benefit from the participation of scholars throughout our disciplines. In none of these, however, does the historically dominant approach entail a privileged understanding of what will be necessary in this effort.

Bibliography

Adolphs, R., and Antonio R. Damasio. 1998. "The Human Amygdala in Social Judgment." *Nature* 393:470–74.

Ahissar, E., E. Vaadia, M. Ahissar, H. Bergman, A. Arieli, and M. Abeles. 1992. "Dependence of Cortical Plasticity on Correlated Activity of Single Neurons and Behavioral Context." *Science* 257 (5075): 1412–15.

Alchian, Armen. 1950. "Uncertainty, Evolution, and Economic Theory." *Journal of Political Economy* 58:211–21.

Alexander, R. D. 1990. "Adaptive Study of Learning and Development." *Ethology and Sociobiology* 11:242–303.

Allais, Maurice. 1997. "An Outline of my Main Contributions to Economic Science." *American Economic Review* 87 (December): 3–12.

Allison, Graham. 1971. *Essence of Decision: Explaining the Cuban Missile Crisis.* New York: HarperCollins.

Allyn, David. 2000. *Make Love, Not War: The Sexual Revolution: An Unfettered History.* Boston: Little, Brown.

Anderson, Steven W., Antoine Bechara, Hanna Damasio, Daniel Tramel, and Antonio R. Damasio. 1999. "Impairment of Social and Moral Behavior Related to Early Damage in Human Prefrontal Cortex." *Nature Neuroscience* 2 (November): 1032–37.

Andreoni, J., and J. H. Miller. 1993. "Rational Cooperation in the Finitely Repeated Prisoner's Dilemma: Experimental Evidence." *Economic Journal* 103:570–85.

Aristotle. 1959. *Nichomachean Ethics.* Translated by David Ross. London: Oxford University Press.

———. 1963. *The Philosophy of Aristotle.* Translated by R. Brambaugh. New York: Mentor.

Arrow, Kenneth J. 1951. "Mathematical Methods in the Social Sciences" In *The Policy Sciences: Recent Developments in Scope and Method,* edited by Daniel Lerner and Harold D. Lasswell, 129–54. Stanford: Stanford University Press.

Arthur, Brian. 1989. "Competing Technologies, Increasing Returns, and Lock-in by Historical Events." *Economic Journal* 99:116–31.

Atran, Scott. 1990. *Cognitive Foundations of Natural History.* Cambridge: Cambridge University Press.

———. 1998. "Folk Biology and the Anthropology of Science." *Behavioral and Brain Sciences* 21:547–609.

Axelrod, Robert. 1980. "Effective Choice in the Prisoner's Dilemma." *Journal of Conflict Resolution* 24:3–25.

———. 1981. "The Emergence of Cooperation among Egoists." *American Political Science Review* 75:306–18.

———. 1984. *The Evolution of Cooperation.* New York: Basic Books.

Axelrod, Robert, and Robert Keohane. 1985. "Achieving Cooperation under Anarchy." *World Politics* 38:226–54.

Bacon, Francis. 1973. *The Advancement of Learning.* Edited by G. W. Kitchin. London: Dent.

Barbieri, Katherine. 1996. "Economic Interdependence: A Path to Peace or a Source of Interstate Conflict?" *Journal of Peace Research* 33:29–49.

Barkow, Jerome H., Leda Cosmides, and John Tooby, eds. 1992. *The Adapted Mind: Evolutionary Psychology and the Generation of Culture.* New York: Oxford University Press.

Baron, Jonathan. 1988. *Thinking and Decisions.* Cambridge: Cambridge University Press.

Barry, Brian, and Russell Hardin. 1982. "Epilogue." In *Rational Man and Irrational Society,* edited by Brian Barry and Russell Hardin, 367–86. Beverly Hills: Sage Publications.

Bar-Tal, Daniel, and T. Leiser. 1981. "The Development of Altruistic Behavior: Empirical Evidence." *Developmental Psychology* 16:516–25.

Batson, C. Daniel. 1991. *The Altruism Question.* Hillsdale, NJ: Lawrence Erlbaum.

Baumgartner, Peter, and Sabine Payr. 1995. *Speaking Minds: Interviews with Twenty Eminent Cognitive Scientists.* Princeton: Princeton University Press.

Baumol, William. 2000. "What Marshall Didn't Know: On the Twentieth Century's Contributions to Economics." *Quarterly Journal of Economics* 115 (February): 1–44.

Beach, L. R., V. E. Barnes, and J. J. Christensen-Szalanski. 1986. "Beyond Heuristics and Biases: A Contingency Model of Judgmental Forecasting." *Journal of Forecasting* 5:143–57.

Becker, Gary. 1976. *The Economic Approach to Human Behavior.* Chicago: University of Chicago Press.

Belsky, Gary, and Thomas Gilovich. 1999. *Why Smart People Make Big Money Mistakes.* New York: Simon and Schuster.

Bendor, Jonathan, and Dilip Mookherjee. 1987. "Institutional Structure and the Logic of Ongoing Collective Action." *American Political Science Review* 81:129–54.

———. 1990. "Norms, Third-Party Sanctions, and Cooperation." *Journal of Law, Economics, and Organization* 6:33–63.

Bendor, Jonathan, and Piotr Swistak. 1997. "The Evolutionary Stability of Cooperation." *American Political Science Review* 91:290–307.

Berlin, Brent, and Paul Kay. 1969. *Basic Color Terms: Their Universality and Evolution.* Berkeley: University of California Press.

Betzig, Laura. 1992. "Medieval Monogamy." In *Darwinian Approaches to the Past,* edited by S. Mithen and H. Maschner. New York: Plenum.

Bicchieri, Cristina. 1990. "Norms of Cooperation." *Ethics* 100:838–61.

Binmore, Ken. 1994. *Game Theory and the Social Contract.* Vol. 1, *Playing Fair.* Cambridge, MA: MIT Press.

———. 1997. "Rationality and Backward Induction." *Journal of Economic Methodology* 4:23–41.

———. 1998a. *Game Theory and the Social Contract.* Vol. 2, *Just Playing.* Cambridge, MA: MIT Press.

———. 1998b. "Evolutionary Ethics." In *Game Theory, Experience, Rationality: Foundations of Social Sciences, Economics, and Ethics,* edited by W. Leinfellner and E. Kohler, 277–83. Dordrecht: Kluwer.

———. 1999. "Why Experiment in Economics?" *Economic Journal* 109:F16–24.

Blair, Clay, Jr. 1957. "Passing of a Great Mind." *Life,* February 25, 1957, 89–90. Quoted in William Poundstone, *Prisoner's Dilemma* (New York: Doubleday, 1992).

Blake, Joseph A. 1978. "Death by Hand-Grenade: Altruistic Suicide in Combat." *Suicide and Life Threatening Behavior* 8 (1): 46–59.

Bolton, Gary E., and Axel Ockenfels. 2000. "ERC: A Theory of Equity, Reciprocity, and Competition." *American Economic Review* 90 (March): 166–93.

Bower, G. W., and T. Trabasso. 1963. "Reversals Prior to Solution in Concept Identification Tasks." *Journal of Experimental Psychology* 63:438–43.

Bowles, Samuel, Robert Boyd, Ernst Fehr, and Herbert Gintis. 1997. "Homo Reciprocans: A Research Initiative on the Origins, Dimensions, and Policy Implications of Reciprocal Fairness." Working paper, University of Massachusetts.

Boyd, Robert, and Peter J. Richerson. 1985. *Culture and the Evolutionary Process.* Chicago: University of Chicago Press.

———. 1990. "Group Selection among Alternative Evolutionarily Stable Strategies." *Journal of Theoretical Biology* 145 (3): 331–42.

———. 1992. "Punishment Allows the Evolution of Cooperation (or Anything Else) in Sizable Groups." *Ethology and Sociobiology* 13:171–95.

Brase, Gary L., Leda Cosmides, and John Tooby. 1998. "Individuation, Counting, and Statistical Inference: The Role of Frequency and Whole-Object Representations in Judgment under Uncertainty." *Journal of Experimental Psychology: General* 127:3–21.

Brewer, Marilyn B. 1982. "Ethnocentrism and Its Role in Interpersonal Trust." In *Scientific Inquiry in the Social Sciences,* edited by Marilyn B. Brewer and Barry E. Collins. San Francisco: Jossey-Bass.

Brown, Donald E. 1991. *Human Universals.* New York: McGraw-Hill.

Brown, Michael H. 1990. *The Search for Eve.* New York: Harper and Row.

Brown, Roger. 1986. *Social Psychology.* 2d ed. New York: Free Press.

Brozen, Yale. 1982. *Concentrations, Mergers, and Public Policy.* New York: Macmillan.

Bueno de Mesquita, Bruce. 1985. "Toward a Scientific Understanding of International Conflict: A Personal View." *International Studies Quarterly* 29:121–36.

Buss, David M. 1999. *Evolutionary Psychology.* Boston: Allyn and Bacon.

Camerer, Colin. 1995. "Individual Decision Making." In *Handbook of Experimental Economics,* edited by John H. Kagel and Alvin E. Roth, 587–703. Princeton: Princeton University Press.

———. 1997. "Progress in Behavioral Game Theory." *Journal of Economic Perspectives* 11 (fall): 167–88.

———. 2002. *Behavioral Economics.* Princeton: Princeton University Press. Forthcoming.

Cameron, Lisa. 1999. "Raising the Stakes in the Ultimatum Game: Experimental Evidence from Indonesia." *Economic Inquiry* 37 (January): 47–59.

Campbell, Donald T. 1987. "Rationality and Utility from the Standpoint of Evolutionary Biology." In *Rational Choice: The Contrast between Economics and Psychology,* edited by Robin Hogarth and Melvin W. Reder, 171–80. Chicago: University of Chicago Press.

Caporeal, Linda R., Robyn M. Dawes, John M. Orbell, and Alphons J. C. van de Kraght. 1989. "Selfishness Examined: Cooperation in the Absence of Egoistic Incentives." *Behavioral and Brain Sciences* 12:683–789.

Cartmill, Mark. 1993. *A View to a Death in the Morning: Hunting and Nature in History.* Cambridge, MA: Harvard University Press.

Cavalli-Sforza, L. L., Paolo Menozzi, and Alberto Piazza. 1994. *The History and Geography of Human Genes.* Princeton: Princeton University Press.

Chagnon, N. A. 1988. "Life Histories, Blood Revenge, and Warfare in a Tribal Society." *Science* 239:985–92.

Charness, Gary, and Matthew Rabin. 2000. "Some Simple Tests of Social Preferences." Working paper, University of California, Berkeley.

Chomsky, Noam. [1957] 1965. *Syntactic Structures.* The Hague: Mouton.

———. 1959. Review of *Verbal Behavior,* by B. F. Skinner. *Language* 35:26–58.

Churchland, Patricia. 1995. "Take it Apart and See How It Runs." In *Speaking Minds: Interviews with Twenty Eminent Cognitive Scientists,* edited by Peter Baumgartner and Sabine Payr, 20–32. Princeton: Princeton University Press.

Clausewitz, Carl von. 1911. *On War.* Translated by J. J. Graham, London: Kegan Paul.

Coase, Ronald. 1960. "The Problem of Social Cost." *Journal of Law and Economics* 3:1–44.

———. 1982. *How Economists Should Choose.* Washington: American Enterprise Institute. Reprinted in *Essays on Economics and Economists* (Chicago: University of Chicago Press, 1994).

Coleman, James S. 1990. *Foundations of Social Theory.* Harvard: Harvard University Press.

Cosmides, Leda. 1985. "Deduction or Darwinian Algorithms? An Explanation of the 'Elusive' Content Effect on the Wason Selection Task." Ph.D. diss., Harvard University, Department of Psychology.

———. 1989. "The Logic of Social Exchange: Has Natural Selection Shaped How Humans Reason? Studies with the Wason Selection Task." *Cognition* 31:187–276.

Cosmides, Leda, and John Tooby. 1992. "Cognitive Adaptations for Social

Exchange." In *The Adapted Mind: Evolutionary Psychology and the Genera-tion of Culture,* edited by Jerome H. Barkow, Leda Cosmides, and John Tooby, 163–228. New York: Oxford University Press.

———. 1994a. "Origins of Domain Specificity: The Evolution of Functional Orga-nization." In *Mapping the Mind: Domain Specificity in Cognition and Culture,* edited by Laurence A. Hirschfeld and Susan A. Gelman, 85–116. Cambridge: Cambridge University Press.

———. 1994b. "Better than Rational: Evolutionary Psychology and the Invisible Hand." *American Economic Review* 84 (May): 327–32.

———. 1994c. "Beyond Intuition and Instinct Blindness: Toward an Evolutionar-ily Rigorous Cognitive Science." *Cognition* 50:41–77.

———. 1996. "Are Humans Good Intuitive Calculators after All?" *Cognition* 58:1–73.

Crawford, Vincent. 1997. "Theory and Experiment in the Analysis of Strategic Interaction." In *Advances in Economics and Econometrics: Theory and Appli-cations: Seventh World Congress,* edited by David M. Kreps and Kenneth M. Wallis, 1:206–42. Cambridge: Cambridge University Press.

Crick, Francis. 1994. *The Astonishing Hypothesis.* New York: Scribner.

Cummins, Denise Dellarosa. 1999. "Cheater Detection Is Modified by Social Rank: The Impact of Dominance on the Evolution of Cognitive Functions." *Evolution and Human Behavior* 20:229–48.

Damasio, Antonio R. 1994. *Descartes' Error: Emotion, Reason, and the Human Brain.* New York: Grosset/Putnam.

———. 1999. *The Feeling of What Happens: Body and Emotion in the Making of Consciousness.* New York: Harcourt Brace.

Danielson, Peter A., ed. 1998. *Modeling Rationality, Morality, and Evolution.* Oxford: Oxford University Press.

Darwin, Charles. [1859] 1909. *The Origin of Species.* New York: Collier.

———. 1871. *The Descent of Man and Selection in Relation to Sex.* London: John Murray.

David, Paul A. 1985. "Clio and the Economics of QWERTY." *American Eco-nomic Review* 75:332–37.

———. 1994. "Why Are Institutions the 'Carriers of History'? Path Dependence and the Evolution of Conventions, Organizations, and Institutions." *Struc-tural Change and Economic Dynamics* 5:205–20.

Davies, Paul C.W. 1999. *The Fifth Miracle: the Search for the Origin and Meaning of Life.* New York: Simon and Schuster.

Davies, Paul Sheldon, James H. Fetzer, and Thomas R. Foster. 1995. "Logical Reasoning and Domain Specificity: A Critique of the Social Exchange Theory of Reasoning." *Biology and Philosophy* 10 (1): 1–37.

Dawes, Robyn M. 1988. *Rational Choice in an Uncertain World.* San Diego: Har-court Brace Jovanovich.

———. 1994. *House of Cards.* New York: Free Press.

Dawes, Robyn M., and Richard Thaler. 1988. "Anomalies: Cooperation." *Journal of Economic Perspectives* 2 (summer): 187–97.

Dawkins, Richard. 1976 [1989]. *The Selfish Gene.* 2nd ed. Oxford: Oxford University Press.

———. 1980. "Good Strategy or Evolutionary Stable Strategy?" In *Sociobiology: Beyond Nature/Nurture?* edited by G. W. Barlow and J. Silverberg. Boulder, CO: Westview Press.

———. 1982. *The Extended Phenotype: The Gene as the Unit of Selection.* Oxford: W. H. Freeman.

———. 1986. *The Blind Watchmaker: Why the Evidence of Evolution Reveals a Universe without Design.* New York: W. W. Norton.

———. 1998. *Unweaving the Rainbow: Science, Delusion, and the Appetite for Wonder.* New York: Houghton Mifflin.

DeBondt, Werner F. M., and Richard Thaler. 1985. "Does the Stock Market Overreact?" *Journal of Finance* 40 (July): 793–805.

———. 1987. "Further Evidence on Investor Overreaction and Stock Market Seasonality." *Journal of Finance* 42 (July): 557–81.

Degler, Carl. 1991. *In Search of Human Nature.* Oxford: Oxford University Press.

Dennett, Daniel C. 1995. *Darwin's Dangerous Idea: Evolution and the Meanings of Life.* New York: Simon and Schuster.

Diamond, Jared. 1992. *The Third Chimpanzee.* New York: HarperCollins.

———. 1997. *Guns, Germs, and Steel: The Fates of Human Societies.* New York: W. W. Norton.

DiMaggio, Paul. 1995. "Culture and Economy." In *Handbook of Economic Sociology,* edited by Neil J. Smelser and Richard Swedberg, 27–57. Princeton: Princeton University Press.

Dixit, Avinash, and Susan Skeath. 1999. *Games of Strategy.* New York: W. W. Norton.

Domar, Evsey. 1970. "The Causes of Slavery and Serfdom: A Hypothesis." *Journal of Economic History* 30:18–32.

Downs, Anthony. 1957. *An Economic Theory of Democracy.* New York: Harper and Row.

Dr. Strangelove or: How I Learned to Stop Worrying and Love the Bomb. 1964. Directed by Stanley Kubrick. 93 min.

Dugatkin, Lee Alan. 1998. "Game Theory and Cooperation." In *Game Theory and Animal Behavior,* edited by Lee Alan Dugatkin and Hudson Kern Reeve, 38–63. New York: Oxford University Press.

Durham, William. 1991. *Coevolution: Genes, Culture, and Human Diversity.* Stanford: Stanford University Press.

Eckel, Catherine, and Philip Grossman. 1996. "Altruism in Anonymous Dictator Games." *Games and Economic Behavior* 16:181–91.

Edgerton, Robert. 1992. *Sick Societies.* New York: Free Press.

Edwards, Ward. 1968. "Conservatism in Human Information Processing." In *Formal Representation of Human Judgment,* edited by B. Kleinmuntz. New York: Wiley.

Einhorn, Hillel J. 1982. "Learning from Experience and Suboptimal Rules." In *Judgment under Uncertainty: Heuristics and Biases,* edited by Daniel Kahneman, Paul Slovic, and Amos Tversky, 268–83. Cambridge: Cambridge University Press.

Ekman, Paul, and Wallace V. Friesen. 1975. *Unmasking the Face.* Englewood Cliffs: Prentice Hall.

Ellickson, Robert. 1991. *Order without Law.* Cambridge, MA: Harvard University Press.

Elster, Jon. 1998. "Emotions and Economic Theory." *Journal of Economic Literature* 36 (March): 47–74.

———. 1999a. *Alchemies of the Mind: Rationality and the Emotions.* Cambridge: Cambridge University Press.

———. 1999b. *Strong Feelings: Emotions, Addiction, and Human Behavior.* Cambridge, MA: MIT Press.

Engerman, Stanley, Elisa Mariscal, and Kenneth L. Sokoloff. 1999. "The Persistence of Inequality in the Americas: Schooling and Suffrage, 1800–1945." Manuscript, University of California, Los Angeles.

Falk, Armin, Ernst Fehr, and Urs Fischbacher. 1999. "On the Nature of Fair Behavior." Working paper 17, University of Zurich.

Fehr, E., and S. Gächter. 2000. "Cooperation and Punishment in Public Goods Experiments." *American Economic Review* 90: 980–94.

Fehr, E., and K. M. Schmidt. 1999. "A Theory of Fairness, Competition and Cooperation." *Quarterly Journal of Economics* 114: 769–816.

Fiedler, K. 1988. "The Dependence of the Conjunction Fallacy on Subtle Linguistic Factors." *Psychological Research* 50:123–29.

Field, Alexander J. 1974. "Educational Reform and Manufacturing Development in Mid Nineteenth Century Massachusetts." Ph.D. diss., University of California, Berkeley.

———. 1976a. "Educational Reform and Manufacturing Development in Mid–Nineteenth Century Massachusetts." *Journal of Economic History* 36 (March): 263–66.

———. 1976b. "Educational Expansion in Mid–Nineteenth Century Massachusetts: Human Capital Formation or Structural Reinforcement?" *Harvard Educational Review* 46 (November): 521–52.

———. 1978. "Sectoral Shift in Antebellum Massachusetts: A Reconsideration." *Explorations in Economic History* 15 (April): 146–71.

———. 1979a. "On the Explanation of Rules Using Rational Choice Models." *Journal of Economic Issues* (March): 49–72.

———. 1979b. "Economic and Demographic Determinants of Educational Commitment, Massachusetts, 1855." *Journal of Economic History* 39 (June): 435–59.

———. 1979c. "Occupational Structure, Dissent, and Educational Commitment, Lancashire, 1841." *Research in Economic History* 4:235–87.

———. 1980. "Industrialization and Skill Intensity: The Case of Massachusetts." *Journal of Human Resources* 15 (spring): 149–75.

———. 1981. "The Problem with Neoclassical Institutional Economics: A Critique with Special Reference to the North-Thomas Model of pre-1500 Europe." *Explorations in Economic History* 18 (April): 174–98.

———. 1984. "Microeconomics, Norms, and Rationality." *Economic Development and Cultural Change* 32 (July): 683–711.

———. 1991. "Do Legal Systems Matter?" *Explorations in Economic History* 28 (January): 1–35.

———. 1998. "Sunk Costs, Water over the Dam, and other Liquid Parables." In *Rationality in Economics: Alternative Perspectives,* edited by Ken Dennis, 123–36. Boston: Kluwer Nijhoff.

———. 2001. *Review of Unto Others: The Evolution and Psychology of Unselfish Behavior,* by Elliott Sober and David Sloan Wilson. *Journal of Economic Literature* 39:132–34.

Fiorina, Morris O. 1990. "Information and Rationality in Elections." In *Information and Democratic Processes,* edited by John A. Ferejohn and James H. Kuklinski. Urbana: University of Illinois Press.

First Contact. 1983. 58 min. Directed by Robin Anderson.

Fisher, Ronald A. 1930. *The Genetical Theory of Natural Selection.* Oxford: Clarendon Press.

Fitzgerald, Frances. 2000. *Way Out There in the Blue: Reagan, Star Wars, and the End of the Cold War.* New York: Scribners.

Flew, Anthony. 1979. *Dictionary of Philosophy.* New York: St. Martins.

Flood, Merrill. 1958. "Some Experimental Games." *Management Science* 5:5–26.

Forsythe, Robert, Joel Horowitz, N. Eugene Savin, and Martin Sefton. 1994. "Replicability, Fairness, and Pay in Experiments with Simple Bargaining Games." *Games and Economic Behavior* 6:347–69.

Fox, Robin. 1989. *The Search for Society: Quest for a Biosocial Science and Morality.* New Brunswick: Rutgers University Press.

Frank, Robert. 1988. *Passions within Reason: The Strategic Use of Emotions.* New York: W. W. Norton.

———. 1994. "Group Selection and 'Genuine' Altruism." *Behavioral and Brain Sciences* 17:620–21.

———. 2000. *Microeconomics and Behavior.* 4th ed. Boston: McGraw-Hill-Irwin.

Frank, Robert, Thomas D. Gilovich, and Dennis T. Regan. 1993a. "The Evolution of One Shot Cooperation." *Ethology and Sociobiology* 14:247–56.

———. 1993b. "Does Studying Economics Inhibit Cooperation?" *Journal of Economic Perspectives* 7 (spring): 159–71.

———. 1996. "Do Economists Make Bad Citizens?" *Journal of Economic Perspectives* 10 (winter): 187–92.

Frank, Stephen. 1998. *Foundations of Social Evolution.* Princeton: Princeton University Press.

Freeman, Derek. 1983. *Margaret Mead and Samoa: The Making and Unmaking of an Anthropological Myth.* Cambridge, MA: Harvard University Press.

Freud, Sigmund. 1962. *Civilization and Its Discontents.* New York: W. W. Norton.

Friedman, Jeffrey, ed. 1996. *The Rational Choice Controversy: Economic Models of Politics Reconsidered.* New Haven: Yale University Press.

Friedman, Milton. 1953. "The Methodology of Positive Economics." In *Essays in Positive Economics,* 3–43. Chicago: University of Chicago Press.

———. 1957. *A Theory of the Consumption Function.* Princeton: Princeton University Press.

Fudenberg, Drew, and David Levine. 1998. *The Theory of Learning in Games.* Cambridge, MA: MIT Press.

Fudenberg, Drew, and Eric Maskin. 1986. "The Folk Theorem in Repeated Games with Discounting or with Complete Information." *Econometrica* 54:533–54.

Fudenberg, Drew, and Jean Tirole. 1991. *Game Theory.* Cambridge, MA: MIT Press.

Garcia, John, and Robert Koelling. 1966. "Relation of Cue to Consequence in Avoidance Learning." *Psychonomic Science* 4:123–24.

Gardner, Howard. 1974. *The Shattered Mind: The Person after Brain Damage.* New York: Vintage Books.

Gauthier, D. 1986. *Morals by Agreement.* Oxford: Clarendon Press.

Gigerenzer, Gerd. 1991. "How to Make Cognitive Illusions Disappear." In *European Review of Social Psychology,* edited by Wolfgang Stroebe and Miles Hewstone, 2:83–115. Chichester: Wiley.

———. 1996. "On Narrow Norms and Vague Heuristics: A Reply to Kahneman and Tversky." *Psychological Review* 103:592–96.

Gigerenzer, Gerd, and Ulrich Hoffrage. 1995. "How to Improve Bayesian Reasoning without Instruction: Frequency Formats." *Psychological Review* 102:684–704.

Gigerenzer, Gerd, Ulrich Hoffrage, and Heinz Kleinbölting. 1991. "Probabilistic Mental Models: A Brunswikian Theory of Confidence." *Psychological Review* 98:506–28.

Gigerenzer, Gerd, and Klaus Hug. 1992. "Domain Specific Reasoning: Social Contracts, Cheating, and Perspective Change." *Cognition* 43:127–71.

Gigerenzer, Gerd, and D. Murray. 1987. *Cognition as Intuitive Statistics.* Hillsdale, NJ: Lawrence Erlbaum.

Gigerenzer, Gerd, Zeno Swijtink, Theodore Porter, Lorraine Daston, John Beatty, and Lorenz Krüger. 1989. *The Empire of Chance: How Probability Changed Science and Everyday Life.* Cambridge: Cambridge University Press.

Gigerenzer, Gerd, Peter M. Todd, and the ABC Research Group. 1999. *Simple Heuristics That Make Us Smart.* Oxford: Oxford University Press.

Gilovich, Thomas. 1991. *Why We Know What Isn't So: The Fallibility of Human Reason in Everyday Life.* New York: Free Press.

Gintis, Herbert. 2000. *Game Theory Evolving.* Princeton: Princeton University Press.

Golding, William. [1962] 1983. *Lord of the Flies.* New York: Coward, McCann and Geoghegan.

Goodall, Jane. 1990. *Through a Window: My Thirty Years with the Chimpanzees of Gombe.* New York: Houghton Mifflin.

Green, Donald P., and Ian Shapiro. 1994. *Pathologies of Rational Choice Theory:*

A Critique of Applications in Political Science. New Haven: Yale University Press.

———. 1996. "Pathologies Revisited: Reflections on Our Critics." In *The Rational Choice Controversy: Economic Models of Politics Reconsidered,* edited by Jeffrey Friedman, 235–76. New Haven: Yale University Press.

Greif, Avner. 1989. "Reputation and Coalitions in Medieval Trade: Evidence on the Maghribi Traders." *Journal of Economic History* 49 (December): 857–82.

Griffin, Dale, and Amos Tversky. 1992. "The Weighing of Evidence and the Determinants of Confidence." *Cognitive Psychology* 24:411–35.

Griffiths, Paul. 1997. *What Emotions Really Are.* Chicago: University of Chicago Press.

Gross, Alan G. 1990. *The Rhetoric of Science.* Cambridge, MA: Harvard University Press.

Güth, W., and H. Kliemt. 1994. "Competition or Cooperation: On the Evolutionary Economics of Trust, Exploitation, and Moral Attitudes." *Metroeconomica* 45:155–87.

Güth, W., R. Schmittberger, and B. Schwarze. 1982. "An Experimental Analysis of Ultimatum Bargaining." *Journal of Economic Behavior and Organization* 3:367–88.

Hamilton, W. D. 1964. "The Genetical Evolution of Social Behaviour." Parts 1 and 2. *Journal of Theoretical Biology* 7:1–16, 17–52.

———. 1967. "Extraordinary Sex Ratios." *Science* 156:477–88.

———. 1975. "Innate Social Aptitudes of Man: An Approach from Evolutionary Genetics." In *Biosocial Anthropology,* edited by Robin Fox, 133–55. London: Malaby Press.

Hardin, Russell. 1977. *The Limits of Altruism.* Bloomington: Indiana University Press.

Harsanyi, John, and Reinhard Selten. 1986. *A General Theory of Equilibrium Selection in Games.* Cambridge, MA: MIT Press.

Hauser, Mark D. 1996. *The Evolution of Communication.* Cambridge, MA: MIT Press.

———. 2000. *Wild Minds: What Animals Really Think.* New York: Henry Holt.

Hebb, Douglass O. 1949. *The Organization of Behavior: A Neurophysiological Theory.* New York: Wiley.

Heller, Joseph. [1961] 1995. *Catch 22.* New York: Alfred A. Knopf.

Henrich, Joseph, Robert Boyd, Samuel Bowles, Colin Camerer, Ernst Fehr, Herbert Gintis and Richard McElventh. 2001. "Cooperation, Reciprocity and Punishment in Fifteen Small-Scale Societies." *American Economic Review* 91 (May).

Hildenbrand, Werner. 1999. "On the Empirical Content of Economic Theories." In *Economics beyond the Millennium,* edited by Alan Kirman and Louis-André Gerard-Varet, 37–55. Oxford: Oxford University Press.

Hinde, Robert A., and Jo Groebel, eds. 1991. *Cooperation and Prosocial Behaviour.* Cambridge: Cambridge University Press.

Hirschfeld, Laurence A., and Susan A. Gelman, eds. 1994. *Mapping the Mind:*

Domain Specificity in Cognition and Culture. Cambridge: Cambridge University Press.

Hirschman, Albert O. 1982. "Rival Interpretations of Market Society: Civilizing, Destructive, or Feeble?" *Journal of Economic Literature* 20 (December): 1463–84.

Hirshleifer, Jack. 1977. "Economics from a Biological Perspective." *Journal of Law and Economics* 20 (April): 1–52.

———. 1982. "Evolutionary Models in Economics and Law." *Research in Law and Economics* 4:1–60.

———. 1985. "The Expanding Domain of Economics." *American Economic Review* 75:53–68.

———. 1987. "On the Emotions as Guarantors of Threats and Promises." In *The Latest on the Best: Essays on Evolution and Optimality,* edited by J. Dupré. Cambridge, MA: MIT Press.

Hirshleifer, Jack, and Juan Carlos Martinez-Coll. 1988. "What Strategies Can Support the Evolutionary Emergence of Cooperation?" *Journal of Conflict Resolution* 32 (June): 367–98.

Hobbes, Thomas. [1651] 1909. *Leviathan, or the Matter, Forme, and Power of a Common-Wealth Ecclesiastical and Civill.* Oxford: Clarendon Press.

Hoffman, Elizabeth, Kevin A. McCabe, and Vernon Smith. 1998. "Behavioral Foundations of Reciprocity: Experimental Economics and Evolutionary Psychology." *Economic Inquiry* 36 (July): 335–52.

Hoffman, Martin L. 1981. "Is Altruism Part of Human Nature?" *Journal of Personality and Social Psychology* 40 (1): 121–37.

Hogarth, Robin, and Melvin W. Reder. 1987. *Rational Choice: The Contrast between Economics and Psychology.* Chicago: University of Chicago Press.

Holmes, Stephen. 1990. "The Secret History of Self Interest." In *Beyond Self Interest,* edited by Jane Mansbridge, 267–86. Chicago: University of Chicago Press.

Houston, Alasdair I., and William Hamilton. 1989. "Selfishness Reexamined: No Man Is an Island." *Behavioral and Brain Sciences* 12:709–10.

Hrdy, Sarah Blaffer. 1979. "Infanticide among Animals: A Review, Classification, and Examination of the Implications for the Reproductive Strategies of Females." *Ethology and Sociobiology* 1:13–40.

Hunt, Morton. 1990. *The Compassionate Beast.* New York: William Morrow.

Hutchinson, Terence. 1938. *The Significance and Basic Postulates of Economic Theory.* London: Macmillan.

Ifrah, Georges. 2000. *The Universal History of Numbers.* New York: Wiley.

International Human Genome Sequencing Consortium. 2001. "Initial Sequencing and Analysis of the Human Genome." *Nature* 409:860–921.

Isaac, F. J. 1983. "Aspects of Human Evolution." In *Evolution from Molecules to Man,* edited by D. S. Bendall. Cambridge: Cambridge University Press.

Isaacs, Jeremy, and Taylor Downing. 1998. *Cold War: An Illustrated History, 1945–1991.* Boston: Little, Brown.

Jones, E. E., and R. E. Nisbett. 1972. "The Actor and the Observer: Divergent Perceptions on the Causes of Behavior." In *Attribution: Perceiving the Causes of Behavior,* edited by E. E. Jones, D. E. Kanouse, H. H. Kelley, R. E. Nisbett, S. Valins, and B. Weiner. Morristown, NJ: General Learning Co.

Kagan, Jerome. 1984. *The Nature of the Child.* New York: Basic Books.

Kagel, John H., and Alvin E. Roth, eds. 1995. *Handbook of Experimental Economics.* Princeton: Princeton University Press.

Kahneman, Daniel, Jack Knetsch, and Richard Thaler. 1986. "Fairness and the Assumptions of Economics." *Journal of Business* 59:S285–300.

Kahneman, Daniel, Paul Slovic, and Amos Tversky. 1982. *Judgment under Uncertainty: Heuristics and Biases.* Cambridge: Cambridge University Press.

Kahneman, Daniel, and Amos Tversky. 1979. "Prospect Theory: An Analysis of Decision under Risk." *Econometrica* 47:263–91.

———. 1996. "On the Reality of Cognitive Illusions." *Psychological Review* 106:582–91.

Katz, Jerrold J. 1962. *The Problem of Induction and Its Solution.* Chicago: University of Chicago Press.

Kavka, Gregory. 1978. "Some Paradoxes of Deterrence." *Journal of Philosophy* 75:282–302.

———. 1986. *Hobbesian Moral and Political Theory.* Princeton: Princeton University Press.

———. 1987. *Moral Paradoxes of Nuclear Deterrence.* Cambridge: Cambridge University Press.

Keil, F. C. 1990. "Constraints on Constraints: Surveying the Epigenetic Landscape." *Cognitive Science* 14:135–68.

Kelly, Robert R. 1995. *The Foraging Spectrum: Diversity in Hunter-Gatherer Societies.* Washington: Smithsonian Institution Press.

Kiefer, Nicholas M. 1988. "Economic Duration Data and Hazard Functions." *Journal of Economic Literature* 26 (June): 646–79.

Kirman, Alan. 1999. "The Future of Economic Theory." In *Economics beyond the Millennium,* edited by Alan Kirman and Louis-André Gerard-Varet, 8–22. Oxford: Oxford University Press.

Kirman, Alan, and Louis-André Gerard-Varet, eds. 1999. *Economics beyond the Millennium.* Oxford: Oxford University Press.

Kissinger, Henry. 1982. *Years of Upheaval,* 245. Boston: Little, Brown. Quoted in Spencer R. Weart, *Never at War: Why Democracies Will Never Fight One Another,* 78 (New Haven: Yale University Press, 1998).

Kitcher, Philip. 1993. "The Evolution of Human Altruism." *Journal of Philosophy* 10 (October): 497–516.

Klein, Daniel B., ed. 1997. *Reputation: Studies in the Voluntary Elicitation of Good Conduct.* Ann Arbor: University of Michigan Press.

Kluckholm, Clyde. 1955. "Ethical Relativity: Sic et Non." *Journal of Philosophy* 52:663–77.

Knowlton, Barbara, Jennifer Mangels, and Larry Squires. 1996. "A Neostriatal Habit Learning System in Humans." *Science* 273:1399–1402.

Koehler, Jonathan J. 1996. "The Base Rate Fallacy Reconsidered: Descriptive,

Normative, and Methodological Challenges." *Behavioral and Brain Science* 19:1–53.

Koopmans, Tjalling C. 1957. *Three Essays on the State of Economic Science.* New York: McGraw-Hill.

Korobkin, Russell S., and Thomas S. Ulen. 2000. "Law and Behavioral Science: Removing the Rationality Assumption from Law and Economics." *California Law Review* 88:1051–1144.

Kotovsky, Laura, and Renee Baillargeon. 1998. "Calibration Based Reasoning about Collision Events in Eleven-Month-Old Infants." *Cognition* 67:311–51.

Krebs, Dennis L. 1987. "The Challenge of Altruism in Biology and Psychology." In *Sociobiology and Psychology: Ideas, Issues, and Findings,* edited by C. Crawford, M. Smith, and Dennis L. Krebs. Hillsdale, NJ: Lawrence Erlbaum.

Krebs, John R., A. Kacelnik, and P. Taylor. 1978. "Test of Optimal Sampling by Foraging Great Tits." *Nature* 275:27–31.

Kreps, D. M., P. Milgrom, J. Roberts, and R. Wilson. 1982. "Rational Cooperation in the Finitely Repeated Prisoner's Dilemma." *Journal of Economic Theory* 27:245–52.

Kropotkin, Peter. 1910. *Mutual Aid: A Factor of Evolution.* London: William Heinemann.

Kunreuther, Howard, L. Ginsberg, L. Miller, P. Sagi, P. Slovic, B. Borkan, and N. Katz. 1978. *Disaster Insurance Protection: Public Policy Lessons.* New York: Wiley.

Kuran, Timur. 1995. *Private Truths, Public Lies.* Cambridge, MA: Harvard University Press.

Kuran, Timur, and Cass Sunstein. 1999. "Availability Cascades and Risk Regulation." *Stanford Law Review* 51:683–768.

Lakatos, Imre. 1970. "Falsification and the Methodology of Scientific Research Programmes." In *Criticism and the Growth of Knowledge,* edited by Imre Lakatos and Alan Musgrave, 91–196. Cambridge: Cambridge University Press.

Lane, Robert E. 1996. "What Rational Choice Explains." In *The Rational Choice Controversy: Economic Models of Politics Reconsidered,* edited by Jeffrey Friedman, 107–26. New Haven: Yale University Press.

Laporta, Rafael, Florencio Lopez-de-Silanes, Andrei Shleifer, and Robert W. Vishny. 1998. "Law and Finance." *Journal of Political Economy* 106 (December): 1113–55.

Lashley, Karl. 1929. *Brain Mechanisms and Intelligence: A Quantitative Study of Injuries to the Brain.* Chicago: University of Chicago Press.

Lazear, Edward. 2000. "Economic Imperialism." *Quarterly Journal of Economics* 115 (February): 99–146.

LeDoux, Joseph. 1996. *The Emotional Brain: The Mysterious Underpinnings of Emotional Life.* New York: Simon and Schuster.

Ledyard, John. 1995. "Public Goods." In *Handbook of Experimental Economics,* edited by John H. Kagel and Alvin E. Roth, 111–94. Princeton: Princeton University Press.

Lepper, Mark D., D. Greene, and R. E. Nisbett. 1973. "Undermining Children's

Intrinsic Interest with Extrinsic Reward: A Test of the 'Overjustification' Hypothesis." *Journal of Personality and Social Psychology* 28:129–37.

Leslie, John. 1996. *The End of the World: The Science and Ethics of Human Extinction.* London: Routledge.

Levin, Laurence. 1998. "Are Assets Fungible? Testing the Behavioral Theory of Life Cycle Savings." *Journal of Economic Behavior and Organization* 36:59–83.

Levy, Jack S. 1988. "Domestic Politics and Wars." *Journal of Interdisciplinary History* 18:653–73.

Lewin, Shira. 1994. "Economics and Psychology: Lessons for Our Own Day from the Early Twentieth Century." *Journal of Economic Literature* 34:1293–1323.

Lewis, Thomas, Fari Amini, and Richard Lannon. 2000. *A General Theory of Love.* New York: Henry Holt.

Lewontin, R. C. 1970. "The Units of Selection." *Annual Review of Ecology and Systematics* 1:1–18.

———. 1972. "The Apportionment of Human Diversity." *Evolutionary Biology* 6:381–98.

Lindert, Peter. 1999. "The Comparative Political Economy of Mass Schooling before 1914." Manuscript, University of California, Davis.

Lorenz, Konrad. 1966. *On Aggression.* New York: Harcourt Brace and World.

Luce, R. Duncan, and Howard Raiffa. 1957. *Games and Decisions.* New York: Wiley.

Lumsden, C. J. 1989. "Does Culture Need Genes?" *Ethology and Sociobiology* 10:11–28.

Lumsden, C. J., and Edward O. Wilson. 1981. *Genes, Mind, and Culture.* Cambridge, MA: Harvard University Press.

———. 1983. *Promethean Fire.* Cambridge, MA: Harvard University Press.

Maclean, Paul. 1973. *A Triune Concept of the Brain and Behaviour.* Toronto: University of Toronto Press.

———. 1990. *The Triune Brain in Evolution: Role in Paleocerebral Functions.* New York: Plenum.

Maine, Henry. 1888. *International Law: A Series of Lectures Delivered before the University of Cambridge, 1887.* London: Murray.

Malotki, Ekkehart. 1983. *Hopi Time: A Linguistic Analysis of the Temporal Concepts in the Hopi Language.* Berlin: Mouton.

Mantzavinos, Chris. 2001. *Individuals, Institutions, and Markets.* Cambridge: Cambridge University Press.

Maoz, Zaev, and Bruce Russett. 1993. "Normative and Structural Causes of Democratic Peace, 1946–1986." *American Political Science Review* 87:624–38.

Marr, David. 1982. *Vision.* San Francisco: W. H. Freeman.

Marwell, Gerald, and Ruth Ames. 1981. "Economists Free Ride, Does Anyone Else?" *Journal of Public Economics* 15:295–310.

May, Ernest, and Philip Zelikow. 1997. *The Kennedy Tapes: Inside the White House during the Cuban Missile Crisis.* Cambridge, MA: Harvard University Press.

Maynard-Smith, John. 1964. "Group Selection and Kin Selection." *Nature* 201:1145–47.

———. [1975] 1993. *The Theory of Evolution.* Reprint, with a new introduction, Cambridge: Cambridge University Press.

———. 1976. "Evolution and the Theory of Games." *American Scientist* 64:41–45.

———. 1982. *Evolution and the Theory of Games.* Cambridge: Cambridge University Press.

———. 1998. "The Origin of Altruism." Review of *Unto Others,* by Elliott Sober and David Sloan Wilson. *Nature* 393:639–40.

Maynard-Smith, John, and George Price. 1973. "The Logic of Animal Conflict." *Nature* 246:15–18.

Mayr, Ernst. 1983. "How to Carry out the Adaptationist Program." *American Naturalist* 121:324–34.

McCloskey, Deirdre. 1983. "The Rhetoric of Economics." *Journal of Economic Literature* 31 (June): 481–517.

———. 1985. "The Loss Function Has Been Mislaid: The Rhetoric of Significance Tests." *American Economic Review* 75 (May): 201–5.

———. 1995. "Modern Epistemology against Analytic Philosophy: A Reply to Maki." *Journal of Economic Literature* 33 (September): 1319–23.

———. 2000. *How to Be Human, though an Economist.* Ann Arbor: University of Michigan Press.

Mealey, Linda. 1995. "The Sociobiology of Sociopathy: An Integrated Evolutionary Approach." *Behavioral and Brain Sciences* 18:523–99.

Mealey, Linda, Christophe Daood, and Michael Krage. 1996. "Enhanced Memory for Faces of Cheaters." *Ethology and Sociobiology* 17:119–28.

Midgley, Mary. 1978. *Beast and Man: The Roots of Human Nature.* Ithaca: Cornell University Press.

———. 1984. *Wickedness: A Philosophical Essay.* London: Routledge and Kegan Paul.

Miller, Gary J. 1997. "The Impact of Economics on Contemporary Political Science." *Journal of Economic Literature* 35 (September): 1173–1204.

Monroe, Kristen Renwick. 1996. *The Heart of Altruism: Perceptions of a Common Humanity.* Princeton: Princeton University Press.

Montagu, Ashley. 1956. *The Biosocial Nature of Man.* New York: Grove Press.

Moore, David S., and George P. McCabe. 1989. *Introduction to the Practice of Statistics.* New York: W. H. Freeman.

Muth, John. 1961. "Rational Expectations and the Theory of Price Movements." *Econometrica* 29:315–35.

Nassar, Sylvia. 1998. *A Beautiful Mind.* New York: Simon and Schuster.

Nicolson, Harold. 1963. *Diplomacy,* 132, 144. 3d ed. London: Oxford University Press. Quoted in Spencer R. Weart, *Never at War: Why Democracies Will Never Fight One Another,* 80 (New Haven: Yale University Press, 1998).

Nisbett, Robert, and Lee Ross. 1980. *Human Inference: Strategies and Shortcomings of Social Judgment.* Englewood Cliffs: Prentice-Hall.

North, Douglass. 1990. *Institutions, Institutional Change, and Economic Performance.* Cambridge: Cambridge University Press.

North, Douglass, and Robert Paul Thomas. 1973. *The Rise of the Western World.* Cambridge: Cambridge University Press.

Nunney, Leonard. 1998. "Are We Selfish, Are We Nice, or Are We Nice Because We Are Selfish?" Review of *Unto Others,* by Elliott Sober and David Sloan Wilson. *Science* 281:1619–21.

Odean, Terence. 1998. "Are Investors Reluctant to Realize Their Losses?" *Journal of Finance* 53 (December): 1775–98.

Oliner, Pearl M., Samuel P. Oliner, Lawrence Baron, Lawrence A. Blum, Daniel L. Krebs, and M. Zuzanna Smolenska, eds. 1992. *Embracing the Other: Philosophical, Psychological, and Historical Perspectives on Altruism.* New York: New York University Press.

Oliner, Samuel P., and Pearl M. Oliner. 1988. *The Altruistic Personality: Rescuers of Jews in Nazi Europe.* New York: Free Press.

Oneal, John R., and Bruce Russett. 1999. "Assessing the Liberal Peace with Alternative Specifications: Trade Still Reduces Conflict." *Journal of Peace Research* 36:423–42.

Ostrom, E. 1990. *Governing the Commons: The Evolution of Institutions for Collective Action.* Cambridge: Cambridge University Press.

———. 1998. "A Behavioral Approach to the Rational Choice Theory of Collective Action." *American Political Science Review* 92 (1): 1–21.

Ostrom, E., J. Walker, and R. Gardner. 1992. "Covenants with and without a Sword: Self-Governance Is Possible." *American Political Science Review* 86:404–17.

Parsons, Talcott. 1937. *The Structure of Social Action: A Study in Social Theory with Special Reference to a Group of Recent European Writers.* New York: McGraw-Hill.

Peters, Pauline E. 1998. Comment on "The Political Economy of Ethnicity." In *Annual World Bank Conference on Development Economics,* edited by Boris Pleskovic and Joseph Stiglitz, 400–405. Washington: World Bank.

Pinker, Stephen. 1994. *The Language Instinct.* New York: William Morrow.

———. 1997. *How the Mind Works.* New York: W. W. Norton.

Pinker, Stephen, and Paul Bloom. 1990. "Natural Language and Natural Selection." *Behavioral and Brain Sciences* 13:707–84.

Poundstone, William. 1992. *Prisoner's Dilemma.* New York: Doubleday.

Premack, David. 1976. *Intelligence in Ape and Man.* Hillsdale, NJ: Lawrence Erlbaum.

———. 1990. "The Infant's Theory of Self Propelled Objects." *Cognition* 36:1–16.

Premack, David, and Anne James Premack. 1994a. "Moral Belief: Form vs. Content." In *Mapping the Mind: Domain Specificity in Cognition and Culture,* edited by Laurence A. Hirschfeld and Susan A. Gelman, 149–60. Cambridge: Cambridge University Press.

———. 1994b. "Origins of Human Social Competence." In *The Cognitive Neurosciences,* edited by M. Gazzinaga, 205–18. Cambridge, MA: MIT Press.

Price, George R. 1970. "Selection and Covariance." *Nature* 277:520–21.

————. 1972. "Extension of Covariance Selection Mathematics." *Annals of Human Genetics* 35: 485–90.

Putnam, Hilary. 1979. "The Place of Facts in a World of Values." In *The Nature of the Physical Universe*, edited by D. Huff and O. Prewett. New York: Wiley.

Rabin, Matthew. 1993. "Incorporating Fairness into Game Theory and Economics." *American Economic Review* 83 (December): 1281–1302.

————. 1998. "Psychology and Economics." *Journal of Economic Literature* 36 (March): 11–46.

Raknerud, Arvid, and Havard Hegre. 1997. "The Hazard of War: Reassessing the Evidence for Democratic Peace." *Journal of Peace Research* 34:385–404.

Rapaport, Anatol. 1991. "Ideological Commitments and Evolutionary Theory." *Journal of Social Issues* 47:83–99.

Rapaport, Anatol, and Albert M. Chammah. 1965. *Prisoner's Dilemma: A Study in Conflict and Cooperation.* Ann Arbor: University of Michigan Press.

Reder, Melvin W. 1999. *Economics: The Culture of a Controversial Science.* Chicago: University of Chicago Press.

Ridley, Matt. 1993. *The Red Queen: Sex and the Origin of Human Nature.* New York: Macmillan.

————. 1996. *The Origins of Virtue: Human Instincts and the Evolution of Cooperation.* Harmondsworth: Penguin.

————. 1999. *Genome: The Autobiography of a Species in 23 Chapters.* New York: HarperCollins.

Riker, William, and Peter Ordeshook. 1968. "A Theory of the Calculus of Voting." *American Political Science Review* 62 (March): 25–43.

Robbins, Lionel. [1932] 1984. *The Nature and Significance of Economic Science.* 3d ed. London: MacMillan.

Rosenberg, Alexander. 1980. *Sociobiology and the Preemption of the Social Sciences.* Baltimore: Johns Hopkins University Press.

Roth, Alvin E. 1995a. "Introduction to Experimental Economics." In *Handbook of Experimental Economics*, edited by John H. Kagel and Alvin E. Roth, 3–110. Princeton: Princeton University Press.

————. 1995b. "Bargaining Experiments." In *Handbook of Experimental Economics*, edited by John H. Kagel and Alvin E. Roth, 253–348. Princeton: Princeton University Press.

Roth, Alvin E., V. Prasnikar, M. Okuno-Fujiwara, and S. Zamir. 1991. "Bargaining and Market Behavior in Jerusalem, Ljubljana, Pittsburgh, and Tokyo." *American Economic Review* 81:68–95.

Ruhlen, M. 1987. *A Guide to the World's Languages.* Stanford: Stanford University Press.

Rule, James. 1997. *Theory and Progress in Social Science.* Cambridge: Cambridge University Press.

Russell, Bertrand. 1974. "On Induction." Reprinted in *The Justification of Induction*, edited by Richard Swinburne, 1–25. London: Oxford University Press.

Sagan, Carl. 1977. *The Dragons of Eden: Speculations on the Evolution of Human Intelligence.* New York: Random House.

Sally, D. 1995. "Conversation and Cooperation in Social Dilemmas." *Rationality and Society* 7:58–92.

Sampson, Geoffrey. 1997. *Educating Eve: The Language Instinct Debate.* London: Cassell.

Samuelson, Larry. 1997. *Evolutionary Games and Equilibrium Selection.* Cambridge, MA: MIT Press.

Samuelson, Paul. 1993. "Altruism as a Problem Involving Group versus Individual Selection in Economics and Biology." *American Economic Review* 83 (May): 143–48.

Sapir, Edward. 1958. "Time Perspective in Aboriginal American Culture." In *Selected Writings of Edward Sapir in Language,* edited by D. G. Mandelbaum, 389–462. Berkeley: University of California Press.

Savage-Rumbaugh, Sue, and Roger Lewin. 1994. *Kanzi: The Ape at the Brink of the Human Mind.* New York: Wiley.

Schaller, Michael, Virginia Scharf, and Robert D. Schulzinger. 1998. *Coming of Age: America in the Twentieth Century.* New York: Houghton Mifflin.

Schelling, Thomas. 1960. *The Strategy of Conflict.* Cambridge, MA: Harvard University Press.

Schweller, Randall L. 1997. "New Realist Research on Alliances: Refining, not Refuting, Waltz's Balancing Proposition." *American Political Science Review* 91 (December): 927–30.

Seligman, Martin, and Joanne Hager. 1972. *Biological Boundaries of Learning.* New York: Appleton Century Crofts.

Selten, Reinhard. 1965. "Spieltheoretische Behandlung eines Oligopolmodells mit Nachfrageträgheit." *Zeitschrift für die gesamte Staatswissenschaft* 121:301–24, 667–89.

———. 1975. "Reexamination of the Perfectness Concept for Equilibrium Points in Extensive Games." *International Journal of Game Theory* 4:25–55.

———. 1998. "Game Theory, Experience, Rationality." In *Game Theory, Experience, Rationality,* edited by W. Leinfellner and E. Kohler, 9–34. Dordrecht: Kluwer.

Sen, Amartya. 1978. "Rational Fools—a Critique of the Behavioral Foundations of Economic Theory." *Philosophy and Public Affairs* 6 (June): 316–44.

Shafir, Eldar. 1994. "Uncertainty and the Difficulty of Thinking through Disjunctions." *Cognition* 50:403–40.

Shafir, Eldar, and Amos Tversky. 1992. "Thinking through Uncertainty: Nonconsequential Reasoning and Choice." *Cognitive Psychology* 24:449–74.

Shefrin, Hersh. 1999. *Beyond Greed and Fear: Understanding Behavioral Finance and the Psychology of Investing.* Boston: Harvard Business School Press.

Shefrin, Hersh, and Meir Statman. 1985. "The Disposition to Sell Winners Too Early and Ride Losers Long: Theory and Evidence." *Journal of Finance* 40 (July): 777–90.

Sibley, C. J., and J. E. Ahlquist. 1984. "The Phylogeny of the Hominid Primates, as Indicated by DNA-DNA Hybridization." *Journal of Molecular Evolution* 20:2–15.

Simon, H. A. 1987. "Rationality in Psychology and Economics." In *Rational*

Choice: The Contrast between Economics and Psychology, edited by Robin Hogarth and Melvin W. Reder, 25–41. Chicago: University of Chicago Press.

———. 1990. "A Mechanism for Social Selection and Successful Altruism." *Science* 250:1665–68.

Simpson, E. H. 1951. "The Interpretation of Interaction in Contingency Tables." *Journal of the Royal Statistical Society,* ser. B, 13:238–41.

Skinner, B. F. 1957. *Verbal Behavior.* New York: Appleton.

Skyrms, Brian. 1996. *Evolution of the Social Contract.* New York: Cambridge University Press.

Smith, Adam. [1759] 1976. *The Theory of Moral Sentiments.* Edited by D. D. Raphael and A. L. MacFie. Oxford: Clarendon Press.

———. [1776] 1937. *The Wealth of Nations.* New York: Modern Library.

Sober, Elliott. 1984. *The Nature of Selection: Evolutionary Theory in Philosophical Focus.* Cambridge, MA: MIT Press.

———. 1992. "Stable Cooperation in Iterated Prisoners' Dilemmas." *Economics and Philosophy* 8:127–39.

———. 1993. *Philosophy of Biology.* Boulder, CO: Westview Press.

Sober, Elliott, and David Sloan Wilson. 1998. *Unto Others: The Evolution and Psychology of Unselfish Behavior.* Cambridge, MA: Harvard University Press.

Spelke, E. S. 1991. "Physical Knowledge in Infancy: Reflections on Piaget's Theory." In *The Epigenesis of Mind: Essays on Biology and Cognition,* edited by S. Carey and R. Gelman, 37–61. Hillsdale, NJ: Lawrence Erlbaum.

Sperber, D. 1995. "Introduction." In *Causal Cognition,* edited by D. Sperber, D. Premack, and A. J. Premack. Oxford: Oxford University Press.

———. 1996. *Explaining Culture: A Naturalistic Approach.* Oxford: Blackwell.

Sperber, D., D. Premack, and A. J. Premack, eds. 1995. *Causal Cognition.* Oxford: Oxford University Press.

Stanley, Steven M. 1996. *Children of the Ice Age: How Global Catastrophe Allowed Humans to Evolve.* New York: W. H. Freeman.

Stanovich, Keith E., and Richard F. West. 2001. "Individual Differences in Reasoning: Implications for the Rationality Debate?" *Behavioral and Brain Sciences* 22 (5). Forthcoming.

Starmer, Chris. 2000. "Development in non-Expected Utility Theory: The Hunt for a Descriptive Theory of Choice under Risk." *Journal of Economic Literature* 38 (June): 332–87.

Stenseth, Nils Chr. 1989. "Can We Afford Not to Believe That Man Is Selfish?" *Behavioral and Brain Sciences* 12:722–23.

Stephens, David W., and John R. Krebs. 1986. *Foraging Theory.* Princeton: Princeton University Press.

Sterelny, Kim. 1995. "The Adapted Mind." *Biology and Philosophy* 10:365–80.

Sterelny, Kim, and Paul E. Griffiths. 1999. *Sex and Death: An Introduction to the Philosophy of Biology.* Chicago: University of Chicago Press.

Stigler, George. 1975. "Smith's Travels on the Ship of State." In *Essays on Adam Smith,* edited by A. Skinner and T. Wilson. Oxford: Clarendon Press.

Street, Philip. 1976. *Animal Migration and Navigation.* New York: Scribner.

Strickberger, Monroe W. 1996. *Evolution.* 2d ed. Sudbury: Jones and Bartlett.

Sugden, Robert. 1989. "Spontaneous Order." *Journal of Economic Perspectives* 3:85–97.

———. 1998. "Normative Expectations: The Simultaneous Evolution of Institutions and Norms." In *Economics, Values, and Organization,* edited by Avner Ben-Ner and Louis Putterman, 73–100. Cambridge: Cambridge University Press

Symons, Donald. 1990. "Adaptiveness and Adaptation." *Ethology and Sociobiology* 11:427–44.

Tajfel, Henri, and Michael Billig. 1974. "Familiarity and Categorization in Intergroup Behavior." *Journal of Experimental Social Psychology* 10:159–70.

Taylor, Paul, and L. Jonker. 1978. "Evolutionary Stable Strategies and Game Dynamics." *Mathematical Biosciences* 40:145–56.

Telser, Lester. 1980. "A Theory of Self Enforcing Agreements." *Journal of Business* 53:27–54.

Thaler, Richard. 1980. "Toward a Positive Theory of Consumer Choice." *Journal of Economic Behavior and Organization* 1:39–60.

———. 1987. "The Psychology and Economics Conference Handbook: Comments on Simon, on Einhorn and Hogarth, and on Tversky and Kahneman." In *Rational Choice: The Contract between Economics and Psychology,* edited by Robin Hogarth and Melvin W. Reder, 95–100. Chicago: University of Chicago Press.

———. 1990. "Anomalies: Saving, Fungibility, and Mental Accounts." *Journal of Economic Perspectives* 4 (winter): 193–206.

Thaler, Richard, and Eric Johnson. 1990. "Gambling with the House Money and Trying to Break Even: The Effects of Prior Outcomes on Risky Choice." *Management Science* 36 (June): 643–60.

Thaler, Richard, and Hersh Shefrin. 1981. "An Economic Theory of Self Control." *Journal of Political Economy* 89 (April): 392–410.

Tooby, John, and Leda Cosmides. 1990. "The Past Explains the Present: Emotional Adaptations and the Structure of Ancestral Environments." *Ethology and Sociobiology* 11:375–424.

———. 1992. "The Psychological Foundations of Culture." In *The Adapted Mind: Evolutionary Psychology and the Generation of Culture,* edited by Jerome H. Barkow, Leda Cosmides, and John Tooby, 19–136. New York: Oxford University Press

———. 1996. "Friendship and the Banker's Paradox: Other Pathways to the Evolution of Adaptations for Altruism." In *Evolution of Social Behaviour Patterns in Primates and Man,* edited by W. C. Runciman, John Maynard-Smith, and R. I. M. Dunbar, 119–44. Oxford: Oxford University Press.

Trefil, James. 1997. *Are We Unique? A Scientist Explores the Unparalleled Intelligence of the Human Mind.* New York: Wiley.

Trinkaus, Eric, and Pat Shipman. 1993. *The Neanderthals: Changing the Image of Mankind.* New York: Alfred A. Knopf.

Trivers, Robert. 1971. "The Evolution of Reciprocal Altruism." *Quarterly Review of Biology* 46:35–57.

———. 1985. *Social Evolution.* Menlo Park, CA.: Benjamin Cummings.

Turner, Frederic, and Ernst Pöppel. 1983. "The Neural Lyre: Poetic Meter, the Brain, and Time." *Poetry* 72:277–309.

Tversky, Amos, and Daniel Kahneman. 1974. "Judgment under Uncertainty: Heuristics and Biases." *Science* 185:1124–31.

U.S. Bureau of the Census. 1975. *Historical Statistics of the United States: Colonial Times to 1970.* Washington: Government Printing Office.

———. 1999. *Statistical Abstract of the United States.* Washington: Government Printing Office.

Vail, Leroy, ed. 1989. *The Creation of Tribalism in Southern Africa.* Berkeley: University of California Press.

van Damme, Eric. 1999. "Game Theory, the Next Stage." In *Economics beyond the Millennium,* edited by Alan Kirman and Louis-Andre Gerard-Varet, 184–214. Oxford: Oxford University Press.

Vasquez, John. 1997. "The Realist Paradigm and Degenerative vs. Progressive Research Programs: An Appraisal of Neotraditional Research on Waltz's Balancing Proposition." *American Political Science Review* 91 (December): 899–912.

Venter, J. C., et al. 2001. "The Sequence of the Human Genome." *Science* 291 (February 15): 1304–51.

von Neumann, John, and Oskar Morgenstern. 1944. *Theories of Games and Economic Behavior.* Princeton: Princeton University Press.

de Waal, Frans. 1982. *Chimpanzee Politics: Power and Sex among Apes.* London: Jonathan Cape.

———. 1989. *Peacemaking among Primates.* Cambridge, MA: Harvard University Press.

———. 1996. *Good-Natured: The Origins of Right and Wrong in Humans and Other Animals.* Cambridge, MA: Harvard University Press.

de Waal, Frans, and Frans Lanting. 1997. *Bonobo: The Forgotten Ape.* Berkeley: University of California Press.

Wade, Michael J. 1978. "A Critical Review of Models of Group Selection." *Quarterly Review of Biology* 53:101–14.

Wagenaar, W. A. 1988. *Paradoxes of Gambling Behavior.* Hove, UK: Lawrence Erlbaum.

Weart, Spencer R. 1998. *Never at War: Why Democracies Will Never Fight One Another.* New Haven: Yale University Press.

Weibull, Jörgen W. 1995. *Evolutionary Game Theory.* Cambridge, MA: MIT Press.

White, Leslie. 1949. *The Science of Culture: A Study of Man and Civilization.* New York: Farrar Straus.

Whorf, Benjamin. 1963. *Language, Thought, and Reality.* Cambridge, MA: MIT Press.

Wiley, J. S. 1988. "Reciprocal Altruism as a Felony." *Ethology and Sociobiology* 9:241–57.

Williams, George C. 1966. *Adaptation and Natural Selection: A Critique of Some Current Evolutionary Thought.* Princeton: Princeton University Press.

———. 1992. *Natural Selection: Domains, Levels, and Challenges,* 49. New York: Oxford University Press. Cited in Elliott Sober and David Sloan Wilson, *Unto*

Others: The Evolution and Psychology of Unselfish Behavior, 43 (Cambridge, MA: Harvard University Press, 1998).

Williams, George C., and R. M. Nesse. 1991. "The Dawn of Darwinian Medicine." *Quarterly Review of Biology* 66:1–22.

Williams, John D. 1954. *The Compleat Strategyst: Being a Primer on the Theory of Games of Strategy.* New York: McGraw-Hill.

Wilson, David Sloan. 1994. "Adaptive Genetic Variation and Human Evolutionary Psychology." *Ethology and Sociobiology* 15:219–35.

———. 1998. "Game Theory and Human Behavior." In *Game Theory and Animal Behavior,* edited by Lee Alan Dugatkin and Hudson Kern Reeve, 261–82. New York: Oxford University Press.

———. 1999. Review of *Evolutionary Psychology: The New Science of the Mind,* by David M. Buss. *Evolution and Human Behavior* 20:279–88.

Wilson, David Sloan, and Elliott Sober. 1994. "Reintroducing Group Selection to the Human Behavioral Sciences." *Behavioral and Brain Sciences* 17:585–654.

Wilson, Edward O. 1971. *The Insect Societies.* Cambridge, MA: Harvard University Press.

———. 1975. *Sociobiology: The New Synthesis.* Cambridge, MA: Harvard University Press.

———. 1978. *On Human Nature.* Cambridge, MA: Harvard University Press.

———. 1998. *Consilience: The Unity of Knowledge.* New York: Alfred A. Knopf.

Wright, Robert. 1994. *The Moral Animal: Why We Are the Way We Are: The New Science of Evolutionary Psychology.* New York: Pantheon.

Wright, Sewall. 1945. "Tempo and Mode in Evolution: A Critical Review." *Ecology* 26:415–19.

Wrong, Dennis. 1994. *The Problem of Order: What Unites and Divides Society.* New York: Free Press.

Wynn, Karen. 1990. "Children's Understanding of Counting." *Cognition* 36:155–93.

———. 1992. "Addition and Subtraction by Human Infants." *Nature* 358:749–50.

Wynne-Edwards, V. C. [1962] 1967. *Animal Dispersion in Relation to Social Behavior.* Reprint, New York: Hafner.

———. 1986. *Evolution through Group Selection.* Oxford: Blackwell.

Young, H. P. 1998. *Individual Strategy and Social Structure: An Evolutionary Theory of Interaction.* Princeton: Princeton University Press.

Zahavi, Amotz, and Avishag Zahavi. 1997. *The Handicap Principle: A Missing Piece of Darwin's Puzzle.* New York: Oxford University Press.

Zihlman, Adrienne et al. 1978. "Pygmy Chimpanzee as a Possible Prototype for the Common Ancestor of Humans, Chimpanzees, and Gorillas." *Nature* 275:744–46.

Index

DATE DUE